Augustus John Cuthbert Hare

North-Western France

Normandy and Brittany

Augustus John Cuthbert Hare

North-Western France
Normandy and Brittany

ISBN/EAN: 9783337326920

Printed in Europe, USA, Canada, Australia, Japan

Cover: Foto ©Thomas Meinert / pixelio.de

More available books at **www.hansebooks.com**

NORTH-WESTERN FRANCE

(Normandy and Brittany)

BY

AUGUSTUS J. C. HARE

AUTHOR OF "PARIS," "WALKS IN ROME," "WALKS IN LONDON," ETC.

GEORGE ALLEN
156, CHARING CROSS ROAD, LONDON
AND
SUNNYSIDE, ORPINGTON
1895

[*All rights reserved*]

CONTENTS.

CHAP.		PAGE
I.	PARIS TO DIEPPE BY PONTOISE, GISORS, FORGES-LES-EAUX, AND NEUFCHÂTEL. FROM THE GARE S. LAZARE	1
II.	PARIS TO HAVRE, BY MANTES, VERNON, GAILLON, ROUEN (JUMIÈGES, CAUDEBEC), AND YVETOT (ETRETAT, FÉCAMP), (LILLEBONNE). FROM THE GARE S. LAZARE	21
III.	PARIS TO CHERBOURG BY EVREUX, LISIEUX (TROUVILLE) (FALAISE), CAEN, BAYEUX, AND VALOGNES. FROM THE GARE S. LAZARE	79
IV.	PARIS TO GRANVILLE, BY DREUX, ARGENTAN AND VIRE. FROM THE GARE MONTPARNASSE	134
V.	PARIS TO CHARTRES, NOGENT LE ROTROU, LE MANS, LAVAL, VITRÉ, RENNES, LAMBALLE, MORLAIX AND BREST. CHEMIN DE FER DE L'OUEST: FROM THE GARE MONTPARNASSE	158
VI.	BAYEUX TO LAMBALLE BY S. LÔ, COUTANCES, AVRANCHES, MONT S. MICHEL, DOL, S. MALO, AND DINAN	304
VII.	PARIS AND LE MANS TO QUIMPER, BY CHÂTEAU-GONTIER, SÉGRÉ, CHÂTEAUBRIANT, REDON, VANNES, L'ORIENT, AND QUIMPERLÉ. CHEMIN DE FER DE L'OUEST.	339

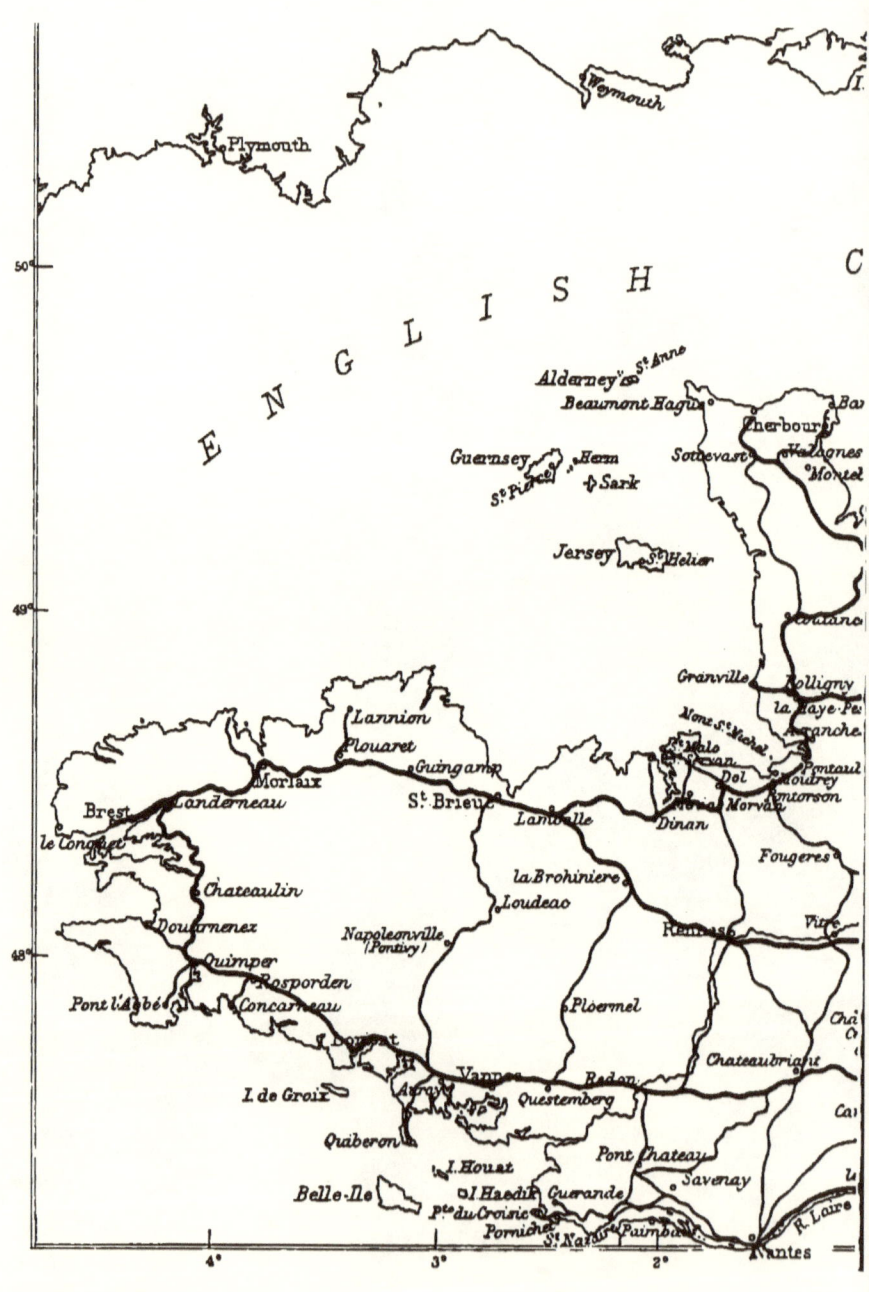

CHAPTER I.

PARIS TO DIEPPE BY PONTOISE, GISORS, FORGES-LES-EAUX, AND NEUFCHÂTEL. FROM THE GARE S. LAZARE.

FOR this route see *North Eastern France*, ch. ii., as far as

32 k. *Pontoise* inclusive.

42 k. *Ws-Marines*. 5½ k. S. is *Marines*, with the château of Chancellor Sillery, and the remains of a monastery of Oratorians, which he founded here in 1618. 5 k. (omnibus) is Vigny, with its fine gothic château: see ch. ii.

50 k. *Chars*, with a church chiefly XIV. c. Here the line to Magny (see ch. ii.) branches off on l.

The line passes (r.) the fine XI. and XII. c. church of *Villetertre*.

57 k. *Liancourt-S.-Pierre*, on the Roman road called *Chaussée Brunehaut*, has a church with tower of XII. c., nave and S. transept XIII. c., choir and N. transept XVI. c.

63 k. *Chaumont-en-Vexin* has some remains of an XI. c. castle. The church (XV. and XVI. c.) has a rich portal and flamboyant galleries. In the principal street is a good timber XVI. c. house. 5 k. W. is *Chambors*, with an old château turned into a farm and a church of 1532. To the r. of the line is the hamlet of *La Bertichère*, with

a chapel of xi. c. or xii. c. and château of xv. c. or xvi. c.

68 k. *Trie-Château*, had an important xv. c. fortress, of which the gothic gateway remains, crossing the Gisors road. The church has a splendid gothic façade. The Hôtel de Ville, which was once the Maison de Justice Seigneuriale, is xii. c. 2 k. S.E. is the dolmen called *La Pierre des Druides*.

71 k. *Gisors*[1] (Hotel: *de l'Écu de France*—very good, but *horrors*), which, ruled in its early existence by the Comtes de Vexin, who had the privilege of bearing the oriflamme of S. Denis before the kings of France, became a constant source of dispute between the kings and the dukes of Normandy. As Philippe Auguste was rushing for refuge to the fortress after the battle of Courcelles, the bridge fell, and the king, who seemed to escape by a miracle, gilt the gate above it all over in his gratitude.

The earliest part of the church of *SS. Gervais and Protais*, the choir and aisles, are due to Blanche of Castille, 1240; the nave, chapels, and towers are xiv. c., xv. c., and xvi. c.; the W. portal is a curious specimen of the Renaissance. The N. portal is splendid flamboyant. The interior has five aisles. The first pillar r.—*le Pilier des Marchands* (1526)—has six sides, each showing different sculptures typical of the guilds who paid for its erection. The fourth pillar of the same aisle—*le Pilier des Dauphins*—is a beautiful wreathed column ornamented with salamanders. In the third chapel (r.) is a skeleton in stone, attributed to Jean Goujon. At the end of the r. aisle is a

---

[1] There are three stations at Gisors. Those leaving by any of the branch lines should be careful to be taken to the right one.

beautiful flamboyant doorway. The baptistery has a huge tree of Jesse. It was this church to which Henri IV. was refused admittance by the curé till he had publicly adored the cross. 'Ventre-saint-gris,' exclaimed the king, as he entered the sanctuary, 'me voilà donc enfin roi de Gisors.' Opposite the E. end of the church, a passage under the houses on the other side of the principal street, leads

CASTLE OF GISORS.

up through the postern gate to the *Château*, the remains of which are amongst the finest in France. It was built in 1097 for Guillaume le Roux by Robert de Bellesme, a great architect of fortresses. Henry I. strengthened it by outer walls and towers, and more towers were added by Henry II., who held here the conference (1175) with Louis VII., in which they agreed to take up the cross. The enclosure is formed by a wide and deep entrenchment, now laid out in gardens, and a wall flanked by twelve towers, most of them square. It had four gates, of which three exist, besides the postern. In the midst, on a high artificial mound, rises the octagonal keep, begun XII. c., which is the earliest part of the existing building. It is surrounded by a circular rampart, flanked by flat buttresses, and with strengthening beams incrusted in the masonry. This encloses a deep well and the remains of a romanesque chapel dedicated to S. Thomas of Canterbury. The keep is flanked by a XV. c. tourelle, enclosing a staircase. The principal buildings for residence occupied the space between the walls and the mound. Where the ramparts of the castle meet those of the town stands the *Tour du Prisonnier*, built by Philippe Auguste, and containing three stories of single-vaulted chambers. In the lowest are preserved a number of rude wall-sculptures, supposed to have been executed by the Chevalier Poulain ('Le Prisonnier de Gisors') in the reign of Louis XI., from the inscription—'O mater Dei, memento mei Poulain.' The *Halles*, built by the Duc de Penthièvre, who was lord of Gisors at the time of the Revolution, are within the enclosure of the castle, at the upper end.

The town has several XVI. c. wooden houses: one in the Rue des Tanneurs bears an inscription to the Virgin. The *Hôtel de Ville* was the XVII. c. Couvent des Carmélites.

[For the line S.W. from Gisors to Vernon see ch. ii.]

[A line leads W. from Gisors to Pont de l'Arche. Descending into the valley of the Epte, it passes l. the *Château de Vaux*; then a stone cross—*Croix percée*—which commemorates the oath of fidelity taken by the Norman barons to Richard Cœur de Lion before he left for the Crusades.

Farther, on l., is *Neaufles-S.-Martin*, which had an important

XII. c. fortress of the Archbishops of Rouen, destroyed by Mazarin.

8 k. *Bézu-S.-Eloi*, has a church, partly XII. c., and a tower called *Tour de la Reine-Blanche*, built into a mill.

9 k. *Bernouville*. The line passes the ruins of a XII. c. priory, turned into a farm.

16 k. *Etrépagny*, on the Bonde. The church has a good XIV. c. tomb.

24 k. *Saussay-les-Andelys* (a railway in progress to Les Andelys). 6 k. hence, on the road to Les Andelys, is the fine church of *Ecouis*, founded by Enguerrand de Marigny (1311-13), who was once represented, with his wife Alips, on the pillars of the principal portal. In the interior is the tomb of his brother, Jean de Marigny, Archbishop of Rouen.

29 k. *Lisors*. 2 k. N. are the ruins of the (XII. c.) *Abbaye de Mortimer*.

32 k. *Ménesqueville-Lyons*. The romanesque church of *Ménesqueville* contains the tomb of Jacques le Court, 1660, and his wife Renée Bigot. The name commemorates the famous *Forest of Lions*. 9 k. (omnibus) is *Lyons-la-Forêt* ('nemus de leonibus'—'silva leonum'), where Carloman received, from a wild boar, the wound of which he died at Les Andelys. It was the favourite hunting ground of the dukes of Normandy, where Guillaume Longue-Épée, second of the race who became dukes of Normandy, had a hunting lodge. Near this the monks of S. Denis built a church, which they dedicated to their patron saint, and which was afterwards replaced by a great ducal castle (now destroyed), in which (Dec. 1, 1135) Henry I. died, and whence his embalmed body was taken for burial in England at the abbey which he had founded at Reading. The church is flanked by a huge square tower coated with slates. Outside Lyons are remains of a convent, with an inscription recording its foundation by Louis XIII. in 1624 in honour of S. Louis.

36 k. *Charleval*. The church has a romanesque portal.

38 k. *Fleury-sur-Andelle*. A road leads hence to (23 k.) Rouen, by (5 k.) *Bourg-Beaudouin*, near which the Girondist minister Roland died by his own hand under a tree, Nov. 15, 1793; and (13 k.) *Boos*, with a very interesting manor-house (now farm) of the XIII. c., which belonged to the abbesses of

S. Amand-de-Rouen. The very curious XVI. c. pigeon-house is decorated with inlaid tiles.

40 k. *Radepont* has a château and a much-restored castle of XII. c. Its church contains a fine retable from the Abbey of Fontaine Guérand, founded in 1198. Turning left on leaving the station, a path through the delightful park of the Marquis de Radepont, richly wooded and watered by the rushing Andelle, leads in 2 k. to the *Abbaye de Fontaine Guérand.* The beautiful ruined church and the neighbouring building are XIII. c. The former contains the tomb of Marie de Ferrières. Opposite the ruins is a XV. c. chapel above a XII. c. crypt. Following the path which leads hence to the forest, we find the XVI. c. *Château de Bonnemare*, adorned with medallions and reliefs representing Charles VII. and Agnès Sorel.

44 k. *Pont-S.-Pierre.* The imposing XV. c. château is approached by a long avenue. There are some small remains of a XII. c. castle which played an important part in the wars of Philippe Auguste with John of England. The road from hence to (10 k.) Boos (see above), passes through *Neuville-Champ-d'Oisel*, which has a fine church, chiefly XIII. c., with XVIII. c. stall work.

47 k. *Romilly-sur-Andelle*, overhung to the S.W. by the *Côte des Deux-Amants*, so called from the legend that the lord of a neighbouring castle refused the hand of his beautiful daughter to any one who should be unable to carry her to the top of the hill without stopping. This her lover had almost accomplished, when he sank down and died, and the maiden instantly threw herself from the rocks.

48 k. *Pitres.* Some early remains discovered here are supposed to belong to a palace of Charles le Chauve, who assembled several councils here between 861 and 869.

54 k. Pont de l'Arche (see ch. ii.).]

75 k. *Eragny.* The church has some interesting fragments of romanesque work. In the XVI. c. château is a good brick staircase.

79 k. *Sérifontaine.* The church (XI. c., XIII. c., and XVI. c.) has good glass, pendants, and a Passion in gilt wood.

88 k. *Neufmarché.* The romanesque church is xii. c., with a sculptured portal. There are some remains of the castle built in 1115 by Henry I. of England, and in which a council of Anglo-Norman bishops and barons met, in 1160, to decide between the popes Alexander III. and Victor III. The remains of a camp made by the English, when besieging Neufmarché in 1419, are to be seen at the *Mont des Boulards.*

S. HILDEVERT, GOURNAY.

Neufmarché is on the edge of the *Pays de Bray,* a curious district, all the upper soil of which has been carried away at an early period, rendering it useless for corn-growing, but admirable for grazing purposes.

96 k. *Gournay Ferrières* (Hotel: *du Lion d'Or*). The ancient town of *Gournay* was formerly walled, but little remains of its fortifications except the xviii. c. *Porte Ibert* and a few towers. The church of *S. Hildevert* is xi. c. and xii. c.,

and was a magnificent building till its interest was destroyed by recent restoration. The common masons'-work which has replaced the original capitals in the principal nave serves as a foil to some grand untouched capitals in the side aisles. The choir remains of the romanesque leper-chapel of *S. Madeleine*. The XVII. c. *Convent of Capucins* is now a gendarmerie and prison. The aged Hugh de Gournay, who fought in the battle of Hastings, left his name to Barrow-Gurney in Somerset, and other places in England. The numerous family of Gurney in England claims Gournay as its ancestral home.

Gerberoi, near Gournay, which had the right of sanctuary, was a refuge to Robert, eldest son of the Conqueror, who ravaged Normandy from thence (1078) with his band of freebooters. The castle was besieged by William, and a regular battle took place under its walls, in which not only Rufus was wounded, but William himself was in the utmost danger when in combat with a single knight, who proved to be his own son.

[A line leads E. to (29 k.) Beauvais by (7 k.) *S. Germer*. Turning r. on leaving the station, by the high road, and then l. to the village buried in trees, we reach at 2½ k. (*Hôtel S. Germer*[1]) a green surrounded by cottages in front of the immense cruciform church, which belonged to the famous *Abbey* founded by S. Germer in 650. It is approached by a fortified gateway of XIV. c. The church is one of the finest specimens of transition in France. The narrow pointed arches round the apse have zigzag mouldings. The romanesque triforium is blocked in the nave, but still open in the choir and transepts. Chapels radiate round the choir, but the E. chapel was destroyed in the XIII. c. to make way for the beautiful passage leading to the *Sainte*

---

[1] S. Germer is more interesting to the architect than the artist.

Chapelle, which recalls that of Paris, and may be anterior to it. Some of its windows bear the arms of S. Louis. The chapel has remains of colour, and contains many incised gravestones; from the principal one the abbot's crozier was stolen by an English traveller. Several of the abbots have been canonised. S. Eustache, who is buried in the centre of the nave, is said [1] to have restored the use of Sunday in England. S. Domana, wife of S. Germer before he became a priest, is buried in the S. transept, where there is a fine S. Sepulcre; and the remains of his son, S. Amalbert, have been brought here from a neighbouring village: both are greatly venerated in the diocese of Beauvais. It is worth while to ascend to the stone corridor which surrounds the roof of the Sainte Chapelle, to see the extraordinary gargoyles, many caricaturing Benedictine friars. It was in the abbey here that William of Normandy met Philip of France, and besought his aid for the invasion of England, promising, if he gave it, to hold England as well as Normandy as a fief of the French crown.]

[A road leads S.W. from Gournay to (32 k.) Ménesqueville, on the line from Gisors to Pont de l'Arche, and a railway is in progress. The road passes (at 10 k.) to the l. of *Mont-Roty*, which is the point of a great pilgrimage to the image of S. Jean du Temple, and (at 29 k.) reaches Lyons-la-Forêt (see p. 5).]

Following the valley of the Epte, the line passes on l. *Cuy-S.-Fiacre*, with a XII. c. church and beautiful cemetery cross, then the (XI. c., XVI. c., and XVII. c.) church of *Beuvreil* and the (XIII. c.) *Château des Huguenots*, transformed into a farm. The neighbouring ($2\frac{1}{2}$ k. W.) church of *Dampierre* has curious timber vaulting and a fine XVI. c. cemetery cross: close to the church is the old *Manoir de Rambures*.

103 k. *Gancourt-S.-Etienne.* At *S. Etienne* (l.) is a XII. c. choir and a XVI. c. farmhouse. The line passes on l.

[1] *Breviarium Romanum.*

Ménerval, with a (XII. c., XIII. c., and XVI. c.) church with good timber vaulting.

111 k. *Saumont-le-Poterie*. The village church (2 k. l.) has a good XVI. c. choir with a *chapelle seigneuriale* of the same date. The church (r.) of *Pommereux* is XII. c. and XIII. c.

116 k. *Forges-les-Eaux* (Hotels: *des Thermes; des Bains*), a prettily-situated mineral watering-place, which was very fashionable in the reigns of Louis XIII. and XIV., and which was frequented by 'La grande Mademoiselle.'

'La vie de Forges est fort douce et bien différente de celle que l'on mène ordinairement: on se lève à six heures au plus tard ; on va à la fontaine ; pour moi je n'aime pas prendre mes eaux chez moi ; on se promène pendant qu'on les prend ; il y a beaucoup de monde ; on parle les uns aux autres ; le chapitre de régime et de l'effet des eaux est souvent traité aussi bien que celui des maladies qui y font venir les gens, et du progrès qu'on fait à les détruire. On sait tous ceux qui sont arrivés le soir ; quand il y a des nouveaux venus on les accoste ; c'est le lieu du monde où l'on fait le plus aisément connoissance. Quand on a achevé de boire, ce qui est ordinairement sur les huit heures, on s'en va dans le jardin des Capucins, qui n'est point fermé de murailles. Forges est un lieu où il vient toutes sortes des gens, des religieuses de même, des prêtres, des ministres huguenots et les grands de tous pays, de toutes professions, cette variété est assez divertissante. Après qu'on s'est promené on va à la messe, puis chacun va s'habiller ; les habits du matinée et ceux de l'après-midi sont fort différens ; le matin on a de la rature et de la fourfure, et l'après-dîner du taffetas. La meilleure saison pour prendre les eaux, c'est la canicule, qui, pour l'ordinaire, est assez chaude ; quand on a bu beaucoup d'eau, on a grand froid. On dine à midi avec beaucoup d'appétit, ce qui m'est nouveau : excepté lorsque je prends les eaux et que je suis fort longtemps sans manger, je n'ai jamais faim. L'après-dîner on venoit me voir ; à cinq heures j'allais à la comédie, une des troupes de Paris était à Rouen, je la fis venir à Forges, ce qui étoit d'un grand secours pour le divertissement. A six heures on soupe, et l'on va se promener aux Capucins, où l'on dit les litanies; presque tout le monde les entend avant la promenade, puis à neuf heures chacun se retire. Les eaux me firent grand bien.'—*Mémoires de Mlle de Montpensier.*

An excursion may be made to (2½ k.) *Riberpré*, an old moated château (5 k.): the church of *Thil-Riberpré*, partly XIII. c., with stalls and an altar from the Abbey of Clair-Ruissel; and (7 k.) the abbey of *Beaubec*, founded 1128, restored, after a fire, in 1450, and ruined at the Revolution: the *Chapelle S. Ursule*, built 1266, was restored in 1780. Another excursion is that to (3¼ k.) the church of *La Ferté-S.-Simon*, whence there is a wide view. The apse is the remnant of a collegiate church founded (x. c.) by Gautier de Gournay. Behind are ruins of a fortress. The hamlet of *S. Samson* has a XIII. c. font. At 10 k. is *Argueil*, with a château of XIII. c., XVI. c., and XVII. c. At 12 k. *Sigy*, with a monastic church, possessing a noble XII. c. choir, with timber vaulting of XVIII. c.

121 k. *Serqueux*, a junction station.

[A line runs E. to (72 k.) Amiens, and west to (45 k.) Rouen by—

18 k. *Montérollier-Buchy*. Near the church of *Montérollier* (3 k. N.) is a tower of the ancient château, and in the cemetery a good XVI. c. cross. At *Bosc-Bordel* (4 k. E.) is a good XIII. c. church, with a fine porch. *S. Martin d'Omonville* (6 k.) has good XV. c. alabaster reliefs. The romanesque church of *Estouteville* is passed on the l. before reaching—

25 k. *Longuerue-Vieux-Manoir.*

29 k. *Morgny.* 5 k. distant is the fine XV. c. collegiate church of *Blainville-Crevon*, founded by Jean d'Estouteville.]

After leaving Serqueux, the line passes (r.) *Beaubec-la-*

Rosière, where the church (XI. c., XII. c., and XIII. c.) is preceded by a square called *La Prèle*, with a XIII. c. cross.

130 k. *Nesle-S.-Saire*. *Nesle-Hodeng* (r.) has a XII. c. and XIII. c. church, a beautiful XVI. c. cross, and remains of an abbey of 1140, turned into a farm. Below the church of *S. Saire* (l.) with XIV. c. glass, is an ancient crypt containing a well. The line now passes (l.) *Neuville-Ferrières*, where the church has a XIII. c. choir.

136 k. *Neufchâtel-en-Bray* (Hotel: *du Grand Cerf*) was the ancient Driencourt.

'But a castle, erected in comparatively modern times by Henry Beauclerc, subsequently caused Driencourt to obtain the denomination of Neufchâtel, which it still retains, like its Helvetic congener. You smell the cheese in every room of your inn. The region is the dairy of Paris.'—*Palgrave*.

Robert, eldest son of the Conqueror, in rebellion against his father, found a refuge here.

The church of *Notre Dame* (XII. c., XV. c., and XVI. c.) has a XVI. c. tower, a late XV. c. portal. A S. Sepulcre, of 1491, is full of expression. Only the apse and a XVI. c. aisle remain of the church of *S. Pierre*. The *Abbaye des Bernardines* is now a *Hôtel de Ville*, and contains a small *Musée d'Antiquités*. Entered by a passage from the l. of the *Grande Rue*, where it opens on the church, is the very picturesque and curious *Maison des Templiers*, with much carved timber-work. The cheeses for which the place is famous are called *bondons de Neuchâtel*.

Historians should make an excursion (carriage 6 fr.) on the road to Aumale to (11 k.) *Mortemer* (*mortuum mare*—stagnant pool), which had a famous castle under the Norman dukes. It lies, embedded in thick foliage, below a low line of hills. The first settlement here originated in the hermitages of Tascio, Guiard, and the noble Guillaume de Fresquiennes, near which a monastery arose, giving an impulse to clearances, which have continued

MAISON DES TEMPLIERS, NEUFCHÂTEL.

through seven centuries, till the Forest of Lions has lost all general sylvan character, though wooded portions are called forests of Bray, Andelys, Gournay, Vernon, Longböel, etc. The remains of the castle—a mere rag of wall surrounded by a tremendous entrenchment—are approached through the garden of a little mansion on the left of the village lane. When William the Conqueror burnt Mortemer, in the XI. c., he gave the fortress to William de Warrenne, who afterwards married his step-daughter Gundrada.

'The castle rises above the surrounding country; the tall dungeon tower, whose walls still crown the rock, became the head station of the French troops, and they filled the fortress with the booty they had gained. The field of Mortemer, and the scattered farmhouses representing Mortemer, are standing immediately beneath that grim grey donjon tower. The Normans diligently dogged the enemy, and when the day emerged from the night, which the French had passed in drunken debauchery, they assailed the fortalice and fired the town. The dark, cavernous, ancient church still exists, in good repair; a score of straggling farmhouses are dotted in the surrounding pastures, and the charred timbers, turned up by the ploughshares, still testify the original extent of the town. . . . The French, thoroughly routed, fled from the field bestrewed with corpses, every pit and dungeon was crowded with captives, and amongst them the Count of Burgundy, his ransom worth a king's.'—*Palgrave*.

Roger de Toeni, climbing up a tree on a hill above the French camp, told the French of their defeat, as was long commemorated in song and lay :—

> ' Franceiz, Franceiz, levez, levez,
> Tenez vos veies, trop dormez ;
> Allez vos amis enterrer,
> Ki sunt occiz à Mortemer.'

Near the church is *La Ferme du Prieuré*, a remnant of a Cluniac Priory, founded by Henry I. The church itself was begun by Henry II. in 1154, and consecrated 1209.

[A road runs N.E. from Neufchâtel to (30 k.) Blangy (on the line from Beauvais to Tréport), by (19 k.) *Foucarmont*, where there are considerable remains of the minor buildings of an abbey founded by Henry I. in 1130. The *Chapelle de l'Espinette* is flamboyant. At 3½ k. is the (XVI. c.) church of *S. Léger aux Bois*, surrounded internally by a sculptured garland interrupted by statues.]

141 k. *Mesnières*, has a fine and important renaissance *Château* now turned into an orphanage. The *Galerie des Cerfs* is named from six stags in stone. The old chapel has ancient glass and statues. In the *Church* the (XIII. c.) Chapelle de la Vierge communicates with the choir by a renaissance arcade of 1618.

145 k. *Bures*. The fine church is XII. c. and XIII. c. In the N. wall of the choir a Latin inscription relates its consecration in 1168. The choir windows deserve notice. The font is XIV. c. A brick house is late XV. c. The old *Manoir de Tourpes*, turned into a farm, is said to have belonged to Gabrielle d'Estrées. The line passes (r.) the (XI. c., XIII. c. and XVI. c.) church of *Osmoy* : on the l. is the old *Manoir de la Valouine* (1602).

152 k. *S. Vaast d'Equiqueville*. The church is XI. c., XIII. c., and XV. c. The house called *La Doyennée* is XIII. c.

159 k. *Dampierre*. The *Château de Senarpont* is late XVI. c. On r. is the church (partly XIII. c.) of *S. Aubin le Cauf*.

164 k. *Arques la Bataille* (Hotel : *du Château*—good), on the little river Arques, with a very picturesque church of 1515-83, where the *Chapelle S. Nicolas*, which has a good renaissance portal, contains a bust of Henri IV. and an inscription relating to the battle of Arques. A convent of Bernardines is turned into a private house. Many who frequent the sea-baths at Dieppe have their lodgings at Arques, and the hotels are full during the season. From the top of the village a steep ascent leads to the *Castle*,

occupying a tongue of land, with its donjon on the neck of the isthmus. It was built in the middle of the XI. c. by Guillaume, Comte d'Arques, half-uncle of William the Conqueror,[1] and fortified by a very deep fosse between the castle

CHURCH OF ARQUES.

and the natural cliffs, so that assailants, who ascended the latter, would only find themselves on a narrow ledge, exposed to the fortress, but far removed from it. Count William turned his castle into a nest of robbers, from which he ravaged the country, so the Conqueror besieged him there

[1] Son of Richard le Bon by his third wife, Papia. He claimed to be the legitimate descendant of Rollo.

and starved him into surrender. He was banished, and Arques was bestowed upon Hélie de S. Saens, but it was reclaimed by Henry I., who fortified it afresh. It was seized by Philippe-Auguste during the captivity of Richard Coeur de Lion, who recovered it in 1196. In 1204 it was the last Anglo-Norman fortress to open its gates to the French. In the last century it was used as a granary for building materials, and its huge indestructible walls, stripped of their hewn stone, are now shapeless masses. The inner enclosure of the castle is divided into two courts, the outer occupied by the buildings of François I., and flanked by enormous towers of brick and stone, which defended the entrance. This court communicated with the second, of the XI. c., by a triple gate fortified with portcullis, containing the XI. c. keep, opposite which is a modern relief representing Henri IV. on horseback.

The neighbouring hamlet of *Archelles*, which has a XVI. c. manor-house, is overlooked by the wooded hill which was the scene of the famous battle of Arques and the great victory of Henri IV. over the troops of Mayenne.

170 k. *Dieppe* (Hotels : *Royal ; de Bristol ; des Bains ; du Rhin ; de la Plage*), which rose to importance under the Anglo-Norman rule as a principal point of communication with England, suffered terribly in the wars of religion, and from the English bombardment of July 1694. Its reputation as a marine bathing-place has restored some of its prosperity, and its *Château* (built in 1435) gives it a certain dignity. Several streets are rather picturesque, but the town contains no especial objects of interest except the (XII.—XVI. c.) church of *S. Jacques*, which has a splendid

rose-window and a rich open flamboyant balustrade in the choir.

Beyond the faubourg of *Pollet*, near the hamlet of *Puys*, is the curious enclosure called *La Cité de Limes*, containing a number of little tumuli. It was probably one of the *oppida* which were the last refuge of the ancient inhabitants at the time of the Roman invasion.

The principal excursion from Dieppe is that to (6 k.) Arques, which may be reached either by rail, by road, or by a boat upon the Dieppette.

2 k. from Dieppe by the shore is *Puys*, where Lord Salisbury has a villa.

6 k. is the pleasant village *Varengeville*, with interesting remains of the manor-house (1530-42) of Jean Ango, the Jacques Coeur (merchant prince) of the time of François I., who frequently lent large sums of money, and even a fleet to his sovereign, but was ruined by jealous cabals after the death of François. In the medallions of the façade François I. and Diane de Poitiers are represented. The picturesquely situated church is of XIII. c. and XV. c. 2 k. hence is the *Lighthouse of Ailly*, on the Cap des Roches.

An excursion may be made to (15 k.) *Envermeu*, passing (7 k.) *Ancourt*, where the XVI. c. church has a XIII. c. tower and good glass; and (8 k.) *Sauchay-le-Bas*, with a restored romanesque church. Only the mound called *Le Câtel* remains to mark the site of the castle which William the Conqueror built at *Envermeu*. The fine (XVI. c.) flamboyant church of *Notre Dame* is a rich and beautiful specimen of the period: in the cemetery is a renaissance cross.

[A road leads N.E. from Dieppe to (30 k.) Tréport, by (8 k.) *Graincourt*, where the church has a romanesque portal and XVI. c. font; (11 k.) *S. Martin en Campagne*, where the cemetery has a XVI. c. cross; (15 k.) *Béville sur Mer*, where the church has a graceful XV. c. choir: and (21 k.) *Criel* (Hotel: *de la Plage*), a small bathing-place.]

[A road leads W. to (34 k.) S. Valery en Caux by (15 k.) *Le Bourg Dun*, with a rather interesting church of many dates; the S. transept is of delicate renaissance of the time of François I.; and (21 k.) *Ouville-la-Rivière*, where the church has an XI. c. tower. 6 k. from Ouville is *Hautot sur Mer*, with remains of an old fortress: the church choir is XIII. c., the cemetery cross of 1520. Near the old house called *La Cohue* is a fine XVI. c. cross called *La Croix à la Dame*.]

[A road leads E. to (69 k.) Nointot, on the line from Paris to Havre by (21 k.) *Bacqueville*, with a XVI. c. church containing a curious painting representing the legend of a Sire de Bacqueville; and (31 k.) *S. Laurent en Caux*, with a remarkable yew tree and a cemetery cross of 1603.]

[For the line to Rouen by Malaunay see ch. ii.]

The country is full of farmhouses, which recall Alphonse Karr's description of a Normandy farm :—

'La masure était une charmante habitation. Le chaume qui la couvrait était tapissé de mousse du côté du nord. Des iris élevaient sur sa crête leurs feuilles aiguës et leurs fleurs violettes; il y avait dans la cheminée un nid dans lequel des hirondelles venaient pondre et couver leurs oeufs tous les ans. Un vieux chèvrefeuille couvrait en partie la façade de la chaumière, et poussait avec un tel luxe de végétation qu'il fallait chaque année couper quelques branches qui auraient obstrué les fenêtres. La cour. . . . on appelle ainsi en Normandie toute autre chose que ce qu'on appelle cour à Paris. Une cour normande est un grand carré de terre couvert d'herbes et entouré d'une haie d'épines entre des chênes et des ormeaux plantés sur un fossé. Il faut ouvrir ici une nouvelle parenthèse pour dire que le mot fossé a également, en Normandie, un sens tout différent de celui qu'il a, je crois, partout ailleurs.

'On appelle fossé précisément le contraire de ce qui s'appelle d'ordinaire un fossé, c'est à dire un talus haut de quatre à six pieds, en forme de petites murailles, qui entoure une cour et sur lequel on plante des arbres. Je disais donc que la cour était remplie de pommiers, vieux arbres rugueux et moussus, qui, tous les ans, se chargeaient au mois de mai de fleurs blanches et roses d'une fraîcheur et d'un éclat enchanteurs. Une grande mare servait d'asile à des canards dont le col vert miroitait au soleil. Outre les pommiers, il y avait dans la cour des groseilliers à maquereaux et des grossilliers à grappes appelés galadiers; l'herbe était parsemée de violettes, les unes de la couleur ordinaire, les autres blanches, et de bassinets jaunes, sorte de boutons d'or à pétales pointus qui couvrent presque entièrement la terre au printemps.'—*Alphonse Karr,* '*Clovis Gosselin.*'

The apple-orchards give a radiant appearance to the country in spring and autumn, and are very profitable to their owners; though Normandy cider-makers, seldom satisfied with their crops, generally say, when asked what sort of season it is with them, 'Pour une année où il n'y a pas de pommes il y a des pommes ; mais pour une année où il y a des pommes, il n'y a pas de pommes.'

CHAPTER II.

PARIS TO HAVRE, BY MANTES, VERNON, GAILLON, ROUEN (JUMIÈGES, CAUDEBEC), AND YVETOT (ETRETAT, FÉCAMP), (LILLEBONNE). FROM THE GARE S. LAZARE.

LEAVING the Gare S. Lazare, the line reaches—

8 k. *Colombes*, where Henrietta Maria, widow of Charles I. of England, died, August 31, 1669, in her château. Here also, was the convent of *Chaillot*, where both Henrietta Maria and Mary Beatrice often took refuge, and to which their hearts were bequeathed.

17 k. *Maisons-Laffitte*. The magnificent château of Maisons was built by François Mansart for René de Longueil, Surintendant des Finances. Voltaire frequently stayed there with the Président de Maisons, and nearly died there of the small-pox. On his recovery, he had scarcely left the château to set out on his return to Paris, when the room he had occupied and the adjoining chambers were destroyed by fire. In 1778 the château was bought by the Comte d'Artois, and an apartment was arranged there for each of the royal family. Maisons was sold as national property at the Revolution, and has since belonged to the Duc de Montebello, and to the banker Laffitte, by whom part of the park has been cut up for villas.

As Maisons is approached by the railway, there is a fine view (on right) of the stately château rising above the west bank of the Seine, with a highly picturesque mill of the same date striding across an arm of the river in the foreground.

At 1½ k. is *Sartrouville*, where the church has a central romanesque octagon, with a stone spire of later date. The nave piers are cylindrical, the arches pointed transitional.

22 k. *Conflans-S.-Honorine.* This place receives its first name from its situation at the confluence of the Seine and Oise; its second from the shrine of S. Honorine, brought hither by a native of Graville for protection from the Normans in 898: her relics are still carried in procession on Ascension Day. The parish church of *S. Maclou* has an admirable romanesque tower of the xii. c. In the choir is the tomb of Jean I., Seigneur de Montmorency, and near it the xiv. c. statue of Mathieu IV. de Montmorency, Admiral and High Chamberlain of France, 1304. A tower, called *La Baronnie*, marks the site of the priory of S. Honorine.

27 k. *Poissy* (Hotel: *de Rouen*, right of station—very humble), on the left bank of the Seine, was the seat of a very ancient royal residence, destroyed by Charles V. If S. Louis was not born he was certainly baptised here, and was wont to sign himself 'Louis de Poissy.'

Close to the railway, in the centre of the tiny town, rises the noble *Church*. Late romanesque, with flamboyant additions, it has a most striking outline. The older portions—the nave, the apsidal choir with its two apsides, and the west and central towers, date from the xi. c., though the massive west tower, supporting a conical stone spire, and the two first bays of the nave, were rebuilt, on the old lines, in the XVII. c. The nave chapels are XVI. c.

WEST TOWER, POISSY.

The west tower formerly served as a porch, but this is now blocked up, and the principal entrance is by a magnificent early XVI. c. porch on the south, with open arches on two sides. The exterior has been injured by coarse restoration, but the interior is exceedingly beautiful and has been well restored. A number of early statues of saints are full of quaint character. The romanesque chapel on the north of the choir contains a fragment of the font in which S. Louis was baptised; a considerable part at least of the rest has been taken as dust in glasses of water by the faithful as a cure for fever. In the same chapel is a tombstone, with a very curious epitaph, recording how Remy Henault, 1630, was twice dead and twice alive; how, after having been consigned to the tomb, he was resuscitated by the devotion of his son, expressed in ardent prayer to S. Geneviève, and rose again a second Lazarus, to be called 'Le ressuscité.' His son, a second Remy, who ordained special worship to S. Geneviève for her favour, now rests with him.

In the opposite chapel, of S. Louis, are relics of the sainted king. This chapel formerly had a stained-glass window representing the birth of S. Louis, and beneath were the XVI. c. lines—

> 'Saint-Louis fut un enfant de Poissy,
> Et baptisé en la présente église;
> Les fonts en sont gardés encore ici,
> Et honorés comme relique exquise.'

The apsidal chapel, filled with *ex-votos* to the Virgin, has modern stained-glass illustrative of the life of S. Louis.

A little behind the church is a fine old gateway, flanked by two round towers, the principal existing remnant of the famous *Abbaye de Poissy*, which Philippe le Bel founded in 1304, in the place of an earlier Augustinian monastery founded by Constance of Normandy, wife of King Robert.

In its refectory, Catherine de Medicis convoked the *Colloque de Poissy* in 1560, when thirty Protestants, with Théodore de Bèze at their head, disputed upon religious subjects with the papal legate, sixteen cardinals, forty bishops, and a number of other theologians. Nothing remains of the magnificent abbey church, a marvel of architectural beauty, begun by Philippe le Bel and finished by Philippe de Valois, which was pulled down in the beginning of the XIX. c. It contained the tombs of Queen Constance, Philippe le Bel, Agnès de Méranie, and of Philippe and Jean of France, children of Louis VIII. and Blanche of Castille. A pewter urn, containing the heart of the founder, Philippe le Bel, was found during some repairs in 1687. Reached by the abbey gate is the house occupied, through thirty years, by the famous artist Meissonier.

On the right of the station is the entrance to the *Bridge* (originally of thirty-seven arches) built by S. Louis, but all its character is destroyed by its being lowered and by the substitution of a cast-iron parapet for the original of stone.

The famous Cattle-market of Poissy, founded by S. Louis, is still held every Thursday.

The line passes (l.) *Medan*, with a château dating from the XV. c., and in which pavilions of that date are connected by galleries of the time of Henri IV. In the XVII. c. church is the font of the famous royal church of S. Paul in Paris, in which many kings and princes have been baptised.

35 k. *Triel.* A considerable place under the hills, on the right. The village of *Vernouillet* (l. of the station) has a steeple of good outline rising from a romanesque

tower. A number of ruined *émigrés* on their return to France after the Revolution united to buy its château, and spent the rest of their lives there in happy harmony! The adjoining village of *Verneuil* has a central romanesque tower with late additions. The cruciform church of Triel itself is chiefly of the XIV. c., with a plain central tower: a street passes beneath the lofty choir. *Vaux* (1 k.) has a romanesque tower and transept, and an elegant semicircular early pointed apse; the nave, which has aisles, but no clerestory, is XIV. c.

41 k. *Meulan-les-Mureaux*. The station is at *Mureaux*, where the modern church contains six curious XIII. c. columns; of these, four, at the entrance, support a kind of triumphal arch of three openings. A stone bridge connects Mureaux with *Meulan*, once the chief town of a countship, which was united to the crown of France by Philippe Auguste in 1203. Louis XIII. established a convent of the Annunciation here for Charlotte du Puy de Jésus-Maria, whose prayers were believed to have removed the barrenness of Anne of Austria. The church of *Notre Dame*, in the lower town, is XIV. c. and XV. c.; that of *S. Nicolas*, on the hill (Le Haut Meulan), has a XII. c. ambulatory. Near Notre Dame is a good XIV. c. house. On the island called *Le Fort* are remains of a XV. c. chapel of S. Jacques, and of a castle, of which Du Guesclin overthrew the donjon, when it was defended by the partisans of Charles le Mauvais. 6 k. N., occupying a square eminence, is the interesting late XV. c. *Château de Vigny*, built by Cardinal Georges d'Amboise.[1]

49 k. *Epône*. The château belonged to the family of

---

[1] See page 1.

Créqui. The church has an octagonal romanesque tower, containing an XI. c. portal: two other portals are XII. c.

[An omnibus runs from the station of Epône to that of *Villiers-Néauphle*, on the line from Paris to Dreux, by the valley of the Mauldre, passing (12 k.) *Aulnay*, where the church contains an ancient tabernacle beautifully sculptured; and (20 k.) *Maule*, where the church was built 1070—1118, has a tower of 1547, and covers an XI. c. crypt: a beautiful XV. c. chapel serves as a sacristy. The château dates from Louis XIII.]

57 k. *Mantes* (Hotel: *du Grand Cerf*, a good old-fashioned inn, with comforts; *du Soleil d'Or*). 'Mantes la jolie' of the old topographers is a charming and interesting old town. It was in 1087, after burning Mantes, which he had reclaimed from Philippe I. of France, that William the Conqueror, whilst riding proudly round the town, received the injury of which he died a few days after at Rouen.

'Comme il galopait à travers les décombres, son cheval mit les deux pieds sur des charbons accouverts de cendre, s'abattit, et le blessa au ventre. L'agitation qu'il s'était donnée en courant et en criant, la chaleur du feu et de la saison rendirent sa blessure dangereuse. On le transporta malade à Rouen, et de là dans un monastère hors des murs de la ville dont il ne pouvait supporter le bruit. Il languit durant six semaines, entouré de médecins et de prêtres, et son mal s'aggravant de plus en plus, il envoya de l'argent à Mantes pour rebâtir les églises qu'il avait incendiées.'—*Augustin Thierry*.

The noble church of *Notre Dame* was built with the money sent by William the Conqueror, and was again rebuilt at the end of the XII. c., at the same time as Notre Dame de Paris, to which it has a great resemblance.

Its façade shows what that of Paris would have been if its completion had not been delayed till the middle of the XIII. c. Of the three grand portals, two are admirable examples of the XII. c.; that on the right was rebuilt in 1300, with a gable copied from the south portal of Rouen cathedral, which adds to the effect of the building by variety. Above the three portals are seven

MANTES.

arches, of which four light the first floors of the two towers. Higher, is a large window in each tower, and in the centre a beautiful rose-window. The graceful gallery above, of slender lancet arches, is comparatively modern. The upper story of the towers, of open arches, is indescribably light and beautiful. The retired space, shaded by trees, in which the church stands, recalls an English cathedral close in the charm of its seclusion.

The church has no transept, and originally it had only

a simple ambulatory, with no radiating chapels; the five chapels which surround the choir only having been added in the xiv. c. The clerestory is exceedingly light, and the triforium, covering the whole space of the aisles, of great width. Two leaden coffins recently discovered are supposed to contain the heart and entrails of Philippe Auguste, who died at Mantes, July 14, 1223. Viollet le Duc mentions the Chapelle de Navarre on the south of the choir, with its four arches meeting at a central pillar, as one of the finest examples of the xiv c. in the Île de France: its four great windows are beautiful in design, have grand fragments of stained glass, and are supported by a graceful arcade. Against the wall of the north aisle is the curious incised gravestone of Robert Gueribeau, 1644, founder of the Ursuline convent.

Below the church, 'the *Grande Rue* presents that precipitous descent which sadly, sorrowfully, and ignobly terminated the Conqueror's earthly career.'[1]

An artist will find attractive subjects in the noble tower of 1340, which is all that remains of the great church of *S. Maclou*, destroyed in the Revolution, and in the gothic entrance (1344) of the old *Hôtel de Ville* (which has a stone staircase of the time of Charles VIII.), with a pretty renaissance fountain in front of it. Many picturesque fragments remain of the ancient walls and towers with which Mantes was surrounded by Charles le Mauvais and Charles le Sage, especially the *Tour de S. Martin* and an old postern gate on the *Quai des Cordeliers*. Of the other gates, the *Porte Chante l'Oie* still exists. There is a very picturesque half-ruined bridge connecting the right

[1] Palgrave.

bank with the island in the Seine, whence there is the best view of Notre Dame, rising in grey grandeur above the broken outline of the old houses, while the whole is mirrored in the Seine.

Beyond the island, with its pleasant promenades, a second bridge leads to the suburb of *Limay*, which has a modern Mairie, of good design, and a church chiefly of the XIII. c. and XV. c., but possessing a very beautiful tower and spire of the XII. c., with a romanesque chapel beneath. On the left of the west entrance is the tomb of Jean le Chenet, grand-écuyer to Charles II., and his wife, brought from the chapel of S. Antoine, which they founded at the Celestine Convent; behind it is a *Pietà* in coloured relief, on either side of which are the founders presented by their patron saints. The low wide font is of the XIII. c.

On the hill above Limay is *Le Château des Célestins*, on the site of a convent founded in 1376 by Charles V.; and a little below the white walls of its vineyard terraces a path leads to the *Hermitage of S. Sauveur* (4 k. from Mantes). The way winds along the edge of the limestone hills, which, ugly in form, especially lend themselves to vineyards, and the views of the windings of the Seine are beautiful. A stone cross stands at a point where there is an exquisite view of Mantes—the noble towers of Notre Dame rising above rich woods and a graceful bend of the river, and the wavy hills, in soft succession of pink and blue distances, folding behind them. The hermitage is very quaint and picturesque—a little establishment enclosed by walls, and a church of considerable size caverned out of the rock and containing a curious old S. Sepulcre, with a number

of other figures full of character, brought from the
Célestins; also the effigy of Thomas le Tourneur, secretary
of Charles V. and canon of Mantes, who died in that
convent.

Those who wish for a longer walk may cross the Seine
by a ferry to the church of *Gassicourt* (3 k. from Mantes),
partly of the XI. c. and XIII c., which belonged formerly

HERMITAGE OF S. SAUVEUR.

to a Cluniac priory, and of which Bossuet always held the
living. The portal is curious. The choir windows have
remains of stained glass given by Blanche of Castile. A
singular sculpture represents Jesus offering to the Queen,
as the Virgin, the portrait of S. Louis as a child. There
are considerable remains of mural paintings, and, in the
Chapelle S. Eloi, a sculptured lavabo.

A road runs north-west from Mantes, evading a wide bend
of the river, by the *Château de Mesnil* to (12 k.) *Vétheuil,*

which has an important collegiate church, partly gothic and partly renaissance, to the ornamentation of which many kings and queens of France have contributed. The porch bears the monograms of François I. and Henri II. The south and west doors are sculptured with scenes from Scripture history. The west portal, surmounted by a triple gallery, has statues of royal benefactors; the central column bears a figure of Charity. The unfinished tower is of 1350. In the interior are considerable remains of mural paintings. The XII. c. choir has good stall-work. At the end of the *Cour de l'Eglise* is a little crypt, a relic of the primitive church of Vétheuil.

At 19 k. from Mantes is the famous castle of *La Roche-Guyon* (see later).

To the south of Mantes is (10 k.) *Rosay*, where the picturesque brick château of the Comtesse de Jobal dates from Henri III., and between Rosay and Septeuil, the little village of *S. Corentin*, which possessed an abbey where the heart and entrails of Agnès de Méranie, wife of Philippe Auguste, and of Blanche of Castille were buried.

63 k. *Rosny.* The XVI. c. *Château* (approached by a turn on the r. of the village street, opposite the fountain), was built by the famous Sully (Maximilien de Béthune), to replace an earlier château in which he was born, December 13, 1550. It was left unfinished in 1610, as he had no longer spirit to continue the work after the murder of his beloved master, Henri IV. The Duchesse de Berri, daughter-in-law of Charles X., inhabited it as a summer residence; and a funeral monument remains behind the altar of the church, which once supported the heart of the murdered Duc de Berri. The château, with its high dormer roofs, red brick walls and stone ornaments, has a singularly cheerful aspect, and its beautiful park and brilliant gardens, most courteously thrown open by its

generous owner M. Lebaudy, are a great delight to the people of the little town on summer evenings.

The line passes by a tunnel under the hill of *Rolleboise*, which bears the remains of a castle taken (1364) by Du Guesclin and destroyed by Charles V.

80 k. *Vernon* (Hotel: *d'Evreux*), which has a great state factory of military equipments. The church has a choir of XII. c., a nave of XIV. c., and chapels of XV. c. In the second

CHATEAU DE ROSNY.

chapel l. is the tomb of Marie Maignard, wife of the Sieur Imbert d'Harcquency. In the r. aisle is a Resurrection by *Annibale Caracci*. Six fine tapestries are of the XVII. c. Of the ancient fortifications, the *Tour des Archives* is preserved. The castle of *Vernonnet*, on the r. bank of the Seine, was built by Edward I. of England. Only the stables remain of the *Château de Bizy*, destroyed in the Revolution, which was the property of the Duc de Penthièvre.

[A line runs N.E. from Vernon to (42 k.) Gisors, by—

12 k. *Gasny.* This is the station for *La Roche Guyon,* 2½ k. distant. Beyond the last house in the village of Gasny, pedestrians may take a footpath on l. which leads over the brow of a hill to a declivity above the Seine, whence the village is seen by the river, with the castle on a chalk bluff above it. There is a small hotel near the suspension-bridge.

The famous Château de la Roche Guyon was founded by Guy de Guyon in 998 (though the existing buildings are of the XIII. c.), and taken by the English in 1418, after a gallant defence

CHÂTEAU DE LA ROCHE GUYON.

by Perrette la Rivière, widow of Guy VI. de la Roche Guyon, who fell at Agincourt. Old ballads tell the story of the lord of the castle murdered in 1097 by his father-in-law, together with his wife, who vainly tried to protect him. The immense substructions are hewn out of the rock. The principal remaining building is the keep. The later château of the Duc de la Roche Guyon—a great building like a barrack at the foot of the cliff—has some traces of the XIII. c. and an entrance gate of the XV. c. The *Salle des Gardes,* inscribed with the family mottoes, '*C'est mon plaisir,*' '*In Deo confido,*' is filled with armour. In the

GAILLON.

Chambre de Henri IV. are the king's bed and bureau. The MS. of La Rochefoucauld's 'Maximes' is preserved here. Lamartine's Meditation, entitled 'La Semaine Sainte à la Roche Guyon,' was written when the beautiful XIV. c. chapel was restored. The xv. c. church contains on r. of the altar the tomb of François de Silly, Duc de la Roche Guyon, 1627, with his kneeling statue, 'Le monde est le tombeau de sa gloire parfaite.' A number of members of the families of La Rochefoucauld, De Rohan, and De Montmorency repose in the vaults. A fountain, below the church and the château, was erected by Duc Alexandre de la Rochefoucauld in 1717.

19 k. *Bray-Ecos.* The village of Bray, near the station, is overlooked by the church and ruined castle of *Baudemont.* 5 k. N.W. is the XIII. c. church of *Ecos*, on the spot where SS. Nicaise, Quérin, and Scubicule were martyred. The xv. c. *Château du Chesnay* near this has been recently rebuilt.

27 k. *Bordeaux-S.-Clair.* The village of S. Clair has the ruins of a castle built by Henry II. of England. 6 k. N.W. is the *Château de Boisdenemetz*, built under Louis XIII., and 6 k. S.W. of this is the *Château de Beauregard*, where the poet Abbé de Chaulieu was born in 1639. 6 k. E. of the station of Bordeaux is the fine church of *Parnes*, partly XI. c. and XII. c., and 3 k. S.E. of this the *Château d'Halaincourt*, of xv. c. and XVI. c.

32 k. *Dangu.* Here was a famous fortress of the XI. c., one of the principal places of defence on the frontier of Normandy. The present château (Comte F. de Lagrange) is of 1567, and is well known from its *haras.*]

[A line leads S.E. to (17 k.) Pacy-sur-Eure, on the line from Dreux to Louviers by (9 k.) *Drouains-Blaru*, near which is the *Château de Brécourt*, of the time of Louis XIII.]

94 k. *Gaillon* (Hotel: *d'Evreux*). 2 k. l. is the town, surmounted by the remains of its *Château*, now transformed into a prison. This once magnificent building was begun, on the site of an earlier castle, by Guillaume d'Estouteville in 1454, and continued in the XVI. c. by Cardinal Georges d'Amboise, minister of Louis XII., and Cardinal de

Bourbon, and finished by Colbert, Archbishop of Rouen. All the great renaissance architects and sculptors of the time were employed upon it; but it was sold, and the greater part of it demolished at the Revolution. The portions which remain are the entrance gate built by Georges d'Amboise, the Grande Galerie, the clock-tower, and a tower of the chapel, in which the Bishops of Normandy met in conclave to condemn the *Maximes des Saints* of Fénélon. The magnificent portico which separated the two courts of the château has been removed to the court of the Palais des Beaux Arts at Paris. 3 k. S. is the hill-set village of *S. Aubin-sur-Gaillon*, where Marmontel is buried in the cemetery.

[Omnibuses (1 fr.) ply between Gaillon and (8 k.) Les Andelys (carriage 8 fr.). The road runs across an exposed plain to *Le Petit Andely*, a picturesque and ancient village on the r. bank of the Seine, which contains the fine xii. c. church of *S. Sauveur*. The interior is remarkably striking and majestic. At the foot of the Roche S. Jacques is the *Hospice S. Jacques*, founded in 1784 by the Duc de Penthièvre.

Above Le Petit Andely the massive ruins of *Château Gaillard* rise boldly from chalk cliffs. It was founded by Richard Coeur de Lion in 1197. 'Qu'elle est belle, ma fille d'un an!' exclaimed the king, after its three lines of defence were finished. But under John (1204) the castle was taken by Philippe-Auguste. In 1313 it served as a prison to Marguerite de Bourgogne, wife of Louis X., and Blanche, wife of Charles le Bel (accused of adultery), the former of whom was strangled here by order of her husband when he wished to marry again, and the latter removed to lifelong imprisonment in the Abbey of Maubuisson. In 1334 the château was inhabited by David Bruce during his exile. Charles le Mauvais was imprisoned there in 1355.

There is a fine view of the windings of the Seine from the ruins, of which the keep is the principal feature. It is almost circular, but has an angle towards the E., and is supported externally by 'buttresses like huge stone quoins.'[1]

'Le donjon du Château-Gaillard était pour le temps une oeuvre tout-à-fait remarquable. Ce donjon, dont le pied est entièrement plein et par conséquent à l'abis de la sape, se composait d'une salle ronde, au rez-de-chaussée de laquelle il fallait descendre d'un premier étage au niveau d'une poterne, d'un second étage au niveau des machicoulis, chemin de ronde crénelé,

CHÂTEAU GAILLARD.

d'un troisième étage en retraite, fermé, propre aux approvisionnements de projectiles, et d'un quatrième étage étendu et couvert, commandant les chemins de ronde et les dehors au loin. Rien de trop, rien d'inutile, rien que ce qui est absolument nécessaire à la défense.'—*Viollet le Duc.*

The tower has an elliptic outwork, offering through three parts of its development, seventeen segments of towers, which are only separated from each other by two feet of curtain wall.

[1] Deville, *Histoire du Château Gaillard.*

In the river, opposite Le Petit Andely, is *Île Contant*, with remains of an octagonal tower called *Boutavant*, built by Richard Coeur de Lion in 1196.]

At *Le Grand Andely* (1 k. farther) the *Hôtel du Grand Cerf* occupies a richly sculptured black-and-white timber building of the beginning of the XVI. c. In the restaurant, formerly the kitchen, is a huge and splendid decorated chimneypiece. The courtyard of the hotel is picturesque.

In the Place du Marché is a statue of Nicolas Poussin, who

HOTEL DU GRAND CERF, LES ANDELYS.

was born June 1, 1594, at the hamlet of *Villers*, 3 k. S.E. of the town. One of his best works, 'Coriolanus yielding to his mother,' and an Adoration of the Shepherds, from his hand, are in the *Hôtel de Ville*.

'Vers Les Andelys, les rives de la Seine, si riantes et si fleuries autour de Rosni et de Mantes, si luxuriantes de végétation sur les pentes des fières collines qui commandent Rouen, prennent un caractère plus sérieux et plus austère; de grands rochers nus et vigoureusement dessinés réfléchissent dans le fleuve leurs masses sévères, et dominent ces iles où jadis les pirates scandinaves abritaient leurs nids d'orfraies, où tomba, plus tard, le boulevard de la puissance anglo-normande, le fameux Château-Gaillard, sous la hache de Philippe-Auguste. C'est là que naquit, en 1594, Nicolas Poussin, et qu'il reçut ces premières impressions dont la pensée de l'artiste garde toujours la trace.' —*Henri Martin*, '*Hist. de France*.'

1 k. from Les Andelys is the village of *Radeval*, once celebrated for the Manoir de Radeval, known in the neighbourhood as 'Le Grand Maison.' This magnificent house was built by Jean Picard, Bailiff of Gisors, Lord of Radeval, and Controller of the Household to François I. His arms constantly appeared in its decorations. In 1820 it was sold to a company of 'vendeurs des monuments en détail,' who pulled it down, and sold its grand oriel window and all its richly sculptured stones, each marked with its price, to Lord Stuart de Rothesay, then British Ambassador at Paris, who used them in building Highcliffe, near Christchurch, in Hampshire.[1]

107 k. *S. Pierre-du-Vauvray*.

[A branch line turns W. to—

3 k. *Le Vaudreuil*, at the confluence of the Seine and the Reuil, which gave its name of 'Vallis Rodolii,' to the home of Sperling, the rich miller, whom Espriota, widow of Richard le Bon, had taken as her second husband. The castle, built by Fredegonde, became the home of William the Conqueror's boyhood, when, in accordance with his father's will he was separated from his mother Arlotta, and educated here by his guardians, Gilbert Crespin, Comte de Brienne, and Thorold. Here he was besieged by William de Montgomery, and his guardian Thorold and his connection Osborne (son of Herfast, brother of the Duchess Gunnora) were murdered by his side; but he was himself saved by his uncle Gontier, and found refuge in a peasant's cottage.

8 k. *Louviers* (Hotels : *du Mouton*; *du Grand Cerf*), a town 'grosse et moulte marchande' in the time of Froissart, but now without commercial consequence.

[1] See Brossard de Reville, *Hist. de la Ville des Andelys*.

The older part is built of timber. It had long a certain importance from its cloth manufactures, but they have fallen into decadence. The rich gothic church of *Notre Dame* is chiefly XIII. c. The S. aisle of the nave and a most magnificent S. porch are splendid specimens of the rich decoration of the xv. c.—completely lace-work in stone—in which flamboyant architecture reaches its apotheosis. The central nave, which is of great height, is lighted by beautiful stained glass. A S. Sepulcre has life-size figures. At the end of the two r. side aisles is a double chapel, with a central pillar bearing a statue of S. Hubert with his legendary stag. A gothic tomb commemorates the Sire d'Esternay, Governor of Normandy, who was sewn up in a sack and drowned in the Eure by order of Louis XI.

A line connects Louviers with (26 k.) Evreux.

For the line from Louviers to Dreux see ch. iii.

A line connects Louviers with (20 k.) Elboeuf: see later.]

On the l. of the line is *Notre Dame du Vaudreuil*, with a fine XII. c. portal. Here Fredegonde had a palace. Further l. is *Léry*, with some small remains of a palace of Queen Blanche, widow of Philippe de Valois, and a little church of XI. c. and XII. c. On the r. is the xv. c. and XVI. c. church of *Alisay*.

119 k. *Pont de l'Arche*. The village is 2 k. distant on the l. Here Charles le Chauve had a palace, and here the council met (in 1310) in which the Templars were condemned. The unfinished church, chiefly xv. c., has a great deal of fine contemporary stained glass. The stall-work comes from the Abbey of Bon-Port. The arabesques of the font are attributed to Jean Goujon, and the organ is said to have been the gift of Henri IV. One of the curious old timber houses has a wooden porch of the XIII. c., supported by five pillars. By a pleasant path along the

r. bank of the Seine (or by the Elboeuf road) we may reach the remains of the *Abbaye de Bon-Port*, founded in 1190 by Richard Coeur de Lion. Its glorious church is entirely destroyed, but its noble refectory still stands, with the ancient kitchen used as a cellar, and several other buildings of the abbey. It is a very picturesque spot. To the

ABBAYE DE BON-PORT.

S. of the abbey extends the *Forest of Bord* or *Pont de l'Arche*.

[For the line from Pont de l'Arche to Gisors see ch. i.]

The line passes (r.) *Sotteville-sous-le-Val*, which has a XII. c. cross in its cemetery.

126 k. *Oissel*. The *Manoir de la Chapelle* has a curious old well, surmounted by a renaissance pyramid.

130 k. *S. Etienne-du-Rouvray*. The church is XVI. c. and XVII. c. At *Belboeuf*, on r. of the Seine, the church has

a XIII. c. font. The cavern chapel of *S. Adrien* is a place of pilgrimage.

140 k. *Rouen* (Hotels: *d'Angleterre*—good but dear, and very noisy; *d'Albion*—dear; *du Nord*—very good and reasonable, well situated near the Grosse Horloge; *de la Poste*—good and quiet), formerly the capital of Normandy, still the seat of an archbishopric and capital of the Département de la Seine-Inférieure, and the seventh town of France as to its population. In the XI. c. Rouen was called Ratuma, and was the capital of the Véliocasses. Under the Romans it became important as Rotomagus. Christianity was preached here in the III. c., and in 260 an oratory of the Virgin, on the site of the present cathedral, was built by S. Mellon, first bishop of Rouen. Several of his successors were canonised, and S. Paulinus, in one of his letters, speaks of Rouen as a town 'famous for its holy places.' In 876 Rollo seized Rouen,[1] and built a new city, with the castle long known as Vieux Palais. Normandy was made an independent duchy for him, being only reunited to France under Philippe-Auguste in 1193. Successive sovereigns — Richard Sans Peur, Philippe Auguste, S. Louis, and Philippe de Valois—surrounded Rouen in turn with six ever wider circles of walls. In 1418 the town was besieged for six months, and eventually taken by Henry V. of England. In 1431 the English were disgraced at Rouen by the execution of Jeanne Darc. In 1449 they were driven out by Charles VII.

Old Rouen, till recently one of the most interesting

---

[1] 'Quand Rou à Roen arriva,
Qui de North hommes amena,
Cil furent Normans appellés,
Por ceu que de North furent nés.'—*Roman de Rou.*

towns in France, has been improved away of late years by its municipal council, and the principal streets are now a feeble and dull imitation of those of Paris. Still there is much to visit, the best points being the Grosse Horloge, the Hotel de Bourgtheroude, Cathedral, Vieux Halles, S. Maclou, the Aitre S. Maclou, and S. Ouen.

For the benefit of sight-seers who are content with a glance, the buildings of Rouen may be taken in the following order.

From the principal station of the Rive Droite, the Rue E. Leroy leads to the modern Rue Jeanne Darc, one of the three great modern streets which have recently pierced and completely altered the character of the *ville aux vieilles rues* of Victor Hugo. By a side street on r. we may visit the restored church of *S. Patrice* (1535), which contains a quantity of very fine XVI. c. glass, especially (l. aisle) the magnificent window representing the Triumph of the Law of Grace, attributed to Jean Cousin.

L. of the Rue Jeanne Darc is the *Square Solferino*, with the *Musée de Peinture*, open to the public daily from 12 to 5. It contains three of the little pictures by *Perugino*, which once, in the church of S. Pietro at Perugia, surrounded the great picture of the Ascension, now at Lyons.

The church of *S. Godard*, at the back of the square, is partly XVI. c., and has a good deal of (restored) XVI. c. glass. *S. Laurent*, in the Rue Thiers, was built 1444—1554. It is now turned into shops. The external balustrade of the nave is of letters forming the verse of a psalm : the fine tower is of 1501.

Farther down the Rue Jeanne Darc to the l. is the magnificent *Palais de Justice*, built by Louis XII. for the

Échiquier de Normandie, which was formed into an independent sovereign court of permanent magistrates, recognised as a parliament by François I., and which held all the powers of communal administration, civil and military. The oldest portion of the building is the l. wing, erected in 1493 as a meeting-place for merchants. The r. wing (which only dated from the XVIII. c.) was rebuilt 1842-52. The splendid central façade, begun 1499, is due to Roger Ango and to Laurent Leroux, architect of the central portal of Notre Dame. The statues, representing all the different classes of society of the time of Louis XII., are modern additions by Le Brun. A staircase (of 1607) leads to the *Salle des Procureurs* or *des Pas Perdues*, which has bold simple timber vaulting. A marble table of 1555 is shown as that where the jurisdiction of the rivers and forests was executed. The parliament chapel, which adjoined the hall and overhung the Rue aux Juifs, was demolished in 1794. A door at the end of the hall (r.) communicates with the restored hall of the *Cour d'Assises*, possessing a beautiful gilt and sculptured chestnut ceiling of the time of Louis XII. The *Chambre du Conseil* contains portraits of the Counsellors of the Parliament of Normandy, and a Crucifixion given by Louis XII.

Farther down the Rue Jeanne Darc, the *Tour de la Grosse-Horloge* (of 1389) is seen spanning the first street on l., with its picturesque arch of 1511. The great clock dates from 1447. The arch unites the tower with the old Hôtel de Ville of 1680, but the latter is broken up into dwellings, and has lost all character, except a portion towards the Rue Thouret.

Turning the other way, down the Rue de la Grosse-

Horloge (r. of Rue Jeanne Darc), we reach (on r.) the *Hôtel du Bourgtheroude* (6, Place de la Pucelle), begun by Guillaume le Roux, lord of Bourgtheroude, at the end of the xv. c., and finished under François I. The S. and W. façades (upon the court) are exceedingly rich in sculpture. The W. façade is covered with reliefs, those in the attic being in higher relief, as suited for more distant view. This façade is flanked by a tower decorated with reliefs of pastoral scenes, and enclosing a cabinet, which retains its carved wooden (xvi. c.) ceiling with pendants, and walls with pictures in the style of Primaticcio. Under the lower windows of the S. façade are five celebrated reliefs of the Field of the Cloth of Gold, representing the interview of François I. and Henry VIII. in 1520.

A little behind is the church of *S. Eloi*, now used as a protestant chapel, ending in a three-sided (xvi. c.) apse. A xvi. c. tomb bears the inscription—'Ici gist ung corps sans âme, Priez Dieu qu'il en ait l'âme.'

In the *Place de la Pucelle*, a fountain by Paul Slodtz (replacing a beautiful xvi. c. fountain, destroyed in 1750), commemorates the execution of Jeanne Darc, though the exact site of her scaffold was more to the W., on the site now occupied by the Théâtre-Français.

'Dix mille hommes pleuraient! . . Quelques Anglais seuls riaient ou tâchaient de rire. Un d'eux, des plus furieux, avait juré de mettre un fagot au bûcher; elle expirait au moment où il le mit; il se trouva mal; ses camarades le menèrent à une taverne pour le faire boire et reprendre ses esprits, mais il ne pouvait se remettre : "J'ai vu," disait-il, hors de lui-même, "j'ai vu de sa bouche, avec le dernier soupir, s'envoler une colombe." D'autres avaient lu dans les flammes le mot qu'elle répetait, "Jésus!" Le bourreau alla le soir trouver frère Isambart; il était tout épouvanté; il se confessa, mais il ne pouvait croire que

Dieu lui pardonnait jamais. Un secrétaire du roi d'Angleterre disait tout haut, en revenant : " Nous sommes perdus ; nous avons brulé une sainte."

' Cette parole, échappée d'un ennemi, n'en est pas moins grave. Elle restera. L'avenir n'y contredira point. Oui, selon la religion, selon la patrie, Jeanne Darc fut une sainte.'—*Michelet, ' Hist. de France.'*

Returning to the Rue Jeanne Darc, on the r. at the corner of the Rue de l'Ours, is the *Tour S. André*, which belonged to a xvi. c. church, and is surmounted by statues of SS. André, Adrien, Pierre, and Jean Baptiste. Close by, is the reconstructed renaissance façade of a house called *Maison de Diane de Poitiers*, destroyed in making the Rue Jeanne Darc. Farther, on r., is the unfinished xvi. c. church of *S. Vincent*. It is of the xvi. c., except the tower (1669) and two modern chapels. The west porch is of the richest flamboyant. The church contains a great deal of exceedingly fine xvi. c. stained glass, especially (on the r. of the apse) *Le vitrail de Chars* (1515), representing the triumph of Religion in the town of Rouen.

On reaching the quay, it is best to turn l. to the *Pont de Pierre* of 1812-29, whence there is a good view. Crossing the bridge, we reach, opposite the suspension bridge, the *Place S. Sever*, containing a bronze group by Falguière and Legrain, in honour of the Abbé de la Salle, founder of the Institut des Frères des Écoles Chrétiennes (1719), whose epitaph (removed from an earlier church) is to be seen in the modern renaissance church of *S. Sever* (1858-61), by Vachot. S. Sever was formerly Hermondeville, where Thibault le Tricheur pitched his camp, and saw his army massacred by the Normans whilst attempting to besiege Duke Richard Sans Peur, stepson of his wife Luitgarda.

Returning by the suspension bridge, the Rue du Grand Port will bring us to (r.) the Place de la Cathédrale, at the angle of which is the ancient *Bureau des Finances*, a beautiful renaissance building of 1509.

The glorious *Cathedral of Notre Dame* is believed to occupy the site of a basilica erected in the III. c. by S. Mellon. This was rebuilt in 400, doubled in size by S. Ouen in 650, and destroyed by the Normans in the IX. c. The cathedral was rebuilt by Duke Rollo (baptised there in 913 and buried there in 931) and his grandson Richard I.; and in 945, Richard Sans Peur, the thirteen-year-old sovereign of Normandy, returned public thanks there for the marvellous victories which his Danish allies had enabled him to gain over the French; but this cathedral also was burnt (with the town) in 1200.

The existing church (except the earlier base of the Tour S. Romain) was entirely built by the architect Enguerrand, in the first twenty years of the XIII. c. The main entrance, flanked by (l.) the Tour S. Romain and (r.) the Tour de Beurre, has three portals decorated with reliefs, mutilated by the Calvinists in 1562: the principal was rebuilt by the Cardinals d'Amboise (1507-30), from plans of Jacques and Laurent Leroux. A tree of Jesse decorates the tympanum of the central portal, and above are a gallery and gable of open work. The tympanum of the l. portal has scenes from the life of S. John Baptist. The daughter of Herodias is represented (as in a fresco at Brunswick) as dancing on her hands and throwing up her legs into the air. The XIII. c. ironwork of the door on r. deserves notice.

'The great western façade exemplifies the corruption of taste in later times. It is viciously florid. It looks like a piece of rockwork, devoid, as it is, of windows, and rough, and incrusted with images and tabernacles and ornaments from top to bottom; yet there is an expanse and grandeur about it which cannot be viewed without admiration.'—*Gally Knight*, '*Arch. Tour in Normandy.*'

The *Tour de Beurre* (1485—1507) has a sixth flamboyant story of 1465-77. At the foot of the tower, on l., is the *Cour de l'Albane*, on the r. of which is a xv. c. hall, used for theological lectures.

The N. transept is entered by the *Portail des Libraires* (1280—1300), reached from the Rue S. Romain by a kind of corridor, with a stone screen towards the street, surmounted by a beautiful open gallery. The corridor was formerly occupied by bookstalls, whose name clings to the portal, which has reliefs partly biblical, partly from pagan mythology. In the seventh bay of the nave, on N., is a simple door with xiii. c. ironwork. Some of the windows on the S. of the nave are round-headed (though xiv. c.). The xiii. c. *Porte des Maçons* has the Presentation of Christ in the Temple in its tympanum. The *Portail de la Calende* (S. transept) is sumptuously decorated with statues and sculpture: the ironwork is xiii. c. The great central *Tour de Pierre* (xiii. c. and xvi. c.) was formerly surmounted by a noble spire, destroyed by lightning in 1822; this has been unhappily replaced by a hideous cast-iron pyramid (by Alavoine), 482 feet in height, which throws everything else out of proportion.

The noble interior is 435 ft. in length, and the height of the nave is $89\frac{1}{2}$ ft. The cathedral is lighted by 130 windows, many of them filled with beautiful XVI. c. glass, some of which, especially that over the Portail de la Calende, is attributed to Jean Barbe, to whom the Château de Gaillon owed many of its best decorations.

The stall-work of the choir is XV. c., and has very curious misereres. The sanctuary formerly contained, with others, the tomb of William, son of Geoffrey Plantagenet and grandson of Henry II., and of Charles V., but the graves were violated by the protestants of 1562, and the remains of the monuments removed by the canons, when a heavy *jubé* (now removed) was put up at the entrance of the choir, in 1774. The beautiful gothic staircase in the corner of the N. transept was erected in the latter part of the XV. c. by Cardinal Guillaume d'Estouteville, as an approach to the cathedral library of 1424.

The last chapel on the S.E. of the nave (*Chapelle du Petit S. Romain*) contains the XIII. c. *Tomb of Rollo*, the Danish jarl who was the supposed founder of the Norman duchy, of which the true founder was Richard Sans Peur. Rollo was first buried in the sacristy: he was moved to the chapel of S. Romanus when Archbishop Maurice rebuilt the cathedral.

'The recumbent statue which represents the Danish Jarl, clad in ducal robe, may date from the reign of S. Louis. The sculptor has happily succeeded in embodying the notion conveyed by tradition and history: the once mighty man of war, thoroughly worn out,—the sunken lips,—the furrowed brow,—the strength of fourscore years come to labour and sorrow.'—*Palgrave.*

The splendid glass of the *Chapelle du Grand S. Romain*, which opens from the S. transept, tells the story of S. Romain.

In the S. choir aisle is a modern monument to *Richard Coeur de Lion* (buried at Fontevrault), with a statue simply and severely treated, and with a larger head than in that at Fontevrault. His heart is preserved here.

In the *Chapelle de SS. Pierre et Paul* is the wooden coffin which contains the remains of *Matilda*, daughter of Henry I., and lawful Queen of England, who died at Rouen, Sept. 10, 1167, widow first of the Emperor Henry V. of Germany, by whom she was childless, and afterwards of Geoffrey Plantagenet, Earl of Anjou, by whom she was the mother of Henry II.

The *Chapelle de la Vierge* contains the noble renaissance *Tomb of Cardinal Georges d'Amboise*, minister of Louis XII., and his nephew (also cardinal), who erected this monument in 1520-25, from designs of Rouland Leroux, master-mason of the cathedral. The cardinals are represented on their knees: the head of the second cardinal is attributed to Jean Goujon.

'Dans les derniers moments de sa vie, le cardinal légat disait à un religieux qui se trouvait auprès de lui: "Ah! frère Jean! frère Jean, mon ami, que n'ai-je été toute ma vie frère Jean!" Puis il ajouta, en se tournant vers les membres de sa famille qui entouraient son lit: "Mes amis, ne vous mettez jamais jusquelà où je me suis mis." Ce cri du repentir pouvait se rapporter à l'élan ambitieux qui avait fait rechercher la tiare au cardinal d'Amboise, par le sacrifice de l'or et surtout du sang des Français; mais la posterité a du l'absoudre, en reconnaissant que jamais le peuple ne fut plus ménagé, la fortune des citoyens plus respectée, la police du royaume plus exactement observée que sous le ministère de cet homme d'état.

'Georges d'Amboise mourut à Rouen, le 25 mai 1510. On raconte que deux cents gentilhommes, douze cents prélats, et onze mille prêtres assistèrent à son enterrement, qui fut accompagné d'une pompe jusqu'alors sans exemple, et d'un concert de regrets et de lamentations. On peut douter, sans trop de scepticisme, de la présence à ce cortège funèbre, d'une armée ecclésiastique qu'il eut été presque impossible de réunir.'[1]— *Touchard-Lafosse*, '*Hist. de Paris.*'

'The two life-size figures are kneeling, robed in splendid long flowing garments, on a black marble slab, supported by consoles. The elder has a characteristically conceived and brutal priestly countenance; the younger is likewise repulsive, but full of energetic life; both are attired in pompous mantles. Under the consoles are pilasters, and between these, niches, containing seated statues of the Virtues. The whole work possesses great decorative beauty, but the figures are unequal; the drapery of several is excellent in style, that of the others displays restless folds. The heads also are occasionally full of animation; others, on the contrary, are insipid and constrained. The splendid wall at the back, which is radiant with gold and colour, exhibits S. George and other saints, likewise unequal in value. The vaulting is adorned with charming gilt cassettes, and above it rises a rich crowning member with statuettes in niches and graceful friezes of children, all in playful renaissance forms, which are repeated in the airy pyramidal points, with which this luxuriant and splendid work terminates in the gothic manner.'—*Lübke.*

A simple stone, below the tomb, covers the remains of Cardinal de Cambacérès, 1818. Opposite is the tomb of the Cardinal Archbishop Prince de Croy, 1844. The altar-piece of the Adoration of the Shepherds is by *Philippe de Champaigne.*

The magnificent *Tomb of Louis de Brézé* (l.), erected by his widow, Diane de Poitiers, is one of the marvels of the Renaissance. Diane kneels at the head of the figure of her dead husband, full of wonderful expression. He is

[1] See *Les Loisirs d'un Ministre d'État* of M. de Paulny, and Daru, *Hist. de Venise*, iii. 520-21.

represented again as an infant in his mother's arms, and a third time on horseback, at the top of the monument which, executed 1535-44, is attributed to Jean Goujon, or Jean Cousin. The adjoining tomb (1488-92), of the transition from gothic to renaissance, commemorates Pierre de Brézé, Comte de Maulevrier, seneschal of Anjou, killed at the battle of Montlhéry in 1465, and Jeanne de Bec-Crespin, his wife.

In the l. aisle of the choir is a modern monument to *Henri Courte Mantel*, brother of Richard I., who died at Martel en Quercy, 1183; and against the N. wall, surrounded by small coloured figures of angels, within a niche, behind three pointed arches, the very beautiful XIII. c. *Tomb of Archbishop Maurice*, the oldest in the cathedral.

The XIV. c. sculptures in the galleries of the transept and upper parts of the façade, as well as the figures at the portal of the S. transept, are very inferior to earlier works.

'The pedestals on which the figures stand are very different in character, their rectangular surfaces being covered with an innumerable quantity of small reliefs in indented medallions, containing, it appears, scenes from the History of Joseph and other Old Testament subjects, with corresponding incidents from the Life of Christ. We here perceive plainly, from the contrast, how the masters of this period had lost all vigour of style in the treatment of large statues, and tried to compensate for this in smaller works by natural, and often charming, touches of actual life.'—*Lübke*.

The first chapel in descending the N. aisle of the nave (*Chapelle de S. Anne*) contains the *Tomb of Guillaume Longue-Epée*, son of Rollo, murdered on an island in the

Somme in 943,[1] and the epitaph of the great regent, John, Duke of Bedford, 1435.

In a chapel off the north choir aisle is the striking *Tomb of Cardinal de Bonnechose*, 1883.

From the S. entrance to the cathedral a street leads S.E. to *Les Anciennes Halles*, of the end of the XIII. c. They are entered by a most graceful little building of the Renaissance, known as *Le Monument de S. Romain*—a little domed portico with staircases, erected in 1512. The *Haute Vieille Tour* behind this was part of the ancient palace in which Prince Arthur was imprisoned and murdered by John.

Returning to the cathedral, turning r. and passing the stately walls of the *Archevêché*, chiefly built by Cardinal d'Estouteville, 1461, but with a portal by Mansart, we reach, a little E. of the cathedral, the church of *S. Maclou*, rebuilt

---

[1] All the descendants of Rollo, from Guillaume Longue-Épée downwards, except the sons of Richard II. and Judith, were born out of wedlock, and legitimised by an after marriage, till William the Conqueror, who was not legitimised at all.

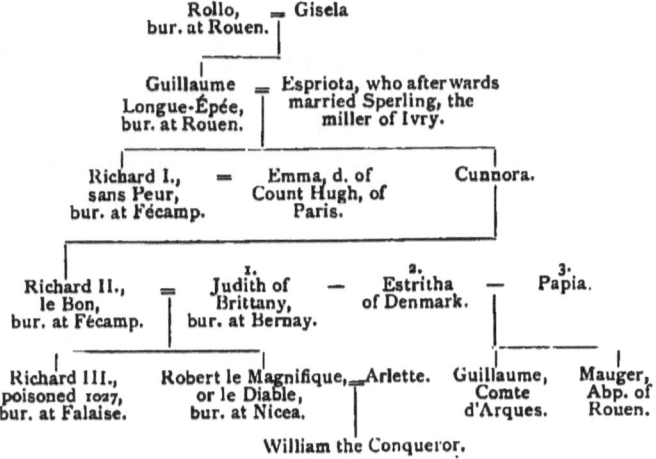

from designs of the architect Pierre Robin, 1437—1520. The W. front has a beautiful flamboyant porch, which once had five entrances (now three) opening upon the five aisles of the church. The wooden doors are sculptured with designs by Jean Goujon, as well as a much mutilated fountain at the N.W. angle of the building. The portal of the N. transept has a central Corinthian pillar, twined with vine tendrils, and supporting a statue of the Virgin. The spire, by Viollet le Duc, is of 1868. The interior has fine but mutilated glass of XV. c. and XVI. c., but the most interesting object it contains is the beautiful tourelle of open flamboyant work, like the most delicate lace in stone, containing a staircase leading to the organ by Arthur Fillon, 1521. The columns supporting the organ are by Jean Goujon.

L'Aitre[1] *S. Maclou*, entered by the gate at 188, Rue Martainville, is a beautiful cloistered court, encircled by buildings of stone and timber of 1526-29. Upon each of the Corinthian columns which surround it is sculptured a scene from the Dance of Death (*Danse macabre*), forming singular contrast with the joyous pagan sculptures near them. One of the galleries, of coarser sculpture, is (1640) later in date than the others. The court, once a cemetery, is now used for a number of schools.

The Rue de la République leads (r.) from the west front of S. Maclou to *S. Ouen*—matchless in its exquisite beauty.

Here a monastery was founded by S. Victrice (393—417), and restored by S. Clotilde (524—530). Having been transformed (630) by S. Ouen into an abbey for men, it took the name of its second founder in the XI. c. Nothing now remains of the romanesque church, repeatedly

---

[1] L'Aitre = atrium.

burnt and ruined, except the circular apside at the N. transept of the church called *Chambre-aux-Clercs*, which is of the beginning of the xii. c., and probably a remnant of the third of the five churches on this site. The existing church, begun in 1318, was not finished till 1846. The W. façade, which has a glorious rose-window, is covered with statues of the kings and saints connected with Rouen; that of S. Ouen occupies the summit of the gable. The statues on the front of the S. transept are those of the principal benefactors of the abbey: its *Portail des Marmousets* is of marvellous beauty. On the N. of the church part of the xvi. c. cloister remains. The magnificent central tower (xiv. c.—xvi. c.) is surmounted by a ducal crown of open-work.

The entire church (453 feet in length, 83 in breadth, 106 in height), in the form of a Latin cross, is surrounded by side aisles: eleven chapels radiate round the choir. The glorious glass has been well restored, and the ancient pavement preserved. The nave has ten bays, and the triforium is all glass. In the 2nd chapel l. of choir are the tombs of an unknown architect (xiii. c. or xiv. c.) and of the master mason Alexander de Berneval (xv. c.).

On the S. side of the pretty public garden which surrounds the E. end of the church an ancient *Necropolis* was discovered in 1871, with tombs extending from the vi. c. to the xiv. c. It was here that Jeanne Darc was compelled to make a solemn abjuration of her supposed errors.

At the corner of the Rue de l'Hôpital (opposite the W. front of S. Ouen) and the Rue des Carmes is a copy (1870) of the beautiful ancient gothic *Fontaine de la Crosse* (xv. c.), now pulled down.

Continuing to follow the Rue de la République, we reach

(r.) the *Fontaine S. Marie* (1879) and (l.) the *Musée d'Antiquités* (open 12 to 4), which occupies part of the ancient Convent of the Visitandines (1680-91) which also contains the *Museum of Natural History* and *Collections of China and Pottery*. Amongst the autographs are charters signed by William the Conqueror—with a cross, for he could not write.

Transported to the garden is the beautiful ancient *Fontaine de la Croix de Pierre* (1515) recently brought hither from the Carrefour S. Vivien, where it has been replaced by a copy.

Hence, by the church of *S. Godard*, chiefly xvi. c., covered with modern mural paintings, and the *Tour de Jeanne Darc*, a remnant of the old château of Philippe-Auguste, said to have been the prison of the heroine, we may regain the railway station.

Near the W. extremity of the city and the railway station is the church of *S. Gervais*, with a very curious crypt, probably built in the iv. c. from Roman materials, and if so, the oldest piece of architecture in Normandy. Here S. Mellon, the first bishop of Rouen, was buried. To the adjoining priory William the Conqueror, after he had received his death-wound at Mantes, was removed from the palace at Rouen for the sake of greater quietude; here he made his will, disposing of his treasure to the church for the good of his soul; hence he sent William Rufus to England and released all his captives, and here he died (Sept. 9, 1087).

'He had striven to make peace with God and man, and to make such provision as he could for the children and the subjects whom he left behind him. And now his last hour was come.

SUBURBS OF ROUEN.

On a Thursday morning in September, when the sun had already risen upon the earth, the sound of the great bell of the metropolitan minster struck on the ears of the dying king. He asked why it sounded. He was told that it rang for the prime in the church of Our Lady. William lifted his eyes to heaven, he stretched forth his hands, and spake his last words: "To my Lady Mary, the holy mother of God, 1 commend myself, that by her holy prayers she may reconcile me to her dear Son, our Lord Jesus Christ." He prayed, and his soul passed away.'— *Freeman.*

When the Conqueror had breathed his last, his nobles and servants plundered his room and fled, and he remained unburied, till the faithful knight Herlwin, at his own cost, undertook the embalming of the body and its removal to Caen.

Omnibuses leave the Place des Arts every two hours for ($3\frac{1}{4}$ k.) the *Chapelle de Bon Secours* (1840-42), whence, and from the neighbouring heights of *Mont S. Catherine*, there is a most beautiful view over Rouen, the islands and windings of the Seine, and the verdant meadows, once the field where the famous Edeline, nephew of Otho of Germany, fell in single combat with Richard Sans Peur, in that important battle (946) before the walls of Rouen in which the Normans were victorious. Below Mont S. Catherine is the little romanesque church of *S. Paul.*

4 k. E. of Rouen is the manufacturing village of *Darnetal*, which has the fine XVI. c. *Church of Long Paon*, and (at the opposite end of the village) the *Tour de Carville*, used as an observatory by Henri IV. when besieging the Fort S. Catherine.

It was at *Chevilly*, near Rouen, that the Conqueror heard of the death of Edward the Confessor, and that Harold had occupied the throne.

At the *Mont au Malades*, a priory founded by Henry II. in

expiation of the murder of Becket, is an admirable XIII. c. gravestone of a lady.

Above the suburb of *Déville* is the *Wood of Roumare*, where for many years hung the bracelet, which showed that the prince of the district had taught his subjects to respect rights of property.

An excursion should be made from Rouen to (10 k.) the famous Abbey of *S. Georges de Boscherville*,[1] which is a little to the l. of the high road to Caudebec. Its splendid *Church* remains intact, and was built, as the inscription over the portal tells us, by the munificence of Raoul de Tancarville, grand chamberlain of William the Conqueror, 1050-66. The portal, adorned with a triple zigzag moulding, is surmounted by two ranges of round-headed windows, and flanked on either side by a square tower, crowned by a campanile with four gothic arcades, surmounted by a hexagonal stone spire, with pinnacles. All round the exterior of the church runs a bold cornice, supported by heads of men and animals. The interior was covered with whitewash, intersected by yellow lines, in 1876, and its beauty entirely destroyed. What it was before that date may be seen by the fragment of a chapel left untouched because covered with frescoes. The three naves are divided by eight romanesque arches. Above, a gallery runs round the whole. Several piscinas are XIII. c. Entered from the orchard on the north of the church, where the old well, formerly in the centre of the cloister, remains under the apple-trees, is the *Chapter House*, of 1157—1200, surmounted by a construction of the XVII. c.: the mutilated portal is of great beauty. The other buildings of the abbey are only of the time of Louis XIV. It is difficult to get any good general view of the abbey, which is much hemmed in by walls and houses. A little restaurant near the west portal can supply luncheon.

[A pleasant excursion may be made in calm weather[2] down the Seine to (135 k.) Havre. There is a daily service of boats from June 1st to Sept. 30th from the Quai du Havre, opposite la Douane (1st class, 6 fr. 50 c.; 2nd class, 5 fr. 50 c. The passage occupies seven hours, and there is a café-restaurant on board.

[1] It may be reached by public carriage from 145, Rue des Charrettes.
[2] The sea is often rough at the mouth of the river.

The boat passes: r. the château and church of *Canteleu*; r. *Croisset*; r. *Dieppedalle*, opposite the *Ile S. Barbe*; r. *Val de la Haye*, where a monument commemorates the shifting of the coffin of Napoleon I. from the steamer La Normandie to La Dorade; r. *Hautot-sur-Seine*, where the church has good XIII. c. glass; r. *Soquence*, with a modern château; l. (20 k.) *La Bouille*. The Seine now makes a great bend, skirting on l. the hills covered by the Forest of Mauny, to l. *Bardouville*, with XI. c. and XIII. c. church. L. *Berville-sur-Seine*, where the river bends again. R. *Duclair* (see later). R. *S. Pierre de Manneville*, with a fine XVI. c. church; r. *S. Martin de Boscherville*. On r. the hills are now clothed by the forest of Jumièges. R. *Mesnil sous Jumièges*, with a XIII. c. manor of Agnes Sorel, 4 k. from the famous abbey. L. *Yville-sur-Seine*, with a XII. c. church tower, a XIII. c. cross in the cemetery, and an XVIII. c. château. After another wooded bend of the river is l. *Heurteauville*, with a church built by the monks of Jumièges in 1730. Passing the Bac de la Mailleraye, we reach l. *Notre Dame de Bliquetuit*, where the church has a good XIII. c. choir. L. *S. Nicolas de Bliquetuit*, with a church of XI. c. altered in XVII. c. R. Caudebec (see later). R. the *Château de Villequier*. L. *Vatteville*, with a XVI. church containing good XVI. c. and XVII. c. glass, a ruined XI. c. castle, and XVI. c. houses. L. The village of *Aizier*, with a romanesque church. L. *Vieux-Port*, and, under the wooded hills, the admirable XV. c. tower and XII.—XVI. c. church of *Norville*. R. *S. Maurice d'Ételan*, with a XV. c. church and another in ruins. R. The *Château d'Ételan* (XV. c.), with a graceful XV. c. chapel. L. *Quillebeuf* (see later). R. *Notre Dame de Gravenchon*, with a XII. c. and XIII. c. church. R. *Port Jerome*, some distance inland from which is Lillebonne (see later). R. the wooded promontory of Tancarville, with its fine château (see later). Beyond this the river almost becomes sea. On l. we pass *Berville-sur-Mer*; r. *Cap du Hode*, the *Château de Gonfreville-l'Orcher*, and the *Pointe du Hoc* below Harfleur, with Havre beyond it. L. The Chapelle de Notre Dame de Grâce is seen above Honfleur.]

[For the line from Rouen to Port Audemer and Serquigny see chap. iii.]

Leaving Rouen by the station of the Rue Verte, we reach—

146 k. *Maromme*, a manufacturing suburb, connected by a tramway with Rouen.

149 k. *Malaunay*.

[A line branches N.E. to (52 k.) Dieppe, by (6 k.) *Monville*, where the church has a massive XI. c. tower and a XVI. c. choir. An excursion may be made by (8 k.) *Fontaine-le-Bourg* to (14 k.) *Cailly*, an ancient town once fortified, 4 k. S. of which is the village of *S. André-sur-Cailly*, where remains of an amphitheatre and many relics of Roman occupation have been found.

22 k. *S. Victor l'Abbaye*. Only a chapter-house (XIII. c.) remains of the abbey, to which a pilgrimage was made by William the Conqueror, of whom there is a statue in a niche outside the chevet of the church. The neighbouring church of *S. Maclou de Folleville* contains the ancient *banc seigneurial* of the family of Giffard de la Pierre, whose old brick XVI. c. manor stands on the opposite hill.

26 k. *Auffay*. The collegiate church is mostly XIII. c.

35 k. *Longueville*, formed into a duchy under Louis XII., has a ruined castle, and a church of XI. c. and XVI. c. Only some buildings of 1700, used as a factory, remain of the Priory of *S. Foy*, founded in 1093.

45 k. *S. Aubin-Offranville*. *S. Aubin-sur-Seine* has an interesting XVI. c. church. The *Château de Miromesnil* is XVI. c. and XVII. c. The church of *Tourville-sur-Arques* has a XVI. c. font and a good bénitier of the time of François I. *Offranville* has a XVI. c. church, where the *Chapelle S. Barbe*, now the sacristy, has remarkable XVI. c. glass.]

157 k. *Barentin*.

[A branch line leads S.E. to—

15 k. *Duclair*. A little town with a quay on the Seine. The church has a romanesque tower, a XIV. c. choir, a renaissance portal, and XIII. c. statues. In the garden of the *Château de Taillis* is the tomb of an abbot of Jumièges.

20 k. *Gainville*. 3 k. distant is the famous *Monastery of*

MONASTERY OF JUMIÈGES.

Jumièges (Hôtel de l'Abbaye, Café de la Place, both tolerable), founded in VII. c., and ruled, during its 1120 years of existence, by eighty-two abbots, including SS. Philbert, Aichaire, Hugues, Thierry, and Gontard. It at one time contained above nine hundred monks.

The original church, as built by Lanfranc, Abbot of Bec (afterwards Archbishop of Canterbury), was destroyed by Raoul Torta, prime minister of Louis d'Outre Mer (940), till 'the wise clerk Clement' reclaimed the towers, which remain. Rebuilt, but pillaged by the Calvinists, and destroyed by the Revolution, the abbey is now only a picturesque and beautiful ruin, in the private grounds of Mme Lepel Cointet, to which strangers (accompanied by the portress) are always admitted. The gateway and *les communes* form the present residence. The arches under the gateway are used as a museum for relics found in the ruins, including the tombstone of Nicolas Leroux, the fifty-ninth abbot, who was one of the judges of Jeanne Darc, and the stone which covered the heart of Agnes Sorel (Saurelle), Dame de Beaulté, the beloved mistress of Charles VII., who died at Mesnil, in 1449, and whose body was buried at Loches. Two much-broken statues are called *Les Enervés*, and are believed to commemorate the two sons of Clovis II., who, in his absence, revolted against their mother Bathilde, and were punished by having the sinews of their arms and legs cut and being sent adrift thus in a boat upon the Seine. They were landed at Jumièges, and being kindly received by the monks, remained in the abbey till their death.

The remains of the enormous abbey-church of *Notre Dame* —beautiful in their pink-grey colouring—consist chiefly of the west front, with its flanking towers, the aisles of the nave (that on the left retaining its vaúlting), the great romanesque arch which supported one side of the tower, and some exquisitely beautiful fragments of the XIII. c. choir. In the S. transept are a number of remnants of statues, etc., found in the abbey. Hence a passage communicates with the church of *S. Pierre*, built under Dagobert, ruined by the Normans in 840, and rebuilt in 930 by Guillaume Longue-Epée, son of Rollo, who, in his youth, would willingly have become a monk of Jumièges. Under the romanesque arcade on the N. wall of this church are medallions with remains of x. c. paintings. From the r. of the church we enter the *Chapelle S. Martin*, where the central boss of the vaulting represents S. Philbert, abbot of Jumièges, with the wolf which is his attribute. At the foot of the S. tower of Notre Dame is the ruin of the gothic *Salle des Gardes de Charles VII*. In the *Salle capitulaire* are tombs of priors. The (destroyed) cloister communicated on the W. with the *Library*, of which three romanesque arches remain. In the house of the proprietress are some vaulted gothic halls.

Many picturesque legends hang about Jumièges. It is said

CAUDEBEC.

that when the second abbot, Alcadre, was dying, he was anxious about leaving behind him too many monks — nine hundred, more than the abbey could support. But, in a vision, he saw an angel mark four hundred and sixty of these with a palm branch, saying: 'Be at rest; I have marked those whom the Lord has found most worthy, and who shall stand in His presence on the third night from this.' Then those monks prepared for death, and on the third night, as 'Amen' was said at the midnight prayers, they passed into eternal peace.

At the nunnery of S. Philbert, where the nuns washed for the monks of Jumièges, a wolf ate the donkey that drew the washing to the river; but the wolf was compelled by the holy monks to take his place, in which it served peacefully for the rest of its life.

The parish church of *S. Valentin*, of XI. c. and XII. c., commemorates in its dedication the deliverance of Jumièges from

RUE DES CORDONNIERS, CAUDEBEC.

an invasion of rats by the intervention of S. Valentin. In a neighbouring wood is the pilgrimage chapel of *La Mère de Dieu*.

31 k. *Caudebec* (Hotels: *de la Marine*—excellent; *du Siècle*) is supposed to occupy the site of the Roman Lotum. It is a most delightful resting-place and centre for excursions. The charming

little, quiet, comfortable hotels are on the little quay of the broad, swiftly flowing Seine, and have a view of green pastures and richly wooded hills. With its fine trees, quaint buildings, and broad reaches of water studded with white sails, it has been painted by Horace Vernet and a thousand later artists. Scarcely any town in France of its size contains more picturesque buildings. The Rue des Cordonniers and the Rue de la Boucherie are almost entirely of xv. c. and xvi. c. houses, bulging, broken into a thousand quaint outlines against the sky, and with an infinitude of quaint projections. An artist will not fail to paint the Caux and another clear rushing stream, which are entirely overarched by old timber houses, glorious in colouring. One stone house, formerly monastic, is xiii. c.; other houses have all their mouldings wreathed in flowering creepers, or are a mass of pink and white roses in their season. The *Church* is an exquisitely beautiful building of the xv. c. and xvi. c., begun from plans of Guillaume Letellier (whose house is close by), in the gothic style, and finished in that of the renaissance. The principal portal (xvi. c.) has three arches, with a veil of richest sculpture; above is a balustrade with caryatides of the time of Henri IV., surmounted by a gallery in gothic letters (from the anthem of the Virgin), the continuation of that which surrounds the roof. In the gable is a rose-window, with two ranges of statuettes of the kings of Judah. The exquisite little portal towards the Place du Marché is xv. c. The noble central tower has a beautiful octagonal spire; it has now only two of its eleven ancient bells.

The interior consists of a vast central nave, with aisles which encircle the choir also, and of nineteen chapels. A doorway on the right, surmounted by a figure of the 'Weary Christ,' is a beautiful artistic subject. In the side aisles is much rich stained glass. The sculpture of the upper part of the S. door represents the Last Supper, the lower a xvi. c. procession in honour of the Sacrament. Behind the choir is the *Chapelle de la Vierge*, with a beautiful pendant. The adjoining chapel has a S. Sépulcre of marvellous expression under a beautiful xv. c. canopy. A rich bracket bears a canopied Descent from the Cross. Much of the glass in the chapels deserves attention. |The wood-carving of the sacristy comes from the abbey of S. Wandrille.

In a house on the Route d'Yvetot (25—27) is a staircase formed by XIII. c. tombstones from the abbey of Jumièges.

The immediate neighbourhood of Caudebec has every charm which wooded terraces above the broad expanses of the river, villas and cottages embosomed in flowers, and endless drives and excursions can give. It is one of the best places in France to choose for a few months' stay, and there are generally many villas to be let for the summer.

An excursion should be made to (3½ k.) *S. Wandrille*, following the Duclair road, and turning to the l. at *Caudebecquet*, where the *Grotte Milon* was once inhabited by the saint of that name. A fine renaissance portal admits to the grounds of the Abbey of *S. Wandrille*, inhabited by monks since it was founded by the saint—a pupil of S. Columban—in 670, except during a hundred years succeeding the Revolution (1793—1893), after which it was repurchased by Benedictines from the Marquis de Stackpoole, who had done much to mutilate the monastic buildings. Strangers are most kindly admitted and received. The abbey first bore the name of Fontenelle, from the rushing brook in its grounds. The buildings which are still inhabited are chiefly due to monks of St. Maur in the XVII. c. But the noble cloister, communicating with the dwelling-house, is of XIV. c. and XVI. c. At its N.W. extremity is a beautiful renaissance lavabo, which stands at the entrance of the refectory, a noble vaulted hall, XII. c. in the lower, XV. c. in the upper part, lighted by eight flamboyant windows. This communicates with the kitchen built under Louis XIV. Beyond the cloister are the remains of the church of 1248—1342, the S. door of which led to XII. c. buildings, comprising the dormitory.

On the wooded hill opposite the abbey is the very curious *Chapelle S. Saturnin* of the XI. c., with a low tower and three apsides somewhat resembling the Chapelle S. Croix at Montmajour. In the rock are several cells inhabited by hermits in the IX. c.

'It is a perfect cross church of the transverse triapsal form, and has a central tower. The semicircular apses spring directly from the tower, and internally have a semi-domical roof. The masonry is rough, some having a herring-bone appearance.

The windows, where they have not been altered, are narrow and round-headed. The nave is without aisles.'—*J. L. Petit.*

The *Parish Church* has tower and S. transept of XI. c., choir of XII. c., and Lady chapel of XIII. c. Several reliquaries were brought from the abbey.

A pleasant walk may be taken from Caudebec by following the r. bank of the Seine to the fisherman's pilgrimage chapel of *Notre Dame de Barre-y-Va,* founded XII. c., rebuilt under Louis XIV., and then by a path on r. to *Villequier,* with its château of *temp.* Louis XV., its XV. c. church with splendid stained glass, and a curious equestrian statue of S. Martin, and its cemetery, where Mme Vacquerie, daughter of Victor Hugo, is buried, with her husband and child, all lost in a shipwreck near this in 1843.

Another excursion may be made (by leaving the Yvetot road to the l., 2 k. from Caudebec) to (4 k.) *S. Gertrude,* which has a beautiful XVI. c. church, with a central tower, noble portal, and flamboyant windows filled with glorious glass. The choir has a beautiful pendant, a curious XVI. c. gravestone, and a stone tabernacle of exquisite grace.

Allouville (see later) is only 6 k. from Caudebec. Lillebonne (see later) is about 10 k.]

159 k. *Pavilly,* where S. Philbert of Jumièges founded a monastery in the VII. c., replaced in the XI. c. by an abbey, of which the XIII. c. church remains. The priory *Chapel of S. Austreberte* is XII. c. The château of the ancient Comtes d'Esneval is of 1460-78. 4 k. N.E. are the village and holy well of *S. Austreberte,* who was abbess of Pavilly in the VII. c.

170 k. *Motteville* has a château of the time of Henri IV.

[A line leads N. to S. Valery en Caux by—

5 k. *Grémonville,* with an unfinished château of *temp.* Henri IV. 4 k. is *Ouville l'Abbaye,* with some remains of an abbey founded in the XII. c.

12 k. *Doudeville,* In the church (XIII. c. and XVI. c.) is the

S. VALERY EN CAUX.

heart of the Marechal de Villars. An omnibus leads by (11 k.) *Bretteville*, with a château of 1730, which belonged to the Marquis de Miromesnil, keeper of the seals under Louis XVI., and where four candles perpetually burn in the church—two for Mme Lebret, daughter of the Marquis, and her husband, and two for Louis XVI. and Marie Antoinette—and (14 k.) *Brametot*, which has a cross of 1550, to (18 k.) *Fontaine-le-Dun*, which has a church of XII. c., XIII. c. and XVI. c., and a cemetery cross of 1547. At *Notre Dame la Gaillarde*, near this, are a cross of 1540, and a chapel of *S. Marguerite du Dun* (XI. c.), used as a barn.

20 k. *S. Vaast-Bosville.*

(A branch line leads to—

7 k. *Cany* (Hotel: *du Commerce*), a pretty town with a XVI. c. church. 2 k. distant, in the valley of the Durdent, is the prettily situated château built by Mansart in the XVII. c. From Cany, a road leads (9 k.) to Veulettes (see below) by (5 k.) *Paluel*, near which rises the (XIII. c., XVI. c. and XVII. c.) *Chapelle de Notre Dame de Janville*, a great place of pilgrimage with sailors. 12 k. from Cany is *Valmont* (Hotel: *du Commerce*), with the interesting old *Manor-house* of the Sires d'Estouteville and de Valmont. The keep dates from the XI. c.; the château is XV. c., and is united on N. and S. to the renaissance *Galerie de François I*. The château belonged at one time to Du Guesclin, who received François I. there. On the opposite side of the river are interesting remains of the *Abbey*, founded XII. c. and mostly rebuilt XVII. c., now a private house. Strangers are admitted to see the ruins of the abbey church, which are chiefly renaissance. The XVI. c. *Chapelle de la Vierge* is intact, and has a retable representing the Annunciation, attributed to Germain Pilon, and tombs of the Sires d'Estouteville. Cany is 8 k. by road from Les Petites Dalles: see later.)

27 k. *Néville* has a cemetery cross of 1582.

32 k. *S. Valery en Caux* (Hotels: *de la Paix; de la Plage; des Bains*), a small seaport and bathing place, which takes its name from the Picardy saint who is said to have dried up here the source of a little river, which was a source of idolatry in the early inhabitants. The church is of XV. c. and XVI. c. The

XVI. c. *Couvent des Penitents*, now used as an arsenal, preserves its cloister. The *Maison de Henri IV.* is XVI. c. At 1 k. is the ruined (XVII. c.) *Chapelle S. Leger*. At 4 k. is *Manneville-ès-Plains*, with a small XVI. c. chateau. At 4 k. is the modern *Calvaire d'Ingouville*. At 5 k. is *S. Sylvain*, where the XIII. c. church has a XVI. c. font and a beautiful churchyard cross of 1519. At 8 k. (on the road to Dieppe) is *Veules* (Hotels: *de Rouen; de la Place; du Casino*), a small sea-bathing place, with a XVI. c. church of *S. Martin*, a very fine XVI. c. cemetery cross and a XVI. c. house called *Le Presbytère de S. Martin*. The neighbouring XVI. c. church of *Blosseville-ès-Plains* (2 k. S.) has good stained glass.]

178 k. *Yvetot* (Hotel : *des Victoires*).

'Il était un roi d'Yvetot
 Peu connu dans l'histoire.
 Oh ! oh ! oh ! oh ! Ah ! ah ! ah ! ah !
 Quel bon petit roi c'était là !' *Béranger.*

The origin of the 'kingdom of Yvetot' is said to lie in the story that Gauthier, lord of Yvetot and chamberlain of Clotaire I., falling into disgrace with his master, was forced to fly to foreign lands, where he distinguished himself in war. After ten years he returned, protected by a recommendation from the pope, and flung himself at the feet of Clotaire as he was attending mass on the Good Friday of 536. The king, infuriated by seeing him, regardless of the holy place, drew his sword and killed him on the spot. Then the pope, enraged at the contempt shown for his safe-conduct, threatened to excommunicate the king, and he only purchased forgiveness by erecting Yvetot into a kingdom for the descendants of his murdered chamberlain.

'On sait seulement avec quelque certitude, que ce fief se composait en plusieurs terres : que la principale, celle d'Yvetot, était positivement franche de toute servitude longtemps avant l'année 1370, et que les autres se trouvèrent également affranchies soit par l'usage, soit par quelque transaction ignorée aujourd'hui.'—*Guibert*, '*Villes de France.*'

The ugly brick church has good woodwork from the Abbey of S. Wandrille. The hospice bears the name of its founder, Asselin. An excursion may be made (carriage 5 frs.) to (6 k.) *Le Chêne d'Allouville*, with a very famous churchyard oak of immense size, in which two chapels have been established, the lower dedicated to *Notre Dame de la Paix*, the upper called the *Cellule de l'Ermite*. This is one of the most curious trees in France, and is believed to be more than nine hundred years old.

The road from Yvetot to (11½ k.) Caudebec passes (3 k.) *Auzebosc*, with a ruined castle and interesting church with handsome altars of Louis XVI., and (8 k.) *Maulevrier*, with a little XII. c. church of *S. Leonard*. The road from Yvetot to (22 k.) Lillebonne passes (13 k.) *Trouville en Caux*, with a XIII. c. church.

The line leaves to r. the remains of the château of *Ecretteville-lès-Baons*, to the l. the church of *Valliquerville*, with a fine XVI. c. tower.

189 k. *Foucart-Alvimare*. At *Alvimare* (1 k. l.) is a renaissance manor-house, now a farm, with the *Chapelle des Blanques* of 1518. Two stone crosses in the hamlet are said to commemorate knights who fell in battle here in the XIV. c. or XV. c.

197 k. *Nointot*. On the walls of the church are seen the mutilated arms of a seigneur de Nointot who, having threatened the life of the aged curé of the parish, was imprisoned in the sacristy till he had promised to respect

him, to pay a large sum to the poor, and to efface his arms. The line passes (r.) the XIII. c. and XVI. c. church of *Mirville.*

203 k. *Beuzeville-Bréauté.* The church of *Beuzeville le Grenier* has an XI. c. tower. The church of (3 k.) *Bréauté* is XI. c. and XII. c.

[A line runs N. to Fécamp by—

12 k. *Les-Ifs-Etretat.* There are diligences from this station by (11 k.) *Les Loges,* with an old manor-house and XVI. c. church, to (15 k.) *Etretat* (Hotels: *Blanquet, Hauville*), a fashionable little sea-bathing place, which owes its reputation to the writings of Alphonse Karr. The church is mostly XII. c., with a XIII. c. lanthorn. Under the *Falaise d'Aval* is the cavern called *Trou à l'Homme,* then the natural arch known as *Porte d'Aval,* near which is the isolated rock called *L'Aiguille d'Etretat.* Beyond this (sometimes known as *le Petit Port*), is the larger chasm called *La Manneporte.* There is a wide view from the *Falaise d'Amont,* beneath which the *Porte d'Amont* may be reached at low water. In the cliff is the platform called *La Chambre des Demoiselles,* from the legend of three beautiful sisters, carried off by the knight of Filleville, who, refusing to yield to his blandishments, were rolled by him over the cliff in a barrel full of spikes, at a point where their harmless apparition is frequently seen. At the end of the cliff on the right is *La Roche de S. Olive,* with a hidden spring, where a poor washerwoman of that name, about to be carried off by pirates, vowed a chapel if God would deliver her, which He did, driving the boats of the pirates out to sea. Excursions may be made by carriage to the little bathing-place of *S. Jouin* (Hotel: *de Paris*), or on foot to *Cap Antifer.*

19 k. *Fécamp* (Hotels: in the town, *Canchy*—good; *Chariot d'Or*—good; *Grand Cerf,* a curious old house opposite the abbey: on the shore, *des Bains, du Casino, de la Plage*), a popular sea-bathing place, which is said to owe its origin to a monastery for women founded in 658 by S. Waninge, on the spot where the waves had thrown up a fig tree, in the trunk of which one Isaac had concealed the precious blood of our Saviour, collected and bequeathed to him by his uncle, Joseph of

Arimathea. Richard Sans Peur, husband of the Danish Gunnora and grandfather of the Conqueror, magnificently rebuilt the abbey—'miro opere, quadris lapidibus, gothica manu,'[1] intending it at once as a minster and a palace—the residence of his later years. Then an angel is said to have transferred the relic to the altar of the new church, with the words 'The price of

TOWER OF S. TRINITÉ, FÉCAMP.

the redemption of the world, which comes from Jerusalem.' After the death of Richard the Fearless, in 996, Fécamp continued to be the especial home of all those descendants of the ducal house of Normandy who embraced the monastic life. Here also Nicolas, son of Richard III., was forced by his uncle, Duke Robert, to become a monk. William Longue-Épée added a palace to the monastery, with a little chapel erected on the site of an earlier shrine of S. Eulalie.

[1] Dudo de S. Quentin.

The great monastic church of *S. Trinité*, dating originally 1082—1107, was almost entirely burnt, and rebuilt 1170—1200. But the E. end of the present fabric probably retraces the lines of the basilica of Duke Richard, whose monastery was colonised with Benedictines from Cluny, under the guidance of S. Mayolus. After his buildings were finished—

'There was one object which excited much speculation. It was a large block of stone, placed right across the path which led to the transept doorway, so close to the portal as to be beneath the drip of the eaves; or, at all events, within the splash of the stream gushing on rainy days from the queer wide mouth of the projecting gurgoil, stretching out his long neck. Fashioned and located by Duke Richard's order, the stone was hollowed out so as to form a huge, strong chest, which might be used either as a coffin or a sarcophagus. Its first employment, however, was for the living, not for the dead. On the eve of every Lord's day, the chest, or whatever it might be called, was filled to the brim with the finest wheat-corn—then a cate, or luxury, as it is considered now in many parts of France. To this receptacle the poor resorted, and each filled his measure of grain, and into each open hand were dropped five dulcet-clinking pennies; while the lame and the bedridden were visited by the almoner as he made his rounds through Fécamp town, and by each was the dole received.'—*Palgrave*, '*Hist. of England and Normandy.*'

When Richard Sans Peur was seized with his last illness, at Bayeux, in 996, he desired to be carried back to Fécamp—which was at once minster and palace—and there, after his death, he was laid in this stone sarcophagus, though his remains were afterwards removed to the interior of the building, where Ware saw his coffin. The central tower of the church is of great beauty. The modern façade was added in 1696. The interior has the splendour of a cathedral, though it has been terribly spoilt by whitewash and restorations. The S. transept contains the *Chapelle de la Dormition de la Vierge*, with a representation of her death by the monk Robert Chardon. A lovely little xv. c. tabernacle contains a stone said to be marked by a footprint of the angel who assisted at the dedication of the church, and was presented by Gilles de Duremont, one of the judges of Jeanne Darc. Opposite the apsidal chapel is the XVI. c. marble tabernacle for the relic of the precious blood, which is still a great object of pilgrimage. Several of the chapels have beautiful renaissance screens. In the *Chapelle S. André*, which has an exquisite screen, are the very fine tombs of Abbot Guillaume de Putot, 1297, and Abbot Robert de Putot, 1329. In the Chapelle S. Jean is the tomb of Thomas, twelfth abbot, 1297. Several tombs of abbots are seen in other chapels, the most ancient being that of Abbot Richard I., who died in 1223. Several even more important tombs were destroyed in the Revolution, especially that of Robert, second son of Richard Sans Peur and the Duchess Gunnora,[1] which was the earliest certificated sepulchral monument in Normandy, and interesting as exhibiting a lion, employed as device or bearing.[2] Marguerite, Comtesse du Maine, who was betrothed to Robert, eldest son of the Conqueror, and died before her marriage, was also buried here.

Of the monastery—where William the Conqueror, with great state, kept the first Easter after the conquest of England—little remains except XVIII. c. buildings, now used for public offices.

The (XVI. c.) *Church of S. Etienne* has good gothic side-portal. In a street to the N.E. of the town is the *Fontaine du Précieux-Sang*, where the sacred fig-tree is said to have been deposited by the waves, and into the cold waters of which children ill with eruptions are often plunged, to their great injury. The *Maison de S. Waninge* (at the end of La Retenue) has a XIII. c. portal.

From the port a steep path leads to the pilgrimage *Chapelle Notre Dame du Salut*, XI.—XIV. c., near which are a lighthouse and the *Fort de Notre Dame de Bourg-Baudouin*. 4 k. S.W. of the town is *Ganzeville*, with a XIII. c. font and XVI. c. cross; the château is XVII. c.

---

[1] Gunnora was probably the third wife of Richard Sans Peur, but her sons were born during the lifetime of his other wives. Her children were Richard le Bon; Robert, buried at Fécamp; a second Robert; Maude, Countess of Tours and Champagne; Havisa, Duchess of Brittany; and Emma, twice queen regnant and twice queen dowager of England. Gunnora had a brother, Herfastus, and three sisters, Sainfrida, Gueva, and Adelina.

[2] See Palgrave, *Hist. of England and Normandy.*

1 k. farther is *Notre Dame de Toussaint*, a romanesque church partly rebuilt (XVI. c.) in the style of the renaissance. In the cemetery is a magnificent cross of 1560.

5 k. W. of Fécamp is the dull little bathing-place of *Yport* (Hotels: *de la Plage; des Bains*), 3 k. from which is the XII. c. church of *Vattetot sur Mer*, with an octagonal stone spire.]

[A line runs S. to—

6 k. *Bolbec*, a great centre of protestantism in the XVII. c. It possesses two fountains which once ornamented the gardens of Marly. At *Fontaine-Martel* is an old castle of great antiquity, and near it the (XI. c.) *Chapelle S. Martin*. At *Val aux Grès* is a leper hospital of the XII. c., rebuilt XVII. c. and turned into a private house.

11 k. *Gruchet la Valasse* has some remains of a Cistercian abbey, built *c.* 1157, and suppressed 1790.

14 k. *Lillebonne* (Hotels: *de France*—good, clean, and reasonable; *du Commerce*). This hot little town, embosomed in wooded hills, once the capital of the Calètes, received the name of Juliobona from Augustus in honour of his daughter Julia. It became the central point of many Roman roads which diverged hence over this part of Gaul. On one side of the Place de l'Hôtel de Ville, an iron railing allows you to look down upon remains of a Roman theatre and baths. Above, in the garden of a modern château, are a fine circular XIII. c. tower and other remains of the castle built by William the Conqueror. In its great hall (1065) all that was wisest and best in the duchy of Normandy collected to listen to and ponder his scheme for the conquest of England. The XVI. c. church of *Notre Dame* has a rich flamboyant spire and a fine portal; the stalls come from the abbey of Valasse.

It is 11 k. from Lillebonne to *Tancarville*—carriage 8 frs. The road crosses marshy meadows, and then skirts the foot of wooded escarpments of chalk to the pretty little hamlet (Hotel: *du Havre*—sometimes closed) in the hollow between the castle hill and that called *La Pierre Gante*. Till 1320 the château belonged to the family of Tancarville, then to the houses of Harcourt, Longueville, la Tour d'Auvergne, and de Montmorency. Charles VI., Talbot, Dunois, Charles VII., and Agnes Sorel have inhabited it. At one time it was possessed by the speculator Law.

Under the Empire, the Duc d'Albufera resided in the château, and Pierre Lebrun, as his guest, wrote his tragedies of *Ulysse* and *Marie Stuart* there. A winding road, lined with fine trees, leads from the village to the château, which has a gateway flanked by round towers. Passing this, we find a triangular space guarded by towers (de l'Aigle, Coquesart, Carrée) at the angles. In the inner space are ruins of the earlier manor-house. The *Château Neuf* was built (1709-17) by Louis de la Tour d'Auvergne. Tancarville will probably be found disappointing by artists: the white walls and rich green are too violent in contrast.

The railway is continued to—

20 k. *Port Jerôme.* This is opposite *Quillebeuf* (to which there is a ferry), the ancient capital of the Roumois, one of the primitive subdivisions of Normandy. It is a prosperous fishing-port, with a lighthouse. The church of *Notre Dame de Bon-Port* has some portions dating from XI. c. The choir windows have curious glass, representing a procession of a charitable confraternity in costume of Henri IV. At Quillebeuf a betrothal confers all the rights of a marriage, but if a swain deserts his affianced bride afterwards he is an outcast from society.]

211 k. *S. Romain de Colbosc* has a fine cemetery *Cross* of 1528, brought from Grosmenil. The *Lepers' Chapel* is now a barn. 6 k. N. is *Angerville-l'Orcher*, with a church of XI. c., XII. c., and XIV. c. S. Romain is 14 k. from Tancarville.

222 k. *Harfleur*, once a place of great importance, ruined by the filling up of its port with sand and by the existence of Havre. The XVI. c. church of *S. Martin* has a noble W. tower, with an octagonal stone spire: it is by a French architect, though Casimir Delavigne has written—

'C'est le clocher d'Harfleur, debout pour nous apprendre,
Que l'Anglais l'a bâti, mais n'a su le défendre.'

In front of the high altar is a fine sepulchral stone of a lady,

1499. Part of the fortifications still exist, by the aid of which Harfleur was bravely defended against the English in 1415 and 1443. The *Château*, on the bank of the Lézarde, is of XVII. c. The *Hôtel de Ville* has a staircase of 1489. At 6 k. is *Gonfreville d'Orcher*, with a XVII. c. château built on the ruins of an ancient fortress.

[A branch line leads N. to 4 k. *Montivilliers*, an ancient town which rose round an abbey founded in 682, which existed till 1791, and of which the abbess had her dean, canons, vicars-general, and all the rights of a bishop. The abbey church, which remains, is XI.—XVI. c. It has a central tower, with an octagonal spire of XII. c. The W. portal is of great richness. A crypt contained 130 skeletons of nuns. Most of the town walls have perished. The *Cimetière de Brise-Garet*, outside the town, has a XVI. c. cloister, and a stone cross mutilated in the Revolution.]

The ruins of the *Abbey of Graville S. Honorine* (see later) are seen on the r. before reaching—

228 k. *Le Havre* (Hotels: *Frascati; de l'Europe; Continental; de Bordeaux; d'Angleterre*), originally called Havre de Grâce, from a chapel of Notre Dame de Grâce, which only dates from the XV. c. The chapel is much frequented, especially on the Whit Monday festival.

'In the chronological table of French trade and commerce, the date of Havre's foundation ranges even with the planting of the *drapeau blanc* on the shores of the S. Lawrence.'—*Palgrave*.

The bastard-gothic church of *Notre Dame* is XVI. c., and contains the graves of Isaac, Pierre, and Jacques Raulin, murdered by the jealousy of the governor Villars in 1599. It is worth while to ascend from the Place de l'Hôtel de Ville (by the Rue Thiers, Grande Rue, and Rue de Montivilliers) to the heights of *Ingouville* for the sake of the view, though no one will agree with Casimir Delavigne (who was born on the quay which is named after him),—' Après Constantinople, il n'est rien d'aussi beau.'

' Ingouville est au Havre ce que Montmartre est à Paris, une haute colline au pied de laquelle la ville s'étale, à cette différence près que la mer et la Seine entourent la ville et la colline, que le Havre se voit fatalement circonscrit par d'étroites fortifications, et qu'enfin l'embouchure du fleuve, le port, les bassins, présentent un spectacle tout autre que celui des cinquante mille maisons de Paris.

' À sa crête, Ingouville n'a qu'une rue ; et, comme dans toutes ces positions, les maisons qui regardent la Seine ont nécessairement un immense avantage sur celles de l'autre côté du chemin auxquelles elles masquent cette vue, mais qui se dressent, comme des spectateurs, sur la pointe des pieds, afin de voir par-dessus les toits. Néanmoins il existe là, comme partout, des servitudes. Quelques maisons assises au sommet occupent une position supérieure ou jouissent d'un droit de vue qui oblige le voisin à tenir ses constructions à une hauteur voulue. Puis la roche capricieuse est creusée par des chemins qui rendent son amphithéâtre praticable ; et, par des échappées, quelques propriétés peuvent apercevoir ou la ville, ou le fleuve, ou la mer. Sans être coupée à pic, la colline finit assez brusquement en falaise. Au bout de la rue qui serpente au sommet, on aperçoit les gorges où sont situés quelques villages, Sainte-Adresse, deux ou trois saints je ne sais qui, et les criques où mugit l'Océan.'—*Balzac*, '*Modeste Mignon*.'

A tramway leads from the Rond Point du Cours de la République to (4 k.) *S. Adresse*, extolled by Alphonse Karr.

In the E. suburb of *Graville S. Honorine* (omnibus) are the important remains of a fortified *Abbey*, built in the XI. c., and situated on a rock, whence its buttresses rise like those of a fortress. The monastic buildings (used as presbytery, mairie, etc.) were rebuilt in the XVIII. c., and the portal of the church in the XIV. c. The nave has six romanesque arches, with capitals covered with curious (XI. c.) sculpture. The choir and its chapels are chiefly XII. c. In 1867 the tomb of S. Honorine was found hidden in the thickness of the wall; it is pierced by a hole through which pilgrims could pass their heads. The graveyard, which contains the tomb of Léon Buquet, author of '*La Normandie poétique*,' has a fine (XIII. c. or XIV. c.) cross. At the foot of the abbey are remains of the château of the Mallets, Sires de Graville. The XIII. c. chapel of *Notre Dame des Neiges* is a barn.

The steam-passage from Havre to Honfleur occupies from 25 to 40 min.; to Trouville, 45 to 50 min.; to Caen, 3 hrs., of which a portion is spent in ascending the Orne.

CHAPTER III.

PARIS TO CHERBOURG BY EVREUX, LISIEUX (TROU-VILLE) (FALAISE), CAEN, BAYEUX AND VALOGNES FROM THE GARE S. LAZARE.

FOR the line from Paris to (58 k.) Mantes, see chap. ii. Leaving Mantes, the line passes through the forest of Rosny.

71 k. *Bréval.* The XVI. c. château of *Gilles* is seen r., then *Gainville*, with a XV. c. and XVI. c. church and the ruins of a XV. c. fortress.

81 k. *Bueil.*

[A line runs S. to (30 k.) Dreux (see ch. iv.) by—

5 k. *Ivry la Bataille*, famous for the victory of Henri IV. over the Duc de Mayenne and the Army of the League, May 14, 1590, and picturesquely connected with the *panache blanc* waving above the royal helm, and for the exhortation of the hero-king to his men:—

'Mes compagnons, si vous courez aujourd'hui ma fortune, je cours aussi la vôtre. Je veux vaincre ou mourir avec vous. Gardez bien vos rangs, je vous prie. Si la chaleur du combat vous disperse un moment, hâtez-vous de vous rallier entre ces trois poiriers que vous voyez là-haut à ma droite, et si vous perdez vos enseignes, ne perdez pas de vue mon panache blanc; vous le trouverez toujours au chemin d'honneur, et j'espère aussi de la victoire.'

A *Pyramid* was raised on the battle-field by the Duc de Penthièvre in the end of the XVIII. c. There are considerable remains of the fortress of Ivry, demolished by Dunois in 1449. A Byzantine portal is a remnant of an abbey founded *c.* 1071 by Comte Roger d'Ivry. The xvi. c. church was built by Philibert Delorme. The *Maison d'Ange* is curious.

In early Norman history Ivry was known from Raoul, Count of Ivry, son of the Duchess Espriota and her second husband, Sperling, the rich miller of Vaudreuil, who was the best friend and counsellor of his half-brother, Richard Sans Peur, and who here slew an enormous bear in single combat.

9 k. *Ezy-Anet.* At *Ezy* (near the station) the xiii. c. *Chapelle S. Germain* recalls the legend that the holy bishop of Paris here miraculously restored the hand of a young washerwoman which had been eaten up by the trout of the adjoining fountain.

At 1½ k., on the opposite side of the Eure, is *Anet* (Hotel: *de Diane*—a good country inn); omnibus, 50 cents. Alnetum (the place of alders), was once famous for its glorious château, the remains of which have been well restored by M. Moreau; what is left being as well cared for as in the palmy days when Diane de Poitiers was its mistress. The earliest building here was of the x. c. About 1340 it was made into a fortress by Charles le Mauvais, Count of Evreux and King of Navarre. In 1378 it was dismantled by Charles V. In 1444 it passed to the family of Brézé. In 1548-52 Diane de Poitiers, widow of Louis de Brézé, demolished the irregular buildings already existing, and began to build the magnificent historic château which became the noblest type of the Renaissance in France, Philibert Delorme being the architect and Jean Goujon the chief sculptor, whilst Jean Cousin painted the windows, so celebrated as *grisailles d'Anet.* The château of Diane surrounded three square courts, the Cour d'Honneur in the midst, with the Cour de Charles le Mauvais and des Cuisines on the right, and on the left the 'Gouvernement' and the Orangerie. Behind was a large garden, surrounded by an open cloister, with a bath on one side; beyond was a vast park. To the N.W. of the court, on the right, were the stables, and, farther on, the Hôtel d' Dieu; to the W. of the court, on the left, was the sepulchral chapel (which contained the tomb of Diane), with the Volière, Héronnière, and Capitainerie behind it. Contemporary writers testify to the enchantments of Anet.

'Me trouvant près du chemin d'Anet, car de tout temps j'ay esté amateur et curieux d'avoir et veoir toutes choses exquises et rares, je me transportay jusques-là, où, il ne fault pas mentir, je fey une conclusion, après avoir tout veu, que la Maison dorée de Neron n'eust sceu estre ni plus riche ni plus belle.'—*Gabriel Simeoni*, 1557.

'La belle Maison d'Anet, qui devoit servir pour jamais d'une telle décoration à la France qu'on ne peut dire de pareille.'—*Brantôme*.

THE ENTRANCE TO ANET.

The first building now seen on approaching the Château d'Anet is the sepulchral chapel; then the beautifully proportioned gateway inlaid with coloured marbles, and supplied with a copy of the famous relief by Benvenuto Cellini (now in the Louvre). It bears an allegorical figure representing Fontaine-Belio (Fontainebleau), with copies of the stag and dogs, now in the possession of the Duc d'Aumale. A black marble tablet is inscribed:

'Phoebo sacrata est almae domus ampla Dianae
Verum accepta cui cuncta Diana refert.'

On the interior was the curious dial inscribed:

'Cur Diana oculis labentes subjicit horas?
Ut sapere adversis moneat, felicibus uti.'

'Diane de Poitiers voulut une oeuvre toute Française; elle confia la construction de son Château d'Anet au génie d'artistes tous ses compatriotes, et leur donna, par cette faveur, l'occasion de lutter avec les artistes étrangers et l'honneur d'assurer et d'affirmer la Renaissance Française. Un fait très-curieux, c'est le caractère des artistes de ce temps-là. Les artistes italiens au palais de Fontainebleau, faisant assaut d'hypocrisie, de malveillance, et de jalousie, se disputaient, se menaçaient, et s'assassinaient entre eux, tandis qu'au Château d'Anet les artistes français, protestants et catholiques, fraternisaient et collaboraient entre eux, chose rare à cette époque de guerres de religion, pour créer un chef-d'oeuvre.'—*P. D. Roussel*, '*Le Château d'Anet.*'

The larger portion of the château was destroyed by speculative proprietors 1799—1810, at which time the portal of the Cour d'Honneur was taken to Paris, where it still exists at the École des Beaux Arts, though without the statue of Louis de Brézé, which was its principal ornament.

'Comme le nom de Diane prête à de nombreuses allégories, l'ornementation de ce Château n'a été faite qu'avec les chiffres, les attributs, les emblèmes et les devises de la Dame du lieu, à laquelle les moindres détails d'ornement faisaient toujours allusion, et de la façon la plus flatteuse. Diane de Poitiers étant veuve a voulu paraître inconsolable toute sa vie: elle n'a jamais quitté le deuil. La manie de Diane était de vouloir persuader à son siècle et à la postérité que la perte de son mari était toujours présente à sa mémoire. Ainsi, la plus grande partie des marbres qui entraient dans la décoration étaient noirs; l'architecture des lucarnes et des cheminées était en forme de tombeau; des palmes étaient enlacées avec son chiffre, et la peinture, comme la sculpture, multipliait à l'infini ces mêmes ornements. D'un autre côté, les chiffres de Diane et de Henri II., harmonieusement enlacés avec des flèches, des croissants et les deltas de l'alphabet grec, ornaient les chapiteaux des colonnes, les frontons, le dessous des entablements, les frises, le dessus des lucarnes, le pavage, les parquets et les portes, les plafonds, les lambris, les vitraux, les bronzes, les serrures, les verrous, les meubles, les tapis, les tapisseries, les faïences du service de table, et jusqu'aux livres de la bibliothèque.'—*Roussel.*

Passing the gate, and entering the beautiful garden beyond, we find on r. the *Chapel*, conspicuous from its two pyramidal towers, finished in 1552, from designs of Philibert Delorme, and formerly built into the E. wing of the château. It was restored in 1840-51, when the façade was added. The crescents and monograms of Diane and Henri II.[1] adorn the doors, bosses, and balustrade of the tribune. The decorations of the interior were by Philibert Delorme and Jean Goujon; but the chapel has been despoiled of all its most precious ornaments, except some sculptures by Jean Goujon. The tribune also is a restoration, yet the whole internal effect of the building is still very beautiful.

The left wing of the château has been restored almost to its original condition, and is shown. The staircase and rooms are very handsome, and M. Moreau has been careful to preserve all old fragments of the original doors, and to collect all that was available of the former tapestry and furniture, much of which bears the chiffre of Diane. In the Salle des Gardes are portraits of the Duc de Vendôme, who possessed the château under Louis XIV., of César de Vendôme, and of the Duc de Penthièvre, the last proprietor before the Revolution.

The exquisite fountain of the Cour de Gauche, representing Diane leaning on a stag, was removed to the Louvre, but has been deprived of its ornamental base, which represented two-thirds of the whole. The Pavillon du Gouvernement retains an ancient ceiling with devices of D and H.

The grounds, kept up in the old French style, with clipped orange and pomegranate trees, are lovely. In the garden on the l. is the *Sepulchral Chapel*, now empty, but built at the end of the XVI. c. by Diane de Poitiers to receive her tomb (now at Versailles).

'La façade se compose de quatre pilastres et d'un entablement corinthiens, que surmonte un attique fort simple avec un

---

[1] Diane was thirty-one and the king only thirteen when she captivated his heart, which was always devoted to her.

amortissement composé d'une espèce d'autel ou tombeau accosté de deux femmes ; un ange est au sommet, à demi caché derrière le tombeau. Sur la porte d'entrée sont deux *Renommées* tenant, d'une main, une trompette, de l'autre, un livre ouvert et une table de la loi sur laquelle on avait écrit, pendant la Révolution: *guerre et mort aux tyrans*. On voit, aux pieds de l'une de ces Renommées, une tête de mort et une serpent, et aux pieds de l'autre un mouton. Aux deux côtés de la porte sont deux niches où se voient des statues de femmes ou d'enfants.'—*De la Guérière*.

All the ornaments of this chapel have been sold, and its altars broken up. The body of Diane was exhumed at the Revolution, and carried to the common cemetery. Her black marble sarcophagus was made into a horse-trough. The other remains of her tomb, which till 1830 were collected at the Beaux Arts, were reclaimed by Louis Philippe for Neuilly, whence, after the Revolution of 1848, they were taken to the Museum at Versailles. It is worth remarking that the tomb is the only thing destroyed by the direct act of the Revolution; all the other devastations at Anet have been due to the ignorance or avarice of its former owners.

Anet possessed a Hôtel Dieu, and the earliest woollen manufactory (filature de laine) in France—of 1815. The parish *Church* (XI.—XVI. c.) is chiefly a rebuilding by Diane de Poitiers, but the apse is XIII. c. It contains the relics of S. Julitte, and (at the entrance of the sanctuary) the tombstone of Anne Louise de Bourbon-Condé, Duchesse du Maine, who inherited Anet after the death of her mother the Princesse de Condé, and her sister the Duchesse de Vendôme. She was buried here in 1753 by the side of her daughter, Louise Françoise, who died in 1743. In the graveyard is a cross of 1555. The altar of the Sacré Coeur had beautiful reliefs by Jean Goujon, mutilated during the Revolution, and now in the Louvre. The church is dedicated to S. Lain.

'Les reliques de S. Latuin, appelé vulgairement S. Lain, premier évêque de Séez, avaient été déposées dans la forteresse d'Anet, vers la fin du IXe siècle ou la commencement du Xe, pour les soustraire à la fureur des Normands. Lorsque les craintes furent dissipées, les habitants de Séez vinrent redemander à Anet le dépôt sacré qu'ils lui avaient confié. Les habitants d'Anet refusèrent de s'en dessaisir. Les Sagiens tentèrent alors d'enlever nuitamment les reliques, et, ayant réussi, prirent le chemin de Nonancourt. Tout à coup, la cloche consacrée au service de la Confrérie de S. Lain sonne à toute volée. Anet est sur pied, se met à la poursuite des Sagiens, qui, dans l'obscurité, obliquant à droite, arrivent à une fontaine, où ils se hâtent de précipiter le coffre contenant les reliques. Elles en sont retirées et portées processionnellement à l'église, d'où le nom du saint·évêque resta à la fontaine.'—*Caraman*, '*Le Château d'Anet.*'

The line passes (r.) *Saussay*, which has a ruined XII. c. chapel and remains of a moated abbey called *Maison-des-Eaux*.

13 k. *Croth-Sorel*. Only the ruins remain of the ancient fortress of Sorel, which existed in 1073. The gateway was built by Marguerite de la Guesle, wife of Pierre Séguier, who bought the domain from Marie d'Albret, Comtesse de Dreux, in 1549.

17 k. *Marcilly-sur-Eure* has ruins of the *Abbey of Breuil-Benoît*, founded in 1137. The nave of the church is restored for worship, and contains a shrine of S. Eutrope. 8 k. is *Illiers l'Evêque*, with the entrenchments of a XII. c. castle, and a graceful XVI. c. chapel in the church.

20 k. *S. Georges-sur-Eure*. The romanesque (XII. c.) church has a tree of Jesse in stained glass of the time of Louis XII. The line passes (l.) the fine (XI. c., XIII. c., and XV. c.) church of *Montreuil*. At the hamlet of *Cocherelle* are a dolmen and the ancient (XII. c.) chapel of *Notre Dame de la Ronde*.]

[A line runs N. to (40 k.) Louviers (see chap. ii.), by

11 k. *Pacy-sur-Eure*, which was ceded by Robert, Earl of Leicester, to Philippe-Auguste as the price of his ransom when he was taken prisoner, and where S. Louis resided for some time in the royal château destroyed by Charles V. In the Rue des Moulins is a curious XVI. c. house. The church is XIII. c. and XIV. c.

'La transition du style roman au beau gothique à lancettes y présente des particularités très dignes d'être étudiées.'—*A. de Caumont.*

26 k. *La Croix S. Leufroy* has ruins of the XII. c. *Tour de Crèvecoeur.* Nothing ancient remains of the *Abbaye de la Croix*

35 k. *Acquigny.* In the cemetery is a chapel built on the spot where S. Maure and S. Vénérand were martyred in the VI. c. The château is of the time of François I.]

92 k. *Boisset-Pacy.* 2 k l. is *Boisset les Prévanches*, with a XVI. c. château, and 3 k. farther the interesting church of *Bretagnolles*, which has a remarkable renaissance baptistery. 10 k. S.W. is *S. André*, which belonged to the family of Terrail, of which Chevalier Bayard was a descendant : his arms and device adorn the walls of the church. Upon the hills overlooking the valley on the r. of the line is seen the ancient church of *Orgeville*, containing the tomb of M. Bonjean, victim of the Commune.

108 k. *Evreux* (Hotels: *du Grand Cerf; du Mouton; de Paris*), the capital of the Department de l'Eure, and seat of a bishopric which dates from the IV. c.

Evreux, which takes its name from the Celtic word *Ebvre*, a forest, was governed in the X. c. by a race of counts, who were the ancestors of the dukes of Normandy. During the captivity of Richard Coeur de Lion, his brother John sold the city to Philippe-Auguste, but regained it, by a cruel and treacherous massacre, upon the release of Richard. It was retaken by Philippe-Auguste, who put almost all the inhabitants to death, and burnt the greater part of the town, which was afterwards a frequent appanage of younger sons of the French kings.

The *Cathedral*, frequently ruined, rebuilt and altered from the XI. c. to the XVIII. c., has still great beauty. The principal portal is renaissance; the N. portal of 1511-31.

The spire was built under the episcopate of the famous Cardinal de la Balue, in the reign of Louis XI. It is of wood coated with lead, and is a favourable contrast to the modern cast-iron spire of Rouen. The interior is a Latin

EVÊCHÉ, EVREUX.

cross, with twenty-three radiating chapels—that of the Virgin, at the E. end, being a splendid specimen of flamboyant. The interest of the nave has been much injured by a recent 'restoration' into conventional gothic, which has destroyed the noble vaulting, with its double ranges of flying buttresses. The wood carving and much of the glass is very fine: a window of the choir has a portrait of Charles le Mauvais, and one in the S. transept that of Louis XI. Two galleries of a gothic *Cloister* remain, but the ignorance of modern 'restoration' has destroyed the very curious upper story, built by Cardinal de la Balue.

Close to the cathedral, with large gardens, is the *Evêché*, built in 1481 on the old city wall, a very beautiful flamboyant edifice, in which Henri IV. resided in 1603. Some remains of a *Roman Wall* of the IV. c. (in the Allée des Soupirs) exist a little to the S.

The church of *S. Taurinus*, at the other end of the city, belonged to an ancient abbey rebuilt by Richard II., Duke of Normandy, in 1026. Of that date is a great part of the church, which occupies the site of a chapel built by S. Candulfe in 660. Part of the nave and tower are of 1407, the W. portal of 1715. The mosaic ornament which fills the round arches of the apse and S. transept is an unusual feature. The church has been ruined by restoration, and has a detestable pavement and much hideous modern glass. The fine old choir windows tell the story of S. Taurinus. Much of the wood carving comes from the Château de Navarre. In the sacristy is the shrine of S. Taurinus, of 1255, one of the most splendid specimens of goldsmith's work of the XIII. c. in existence.

The *Tour de l'Horloge* is of the end of the XV. c. At the angle of the Rue de l'Horloge is the *Musée*. In the Grande Rue is a good house of the XV. c. (No. 78), and another (No. 50) of the renaissance.

2 k. from Evreux was the famous *Château de Navarre*, built by the kings of Navarre in the XIV. c. and destroyed in 1834. 3 k. N. is the XVI. c. *Château de Carambouville*, built by Cardinal

de Bourbon, archbishop of Rouen, proclaimed king by the Leaguers in 1589 as Charles X.

19 k. from Evreux, on the road to Nonancourt, is *Damville*, with remains of an XI. c. castle, burnt by Henry II. of England in 1173 and 1188, and rebuilt by Richard Coeur de Lion in 1198.

[A line leads N. to join the line from Serquigny to Rouen at (48 k.) Clos-Montfort, by—

THE TOWER OF BEC.

25 k. *Le Neubourg*, with remains of a remarkable machicolated fortress, where Henry, the rebellious eldest son of Henry II.—known as Henri Courte Mantel—was married to Marguerite de France, daughter of Louis VII. During the reign of Louis XIV. and the ownership of the Marquis de Sourdiac de Rieux, some of the earliest attempts at operas in France were exhibited here. 9 k. W. of Le Neubourg is *Harcourt*, cradle of the famous family of the name (barons in 1333, counts 1342, dukes 1700), by whom a fortress was built here *c.* 1090. Only two ancient towers and

some vast buildings of the XVII. c. remain of the château, where the English garrison were obliged to capitulate to Dunois in 1449. The choir of the church is XIII. c., the nave XV. c. A neighbouring house bears the date 1551.

43 k. *Le Bec Helloin*, a most interesting spot. The lovely wooded valley is watered by the rapid stream of the Bec. 1 k.

ABBEY GATE, BEC.

r. of the station the grand (XV. c.) tower of the abbey of Bec—yellow grey, like many Somersetshire towers—rises amongst the trees. The gardens of a modern château are entered from the village green by the old abbey gateway, flanked by two high-roofed towers. The cloister and the (XVII. c.) abbot's residence are now a gendarmerie.

LE BEC HELLOIN.

The lasting fame of Bec is due to Lanfranc, son of the lawyer Hanbald, who came to Normandy from the University of Pavia, and founded a school at Avranches in 1039. As he was travelling from Avranches to Rouen in 1042, he met with an adventure in the forest of Ouche which resulted in his becoming a monk.

'His track conducted him through the forest, of which the essarts still constitute the prominent features of the pleasant region. Robbers attacked him. No use raising the *clameur de haro*—no one to hear. Stripped, and bound to a tree, he waited for the opening dawn, and attempted to repeat the service appertaining to the circling hours—the three Hallelujah Psalms, concluding the cycle of each day's prayer and praise. But he could not: he had never committed them to memory; and deeply was he stung by the sense of his neglect of holy things, and the preponderating worth he had attached to secular learning. The silent hours continued, and he endeavoured again to repeat the opening services; but he could not. Struck with compunction, he poured forth his mind in prayer; deploring the time he had given to human learning, the labour he had bestowed on literary studies; and now, when he ought to pray, he was unable to perform his duty to the Church; and he would henceforth devote himself body and soul to the Donor of all blessing. In the early twilight morning he heard footsteps approaching—some peasants released him.'—*Palgrave.*

Under his new impulses, Lanfranc sought the still humble monastery of Bec, where he was joyfully received by the abbot Herlouin. Being soon advanced to the rank of prior, his teaching made the abbey both rich and famous, and the abbot Herlouin was induced to build a larger and statelier monastery near the old site. Meantime Duke William had heard the fame of Lanfranc, and made him his most trusted counsellor, and at the synods of Rome and Vercelli he was famous as the most learned doctor of his time. In 1070 he became Archbishop of Canterbury, to which see Bec afterwards gave two other famous monks—Anselm (1093), the brave supporter of the oppressed and friend of the poor, and Theobald (1139), the early patron of Thomas à Becket.

'It is hardly too much to say that the character of the abbey of Bec influenced not merely Norman monasticism, but the whole progress of learning, education, and religious thought and feeling in Normandy, more than any other institution.'—*Dean Church.*

The XIV. c. parish church contains the tomb of the founder— a wooden slab resting on marble pillars and bearing his painted figure. The Bienheureux Herlouin, or Herlwin, was the son of one Ausgood (of Danish descent) and Heloise, who, after forty years of knighthood and military exploits, took the monastic habit in 1034, at Burneville, near Brionne. Here he worked with his own hands at the building of a church, and learnt to read, his mother Heloise becoming a serving sister to the brotherhood. In 1035 Herlouin moved his monastery to the valley called Bec (Beccus) from the river which watered it, and there he survived as abbot for forty-four years. The beck which gave the place its name is now the only memorial of those early times. The minster of Herlouin has perished, and no existing remains are earlier than the XIV. c. Some tombs from the abbey church are in S. Croix at Bernay.

117 k. *La Bonneville* retains some remains (church and XIII. c. barns) of the *Abbaye de la Noê* or *de S. Florentin*, founded in 1144 by the Empress Matilda, daughter of Henry I. of England. The (XV. c.) parish church has fine stained glass.

126 k. *Conches* (Hotel: *de la Croix Blanche*), where Robert I. of Normandy founded, in 1035, an abbey, which was greatly enriched by his successors. The late XV. c. church of *S. Foy* has seven magnificent choir windows filled with stained glass by Aldegrevers, pupil of Albert Durer, and telling the story of the patron saint. The aisles also have remarkable XVI. c. glass, and most of the windows are dated. The ironwork of the sacristy door deserves notice. A vaulted arcade near the church leads to the ruins of the (XI. c.) castle, the entrenchments of which are

BEAUMONT-LE-ROGER. 93

used as a public garden. The ruins of the *Abbaye des Bénédictins* are XIV. c.

14 k. S. is *Breteuil*, where William the Conqueror, in 1060, built a castle, of which some fragments exist. For the road leading N. to (39 k.) Elbeuf see later.

[A line leads S.W. to join the line from Paris to Granville at (ch. iv.) L'Aigle, by—

27 k. *Rugles-Bois-Arnault.* At *Rugles* (1 k. S.E.) is a fine parish church, chiefly XVI. c., with a XIII. c. nave and XV. c. tower. The church of *S. Jean*, now a warehouse, is X. c. A château, built by the Comte de Rugles, is XVI. c. 4 k. W. is the little church of *S. Antonin de Sommaire*, with XIII. c. glass. 8 k. E., in the forest of Breteuil, is the chapel of *Notre Dame du Désert*, being the choir of an ancient priory church founded in 1135.]

133 k. *Romilly la Puthenaye.* 7 k. S. is *La Ferrière sur Rille*, with a XIII. c. tower, 4 k. W. of which is the *Tour de Thevray* (1489), which is at once one of the last fortresses of the middle ages, and one of the first buildings in which brick was employed after Roman times. The vaulting of all the different stories of the interior is supported by a central pillar.

144 k. *Beaumont-le-Roger* (Hotel: *de Paris*), often made a countship for younger sons of the French kings, is prettily situated in the valley of the Rille. The church of *S. Nicolas*, in front of which stands an ancient cross, is XIV. c., XV. c., and XVI. c. The flamboyant tower has a clock, where a figure named Regulus strikes the hours. At the foot of the tower is the gravestone of the founders of the priory of Beaumont, 1300. The beautiful S. portal is flamboyant. The interior has admirable XV. c. glass; the pendants of the vaulting in the r. aisle have subjects taken

from Ovid's 'Metamorphoses.' Very little remains of the castle built on the hill by Count Roger, c. 1040, but beneath it are picturesque ruins of the Priory of *La Sainte-Trinité*, founded XII. c. The remains of the church are XIII. c. The XVI. c. church of the *Faubourg de Vieilles* is now a barn. 1 k. on the road to Bernay is the fine XVI. c. church of *Beaumontel*. 10 k. on the road to La Barre is the fine Château de *Beaumesnil* (Comte de Maistre), built 1633-40 by Jacques Leconte-Duquesne, Seigneur de Beaumesnil.

149 k. *Serquigny*. The church has a fine XI. c. portal.

[A line runs from Serquigny to (73 k.) Rouen by—

6 k. *La Rivière Thibouville*. The fine château was built by the farmer-general d'Augny, just before the Revolution. Only the chapel remains of the old fortress taken by the Duke of Clarence in 1417.

11 k. *Brionne*, on the Rille, with a castle on a height. In XI. c. it had an island palace with a great fortified hall (*aula lapidea*) where Count Guy of Burgundy, who had joined in the rebellion of the Norman Barons, and fled from the battle of Val ès Dunes, was besieged by Duke William, and only taken, it is said, after a blockade of three years. The Tombeau du Druide, on the W., was a Roman camp.

15 k. *Pont-Authou*. At 2½ k. S.E. are the remains of the important abbey of *Bec-Hellouin*. (See p. 90.)

19 k. *Glos-Montfort*.

[A branch line turns aside N. to Pont-Audemer by—

3½ k. *Montfort S. Philbert*. L. is the old fortified village of *S. Philbert*, with a XV. c. château. R. is the picturesquely situated *Montfort sur Rille*, with the remains of the once magnificent fortress, which had its origin in Roman times, but was rebuilt by Hugues à la Barbe in the XI. c. It was destroyed by John of England to prevent its falling into the hands of Philippe-Auguste. The chapel of *S. Nicolas* was afterwards rebuilt and endowed, and dedicated to Notre Dame by the kings of France. Queen

Margaret of Anjou and her son were amongst its pilgrims; its ruins are still visited on pilgrimage. The church dates from the XI. c., but has lost its character. It contains a statue of *Notre Dame de Pitié*, by the side of which is a chained stone, said to have been attached by one of the lords of Montfort to the neck of his wife, whom he wished to drown, and to have been a votive offering from her when she escaped in safety by the intercession of Notre Dame de Montfort.

16 k. *Pont-Audemer* (Hotel: *du Lion d'Or*), on the Rille. The church of *S. Ouen*, of XI. c. (choir), XV. c., and XVI. c., has fine stained glass. The church of *S. Germain* is XIII. c. and XIV.c. The *Pointe de la Roque* and its lighthouse mày be visited by the steamer down the Rille.]

The line now turns E. by—

26 k. *S. Leger-Boisset.* 4 k. S.E. is *Boisset le Châtel*, with the ruined castle of *Tilly*, and a renaissance château with beautiful brick decorations.

33 k. *Bourgtheroulde.* The village (3 k. r.) retains only the entrance pavilion and the dovecot of its magnificent château, destroyed 1794. It was one of its lords who built the Hôtel du Bourgtheroulde at Rouen. The church has fine renaissance glass.

41 k. *La Londe La Bouille.* At 5 k. is *La Londe*, which has a church with an XI. c. apse, ruins of the XVII. c. château of the Marquis de la Londe, destroyed at the Revolution, and a beautiful rênaissance cemetery cross.

50 k. *Elbeuf-S. Aubin.* *Elbeuf* (Grand Hotel: *de l'Europe*) is famous for its woollen factories. The renaissance church of *S. Etienne* has fine XVI. c. glass. *S. Jean* (chiefly XVI. c. and XVIII. c.) has very fine glass of XV. c. and XVI. c., representing the local industries, especially in the choir, the window given by the Drapers' Guild in 1466.]

159 k. *Bernay* (Hotel: *Cheval Blanc*—good), a bright, clean little town, backed by wooded hills and watered by rushing streams. It was part of the dower of the first wife of Richard II., Duke of Normandy—Judith de Bretagne,

who founded a Benedictine *Monastery* here in 1013, which was sacked in the XVI. c., with horrible massacre of the clergy by the Calvinists, and rebuilt by the Abbot Hennequin de Villenoce in 1628. The poor remains of the Norman abbey are hemmed in by ugly buildings, and faced on the E. with red brick. They are used as a prison and for public offices. The refectory, occupied as a law court, has good gothic vaulting of XVII. c. The church, now a corn exchange, has some remains of the early building of Judith.

In the Grande Rue is the church of *S. Croix*, rebuilt in 1374 and enlarged in 1497. Its beautiful and picturesque XV. c. tower was formerly surmounted by a spire, which was destroyed by a storm in 1687. In the interior, the enormous width of nave and transepts are remarkable. On either side of the west door are tombs of abbots of Bec, and, in the S. transept, is the splendid monument of 'Guillaume Avvilarensis,' 1418, Abbot of Bec, on which his coloured effigy is represented in low relief, robed and croziered. The little figures of saints on the side ornaments are full of character.

The church of *Notre Dame de la Couture*, in a pretty village on the l. of the railway, stands in a cemetery like a garden. Its low slated spire, with pinnacles and ornaments, is quaint. The N. porch is good flamboyant. The interior, modernised in the worst taste, has nothing to recommend it, except its curious old pews.

[A line leads S.E. from Bernay to (87 k.) Mortagne (see ch. iv.) by—

12 k. *Broglie* (Hotel: *du Lion d'Or*), possessed by the family of Broglie from 1716. The church is partly (XII. c.) romanesque. The château was built on the site of an ancient fortress in the

time of Louis XIV. It contains a good library and a number of portraits, including one of Mme de Staël.

16 k. *La Trinité de Réville.* The line to Orbec and Lisieux turns off r. See later.

38 k. *S. Évroult Notre Dame du Bois*, with the ruins of a famous abbey of romantic foundation. In the VI. c. lived Evroul at the court of Hlothar, son of Hlodwig,—fulfilling the life of a saint. At last he forsook the world. He and his wife both took monastic vows. Evroul soon forsook his monastery, with three companions, for a hermitage in the forest of Ouche, on the edge of the forests of Lisieux, Evreux, and Séez. His life was full of miracles, and his cell became the nucleus of a monastery. This was ravaged in the x. c. by Duke Hugo, and fell into decay. Afterwards it was forgotten, till Restold, priest of Beauvais, was moved by a dream to its restoration. William, son of Geroy, becoming a monk of Bec, granted S. Evroul to that abbey, of which it became for a time a dependency, and was colonised by a few monks, with Lanfranc at their head. But Hugh and Robert of Grantmesnil, his nephews, wishing to join with William in a great religious foundation, obtained S. Evroul again in exchange for other lands, and magnificently restored the monastery, filling it with monks from Jumièges in 1050. Samson the Breton became a monk here, to escape the sentence of having his eyes put out, imposed by the Conqueror when he discovered that he had been the means of transmitting large sums of money from Matilda of Flanders to her eldest son Robert, then in Italy, and in rebellion against his father. The abbey of S. Evroul was also the home of Ordericus Vitalis (son of Odelerius, a priest of Orleans), on whose chronicles so much of our knowledge of Norman times depends.

41 k. *Echaffour*, with three menhirs known as *Les Croûtes*. Here we join the line from Paris to Granville: see ch. iv.]

173 k. *S. Mards-Orbec.* At 3 k., *S. Germain la Campagne*, is a church with a good xv. c. choir.

191 k. *Lisieux* (Hotels: *de France* ; *d'Espagne*), a pleasant old town of timber houses—the Chester of France—delightfully situated in the valley of the Orbiquet and

Touques. At the time of the Roman conquest it was the capital of the tribe of Lexoviens; it has some small remains of a Roman theatre and walls.

The former Cathedral of *S. Pierre* had a line of bishops, many of them very illustrious, from the VI. c. to the present century, when the see was suppressed. It is a very remarkable edifice of the transition. Begun in 1045, it was burnt in 1136; rebuilt 1141-82, enlarged 1218, injured by fire in 1226, and completed 1233, and is the most remarkable specimen of transition in Normandy. The W. façade is very severe and simple. The interior—a Latin cross with radiating chapels, where Henry II. of England was married to Eleanor of Guyenne, is a pure and harmonious example of its time. At the cross is a lanthorn tower of the XIII. c. A range of simple lancet-windows surrounds the upper story of the church. Against the N. wall of the transept are two XII. c. tombs. The *Chapelle de la Vierge*, behind the sanctuary, paved with ancient gravestones, was an expiatory offering from Bishop Pierre Cauchon, the wicked judge of Jeanne Darc, who had been expelled from his former bishopric of Beauvais by his diocesans.

The *Évêché*, now used for law courts, is of the XVII. c. and XVIII. c. It opens upon a dull public garden.

The church of *S. Jacques* was built 1496—1501 by the architect Guillemot de Samaison, and is a remarkably uniform and beautiful edifice, though injured by vulgar restorations.

But the chief characteristic of Lisieux is its beautiful old timber houses of the XIV. c., XV. c., and XVI. c., some of them very rich in sculpture. The best are two in the Grande Rue, near the S. door of the cathedral, and the

Vieux Manoir in the Rue des Fevres, which abounds in XIV. c. houses.

3 k. S. is *Beuvillers*, with a curious old XVI. c. manor-house. 12 k. N.E. is *Fumichon*, with a remarkable château, chiefly XVI. c. 13 k. E. is *Marolles*, where the church, partly romanesque, has much curious sculpture. The château is XVI. c. 11 k. W. is the abbey of *Val Richer*, founded 1167, and transformed by M. Guizot into a château (M. de Witt), which was long his residence, and which abounds in historic souvenirs of the reign of Louis-Philippe.

[A line leads N. from Lisieux to (29 k.) Trouville by—

2 k. *Le Grand Jardin*. The line passes (r.) within sight of the ancient church (IX. c. or X. c.) of *Ouilly le Vicomte*, then (r.) the moated (XVI. c. and XVIII. c.) *Château de Bouttemont*; on l. the church (partly XII. c.) of *Coquainvillers* and the ruined *Manoir de Prie*, whence came the famous Marquise de Prie, mistress of the Duc de Bourbon, minister during the minority of Louis XV. Opposite Coquinvillers, on the side of a wooded hill, is the church (partly XVI. c.) of *Norolles*, and the *Château de Malon*, with a fine old gateway, of *temp*. François I., decorated in patterns of brick and stone. The *Ferme de la Vallée* has a great square tower and renaissance chimneypiece. The village of *Manerbe* (4 k.) has an interesting XV. c. church.

10 k. *La Breuil-Blangy*. *Blangy* (6 k.) has a fine late-gothic church and remains of a castle. The line passes (r.) *Parcs Fontaines*, which has a magnificent retable in its XVI. c. church, (l.) *Pierrefitte*, with a church chiefly XIII. c., (r.) *Manneville-la-Piparde*, with a church of XII. c. and XIII. c., (l.) the *Château de Betteville*, (r.) the *Château de Perrey*.

17 k. *Pont l'Evêque*, owes its name to a bridge over the Touques, built by the early bishops of Lisieux. The fine XVI. c. church has good stained glass. At 9 k. (to the r. of the Caen road) is *Beaumont-en-Auge*, with the house which was the birthplace of Laplace, March 22, 1749, and the ruins of a Benedictine priory, founded in 1060.

[A line diverges N.E. to (15 k.) *Honfleur* (Hotel: *du Cheval Blanc; de la Paix*), a port on the r. bank of the Seine, near its mouth, opposite Havre. The curious timber church of *S. Catherine* is xv. c. *S. Leonard* is xvii. c. On the platform of the hill above the town is the pilgrimage chapel of *Notre Dame de Grâce*, built 1606, but said to have been originally founded by Robert the Devil, father of the Conqueror; it has a wide view. It was at Honfleur that Louis Philippe and Marie Amélie embarked for exile.

'Au dernier moment, un commissaire de police voulut faire du zèle. Il se présenta sur le bâtiment où était le roi en vue de Honfleur et le visita du pont à la cale.

'Dans l'entrepont, il regarda beaucoup ce vieux monsieur et cette vieille dame qui étaient là assis dans un coin et ayant l'air de veiller sur leurs sacs de nuit.

'Cependant il ne s'en allait pas.

'Tout à coup le capitaine tira sa montre et dit :—

'" Monsieur le commissaire de police, restez-vous ou partez-vous ?"

'" Pourquoi cette question ?" dit le commissaire.

'" C'est que, si vous n'êtes pas à terre en France dans un quart d'heure, demain matin vous serez en Angleterre."

'" Vous partez ?"

'" Tout de suite."

'Le commissaire prit le parti de déguerpir, fort mécontent et ayant vainement flairé une proie.'—*Victor Hugo*, '*Choses Vues.*'

26 k. *Touques*, where William Rufus embarked after the death of his father to claim the crown of England. The desecrated church of *S. Pierre* is partly xi. c., with a tower of xii. c. At the entrance of the town from Pont l'Evêque is the fine old *Manoir de Meautrix*, of xvi. c. and xvii. c.

On the r. bank of the river are the ruins of the fortress of *Bonneville sur Touques*, a favourite residence of William the Conqueror. Its outer circuit of walls are late xii. c. or early xiii. c. One of the five towers which circle round the keep is called the *Tour du Serment*, because there William is supposed to have received Harold's oath of fidelity. It is lighted by a window called *Fenêtre de la Reine Mathilde.*

29 k. *Trouville-Deauville* (Hotels: *des Roches Noires; de Bellevue; de Paris*—beware of touters at the station), a sea bathing-place, which suddenly came into fashion through the marine landscapes of Charles Mozin and his followers in 1825 ; now it is crowded in summer by above 15,000 visitors. The town of villas has no interest. It was at No. 5, Rue des Rosiers, then belonging to M. Victor Barbey, that Louis Philippe took refuge for thirty hours before his flight from France. The town of *Deauville* (Hotel: *du Casino*) is only separated from Trouville by the Touques.

Pleasant excursions may be made—
1. By the forest of Touques to (16 k.) the *Château d'Hébertot* (of which the oldest part is a machicolated tower of the time of Louis XIII.). 2. To (3 k.) Touques, and (4 k.) Bonneville. 3. By the ruins of the *Château de Lassay*, built by the Marquis de Lassay to receive La Grande Mademoiselle, and those of the *Priory of S. Arnoult*, founded in the XI. c., to (9 k.) the *Château de Glatigny*, a fine building of the XVI. c. and XVII. c. 4. To (13 k.) the *Croix d'Heuland*, of the XVI. c., but sometimes called *Croix de Rollon*, from the legend that, in his delight at the improvement in honesty which had resulted from his laws, Duke Rollo left all his jewels hanging from the arm of this cross, to show his confidence in a people whom he believed incapable of touching them.]

[A line runs S.E. from Lisieux to Echaffour (see p. 97), and (102 k.) Mortagne by—
11 k. *S. Pierre de Mailloc*, with a good XVII. c. château.
19 k. *Orbec*, with a church of XV. c., *Hôtel Dieu* of XVI. c., and several good XVII. c. houses.]

Leaving Lisieux, the main line passes (l.) *Lécaude* with a XII. c. church; and (r.) *Mouteille* with a XII. c. church, overlooked by a hill bearing the ruined (XV. c.) *Château de Mont à la Vigne.*

209 k. *Le Mesnil-Mauger*, with an old moated timber manor-house and a church with a romanesque tower. 2 k. S. is *S. Marie aux Anglais*, with a fine church, chiefly romanesque, and an interesting old manor-house. 4 k. N. is *Crèvecoeur*, with a XIV. c. and XV. c. castle, possessing a XII. c. chapel. The *Château de Grand Champ*, a little S., is XVI. c. and XVII. c.

[A line leads S.E. to (97 k.) Mortagne by—
14 k. *Livarot*, famous for its cheese, with ruins of a XII. c. castle.
24 k. *Vimoutiers*, with some richly sculptured timber houses. The road to Argentan passes near *Roncerai*, with the cottage where Charlotte Corday was born in 1768.
46 k. *Gacé*, with the old château of the Matignon family.
57 k. *Echaffour* (see p. 97)].

216 k. *Mézidon*, on the Dives. The church is XII. c. or XIII. c.

[A line runs N. to Dives and Villers-sur-Mer by—
7 k. *Lion d'Or-Croissanville*. A road leads E. by (8½ k.) *Notre Dame d'Estrées*, where the church has a XIII. c. choir and XVI. c. tower, to (12 k.) *Cambremer*, an old town with a romanesque tower.
14 k. *Hôtot en Auge*. The church, originally romanesque, was rebuilt in the XV. c.; the tower is renaissance. Near it is a very curious old feudal manor-house, containing a fine chimneypiece.
16 k. *Beauvron en Auge*, a very picturesque village, with old timber houses, etc.
20 k. *Dozulé-Putot*. The church of *Putot* (1 k.) is partly XII. c. Here a line branches E. to Troarn and Caen: see later.
28 k. *Cabourg* (Hotels: *de la Plage; des Ducs de Normandie*), a most dreary bathing-place at some distance from the mouth of the Dives.

29 k. *Dives* (reached by tram from Caen,—Hotel: *Guillaume le Conquerant*). This was once an important place, and it was in the harbour at the mouth of the Dives that the Conqueror assembled his army and fleet in 1066 for the invasion of England. Now the sea has retired for 2 k., and the former site of the port is occupied by the dry land of the *Pointe de Cabourg*, formed, between 1790 and 1809, by accumulation of sand. In 1861 a pillar was erected to mark the spot where William is supposed to have embarked with 50,000 men on Sept. 12, 1066, to sail to S. Valery, whence, in the *Mora*, he led his fleet to England on Sept. 27.

In spite of the retirement of the sea, Dives is still a very attractive spot. L'Hostellerie de Guillaume le Conquerant is the most picturesque of XVI. c. inns, and at least three good pictures may be made in its courtyard, surrounded by open galleries, carved rafters, sculptured reliefs, and outside staircases, festooned with roses and wistaria. The village contains many new and some old timber houses; one, sculptured with figures of knights and monks, especially curious. The church of *Notre Dame*, XV. c. and XVI. c., has a grand and rich W. portal. On the interior, the western wall is inscribed with the names of all the knights who sailed with the Conqueror. The massive central arches date from the XI. c. In the S. aisle is a flamboyant gallery over the baptistery. The little sculptured stile of the churchyard deserves notice for its design.

5 k. distant is *Grangues*, with a church of XI. c., XV. c., and XVI. c. It was on the bank of the Dives that the Danes, fighting in behalf of Richard Sans Peur, gained, in 944, the great victory over the French, in which Harold Blaatand is said to have taken the French king Louis prisoner in single combat.

31 k. *Houlgate-Beuzeval* (*Grand Hôtel; Beauséjour; Imbert*), twin bathing-places devoid of attractions.

38 k. *Villers-sur-Mer* (Hotels: *du Casino; du Bras d'Or*), a pleasant bathing place.

[A line leads S. to (167 k.) Le Mans, by—

7 k. *S. Pierre sur Dives*. Here a great Benedictine abbey was founded early in the XI. c. by Lesceline, wife of Guillaume, Comte d'Eu, illegitimate brother of Duke Richard II. But her

abbey church, erected in 1067, was rebuilt in the XII. c. with the exception of the tower. The present glorious abbey church of *S. Pierre* was built under the abbot Jacques de Silly in XIII. c. and XIV. c. On the l. of the sanctuary an incised slab commemorates the foundress Lesceline. The *Halles*, of the XIII. c., belonged to the abbey buildings.

On the bank of the Dives, near a mill, is a very curious stone house of the XV. c., supposed to have been the Abbot's Court of Justice. The octagonal tower at one of its angles contains a

AT S. PIERRE SUR DIVES.

graceful oratory. 2 k. S. is the *Château de Carel*, of the time of Louis XIII. 4 k. W. is *Escures*, with a XII. c. church and old manor-house.

A little N.E. is *Vieux Pont en Auge*, where the church is a most curious and rare specimen of the small masonry of the primitive romanesque, divided by bands of brick. The most remarkable portion is the west front, but here the portal has been reconstructed in the XI. c. or XII. c., and the niche above made in the XVI. c.

3½ k. S.W. is *Grisy*, with an early gothic church and XVII. c. château.

13 k. *Vendeuvre Jort*. 7 k. S.W. is the picturesque ruined *Priory of Ferrières*, dependent on the Abbey of Marmoutiers; chiefly XIII. c. 3 k. E. of Jort is *Courcy*, with a ruined XIII. c. castle and a church with a XII. c. choir.

19 k. *Couliboeuf*. 1 k. is the church of *Damblainville*, partly XIII. c.

[A line branches off W. to
6 k. *Falaise*[1] (Hotels: *de Normandie*; *de France*—both very indifferent).

In the middle of the x. c. Falaise was already the principal town of the Comté de Hiémois, and had its own viscounts. It was strongly fortified by Duke Richard, and became the favourite residence of his son, Robert the Devil, who there fell in love with Arlette, daughter of the tanner, Fulbert, who worked in the valley below the castle.[2] Their son, William the Bastard, born at Falaise in 1027, became Duke of Normandy at seven years old, and was afterwards known as William the Conqueror. At his birth the babe had seized the straw on the chamber floor with such vigour as foretold that he would never let go what he had once laid hands upon. Still, in the streets of Falaise is heard the old Norman song beginning—

> 'De Guillaume le Conquérant
> Chantons l'historiette.
> Il naquit, cet illustre enfant,
> D'une simple amourette.
> Le hasard fait souvent les grands.
> Vive le fils d'Arlette !
> Normands,
> Vive le fils d'Arlette !'

William the Conqueror, who made his first essay at arms in retaking the castle of Falaise from the treacherous governor

---

[1] From its steep rocks.

[2] Fulbert was made ducal chamberlain, and Walter, Arlette's brother, was raised to honourable office. After the death of Duke Robert, in 1035, Arlette married Count Herlwin de Conteville, by whom she was the mother of two sons.

Toustain, loaded his native place with benefits. His grandparents, 'Robertus Pelliparius' (Fulbert, burgess and tanner of Falaise) and his wife Doda lived in the market-place near the old exchange—'Manentes ad veteras cambias in fore Hoiense.'[1] On the Place de la Trinité an equestrian statue of the Conqueror by Rochet was erected in 1851.

The beautiful gothic church of *La Trinité* has a XVI. c. porch, transformed into a chapel, and a renaissance portal. The transept is XIII. c.; the choir, nave and side aisles, of XV. c. and XVI. c., have very rich pinnacles and open-work balustrades, and in the interior the vaulting and capitals are of great richness.

The fine church of *S. Gervais*, begun XI. c., was consecrated 1134 in the presence of Henry I. It has a romanesque tower and wide gothic portal. The l. aisle is XIII. c., the choir XVI. c., of which date there is much fine glass and sculpture.

The *Château* (visitors are not allowed to enter except accompanied by a guide from the gate) is one of the most important fortresses in Normandy. It is chiefly of XII. c. The whole outer wall remains, with its twelve towers, and the ramparts form a long terrace walk planted with trees, and with pleasant views towards the suburb of Guilbray. But the main buildings have been terribly 'restored,' and look almost new. The principal remains are a small XII. c. chapel, a gate of XIII. c., and a square keep, with the great circular tower built by Talbot, who was made governor of Falaise for Henry V. of England. A window in the keep is pointed out as that from which Duke Robert first saw the beautiful Arlette, or Harleva, daughter of Fulbert the tanner, either dancing, or washing at a fountain in the valley, and forthwith fell in love with her; though it is impossible that he could have discovered her beauty at that distance. It is said that in the night on which she was brought to the castle she dreamt that a tree sprang from her which overshadowed all England and Normandy. A room also is shown as that in which William the Conqueror 'fut engendré et naquit,' though the existing keep is probably of a later date than his birth, and we know from the charter of the Church of La Trinité that William was born in the house belonging to his maternal grandfather

---

[1] Alberic de Troisfontaines.

FALAISE. 107

in the old market-place, and that he was baptised in the church at Longevin.[1] A prison in the keep is pointed out, which is entirely built of cut stone, but only retains four of its five original stories.

From the castle the visitor should descend to the l., to an open space planted with trees, whence the best general view

PORTE DES CORDELIERS, FALAISE.

of the building is obtained. Hence a pleasant walk winds below the castle rocks to the *Val d'Ante*, where a fountain is pointed out as that frequented by Arlette, and the town may be re-entered by the picturesque *Porte des Cordeliers* of the XIII. c. Two other ancient gates remain—the *Porte Philippe-Jean* and the *Porte Lecomte*.

In the *Faubourg de Guibray* is a very fine church, begun by William the Conqueror and finished by Philippe-Auguste. The choir is XI. c., nave XII. c., aisles and buttresses XV. c.

[1] *Recherches Hist. sur Falaise*, 1814, p. 134.

Some buildings remain of the *Abbaye de S. Jean*, founded in 1127 by Godefroy de Rou. The prettily situated church of *S. Laurent*, approached by a staircase from the Val d'Ante, is is xv. c. and xvi. c.

1 k. distant is the xvi. c. *Château de Longpré*, a square building with tourelles; 2 k. the xvii. c. *Château d'Aubigny* and the church, with six sepulchral statues of its lords. 4 k. N. the xviii. c. *Château de Versainville*. 4 k. the *Château de la Tour*, where the beautiful Mme de Séran received Marmontel and a numerous literary circle. 8 k. the picturesque *Brêche au Diable* and the *Gorge de S. Quentin*, above which, on *Mont Joly*, the actress Marie Joly is buried.]

53 k. *Argentan* (see ch. iv.), on the line from Paris to Granville.]

Leaving Mézidon, the line passes the château and xiii. c. church of *Canon*; l. (2½ k.) *Vieux-Fumé*, with a xii. c. church; r. *Ouézy sur Laizon*, with a xiii. c. church and ruined priory; r. *Cesny aux Vignes*, then *Airan*, with a beautiful transition portal.

225 k. *Moult-Argences*. The church of *Moult* has a rich romanesque choir. At *Argences* (3 k.) the church of *S. Patrice* (xi. c., xii. c., and xv. c.) is converted into a warehouse. The line passes (r.) *Vimont*, with a column commemorating the victory of Val ès Dunes, gained, 1047, over the rebel lords by William the Conqueror. Farther on r. is *Bellengreville*, where the church has an early gothic choir and rich romanesque portal.

231 k. *Frenouville-Cagny*. The church of *Frenouville* has a romanesque nave, with xiii. c. windows. At *Cagny* are a romanesque church, a ruined priory, and xvi. c. château. Towers and churches are seen on l. before reaching—

239 k. *Caen* (Hotels: *de la Place Royale*—very good; *d'Angleterre; d'Espagne; de la Marine*), capital of Cal-

vados and La Basse Normandie. The town owes its importance to William the Conqueror, who surrounded it with walls, built two palaces, founded abbeys and hospitals, and fixed his exchequer here. Lanfranc, being appointed abbot of S. Etienne, attracted hither a vast number of illustrious followers; and it was a provincial council, summoned here in 1061, which imposed the law of *Trêve de Dieu* upon the Norman lords, and promulgated that of *Couvre-feu* for the repression of disorders. In 1083 Queen Matilda was buried in the abbey of S. Trinité, and in 1087 William was brought from Rouen to that of S. Etienne. Robert Courte-Heuse, eldest son of the Conqueror, made the two canals which now form the Isle de S. Jean. His brother Henry I. raised the walls of the castle and built its keep. In 1204 the oppressions of King John caused Caen to revolt to France, but the town was retaken and sacked by Edward III. of England. Du Guesclin expelled the English in 1370, but Caen was retaken by the army of Henry V. in 1417, and was only finally acquired by France in 1450.

The musical composer Auber, and the poets Moisant De Brieux and Malherbe were natives of Caen. George Brummel, the friend of George IV., died here.

> 'Caen, O Caen, si de ma mémoire
> Jamais je songe à te bannir,
> Si de ton charmant souvenir
> Je ne fais ma plus grande gloire,
> Que je sente engourdir mes doits,
>   Qu'aussi tout ma langue séchée,
> Au palais enroüe se trouvant attachée,
>   Perde l'usage de la voix.'
>
>   *Moisant de Brieux,* '*Norman chanson.*'

Several days may well be spent in visiting in detail the antiquities of Caen and its environs, and it will be found an admirable centre from whence to study the interesting architecture of the Norman village churches. Those who only give one day to the town may follow the Rue de la Gare to the quay. Here, crossing the Orne by the Pont des Abattois, they may turn l. to the Place Dauphine, from the middle of which opens the *Rue S. Jean*, the principal artery of the town. This street, and, even more, the Rue S. Pierre, are picturesque in the varied outline and the red-grey tones of their houses, broken here and there by trees, and with beautiful towers and spires rising behind them. Even the efflorescence of a church like S. Sauveur, covered with interlaced sculpture, has its own charm when subdued into harmonious tints of grey and tinted with golden lichen. The magnificent 'subject' behind S. Pierre, painted by a thousand artists—when the east end of the church rose abruptly from water—has, however, been destroyed by the Orne having been diverted from this point and a hideous market built upon the site—as ruthless an injury to the beauty of Caen as could have been inflicted.

In the *Rue S. Jean*, which contains many old houses,[1]

---

[1] No. 148, Rue S. Jean, occupies the site of the house where Charlotte Corday lived with her aunt, Mme de Bretteville.

'Dans une rue large et populeuse qui traverse la ville de Caen, capitale de la basse Normandie et centre alors de l'insurrection girondine, on voyait et l'on voit encore aujourd'hui, à côté de l'antique demeure aux murailles grises, délavées par la pluie et lezardées par le temps, qui s'appelle le *Grand Manoir*, une maison à deux étages, ne se recommandant à l'attention que par les souvenirs qu'elle réveille. Une porte basse, rarement ouverte, laissait voir, au bout d'une allée obscure, une cour étroite, et, au fond de cette cour, les marches de pierre d'un escalier, en spirale montant à l'étage supérieur. Deux fenêtres à croisillons, dont l'une ouvrait sur cette même cour, et l'autre avait vue sur la cour du Grand Manoir, laissaient filtrer à travers leurs vitraux octogones, enchâssés dans des compartiments de plomb, un jour pâle et morne, qui éclairait faiblement une chambre simple et nue, n'ayant d'autre décoration is the late gothic church of S. Jean. Its portal is surmounted by a square XIV. c. tower; the rich central tower is XVI. c.

The Rue S. Jean ends in the *Place S. Pierre*, one side of which is occupied by the beautiful church of *S. Pierre*, celebrated for its exquisite gothic tower of 1308, with hexagonal pinnacles.

'Cette tour est surmontée d'un trottoir garni d'une balustrade en pierre, et de huit clochetons à jour, délicatement travaillés. La pyramide terminale, construite en pierres de six à sept pouces d'épaisseur, liées les unes aux autres au moyen de crampons de fer, et percée, sur les faces de l'octogone, de quarante-huit ouvertures en forme de rosaces, et garnie de crochets sur les angles : elle est d'une telle solidité, que les intempéries de la saison ne l'ont point altérée.'—*A. de Caumont.*

The sculptures of the great XIV. c. portal—*le portail neuf*—have been destroyed by the Protestants. The aisles, of XV. c., and apse of XIV. c., have been restored (1521) in the style of the renaissance, but are exceedingly graceful. The E. end of the church overhung the Orne, and was indescribably picturesque, but a senseless modern boulevard has destroyed this. The rich vaulting of the choir and apsidal chapels is by Hector Sohier of Caen, 1521. The door of the sacristy, in the chapel of Notre Dame des Sept-Douleurs, has sculptured panels from the Abbey of Ardennes, representing the stories of S. Augustin and

que la grande cheminée antique. Ce jour pâle imprimait à cette chambre reculée, loin des bruits de la rue, dans sa vetusté et dans son obscurité, ce caractère de délabrement, de mystère et de mélancolie que l'imagination humaine aime à voir étendu, comme un linceul, sur les berceaux des grandes pensées et sur les séjours des grandes natures. . . . C'est là que vivait, au commencement de 1793, Charlotte Corday d'Armont.'

Lamartine, '*Hist. des Girondins.*'

S. Norbert. The third capital on the l. of the nave has curious sculpture.

Near S. Pierre the Rue du Marché au Bois leads to the *Château*, founded by the Conqueror, and where his son Henry I. built a magnificent keep. Everything of interest is now destroyed except the xv. c. *Porte des Champs* on the N.E., and the little church of *S. Georges*, a reconstruction of the xv. c., which retains a romanesque arch and capitals. Near this is a building of the xi. c., which served as the Exchequer of Normandy.

From the Rue du Marché au Bois, the Rue du Montoir and Rue des Chanoines lead to the famous church of *La Trinité*, or the *Abbaye aux Dames*, founded by Matilda of Flanders (1062), as that of S. Etienne was by William the Conqueror, as an expiatory offering for their irregular marriage, which had been condemned by the Church of Rome.[1] At its consecration (June 18, 1066) their infant daughter Cecilia, afterwards its second abbess (1113-27), was placed upon the altar by her parents, and offered to the Church.

The central tower has a pyramidal roof, which adds to its picturesqueness : those on either side of the romanesque W. portal had octagonal spires (like S. Etienne), pulled down by Du Guesclin in 1360; the unsuitable balustrades are xviii. c. In the choir, which is reserved for the nuns of the hospital, is the tomb, once rich with gold and gems (with an xi. c. inscription) to Matilda—

'Consolatrix inopum, pietatis amatrix.'

'As for Matilda, a true woman, her goodness, her virtues,

---

[1] Matilda was cousin to her husband William, her mother having been Eleanor, youngest daughter of Richard le Bon.

may be frequently traced in history—her interference, never. Her patience under trouble and tribulation constitutes the main feature of her biography.'—*Palgrave*.

Beneath, is a crypt of the XI. c., where the abbesses, including the Princess Cecilia, are buried. The S. transept has a beautiful XIII. c. chapel.

Behind the church are the vast buildings (1704-26) of the *Hôtel Dieu*, originally founded by Henry I. of England. Opposite the W. end of the church is the nave (XII. c. and XV. c.) of the ancient church of *S. Gilles*, with a very graceful S. portal of delicate and unusual renaissance sculpture.

Returning to S. Pierre, we should follow the *Rue S. Pierre*. Nos. 18-20 are admirable timber houses. In the *Cour de la Monnaie* (r.) are some curious buildings erected in the XVI. c. by Etienne Duval de Mondrainville, and which belonged to the *Hôtel des Monnaies*. A tourelle, bearing two medallions, is surmounted by a lanthorn with a statue.

On the r. of the Rue S. Pierre is the church of *S. Sauveur* (formerly Notre Dame)—one of the triumphs of flamboyant architecture, being chiefly XIV c., with renaissance additions. The tower is XIV. c.

By the Rue Ecuyère and Rue Guillaume le Conquerant we reach the magnificent historic church of *S. Etienne*, which belonged to the *Abbaye aux Hommes*, founded *c.* 1064 by the Conqueror, to expiate his marriage (in spite of the pontifical prohibition) with Matilda of Flanders, who was married already, and whose divorce had not received the papal sanction. The church was begun in 1066 by the famous Lanfranc, who ruled the abbey for four years, after having been abbot of Bec and before becoming (1071)

Archbishop of Canterbury. It was consecrated in 1077 by the Archbishop of Avranches. William endowed it with an arm of the first martyr, which he obtained from Bésançon. The choir was reconstructed on a larger scale in the middle

HÔTEL DES MONNAIES, CAEN.

of the xii. c., when the steeples of the W. towers were added. In 1562 the church was half ruined by the Calvinists, and their injuries caused the fall of the great central spire. The nave was restored by Prior Jean de Baillehache (1609-26), and recently there has been a general, though in most respects a harmless, restoration.

To the first bays of the N. aisle the *Chapelle Hallebout* is united, a gothic edifice of 1315, rebuilt in XVI. c., and which served as the monastic choir, after the destruction by the Protestants, and before the restoration of the nave. The lower story of the central tower forms a lanthorn. In the (XIII. c.) choir a rhyming inscription gives the name of the architect, Guillaume. In the apse of S. Gabriel, between the high altar and the choir, the Conqueror was buried.

'At the gates of Caen, clergy and laity came forth to receive the body, but at that very time flames arose, the streets were filled with heavy smoke: a fire had broken out which destroyed good part of the city; the procession was dispersed, and the monks alone remained. They brought the body to S. Stephen's monastery, and took orders for the royal sepulture. The grave was dug deep in the presbytery, between altar and choir. All the bishops and abbots of Normandy assembled. After mass had been sung, Gilbert, bishop of Evreux, addressed the people; and when he had magnified the fame of the departed, he asked them all to join in prayers for the sinful soul, and that each would pardon any injury he had received from the monarch. A loud voice was now heard from the crowd. A poor man stood up before the bier, Asceline, the son of Arthur, who forbade that William's corpse should be received into the ground he had usurped by reckless violence.

'The bishop forthwith instituted an inquiry into the charge. They called up witnesses, and the fact having been ascertained, they treated with Asceline, and paid the debt, the price of that narrow little plot of earth, the last bed of the Conqueror. Asceline withdrew his ban; but as the swollen corpse sank into the grave, it burst, filling the sacred edifice with corruption. The obsequies were hurried through, and thus was William the Conqueror gathered to his fathers, with loathing, disgust, and horror.'—*Palgrave,* '*History of England and Normandy.*'

A magnificent monument, adorned with gold and

precious stones by Otto the goldsmith, and supported on three small white marble columns, was erected at the cost of William Rufus over his father's grave, and inscribed with an epitaph by Archbishop Thomas of York, which told how William the Conqueror ruled the Normans, conquered the Bretons, and subdued Maine, but in which the conquest of England was never mentioned.[1] When the church and monastery were plundered in the wars of the XVI. c., the shrine was destroyed, and the coffin of the Conqueror[2] broken open and his bones dispersed. A single thigh-bone, preserved by a monk of the abbey, was replaced in a new tomb after the church was repaired in 1626. In 1742, this second tomb, being considered to be in the way of the services in the church, was removed to another part of the choir, where it was destroyed and rifled in 1793, when the one remaining fragment of the body of William was lost for ever. A modern stone commemorates the spot where it once rested.

The *Abbey of S. Etienne*, rebuilt in the XVIII. c., is now occupied by the *Lycée*. In one of its courts is the beautiful but mutilated XIV. c. building known as the *Salle des Gardes*. A curious octagonal XIV. c. building with a cupola,

[1] 'Qui rexit rigidos Normannos, atque Britannos
  Audacter vicit, fortiter obtinuit,
Et Cenomannenses virtute coercuit enses
  Imperiique sui legibus applicuit,
Rex magnus parvâ jacet hic Guillelmus in urnâ,
  Sufficit et magno parva domus domino.
Ter septem gradibus se volverat atque duobus
  Virginis in gremio Phoebus, et hic obiit.'

[2] William was known to his contemporaries as William the Bastard; afterwards he was distinguished from his successor as William the Great, and so spoken of in charters of William Rufus. Ordericus Vitalis is the first to speak of him as the Conqueror—'Guillelmus Magnus, id est Conquæstor, Rex Anglorum.'

now destroyed, was known as 'Le Cuisine de Guillaume le Conquerant.'

A street, turning r. from the W. door of S. Etienne, leads from the Place de l'Ancienne Boucherie to the church of *S. Nicolas*, now a barn, but unusually picturesque in outline, and a fine specimen of xi. c. architecture. The W. tower is romanesque below, and has a xv. c. upper story. The apse and its apsides have stone roofs. A little to the S.E. of the church is a picturesque and simple gateway with a Norman arch and moulding.

The rich xv. c. church of *S. Etienne le Vieux*, on the Boulevards, a little beyond S. Etienne, is now a warehouse. A much mutilated equestrian figure on its walls is pointed out as intended for the Conqueror. The church of *La Gloriette*, or *Notre Dame*, near the Boulevard Bertrand, is of 1684-87.

Behind the Place de la Préfecture is the *Place Royal*. Here is the *Musée*, open from 11 to 4 on Thursdays and Sundays (daily to strangers). It contains—

> *Perugino.* The Marriage of the Virgin—a very beautiful picture, from the cathedral of Perugia.
> *Perugino.* S. Jerome in the Desert—from Fontainebleau.

In the *Hôtel de Ville* is the *Bibliothèque* (open 10 to 4), containing more than 80,000 vols.: some curious books come from the library of Diane de Poitiers.

> 'Jadis renommée comme "ville de sapience," Caen est toujours l'une des cités les plus savantes de la France, du moins si l'on en juge par ses établissements d'instruction supérieure et secondaire et surtout par ses nombreuses sociétés libres. La lycée de Caen est le plus beau de France.'—*Elisée Reclus.*

On the opposite side of the railway is the church of

Vaucelles (Vauxhall), chiefly XV. c., with a curious romanesque tower of XI. c. or XII. c., crowned by a pyramidal four-sided roof.

Several old houses are interesting, especially the *Hôtel du Valois* or *d'Ecouville*, of 1538, in the Place S. Pierre; the *Hôtel de Thaon*, XVI. c., in the Rue S. Jean; the *Hôtel de Loraille*, built by Thomas de Loraille, Bailli de Caen, in 1463; and a house in La Venelle-Quatrans (between Rue de Geôle and Rue des Teinturiers), of rare XIV. c. architecture, which belonged to Jean Quatrans, tabellion de Caen 1380-90.

> 'Si vous prenez la peine d'aller visiter cet édifice, vous verrez qu'il se compose de deux étages au-dessus du rez-de-chaussée, qu'il n'a point de pignon sur la rue comme beaucoup d'autres; qu'il était éclairé par un assez grand nombre de fenêtres étroites et carrées; que les boiseries offirent peu de moulures; que chaque étage est un peu en saillie sur l'étage inférieur; qu'enfin deux grandes lucarnes dominaient le dernier entablement et dissimulaient la monotonie du grand toit qui couvrait l'édifice.'— *De Caumont.*

Beyond the Faubourg S. Gilles and the Abbaye aux Dames, and not far from the canal, are the curious remains of an hotel, built under Louis XII. by Gérard de Nollent, with a tower and wall encrusted with medallions; the former bearing on its battlements some armed statues, which have given it the name of *Maison des Gendarmes.*

2 k. W. of the town are the remains of the Premonstratensian *Abbaye d'Ardennes*, founded *c.* 1121, now turned into farm buildings. The gate-tower has a semicircular-headed gate and pointed wicket. The W. façade of the XIV. c. church has a triple portal, surmounted by a flamboyant rose-window in a pointed arch, with tracery of remarkable grace, formed 'by throwing out six leaves from the centre, bisecting these by other leaves, doubling these at the extremities, and trefoil-feathering each point thus produced.'

The neighbourhood of Caen is the especial district of beautiful steeples, which are all much on the same plan.

'The tower, which is square, whether central or rising from the ground, has, resting upon a lower stage of less ornament, a tall belfry story, also square, without buttresses, or at least any projecting beyond the slope which finishes the cornice of the stage beneath. This belfry has four lofty and deeply-moulded arches in each face, of which the outer ones are narrower than the others, and unpierced; the two in the middle being open as windows. These are often divided by a mullion,

MAISON DES GENDARMES, CAEN.

and sometimes have small plain transoms, without arch or foliation. Above is a rich cornice. From the tower rises an octagonal spire, flanked by four lofty pinnacles of open work, which vary in their plan, some being hexagonal, others octagonal, but they are always finished with spires. On the cardinal points are spire-lights, rising to the same height with the pinnacles, and often finished at the top with a quadrangular pyramid. The spire in many cases is pierced with foliated openings, such as might be described in a circle, the number of cusps decreasing according to the size of the aperture; the lowest range, perhaps, consisting of septfoils, and the highest of trefoils. The masonry is also, as usual, worked in scales.'—*J. L. Petit.*

An excursion of twelve churches may embrace Cambes, Mathieu, Douvres, Luc, Langrune, Bernières, Bény, Fontaine-Henri, Thaon, Cairon, Rosel, S. Contest.

A second excursion of ten churches may be made to Authie, Rost, Séqueville, Bretteville l'Orgueilleuse, Norrey, Cheux, S. Manvieu, Mouen, Fontaine-Etoupefour, Verson.

On the evening of Easter Sunday, or morning of Easter Monday, bands of poor men go to the doors of the villages near Caen, singing—

> 'Séchez les larmes de vos yeux,
> Le Roi de la terre et des cieux,
> Est ressuscité glorieux!
>   Alleluja!
>
> Donnez quelque chose au chanteur,
> Qui chant les louanges du Seigneur.
>   Un jour viendra
>   Dieu vous l'rendra.
>   Alleluja!'

And they receive some sous or a few eggs. But if the person begged from is too poor to give, he replies—

> 'Pauvre chanteur, t'es mal venu;
> Not' poul' n'a pas encore pondu,
>   Demain viendra,
>   Not' cat (chat) pondra.
>   Alleluja!'

The port of Caen, *Ouistreham* (a purely Saxon name), was the great port of communication between the duchy and the kingdom at the time when the dukes of Normandy were kings of England.

EXCURSIONS FROM CAEN.

No one should visit Caen without making an excursion to Dives and its beautiful old inn (see p. 102). This is best accomplished by the tramway, which has its station at the head of the western canal behind S. Pierre. The open tramcars are pleasantest in summer. Artists should on no account miss giving a day to Dives.

5 k. S. of Caen is the vast corn-plain (bright in summer with poppies—'roses de vipères'). To the r. of the road to Falaise is *Ifs*, where the church has a noble tower, romanesque in the lower story and pointed in the upper.

8 k. S.W. is the fine *Château de Fontaine-Etoupefour*, built under Louis XI. and XII. The gateway is flanked by towers, which are circular in the lower and octagonal in the upper story. Between them is a richly-ornamented gabled front, and behind them a moated courtyard.

2 k. S. are the remains of the XII. c. church and XV. c. monastery of *Bretteville sur Odon*, a dependency of Mont S. Michel.

10 k. N.W., in a valley on the r. of the road to Creully, is the picturesque little deserted church of *Thaon*, a very perfect specimen of romanesque, chiefly XII. c., with a tower of the XI. c. having two stories of double windows of the XI. c., and a four-sided stone roof, with heads of animals at the angles; the walls are richly ornamented with arches. A neighbouring chapel is said to have been used for lepers. 2 k. farther is the very fine renaissance *Château Fontaine-Henri* (Marquis de Canisy), of XV. c. and XVI. c., with walls rich in arabesques, tall roofs, and beautifully decorated tourelles and chimneys. Visitors are admitted to the grounds, but the interior is not shown. The chapel of the château is XIII. c. The church has a romanesque choir. Artists will delight both in Thaon and Fontaine-Henri.

7 k. W. of Fontaine-Henri is *Creully*, with a large church, chiefly romanesque, with tombs of the family of De Sillans. In the grounds of the château are important remains of an old castle, the stronghold of Hamon 'Dentatus,' the famous baron who unhorsed Henri I. of France at the battle of Val ès Dunes, who conspired in 1047 against Duke William (the Conqueror), and who was the father of Robert Fitz Hamon, who built Cardiff Castle after the Conquest, and surrounded it with twelve smaller fortresses. In 1100 Creully belonged to Robert of Kent, natural

son of Henry I.; in the XVI. c. to the family De Sillans, and later to the minister Colbert. The ruins of the castle are well seen from the bridge of La Seulles, beyond the mill. 2½ k. S.W. of Creully are the beautiful ruins of the *Priory of S. Gabriel*, founded by Richard, Lord of Creully, in the XI. c. The remains consist of a xv. c. manor, a keep which serves as a belfry, and the choir of the conventual church. The latter terminates in a semi-circular apse; the vaulting is divided by a transverse arch; the arches are principally semicircular, and much ornamented with the chevron. The parish church is remarkable for its tower, supported by a single arch springing segmentally a short distance from the floor.

A more direct route may be taken from Caen to (17 k.) Creully by (8½ k.) *Vieux-Cairon*, l. of which is *Rosel*, with a XIII. c., XIV. c., and XV. c. church; (10 k.) *Cairon*, 1 k. S.W. of which is the fine *Château de Lasson*, chiefly of the time of François I., (14 k.) *La Fresne-Camilly*, with a fine church, partly XIII. c.; (16 k.) *Pierrepont*, where the church has a romanesque portal. Robert, Lord of Pierrepont, came to England at the Conquest in the suite of William de Warenne. Hurst Pierrepont in Sussex, and Holme-Pierrepont in Nottinghamshire, have Norman designations which his descendants, now represented by the Earls Manvers, added to the English localities. Near Pierrepont is the handsome *Château de Lantheuil*.

Varaville, N.E. of Caen, is an old battle-ground of France and Normandy, where the river was crossed by a ford called Gué-Beranger, in the XI. c., where Duke William gained (August 1058) a great victory over the French army under Henri I.

[A branch line runs N. from Caen to its especial bathing-places, offering facilities for visiting many churches of interest; passing by—

11 k. *Cambes*, where the church is partly romanesque, partly XV. c.

15 k. *Mathieu*. The church has a curious late XI. c. roman-esque nave. A tablet marks the house where Jean, father of Clement Marot, was born.

20 k. *Douvres* has some remains of a (XIV. c.) château of the

LA CHAPELLE DE LA DÉLIVRANDE. 123

bishops of Bayeux. The church, with a XII. c. nave and XIV. c. choir, has a very fine romanesque tower, in which the arches of the upper story are slightly pointed.

20½ k. *La Chapelle de la Délivrande.* This famous place of pilgrimage was founded by S. Regnobert in the VII. c., but has been constantly rebuilt. Its celebrated image of the Virgin, which is said to have fallen down from heaven, is of great antiquity, and often attracts 150,000 pilgrims annually. The chapel has been recently rebuilt. Near it are a convent, school, orphanage, mission-house, and many booths for the sale of rosaries, candles, and medals.

23 k. *Luc sur Mer*, a sea-bathing place. The modern church possesses a porch and tower from an earlier building, and a cross of 1662. 3 k. E. is *Lion sur Mer* (Hotel: *de Calvados*), with a renaissance château. The choir of the church is XIV. c.

24½ k. *Langrune* (Hotels: *du Casino; de Bellevue*). The very noble church, XII. c. and XIII. c., has a good central tower, with a low, open stone spire. It has simple, heavy columns, and a stone pulpit. Near this are the *Roches du Calvados*, so called from a Spanish vessel of the Armada which was wrecked there. After the Revolution, the name was taken as that of the Department.

26 k. *S. Aubin sur Mer*, a small bathing-place.

28½ k. *Bernières*. The fine church has a noble XIII. c. tower with a stone spire. The vast choir has fine retables and stall-work of XVII. c. The nave and its aisles are romanesque of XI. c. and XII. c. About 2 k. W. are the Roman excavations known as *Tombelle S. Ursin.*

31 k. *Courseulles* (Hotel: *des Etrangers*) famous for its oyster beds. The difficult entrance of its port is known as *Fosse de Courseulles*. The château is of the time of Louis XVII.

(The road from Courseulles to (21 k.) Bayeux passes (7 k.) *Tierceville*, where the transition church has a XV. c. tower; (9½ k.) *Villers-le-Sec*, where the XIII. c. church has a curious tower with a stair-turret, and r. of which is *Bazenville*, with an admirable XIII. c. tower and XV. c. porch, and a leper hospital (made into a farm), with a flamboyant chapel; (12 k.) *Le Manoir*, l. of which are the XIII. c. church and the XV. c. and XVI. c. château of *Vienne*, and the XVIII. c. château of *Esquay sur Seulles*; (16 k.) *Sommervieu*, where the church has a perfect XIII. c. choir, and a modernised château of the bishops of Bayeux; and (20 k.) *S. Vigor le Grand*, where, in the sacristy, a curious old marble seat is preserved, in which the bishops were seated on taking possession of their diocese, and which is supposed to date from Odo, brother of the Conqueror. The gateway and a XIII. c. barn of a priory remain.)

A hill, formerly called Mout Faunus, where S. Vigor in the VI. c. destroyed an idol which was adored by the ancient inhabitants, is now called *Mont Chrismet*, because at Easter and Pentecost he administered baptism there. The fragments of the very curious font which he is said to have used are now in the museum at Caen.]

[A line leads E. from Caen to Trouville by—

5 k. *Giberville*, 1. of which is *Démouville*, where the church has a good XIV. c. porch.

12 k. *Troarn*, with remains of an XI. c. abbey.

15 k. *Bures*, where Mabile de Bellême was murdered in his bath in the XI. c.

24 k. Dozulé-Putot, on the line from Paris to Trouville.]

[A line leads S. from Caen to (157 k.) Laval, by—

9 k. *Feuguerolles-S.-André*. Of the neighbouring villages *Feuguerolles-sur-Orne* has a XII. c. church, *S. André de Fontenay* has a XIII. c. nave, and slight remains of the *Abbaye de Fontenay*, founded in XI. c.; the church of *S. Martin de Fontenay* is partly romanesque. The village of *Vieux* (church of XIII. c. and XIV. c.), 3 k. S.W., occupies the site of the ancient capital of the Viducasses.

14 k. *Mutrécy-Clinchamps*. The church of (2 k.) *Clinchamps* has a beautiful romanesque tower. The church of (2 k.) *Mutrécy* is a very remarkable specimen of herring-bone masonry.

(A road of 32 k. connects this station with Falaise, passing (2 k.) *Laize la Ville*, 2½ k. from which is the church of *Fontenay-le-Marmion*, chiefly XIII. c., and the foundation of a castle. To the N.W. of the village are remains of a remarkable tumulus.

' Il est formé de pierres sèches tassées les unes sur les

autres. Son diamètre actuel, vers la base, est d'environ cent cinquante pieds; mais il a dû être plus considérable, car on a pris tout autour beaucoup de pierres pour la réparation des chemins de la commune. Cette éminence, dont la hauteur n'est plus aujourd'hui que de vingt à vingt-cinq pieds, renferme plusieurs caveaux ou loges sépulcrales grossièrement arrondies, dont les murs construits en pierres plates et brutes superposées, sans aucune espèce de ciment ni de mortier, s'élèvent en se rétrécissant. Après l'enlèvement des décombres, on a constamment découverts, à une profondeur de dix à douze pieds, une couche d'argile épaisse de vingt-cinq à trente pouces, dans laquelle reposaient des ossements humains brisés, dont les uns avaient éprouvé l'action du feu, tandis que les autres étaient dans leur état naturel.'—*De Caumont*, '*Antiquités Monumentales.*'

3 k. r. of the road is *Fresney-le-Puceux*, with a château built in 1580 by Pierre d'Harcourt. At 25 k. is *Bretteville sur Laize*, with a church, originally XIII. c., but much altered; at 26 k. the XVI. c. *Château d'Outrelaize*.

22 k. *Grimbosq*. 3 k. E. is *S. Laurent-de-Condet*, where the church has a nave of XI. c., choir of XIII. c. 1 k. farther is the interesting XI. c. and XII. c. church of *Montiers-en-Cinglais*.

28 k. *Croisilles-Harcourt. Croisilles* has a XIII. c. church. *Thury-Harcourt*, which was made a duchy by Louis XIV. in favour of Henri d'Harcourt, has a good gothic church. The XVII. c. and XVIII. c. *Château* occupies the site of a XIV. c. castle. 18 k. E., in the direction of Falaise, is the fine XIII. c. church of *Ussy* and its XVI. c. manor-house. The *Ferme du Post*, at Ussy, is a moated and fortified manor. At 20 k. are some small remains of the *Abbaye de Villers*.

34 k. *S. Remy* has a romanesque church.

42 k. *Clécy* has a XV. c. church, with flamboyant windows. The XVI. c. *Manoir de Placy* has two square towers.

46 k. *Berjou-Cahan*. Hence there is a branch line by (30 k.) Falaise (see p. 105) to join the line from Mezidon to Argentan at Coulibeuf.

53 k. *Conde-sur-Noireau*. The fine church of *S. Martin*, near the station (XIII. c. to XV. c.), has been much restored. Near the church of *S. Sauveur* are insignificant remains of a

XII. c. castle. The church of (5 k.) *S. Germain du Crioult* has some architectural interest.

58 k. *Caligni.* 3 k. S.W. are the (XV. c.) remains of the *Abbaye de la Belle-Etoile.* Here we reach the line from Paris to Granville (see ch. iv.).]

[A line leads S.W. from Caen to (77 k.) Vire by—

8 k. *Verson.* The choir of the church is early XIII. c., the nave XIV. c.

12 k. *Mouen* has a romanesque (XII. c.) church.

Mondrainville (6 k. S.W.) has a XIII. c. church.

18 k. *Noyers* has a fine early gothic church and a XIV. c. tithe-barn.

34 k. *Aulnay-sur-Odon.* To the S.W. of the town are ruins of the Cistercian *Abbaye d'Aulnaye,* founded 1131. 2 k. N.W. are remains of a castle, taken by Geoffrey Plantagenet in 1141.

54 k. *La Gauterie.* Here we join the line from S. Lo to Vire: see later.]

Leaving Caen, the main line passes—

253 k. (from Paris) *Bretteville-Norrey.* On r. is the church of *Bretteville l'Orgueilleuse,* which has an early gothic choir; its noble tower has been ruined by lightning. L. is the very important church of *Norrey*—a village cathedral—which has a nave of XIII. c., transept, choir and chapels of XIV. c. The tower is of great beauty.[1]

At 4½ k. N. is *Secqueville-en-Bessin,* with the beautiful (XIII. c.) church tower in which Robert Fitz-Hamon, partisan of Henry I. of England, took refuge from the soldiers of Robert, Duke of Normandy, who lighted a fire under it to force him to surrender.

259 k. *Audrieu* has a good cruciform church of XIII. c. and XIV. c. The church of (5 k.) *Tilly-sur-Seulles* has an

---

[1] This church is described at length in Whewell's *Architectural Tour in Normandy and Picardy.*

XI. c. nave and XII. c. choir, XIV. c. tower and XV. c. porch. The *Chapelle de Notre Dame du Val*, in the middle of the town, is late XII. c.

269 k. *Bayeux* (Hotels: *du Luxembourg*—tolerably good; *Grand-Hôtel Achard*), the capital of the Viducasses, then the ancient Augustodurus. Rollo stormed and captured the town, and with it Popa (the poupée or poppet), daughter of the Count of Senlis-Vermandois, who became the mother of his line. After this Bayeux became a frequent residence of the dukes of Normandy, and was the capital of the Bessin. Harold took the oath of fealty here to William the Conqueror, swearing, it is said unwittingly, upon a chest which had been purposely filled with relics of Norman saints.

Bayeux is a picturesque and curious, but inanimate, town. The noble *Cathedral* (1 k. from station) is a rebuilding, early in the XII. c., of a church consecrated in 1077 in the presence of William the Conqueror, Queen Matilda, and their son, which was burnt in 1166. The W. façade has two towers, with spires of XII. c. The octagonal central tower (restored) is of 1479. All round the roof is a rich gothic gallery. The *Portail du Doyenné* is only opened for the first reception of the dean, or for his body after death. In the interior, tall gothic windows are grafted upon the magnificent romanesque pillars and arches. The chapels have remains of curious XV. c. and XVI. c. paintings. Under the sanctuary is a crypt, believed to date from XI. c., and, with the W. towers, to have been built by Odo, son of Herlwin de Conteville and Arlette, mother of the Conqueror, who, a boy-bishop at the time of his appointment, ruled the see of Bayeux for fifty years. He also built the monastery of S. Vigor.[1] The chapter-house (XIII. c. and XIV. c.) has a curious inlaid pavement. That daughter of William the Conqueror and Matilda who had been betrothed to Alphonso of Spain is buried in the cathedral. It is said that she prayed that she might never be united to the Spaniard, and died on her way to him, and that when her body was brought back here, her knees were found to have grown hard by her long prayers.

Opposite the N. transept is the ancient *Evêché*, used as a Palais de Justice. Several interesting outlying fragments of the cathedral on this side are (1895) in danger of being 'restored' away.

In the Place S. Sauveur is the *Musée*, now containing the famous *Tapestry of Queen Matilda*, on which the queen, with the ladies of her court, has represented, in fifty-eight groups, the whole history of the conquest of England, and the events which led to it. They are all named and described where they stand. Six hundred and twenty-three persons are represented. Nothing can exceed the historic interest and importance of these graphic pictures worked in worsted upon canvas, and evidently executed with the intention of conveying the impression that Harold was a perjured usurper, and William owed his success to his righteous cause.

The tapestry—which used to be known as 'La Toilette du Duc Guillaume'—is undoubtedly contemporary with him, but some authorities consider that it was not the work of the queen, but made by order of Odo, bishop of Bayeux, half-brother of the Conqueror.

[1] He died on his way to the Crusades, and is buried at Palermo.

'I think no one can see the end of the battle—the Housecarls, every one lying dead in his harness, while the light armed are taking to flight, some of them on the horses of the fallen—and not feel that he is in the presence of a work traced out by one who had himself seen the scenes which he thus handed down to later ages.'—*Freeman.*

Bayeux contains a great number of curious old houses, especially 4, Rue S. Malo (xv. c. and xvi. c.); 4, Rue Bienvenue; 1, Rue Franche (xiv. c.); 3, Rue Franche (xv. c.); 8, Rue Laitière; and the *Maison du Gouverneur* in the Rue Bourbeneur. The Rue S. Nicolas is full of picturesqueness. The suburban church of *S. Loup* has a beautiful xii. c. tower, with long arches, and a relief of S. Loup subduing a dragon over its portal.

A diligence (1 fr.) connects Bayeux with (9 k.) *Port-en-Bessin* (Hotel: *de l'Etoile du Nord*), a small bathing-place; also with (10 k.) *Arromanches* (Hotel: *de la Marine*); also with (14 k.) *Asnelles* (*Grand Hôtel*), passing (9 k.) *Ryes*, where the faithful Hubert, Seigneur de Ryes, received William (the Conqueror) flying from Valognes and the rebel barons, set him on a fresh horse, and bade his three sons ride with him and never leave him till he was safe in his own castle of Falaise. The church is xiii. c., and there are several curious old houses.

[A road leads N.W. to Grandcamp by—

6 k. *Tour*, where the church has a fine xiv. c. choir and early gothic tower, stone seats, and interesting reliefs.

17 k. *Formigny*, where the English met with the great defeat from the troops of Charles VII., which caused them to evacuate Normandy. Thirty-five years after his victory, the French general, the Comte de Clermont, erected a chapel on the battle-field and dedicated it to *S. Louis*. This was used as a warehouse after the Revolution, but was restored by Louis-Philippe. Over the W. portal of the church is a curious equestrian statue of S. Martin.

33 k. *Grandcamp* (Hotels: *de la Plage; de la Croix Blanche*), a sea bathing-place, famous for its oysters.]

[A road runs S.W. from Bayeux to (37 k.) S. Lo (see later), passing (at 15 k.), 2½ k. r. of *Balleroy*, a fine château built by Mansart (1626-36), with decorations by Lemoine and Mignard. At 21 k. the road passes 4 k. to the l. of *Cérisy-la-Forêt*, where the fine church of the xi. c. belonged to an abbey founded by S. Vigor, bishop of Bayeux, in 560.]

283 k. *Le Molay-Littry.* 3 k. S. is *Littry*, with important coal-mines. The church is xii. c. An omnibus runs from the station to (10 k. N.) *Trévières*, where the church is partly xii. c. 3½ k. N.E. of the station is the church of *Saon*, containing the fine tomb of Robert Davaynes, Seigneur de Grouchy, and Jeanne Daché, his wife, 1616.

296 k. *Lison* (Buffet).

[For the line from Lison to S. Lo, Coutances, etc., see ch. vi.].

305 k. *Neuilly.* The château was a summer residence of the bishops of Bayeux.

314 k. *Carentan*, in unhealthy plains, has a richly ornamented church of xiv. c. and xv. c.

[A road leads from Carentan to (26 k.) Grandcamp by (16 k.) *Isigny*, with a little port, whence enormous quantities of Normandy butter are conveyed to England.]

326 k. *Chef-du-Port.* The church is partly romanesque. 4 k. N.E. is the church of *S. Mère Église* of xii. c. and xiv. c.

343 k. *Valognes*, rich in Roman remains. The church is xiv. c., xv. c., and xvi. c. The rich varied outline of

the gothic cupola is a striking object. It was at Valognes that Duke William was suddenly roused from sleep by his fool, Golet, and made to fly at midnight from his rebel barons and Grimoald of Plessis, who was about to murder him.

[A road leads N.E. to (7 k.) *Montebourg*, which had an ancient abbey, consecrated in 1152, of which only the abbot's house remains. The church was built at the expense of Baldwin de Reviers, Earl of Devon, a staunch partisan of Matilda, who had fled to Normandy from the vengeance of Stephen. Nothing remains but the foundations. 2 k. S. is the curious church of *S. Floxel*, partly XI. c.; and 2 k. E. the interesting *Cross of Eroudeville*. At 14 k. the road reaches the little bathing-place of *Quinéville*, whence an excursion may be made to (7 k.) *S. Marcouf*, with a curious church of XI. c. to XIV. c. The *Fontaine de S. Marcouf* is an interesting little XIII. c. building enclosing a spring, where the statue of the saint is invoked in cases of skin disease.]

[A road leads N.E. to (26 k.) the little port of *Barfleur*, now almost deserted, but the only and much frequented port of the Cotentin through the middle ages, which offers a perilous entry or departure, and is haunted by a gloomy celebrity arising from the shipwreck of the '*Blanche Nef*,' and the unhappy loss of that wayward prince, none the less mourned by reason of his errors, the Atheling William, in whom the main line of the Conqueror became extinct, and after whose death his royal father, Henry I., never smiled again.]

353 k. *Sottevast*.

[A line diverges S. through the Cotentin to (87 k.) Coutances, by—

8 k. *Bricquebec*, which has picturesque ruins of a château, begun XIV. c., finished at the end of XVI. c. Its lord, Guillaume Bertram, son of Oslac, passed over to England with the Conqueror, and became (in the female line) the ancestor of the Earls of Huntley and Dudley.

'The Cotentin castles, wide in their range and richly varied in their architectural style, constitute the ornament of the landscape; and after all the dilapidations, restorations, or destructions which they sustained, whether occasioned by war or consequent upon peace, effected by violence or dictated by taste or necessity, more than one hundred of these structures still survive.—We read the history of the country on the face of the country.'—*Palgrave.*

23 k. *S. Sauveur le Vicomte.* The town is surmounted by ruins of an ancient castle, and of an abbey founded 1080. The church of the latter is transition, and highly picturesque.

'The seigneurs of S. Sauveur long treasured, amongst their archives, a copy of the grant by which the territory had been bestowed upon their ancestor, Richard, one of Rollo's principal commanders. The domain is described as principally consisting of wood and waste land. Herbert, Bishop of Coutances, consecrated the domestic chapel.'—*Palgrave.*

35 k. *La Haye-du-Puits* has remains of an old castle. An excursion may be made to the ruined abbey of *Blanchelande,* founded by Richard de la Haye, a favourite of Henry II. The abbot's residence is now a farmhouse. Part of the church (consecrated 1185) remains.

43 k. *Lessay,* which had a Benedictine abbey, founded 1140. The church is an interesting building of XI. c., and has stalls from the abbey of Blanchelande.

51 k. *Périers.* The church is a fine building of XIV. c. and XV. c.]

365 k. *Martinvaast.* 14 k. W. is *Les Pieux,* 4 k. from which is the XIII. c. château of *Le Rozel.*

371 k. *Cherbourg* (Hotels: *du Casino; de l'Amirauté; de l'Univers; de France*). Caesaris Burgus was the port to which the Romans first directed their care. From the time of Philippe-Auguste this has been one of the chief

ports of France, and since the XVIII. c. it has been its chief military post.

The church of *La Trinité* is xv. c.

'When the bastions of Vauban arose, the relics of classic antiquity disclosed how sagaciously the Caesars had anticipated the great teacher of modern strategy.'—*Palgrave*.

'Malédiction, Cherbourg, à tes parages sinistres! C'est auprès de Cherbourg que le vent de la colère jeta Edouard III. pour ravager notre pays; c'est non loin de Cherbourg que le vent d'une victoire ennemie brisa la flotte de Tourville; c'est à Cherbourg que le vent d'une prospérité menteuse repoussa Louis XVI. vers son échafaud; c'est à Cherbourg que le vent de je ne sais quelle rive à emporté nos derniers princes. Les côtes de la Grand-Bretagne, qu'aborda Guillaume le Conquérant, ont vu débarquer Charles le dixième sans pennon et sans lance; il est allé retrouver à Holyrood les souvenirs de sa jeunesse, appendus aux murailles du château des Stuarts, comme de vieilles gravures jaunies par le temps.'—*Chateaubriand*, '*Mémoires d'Outre-Touché.*'

17 k. N.W. of Cherbourg is the village of *Beaumont-Hague*, near which may be seen the remains of the curious intrenchment called *Hague Dicke*, 4 k. in length. It is believed to date from the time of the earliest Norman invasions, sometimes supposed to have been intended to cover their embarkations in case of retreat, sometimes attributed to the early inhabitants of Gaul.[1] 3 k. S.W., near Vauville, is the covered stone alley called *Pierres pouqueleés*—worshipped stones. Near (26 k.) the *Cap de la Hague* is the great lighthouse of *Gros-du-Raz*.

[1] See Ernest Desjardins, *Géographie de la Gaule romaine*, I. 333.

CHAPTER IV.

PARIS TO GRANVILLE, BY DREUX, ARGENTAN AND VIRE. FROM THE GARE MONTPARNASSE.

THE *Gare Montparnasse* is on the Boulevard Montparnasse, on the l. bank of the Seine, at a great distance from the hotels usually frequented by English visitors. The trains as far as Versailles run every half-hour from 6.35 to 9.5 a.m.; after 10.5 at every hour.

The places to the r. of the carriages are best for the view.

6 k. *Clamart*, after which the railway passes beneath the fort of *Issy*. On the l. the villages of *Val* and *Fleury* are seen, then Meudon with its terrace. On the r. there is a fine view over the valley of the Seine, with Paris, the Bois de Boulogne, Mont Valérien, S. Cloud, and Sèvres. The gorge of *Val-Fleury* is crossed before reaching—

8 k. *Meudon*. It is an ascent of 1½ k. from the station, in a straight line, to the famous *Terrace* of Meudon, which is always open to the public, and which has incomparably the most beautiful and pictorial view in the neighbourhood of Paris. To the l. the great mass of the city is seen, backed by the heights of Montmartre and by fainter blue distances. The dome of the Invalides glitters to the r. of the windings of the Seine with its bridges, and, farther to the r., southern Paris extends into long lines of houses

for miles, only broken by S. Sulpice, S. Germain, and the Panthéon.

After 'Monseigneur,' the son of Louis XIV., became the owner of Meudon, he lived there whenever he could escape from the Court, and amused himself in the creation of gardens and buildings, as his father did at Versailles: he especially loved, by taking refuge at Meudon, to avoid the tedious monotony of the Voyages de Marly. His morganatic wife, known by the name of Mlle Chouin, resided at Meudon, was united to him *c.* 1695 in secret bonds of matrimony, as Mme de Maintenon was to Louis XIV., but occupied a very different position, living in one of the attics of the house, and seen by none but Monseigneur. The King never came to Meudon, which, after all, he disliked as alienating his son from the Court, till he was summoned thither (1711) by the news of Monseigneur's dangerous illness. Then he established himself there till his son's death (from small-pox), which was very sudden at last.

In the reign of Louis XV., the Duchesse de Berry exchanged Amboise for Meudon, which was reunited to the crown in 1726. In 1736, Stanislaus, King of Poland, was lodged here. In 1789, the first Dauphin, son of Louis XVI., died here. During the Revolution the older château was transformed into a fortress, and Napoleon I. pulled it down, using some of its marbles in building the arch of the Place du Carrousel. A second château, which had been built by the second Dauphin, was repaired and intended to be used as a college for kings! Marie Louise and the King of Rome lived there during the Russian campaign. Afterwards (1833) Pedro, king of Portugal, his daugther, Doña Maria, the Duc d'Orléans, and Marshal Soult, inhabited it in turn. Under the Second Empire it was the residence of Jerome Napoleon, once King of Westphalia. It was destroyed during the Franco-German war of 1870, and the terraces are now the only memorials of the two châteaux. Only the lower terrace is open to the public; at the end is an observatory.

Le Bois de Meudon is a favourite resort of Parisian pedestrians. Mme Roland used to be brought thither in her childhood.

9 k. *Bellevue* (Hotel: *de la Tête Noire*). Here Mme de Pompadour, admiring the view from the hill above the l. bank of the Seine, built a château, 1748-50, which Louis XV. frequently used as a residence, and which he purchased in 1757. After the death of Louis XV. the château became the private residence of his daughters, Mesdames, Tantes du Roi, till their flight before the coming Revolution in 1791.

During the Revolution the château of Mesdames was sold, and has been almost entirely destroyed. The only remaining fragment, now known as *Brimborion* (a pavilion inhabited by Louis XV. whilst the château was building), is in private hands. A fine view over Paris (though inferior to that from Meudon, turning to the l. from the station and taking the second turning to the r.) is to be obtained from the terrace at the end of the Avenue Mélanie.

13 k. *Chaville* possessed a magnificent château, built by Louvois, but it was utterly destroyed at the Revolution.

14 k. *Viroflay.* There is a pleasant walk from hence to Versailles (4 k.) by *Joug* and *Buc*.

18 k. *Versailles.*[1] See 'Excursions from Paris' in *North-Eastern France.*

22 k. *S. Cyr.* This place derives its name from the little Gaulish Christian Cyrus, who was thrown from a rock by the Roman governor, at three years old, for refusing to change his religion after the martyrdom of his mother. A convent afterwards existed here. But S. Cyr was of no importance till Mme de Maintenon received it as a wedding present from Louis XIV., and transferred hither the college for indigent young ladies of noble birth, which she had previously instituted in the Château de Noisy near Versailles, and which she placed under the care of her friend Mme de Brinon, an ex-Ursuline nun. Mansart was employed by Louis XIV. to build the immense edifice, which still exists, to please Mme de Maintenon, who was especially proud of her title of 'Marquise de Maintenon, supérieur de l'abbaye royale de S. Cyr.' Whilst still living at Versailles, she would often amuse Louis XIV. by making the young ladies of S. Cyr get up the newly-written plays of Racine and act them in his presence. Even during the King's lifetime Mme de Maintenon ruled the institution of S. Cyr as an autocrat; and when he was on his death-bed, as soon as he had lost consciousness, she obeyed his wishes by retiring there altogether, probably to avoid complications with his family, having lost those members of it who were fond of her, and having reason to distrust the rest. The day after she reached S. Cyr, the King died. Mlle d'Aumale came into the room and said, 'Madame, toute la communauté est à

---

[1] For a detailed account of Versailles and its historic associations see *Days near Paris.*

l'église.' She understood, rose silently, and went herself to the church, where the office of the dead was being recited. The King had left her nothing in his will, but had simply recommended her to the care of his nephew, afterwards Regent. The Duc d'Orléans was worthy of this confidence. A few days after the King's death he paid her a visit, and continued her pension of 48,000 livres, inserting in the brevet that 'son rare désintéressement la lui avait rendue nécessaire.'

The retreat of Mme de Maintenon was once interrupted. When the Czar Peter came to France, in 1717, he insisted upon seeing the woman who, for thirty years, had played such an important part in the world. She died at S. Cyr, April 15, 1719. She had desired to be simply buried in the churchyard of S. Cyr. But the Duc de Noailles, who had married her niece, erected a magnificent tomb to her in the middle of the choir, which was destroyed in the Revolution. Neither of her two husbands was mentioned in her epitaph.

The Emperor Napoleon I. restored S. Cyr—pillaged at the Revolution—as a military school. Its enormous monotonous white buildings, with high slated roofs, contain 350 pupils, and it annually gives about 140 young officers to the army. The greater part of the former gardens is now a *Champ de Mars*. A black marble slab in the chapel covers the remains of Mme de Maintenon, collected after the Revolution, and is inscribed—'Cy-gît Mme de Maintenon, 1635—1719.—1826.'

29 k. *Villepreux-les-Clayes.* In the woods of *Arcy*, near Villepreux, a fête is held on Whit-Monday, at the *Chapelle S. Jouan.*

MONTFORT-L'AMAURY. 139

33 k. *Plaisir-Grignon.* An omnibus takes travellers in fifteen minutes to the great agricultural institution of Grignon, founded in 1827. The handsome church of Grignon is XIII. C.

40 k. *Villiers-Néauphle.* On the r., in the valley of the Mauldre, at *Néauphle-le-Vieux,* are considerable remains of a Benedictine abbey and church, founded 1066, and now turned into a farm. 2 k. l. of the station is the noble moated *Château de Pontchartrain,* built by Paul Phélypeaux, Secretary of State (*ob.* 1621), and enriched by his descendants, who for four generations filled high government offices. It is now occupied by Comte Henchel de Donnersmack.

An omnibus connects the station with *Beynes,* where the church contains a magnificent renaissance retable, and which has remains of a moated castle, flanked by eight towers.

45 k. *Montfort-l'Amaury.* It is 2 k. from the station, by a straight avenue of planes, to the quaint, seldom-visited town (omnibus 40 c.; Hotels: *des Voyageurs; de Paris—* good restaurant), which is overlooked by the ruined castle of the Comtes de Montfort. This famous family descended from Charlemagne, through Judith (daughter of Charles le Chauve), who married Baudouin Bras-de-fer, Comte de Flandre. Their grandson, Guillaume, Comte de Hainaut, married the heiress of Epernon and Montfort. He fortified the latter place, which took the name of his son, Amaury. Simon, son of Amaury, was the father of the famous Bertrade, who fled from her first husband, Foulques de Réchin, Comte d'Anjou, to marry Philippe I. of France, who was already married himself. The pair were excommunicated, nevertheless Bertrade lived prosperously with the King for

sixteen years, and even contrived to reconcile her first and second husbands, and dine with them together at Angers, and sit with them under the same canopy at church—the King by her side, Foulques on a stool at her feet. Bertrade died a nun. Her brother, Amaury IV., a famous warrior, sometimes the ally and often the enemy of his sovereign, was the grandfather of the celebrated and cruel Simon de Montfort, who overthrew the Counts of Toulouse, and acquired their dominions. His son, Amaury VII., resigned the countship of Toulouse to Louis VIII., for the dignity of Constable.

But the family history was by no means ended yet. The son of Amaury VII. only left a daughter, Yolande, who married (1250) the Comte de Dreux, and secondly Arthur II., Duc de Bretagne. The son of her second marriage, Jean de Montfort, disputed the ducal crown with his niece, Jeanne, wife of Charles de Blois. The son of Jean de Montfort, of the same name, after gaining the battle of Auray, where his rival was killed, became duke, and the Dukes of Brittany continued to be also Counts of Montfort till the marriage of Anne of Brittany with Charles VIII., and afterwards with Louis XII. In 1537, François I. gave up to Spain the countship of Montfort-l'Amaury, but recovered it seven years after. It afterwards belonged to Catherine de Medicis, to her son, the Duc d'Anjou, then to the Duc d'Alençon. At the death of the latter, Henri III. gave it to the Duc d'Epernon. Returning to the crown, it was exchanged, in 1692, by Louis XIV. with the duchy of Chevreuse. Never had fortress so many illustrious owners.

The splendid *Parish Church*, chiefly renaissance, has

some small remains of the original building, given to the
abbey of S. Magloire at Paris, in 1072. The choir is xv. c.,
except the flying buttresses added in the xvi. c., to which
the nave belongs. The tower is of 1613. The vaulting of
the side aisles has very rich pendants. A great deal of fine
stained glass of 1578 remains, most of the windows—superb

PORTE BARDOU, MONTFORT-L'AMAURY.

in colour—representing scriptural subjects, with the donors
kneeling in front, often presented by their patron saints.
In the first window (r.) kneel Henri III. and Catherine de
Medicis, attended by pages and ladies. Facing the church
is the castle on its hill, and *La Porte Bardou* closing the
uphill street, and supposed to derive its name from Hugues
Bardoulf, father-in-law of Simon. From a side street on the

r., in ascending the hill, a pretty flamboyant portal gives access to the xv. c. cloisters of a convent, with good wooden vaulting, the enclosed space being now used as a cemetery. Amongst the tombs is that of the Duchesse de Béthune-Charost, daughter of the Marquise de Tourzel, governess of Louis XVII. Little remains of the castle except two towers, one hexagonal, of admirable brick- and stone-work. There are some ruins of another castle near the château of *Groussaye*.

The modern chapel of *Notre Dame du Chêne*, on the road to Artoire, contains a 'miraculous' statue of the Virgin, said to have been found in an oak. Near this is the xvii. c. château of *Mesnuls*, which belongs to the Comte de Nogent. In the neighbouring forest of *S. Léger* was the *Château de S. Hubert*, a richly-decorated hunting lodge, built by Gabriel for Louis XIV. and destroyed by Louis XVI.

56 k. *Tacoignières*. To the r. of the line is *Richebourg*, which has a fine xv. c. church, with a peculiar and graceful spire.

63 k. *Houdan* (omnibus, 25 c.), the ancient Hodincum, retains its old fortress-tower, built by Amaury III. de Montfort *c*. 1130. It has a fine unfinished gothic church, and (39 Rue de Paris), a richly-ornamented old timber mansion. 6 k. E., at *Gambais*, is a large moated château of the xiv. c.

82 k. *Dreux* (Hotel : *du Paradis*—good), crowned by its royal burial-place, and the remains of the castle of the Comtes de Dreux.

The town—said to have been the capital of the Durocasses in the reign of Agrippa—has sustained many sieges, and (December 19, 1562), was the scene of a sanguinary battle, between the Protestants under Condé and Coligny, and the Catholics under the 'triumvirate' of the Constable de Montmorency, the Duc de Guise, and Maréchal S. André. Eight thousand men fell in the battle, in which the Catholics were victorious, the Prince de Condé on the Protestant side, and Montmorency on the Catholic side, being taken prisoners, and S. André being killed.

The magnificent *Church of S. Pierre* is chiefly flamboyant, but the choir and columns of the nave are XII. c. and XIII. c. The fine gothic portal is by Clément Métézeau, a native of Dreux. The stained glass is of great beauty and interest. In the nave are remains of a series of the Apostles; in the choir several noble life-size figures of saints; in the S. transept the Descent from the Cross and the Sacrifice of Isaac. In the side chapels are a Crucifixion; scenes from the story of the sainted shoemakers, Crispin and Crispinian; the Ascension; the Baptism of Clovis; S. John; Notre Dame de Pitié; S. Blaise; S. Sebastian; fragments of the story of Notre Dame de Lorette, and of that of S. Fiacre. The (restored) windows of the Chapelle de la Vierge narrate the history of the Virgin. Some of the side chapels of the nave have remains of frescoes representing the pilgrimage of the inhabitants of Dreux to S. James of Compostella, in the XVII. c. and XVIII. c. On the wall facing the altar is an armed knight, with the epitaph of Mercoeur of France, 1562. A curious *bénitier* of XII. c. comes from the old collegiate church of S. Etienne. The organ is of 1614.

Near the church is a very fine old clock-tower. The renaissance *Hôtel de Ville* was built 1512-37. It contains a sculptured portal from the Château de Crécy, and armour found on the battlefield of Ivry. The bell, founded under Charles IX., is surrounded with a representation of the Procession des Flambarts, which formerly took place at Christmas at Dreux.

The Orleans Chapel rises picturesquely on the hill at the end of the principal street. There are two ascents, one

DREUX.

for carriages, and a shorter one for pedestrians, winding up to the grounds of the château, which are open to the public. Very little of the ancient castle remains, but its enclosure is occupied by a garden, in the centre of which is the *Chapelle royale*, built by the Dowager Duchess of Orleans in 1813, and gothicised by Louis-Philippe in 1839. The architecture is wretched, but the contents are of the deepest interest. For admission apply to the *concierge* on the left of the entrance to the garden. Only funeral services are now held here. Since the 'château en planches' was destroyed, in 1848, the family have arrived for the services in the morning, leaving again in the afternoon.

The beautiful stained windows of the antechapel represent Christ in the Garden of Olives; the Deposition; S. Arnould washing the feet of pilgrims; and S. Adelaide, Queen of Hungary, distributing alms.

The rotunda or choir is the original part of the church. The beautiful glass of the windows has figures of saints—the Duc d'Orléans is represented as S. Ferdinand, Princess Louise as S. Amélie, Louis-Philippe as S. Philippe. A stair descends behind the altar to the crypts and chapel of the Virgin, entirely occupied by the royal monuments.

R. of the steps. The tomb of Mlle de Montpensier, the two-years-old daughter of Louis-Philippe, by Pradier.

L. of the steps. The Duc de Penthièvre, eight-years-old son of Louis-Philippe.

Facing the steps. The huge tomb of King Louis-Philippe and Queen Marie Amélie, arranged to support their effigies—that of the king standing, with his hand resting upon the kneeling queen.

R. Princess Marie, Duchess of Wurtemberg. The angel above was her last work in sculpture.

R., in the sanctuary. The Duc d'Orléans, eldest son of Louis-Philippe, 1842. The tomb was designed by Ary Scheffer, and is very noble and touching. Behind (in a separate chapel, being a Protestant) is Hélène de Mecklembourg-Schwerin, Duchesse d'Orléans (1858), her hand outstretched from the dark chapel, so as almost to touch her husband.

R. Maria Clementina of Austria, Princess of Salerno, mother of the Duchesse d'Aumale.

L. Mme Adélaïde, 1847, sister of Louis-Philippe, beautiful in lace and ermine; by Millet.

L. The crowned figure of the Duchesse d'Orléans, mother

of Louis-Philippe, and foundress of the chapel. Exquisitely beautiful.

L. The Duchesse de Bourbon Condé, aunt of the king and mother of the Duc d'Enghien.

Turning l. from the steps. Two children of the Comte de Paris—an exquisite work of Franceschi. A child, bearing a cross with one hand, lifts his baby brother to eternity with the other.

L. Prince Ferdinand, son of the Duc de Montpensier; by Aimé Millet. An exquisitely beautiful tomb, and simple touching figure.

R., opposite. Prince Louis, son of the Duc de Montpensier; by Millet. A veiled figure.

L. Six children of the Duc d'Aumale.

L. Louis-Philippe, Prince de Condé, eldest son of the Duc d'Aumale, who died at Sydney in his twenty-first year, September 1866.

L. François, Duc de Guise, last son of the Duc d'Aumale, who died at eighteen, July 25, 1872.

R., opposite. Caroline, Duchesse d'Aumale, 1869, with a beautiful statue by Alfred Lenoir.

Turning r. from steps. Prince Robert, son of the Duc de Chartres, aged eighteen.

A beautiful series of windows represents the life of S. Louis. The tomb of the Duc de Penthièvre, maternal grandfather of Louis-Philippe (father-in-law of the Princesse de Lamballe), was violated in 1793. In side passages are some exquisite windows, each being a picture on a single sheet of glass, executed at Sèvres by Brongniart and Robert.

A little N.E. of Dreux is *Abondant*, whither Mme de Tourzel, governess of the children of Louis XVI., retired after the death of Robespierre, having escaped miraculously from the guillotine, with her two daughters—the Duchesse de Charost, and Pauline, afterwards Comtesse de Béarn and authoress of *Souvenirs de Quarante Ans*. Here this faithful friend of Marie Antoinette is buried, with the epitaph—

'Hic jacet L. E. F. T. A. M. J. de Croy, Ducissa de Tourzel, regiae sobolis gubernatrix. Fortis in adversis, Deo regique fidelis, vere mater pauperum, pertransivit benefaciendo, omnibus veneranda, magno prolis amore dilecta. Obiit anno aetatis 82. Requiescat in pace.'

The church is very ancient, with a monolith font and good stained glass. Above the Eure are the remains of the *Château de la Robertière*.

[A road leads S.E. from Dreux to (23 k.) Maintenon by (17 k.) *Nogent le Roi*, a small fortified town upon the Eure, with four gateways and a fine renaissance church. On the opposite side of the river is (1 k.) *Coulombs*, with remains of a Benedictine abbey founded VIII. c., especially a fine XI. c. portal and ruins of the tower, whose beautiful bells gave rise to the song called *Le Carillon de l'Abbaye*.]

[A line leads S. to (42 k.) Chartres, passing (19 k.) the station of *S.-Sauveur-Châteauneuf*, near which are remains of the fortress of *Chateauneuf-en-Thymerais*, destroyed in 1600.]

91 k. *S. Germain—S. Remy. S. Remi-sur-Avre* has a fine gothic church.

97 k. *Nonancourt* was fortified by Henry I. to defend the frontier of Normandy. At 1 k. (omnibus) is *S.-Lubin-des-Joncherets*, with a XII. c. church, restored XV. c. and XVI. c. The tomb of the Président de Grammont was destroyed at the Revolution, but the statue remains.

118 k. *Verneuil* (Hotel: *du Commerce*), strongly fortified by Henry I. and II. Only one tower—*La Tour Grise*—remains of their castle. The church of *La Madeleine*, of various dates from XI. c. to XVII. c., has a rich tower of 1506-30. *Notre Dame* is chiefly XII. c. *S. Jean*, used as a corn exchange, has a fine XV. c. tower. The gabled

buildings called *Les Perrins* were military warehouses of the time of Henry I. Several houses are picturesque or curious.

141 k. *Laigle*, a town which prospers on factories of pins, nails, wire, etc. The church of *S. Martin*, of many dates, has a picturesque xv. c. tower. *S. Jean* is chiefly xv. c. The *Château*, of the xvii. c., replaces that where William Rufus and Henry Beauclerc insulted their elder brother, Robert, by pouring dirty water (or worse) through the boarded floor of an upper chamber upon his head.

In the history of science, the name of Laigle has become celebrated by the shower of stones which fell there in 1803—the first authentic fall of aerolites known.

[For the line from Laigle to Conches see ch. iii.]

157 k. *S. Gauburge* has fine flamboyant ruins of a priory.

[For the lines towards Lisieux and Caen see ch. iii.]

[A line leads S. to (35 k.) *Mortagne* (Hotels: *du Grand Cerf; de la Bouteille*). The town, on a height 1½ k. from the station, is utterly uninteresting. It has a very large featureless church of xv. c. and xvi. c.]

173 k. *Nonant-le-Pin.* 2 k. N.E. is *S. Germain de Clairfeuille*, where the church (xiv. c. and xv. c.) is famous for its beautiful oak screen. 17 k. N.W. is *Chambois*, with very interesting remains of a xii. c. castle.

182 k. *Surdon* (Buffet). For the line from hence to Caen see ch. iii.

[A line runs S. to—

7 k. *Seès* (Hotel: *du Cheval Blanc*). In the view from the

railway the beautiful gothic cathedral rises above the houses of the town and green meadows. It replaces three churches founded 440, 996, and 1053, and is chiefly XIII. c. and XIV. c. The W. front, with its two spires, its deeply-receding porch, with vast buttresses, is very peculiar. Its E. end, of XIII. c., very graceful and refined, is over-restored. Only a fragment of a cloister remains on the N.

SEÈS.

'La nef, bâtie au commencement du XIII. c., fut remaniée dans sa partie supérieure 50 ou 60 ans après sa construction ; le choeur, élevé vers 1230 et presque entièrement détruit par un incendie, dut être repris vers 1260, de fond en comble, sauf la chapelle de la Vierge, que l'on jugea pouvoir être conservée. Le maître de l'oeuvre du choeur, ne se fondant que sur des maçonneries très insuffisantes, avait cherché par l'extrême légèreté de sa construction, à diminuer le danger d'une pareille situation, et, en ne considérant même le choeur de la cathédrale de Seès qu'a ce point de vue, il mériterait d'être étudié. Les chapelles absidales, présentant des murs rayonnants étendus, se prêtaient d'ailleurs à une construction légère. En effet, les travées intérieures du sanctuaire sont d'une légèreté qui dépasse tout ce qui a été tenté en ce genre.'—*Viollet le Duc.*

[9 k. from Seès, on the road to Mortagne, is the little town of *Essai*, once strongly fortified. A xv. c. chapel remains of its ancient château.]

28 k. *Alençon* (Hotel: *du Grand Cerf*—very good indeed; *de la Gare*), capital of the département de l'Orne. In 1296 it was taken by Duke William (the Conqueror), who had sworn 'by the splendour of God' to avenge himself for the insult of its defenders, who had beaten skins and leathern jerkins on its walls, crying, 'Hides, hides for the tanner!' The town became a stronghold of Calvinism in the xvi. c. under Marguerite d'Angoulême, who married Charles IV., Duc d'Alençon. It was ruined by the revocation of the Edict of Nantes, but prosperity was restored soon afterwards by the introduction of the famous lace manufacture (*point d'Alençon*) by a native lady named Gilbert; this even now employs above two thousand women. Alençon is still an important place. The beautiful xv. c. church of *Notre Dame* (in the Rue du Bercail) is especially remarkable for the extreme magnificence of its flamboyant portal, covered with lacelike sculpture of indescribable richness. It is adorned with six statues representing the Transfiguration. Of these, S. John is supposed to have turned his back (as he is now seen) when the church was pillaged by the Protestants in 1562—a demonstration which so astounded them that they abstained from further injuries. The vaulting of the nave is very rich and complicated. The flamboyant windows have much good xvi. c. glass.

The church of *S. Léonard* was begun by René, duc d'Alençon, *c.* 1489, and finished by his widow Marguerite. Adjoining the Hôtel de Ville are two towers of the ancient *Château*, of which an over-restored xv. c. gateway remains. There is a large, dull public garden.

[For the line from Alençon to Le Mans see ch. v.]

186 k. *Almenèches*. The town, 2 k. from the station, has a richly-ornamented church of xvi. c., rebuilt by

Marguerite de Navarre, Duchesse d'Alençon. The abbey was founded by S. Evroult, and had as an abbess S. Opportune, whose miracle in suddenly covering with salt the lands of a man who had stolen her ass, is still commemorated in the name of *Le Pré-Salé*.

CHÂTEAU, ARGENTAN.

[At 6 k., near *Mortrée*, is the famous *Château d'O* (Marquise d'Albon), chiefly of rich (XVI. c.) renaissance with an XVIII. c. façade. The last of the d'O was one of the mignons of Henri III.

3. k. S.E. of Mortrée is the fine XVI. c. château of *Clerai*.]

10 k. S.E. of Almenèches is the magnificent *Château de Sacy* (Duc d'Audiffret Pasquier).

197 k. *Argentan* (Hotel: *des Trois Maries*, good; *de Normandie*), a prettily situated town. A picturesque street

leads uphill to the large flamboyant church of *S. Germain*, on a height, of 1410—1609, with a very rich N. portal and heavy renaissance tower. One of the pillars near the choir is sculptured with the figure of an ass—l'âne d'Argentan—in strong relief. A little behind the church is the picturesque xv. c. *Château*, now used for public offices. The *Tour Marguerite* is a relic of the old fortifications. On the N. side of the town is *S. Martin*, a very good specimen of the xvi. c.

207 k. *Ecouché*, where the chapel of the hospital has a remarkably sculptured retable.

[13 k. S.W. is the curious *Château de Ranes*, before which thirty Frenchmen are said to have vanquished thirty Englishmen in single combat, in 1432. Its fine square battlemented tower is early xvi. c.]

226 k. *Briouze*.

[A line runs S. to—
23 k. *La Ferté-Macé*. The Hôtel de Ville is partly xiv. c. and xv. c.

33 k. *Bagnoles les Eaux* (Hotels: *des Bains; de Bagnoles*), a little bathing-place in the midst of wooded and rocky scenery, which has given it the name of the Norman Switzerland. The mineral baths of Balneum were probably known to the Romans. Excursions may be made in the forests of Andaine and La Ferté. 4 k. distant is the curious old pilgrimage chapel of *Lignou*, under an old yew.]

243 k. *Flers*, a handsome modern town, rich in prosperous cotton factories. A pool near this is believed to mark the site of a convent of dissolute monks, who met in an orgy on Christmas night, when it was overwhelmed by the waters as they were blasphemously drinking to the health of the newly-born Christ.

[For the line from Flers to Caen see ch. iii.]

[A line leads S. to (91 k.) Laval, by—

23 k. *Domfront* (Hotels: *Trouillard; de Commerce*—very good), a picturesque place, the ancient capital of the district of Houlme, now of the Orne—

'Ancienne ville de cour, devenue cité bourgeoise.'—*Elisée Reclus.*

DOMFRONT.

Near the station is the very interesting church of *Notre Dame sur l'Eau*, on the bank of the Varenne, built in the XI. c. by Guillaume de Bellême, who is said to be commemorated by a good gothic (XIV. c.) tomb in the N. transept. Of the *Château* on a rock above the river, which served as a refuge to the Empress Matilda, little remains beyond a portion of the keep, in a small public garden. Fourteen towers still exist out of the twenty-four towers and four gates which once encircled the town, the most important being known as the *Tour de Godras.*

'The town, still largely girdled by its ancient walls, abides to this day perched on its ancient eyrie, and has not, like so many greater cities, descended into the plain below. The shattered donjon, reared, like that of Falaise, on wild and craggy rocks, looks forth on the wilder and heath-crowned rocks of a rival height, whose distorted strata bear witness to the struggles and revolutions of days before man had yet appeared on the earth.'—*Freeman.*

In the neighbourhood are the ruined *Châteaux de la Guyardière* and *de la Saucerie* and the XVI. c. *Château de la Challerie.*

45 k. *Ambrières,* near the point where the Mayenne joins the Varenne, has a ruined castle built by Duke William (the Conqueror), which was unsuccessfully besieged (1049) by Geoffrey Martel and his allies, Peter of Aquitaine and Odo of Brittany. The church is a beautiful building of XII. c. 5 k. W. are the fine ruins of the *Abbaye Fontaine-Daniel.*]

271 k. *Vire* (Hotel: *S. Pierre*—good; *du Cheval Blanc*), capital of the Norman Bocage. The town, of dull streets of white slate-roofed houses, is well placed on a height, approached by a long hill from the station, and surrounded on three sides by green gorges with the windings of the Vire. The picturesque *Tour de l'Horloge* has a XIII. c. gateway over a street. Beyond it, at the end of a very dull public garden, on the edge of the promontory, is a rag of the once famous XII. c. castle founded by Henry I. The interior of the church of *Notre Dame,* of XIII. c., XIV. c., and XV. c., is rather handsome, with curious old pews; the little Porte de la Petite Poisonnerie is renaissance. Beneath the town opens the picturesque valley of *Vaux-le-Vire,* which has given a name to the Vaudivires or Vaudevilles of the modern theatre. In the middle of the XIV. c. the owner of a water-mill there was Olivier Basselin, the minstrel of drinking-songs. His verses were never written down till

a century later, when Jean le Houx, of Vire, collected them from the lips of the people.

[For the line from Vire to Caen see ch. iii.]

TOUR DE L'HORLOGE, VIRE.

[A line runs S.W. from Vire to (59 k.) Avranches, through very pretty and wild country, passing—

37 k. *Mortain le Neubourg* (Hotel: *du Cheval Blanc*). The station (omnibus) is 1½ k. from the town. The road passes on l. the remains of the *Abbaye Blanche*, founded 1105 by a son of Count Robert de Conteville. The church and part of the

cloister exist in the grounds of a large ugly seminary. On the r. are pretty little cascades of the Cance falling amongst woods and rocks. The town is terraced along the side of the hill, with a wide view over the thickly wooded country. William the Conqueror gave Mortain (which had belonged to William the Warling, who had rebelled against him), to his half-brother, Robert de Conteville, son of Arletta and Herlouin, who supplied 120 ships for the expedition to England; and it remained a royal possession from that time till the Revolution. Count Robert's castle has been destroyed. The church, grim and grey, with massive pillars, is chiefly XII. c. but retains a portal from an earlier edifice of 1082. The cliffs, glades, and miniature waterfalls of the neighbourhood are attractive. There is a little cascade near the transition church of *Neufbourg*.]

285 k. *S. Sever*, where the church belonged to a famous Benedictine abbey, of which the other buildings serve as public offices. In the neighbouring forest is (4 k.) *L'Ermitage*, once a Carthusian convent, but little ancient remains. 2½ k. N.W. of the station is the church of *Courson*, with a very fine gothic porch and a magnificent yew-tree.

298 k. *Villedieu-les-Poëles*. The church (xv. c. and xvi. c.) has curious external sculptures.

320 k. *S. Planchers*. *Anctoville*, with a fine flamboyant church (xiv. c. and xv. c.) is passed before reaching—

328 k. *Granville* (Hotels: *du Nord ; des Trois Couronnes ; de France*), a seaport partially built on the promontory of *Cap Lihou*, and separated from the mainland by the ravine called *Tranchée aux Anglais.* The *Ville-Haute* is encircled by walls rebuilt 1720, and defended on the W. by a fort. The *Rue des Juifs* and various staircases connect it with the *Ville Basse*. The church of *Notre Dame*, on the highest point of Cap Lihou, is built of granite, and is chiefly flamboyant.

[Omnibuses (50 c.) connect Granville with the pretty bathing-place of *S. Pair*, where the church is partly XI. c. and XII. c.

Steamers (2 fr. 50 c.) run on Sundays, Wednesdays, and Saturdays between Granville and the *Iles Chaussey* (11 k. N.W.). The lighthouse on the *Grande Ile* may be visited.]

The deep little gulfs on the shore in this district are called *flieurs*, or *fleurs*, from the Scandinavian word *fjord*.

CHAPTER V.

PARIS TO CHARTRES, NOGENT LE ROTROU, LE MANS, LAVAL, VITRÉ, RENNES, LAMBALLE, MORLAIX, AND BREST. CHEMIN DE FER DE L'OUEST: FROM THE GARE MONTPARNASSE.

SEE ch. iv. for the line from Paris to—

22 k. *S. Cyr.* The line to Granville is left to the right.

28 k. *Trappes.*

[4 k. S. by the Bois de Trappes are the remains of the famous *Abbey of Port Royal des Champs.* A Benedictine abbey was founded here in 1204, by Eudes de Sully, Bishop of Paris. It was a poor establishment, and only intended for twelve nuns. The lords of Montmorency and Montfort were its principal benefactors. Gradually it increased in prosperity. Honorius III. authorised the celebration of the sacred office within its walls even when the whole country might lie under interdict, and a nun was permitted to keep seven fragments of the wafers consecrated on her profession, and with them to administer the Holy Sacrament to herself on as many successive days. Still, for four centuries, Port Royal was not remarkable. In the XVI. c. the rule of the convent had greatly relaxed, when Marie-Angélique, one of the twenty children of Antoine Arnauld, having become a nun at eight, was appointed abbess at eleven years old (in 1602), her sister Agnes, of five years old, becoming abbess of S. Cyr. Six years later the young abbess of Port Royal became its reformer, secluding Port Royal from the world, and herself setting the example of cutting off unnecessary communication with it by refusing admittance to her own parents and her sister Mme le Maître, when they came to visit her on a day ever after known as 'la journée du guichet.'

The success which crowned the labours of the brave Angélique for the reformation of her own abbey led to her being employed in the reform of other religious houses, especially that of Maubuisson, which had fallen into great licence under the rule of a sister of the famous Gabrielle d'Estrées. Many of the nuns from this convent afterwards sought a refuge at Port Royal, but fever soon drove them from the overcrowded buildings, and the whole community was obliged to take refuge in the Rue S. Jacques at Paris, where a house had been purchased for them by Mme Arnauld, mother of the Mère Angélique. Here—in the 'Convent of Port-Royal de Paris'—it was that they became intimate with S. Cyran, then a prisoner at Vincennes, and that they first began to follow him and Jansenius as their teachers.

Meanwhile the deserted buildings of Port-Royal des Champs were occupied by three nephews of the Mère Angélique, the brothers Lemaître, one of whom, Simon Lemaître de Sacy, had translated the Bible and Terence; and another, Antoine, was famous as an advocate. The band of recluses known as the 'solitaires de Port-Royal' was also joined by Antoine d'Andilly, father of the Mère Angélique. With some of his companions, including the well-known author Nicole and the Hellenist Lancelot, he devoted himself to the work of education. Amongst their pupils the most illustrious was Jean Racine, who became the historian of a community in which his sister had taken the veil, and to which his mother had retired. Many of the best known literary works of the age emanated from Port Royal. The *Logique* of Arnaud, the *Traités rudimentaires* of Lancelot, the *Ethiques* of Nicole, the *Histoire ecclésiastique* of Le Nain de Tillemont were written there. The abbey became a famous school, in which statesmen were proud of having studied. 'Ils sont marqués au coin de Port-Royal' became a phrase of literary or religious commendation.

Twenty years had elapsed since the flight of the nuns from the malaria of Port Royal, when S. Cyran, who guided their actions from his prison at Vincennes, bade them return. 'If the site was unhealthy, it was as easy to serve God in a hospital as in a church, and no prayers were more acceptable to Him than those of the afflicted.' The Mère Angélique answered that, in a church, where the presence of angels and an ever holier Power had once rested, it must be resting still, and therefore she would do his bidding. Many of her nuns accompanied her. They were welcomed on their arrival by the 'solitaires,' who included the nearest relatives of the abbess. It was their only meeting. The men returned to the farm of Les Granges. The gates of the abbey were closed upon the nuns. Gradually the report of the holy atmosphere of Port-Royal des Champs led many great persons, weary of the turmoil of life, to establish themselves in their neighbourhood. The Duc and Duchesse de Luynes built a château there, and the Duchesses de Liancourt and de Longueville made frequent retreats at the abbey.

As advocate to Parliament, Antoine Arnauld, the father of the Mère Angélique, had pleaded before the Sorbonne for the expulsion of the Jesuits. This is supposed to have been the first cause of the remorseless vindictiveness of the Jesuits against his family. Arnauld also had praised the *Augustinus* of Jansenius, a Flemish bishop, unknown to ordinary readers, in which the Jesuits pretended that five heretical propositions were to be found, attacking the mystery of divine grace. The very existence of these propositions in the work he had approved was utterly denied by Arnauld. On this insignificant subject arose the great quarrel of Jesuits and Jansenists. The work of Jansenius had been condemned by the Pope, and the Port-Royalists were condemned by the Jesuits for not finding in that work the passages which the Pope said were to be found there. Anne of Austria was appealed to, and sent her officers to eject the nuns and recluses of Port Royal, but for the time the abbey was saved by an apparent miracle. Mlle Perrier, niece of Blaise Pascal, a scholar eleven years old, was apparently cured of *fistula lacrymalis* upon her eye being touched by a thorn from the Holy Crown preserved at Port Royal! The Court surgeon confirmed the truth of the story, and the queen-mother revoked her mandate against the place to which so great a grace had been granted.

The quarrel between the Jesuits and the Port-Royalists lasted sixty years, during which the Jesuits represented scholastic, the Jansenists spiritual, religion. During this time Blaise Pascal, who had joined the recluses of Port-Royal des Champs, published his *Lettres Provinciales*. This for a time assisted to ward off the fall of the abbey, but at length an edict was obtained from Louis XIV., closing its schools, and forbidding the further admission of postulants to the convent; the number of the nuns was reduced by three-fourths.

At this time the Mère Angélique was in extreme old age. She went to die in the convent at Paris, and on her arrival found the royal officers already in possession, and employed in dispersing the inmates. But she was permitted to expire within the monastic walls, and was brought back for burial to Port-Royal des Champs, where the spot selected for her grave was just outside the grille of the nuns' choir.

After the death of their mother, the society ol Port Royal, both at Paris and in the country, underwent renewed persecution from the Archbishop of Paris. 'They may be pure as angels,' he said, 'but they are proud as devils,' and he set himself to grind them to submission. But they found a new defender in Anne Geneviève de Bourbon, Duchesse de Longueville (sister of the great Condé and the Prince de Conti), the heroine of the Fronde, who, at the close of its cruel and last war, had retired to the valley of Port Royal, and whose disinterested and generous conduct had obtained for her not only the pardon, but the reverence of Louis. By her personal influence with the king, and by her eloquent letters to the Pope (Clement IX.), the imprisoned Port-Royalists were set at liberty, and the abbey and schools were reopened. Mme de Longueville herself came to reside permanently at Port Royal, in an hotel which she built close to the abbey. It was here that she heard of the death of her son killed in battle (1672).

Ten years of rest passed over the valley, during which the most distinguished of the original recluses passed away, and were laid in its peaceful cemetery, with Racine, the warrior Prince de Conti, and the Duc de Liancourt, who had also sought a retreat there. In 1679 the Duchesse de Longueville also died; Mme de Maintenon, herself governed by the Jesuits, was now ruling the conduct of Louis XIV.; the disreputable Harlay was Archbishop of Paris, and Port Royal was doomed. The famous recluses were banished; the nuns were despoiled of their estates; they were interdicted the sacraments of the Church; and, on

October 29, 1709, the last fifteen nuns who remained were driven out of their convent by an armed force, some being so old and infirm that they had to be carried away in litters, and died from their removal.

In January 1710 the destruction of the buildings of Port Royal was ordained by royal edict, and in 1712 the church was pulled down. The bodies of the Arnauld family, of Racine, De Saci, and Le Maitre had already been removed by their relations, but

PORT ROYAL.

the tombs of the other Port-Royalists were desecrated, and their remains exhumed.

Port Royal is now the property of the Duc de Luynes, who has cleared out the area of the noble church (built by the architect of Amiens cathedral), showing the bases of its columns. A walnut tree is pointed out as contemporary with the Mère Angélique, and a well which is called 'la fontaine de la Mère Angélique.' The cellars of the Hôtel de Longueville exist, and considerable remains of Les Granges. Amongst the many monumental slabs torn up from the church were those of the

Arnaulds and Sacys, of Nicole, Pascal, and Racine. The last, after finding a temporary resting-place in the church of Magny-les-Hameaux, is now in S. Etienne du Mont at Paris. Many of the bodies from Port Royal were removed to the church of S. Lambert, on the road to Chevreuse, where some monuments to the nuns may still be seen.

A drive from Versailles or Trappes to Port Royal may easily be continued to embrace Dampierre and Chevreuse, whence one may return to Paris by the line from Limours. It is 5 k. from Port Royal to Dampierre, 6 k. (direct) to Chevreuse, which is 4 k. from Dampierre. The great agricultural institute of *Grignon*, established in a Louis XIV. château, which was sometimes used as a residence by Napoleon I., may also be visited from Trappes.

33 k. *La Verrière*, which takes its name from a château which belonged to the Comte de la Valette.

An omnibus leaves the station of La Verrière twice a day for Dampierre, 13 k. (75 c.; 50 c.). The road passes *Mesnil S. Denis*, a château of temp. Louis XIII. In the church are two XVI. c. statues of SS. Fiacre and Catherine. To the south is the pretty little valley of the Yvette, on the north bank of which is a XIII. c. chapel, which is the only existing remnant of the *Abbey of Notre Dame de la Roche*. In the interior of the nave and transept are a number of gravestones of abbots, and in the choir tombs of the family of Levy, followers of Simon de Montfort in the Albigensian crusade. The keys of the chapel are kept at the farmhouse, which has a fine old chimneypiece.

Twenty minutes of descent takes us from the chapel to *Levy-Saint-Nom*, a picturesque village on the Yvette. In the church is an ancient (stucco) image of the Virgin, brought from the chapel of Notre Dame de la Roche, and supposed to have been originally dug up by a bull with his horns. It has a miraculous reputation, which twice a year (March and September) brings mothers to touch it with the linen of their children. A payment of 10 c. is demanded for every shirt which touches the holy image. At the bottom of the valley are the ruins of an unfinished château, begun in the XVI. c. by Jacques de Crussol, 'grand-panetier de France.'

(An omnibus runs between La Verrière and Montfort l'Amaury, 12 k. distant. The road passes the ruined castle of *Maurepas*, one of the domains which Louis XIV. gave to his minister, Louis Phélippaux, in exchange for Marly. When this castle was taken by the English, in the reign of Charles VI., and its garrison were tried, one of them, named Moniquet, confessed to having thrown down seven men alive into the castle well and crushed them by hurling huge stones upon their heads.[1] The village of *La Tremblay* is remarkable for its château, which belonged to the family of Leclerc du Tremblay, of which the famous Père Joseph, the confidential friend of Cardinal Richelieu, was a member.)

A little east is the moated *Château de Pontchartrain* (see ch. iv.)

38 k. *Les Essarts du Roi.* To the r. of the railway, before reaching this station, the train passes the site of the *Priory of Haute-Bruyère* (destroyed at the Revolution), which was founded by the notorious Bertrade de Montfort, queen of Philippe I. Its chapel contained her tomb, with those of her illustrious descendants the Comtes Simon and Amaury de Montfort. Here also the heart of François I., afterwards moved to S. Denis, was long preserved in a vase of white marble. Nothing remains except the Chapelle des Pères, for in the order of Fontevrault a convent for men was always attached to a monastery for women.

The château of *Artoire* was built under Louis XIV. Pedestrians may reach the ruins of Vaux le Cernay in a walk of 1½ hour from Les Essarts.

48 k. *Rambouillet* (Hotels: *du Lion d'Or; Dauphin; Croix Blanche*). A town almost confined to a single street, La Grande Rue, 3 k. in length. In it is a Hospice founded by the Comte de Toulouse (1731).

[1] '*Journal du Règne de Charles VI.*'

The *Château*, preceded by a Cour d'Honneur, has an enormous round tower, battlemented and machicolated, the only remnant of the ancient moated castle, which was entered by a drawbridge, and which belonged to the family D'Angennes, of whom Jean d'Angennes sold Cherbourg to the English. The last of the family was Charles d'Angennes,

CHATEAU DE RAMBOUILLET.

whose wife, the Marquise de Rambouillet, was celebrated as the literary leader of the XVII. c. Her eldest daughter brought Rambouillet by marriage to the Duc de Montausier, governor of 'Monseigneur,' son of Louis XIV. The property was sold by Fleuriau d'Armenonville to the Comte de Toulouse, the legitimised younger son of Louis XIV. and Mme de Montespan, whose son, the Duc de Penthièvre, sold it for sixteen million francs to Louis XVI. The King was devoted to the place, but Marie Antoinette detested it. 'Que voulez-vous que je fasse dans cette crapaudière?' she said, when the King wanted to take her there. Rambouillet became national property under the Republic; it was part of the civil list of Napoleon I., Louis XVIII., Charles X., and Napoleon III.

GARDENS OF RAMBOUILLET.

The main buildings of the château date from the xv. c., but have been altered in the xvi. c. and xvii. c. They are very picturesque as seen from the gardens, which were adorned by the Comte de Toulouse with tanks, lime-avenues, and statues, after the fashion of Versailles.

Cardinal de Bellay was frequently here in the time of D'Angennes, to whom he was nearly related; and in his suite, as a doctor, came Rabelais.

'Il y a au pied du château, une forte grande prairie, au milieu de laquelle, par une bizarrerie de la nature, se trouve comme un cercle de grosses roches, entre lesquelles s'élèvent de grands arbres qui font un ombrage très-agrèable. C'est le lieu où Rabelais les divertissait, à ce qu'on dit dans le pays. Et encore aujourd'hui, on appelle une certaine roche creusée et enfermée la marmite de Rabelais.'—*Tallemant des Réaux*, 1658.

The spot thus spoken of is now surrounded by water and called *L'Ile des Roches*, but the cave of Rabelais is still to be seen there. The *Ferme expérimentale* is due to Louis XVI., and the *Laiterie de la Reine* was made by him for Marie Antoinette, to console her in temporary absences from her beloved Trianon. It was afterwards a favourite spot with Marie Louise, for whom Napoleon I. redecorated the little temple, the original decorations having been removed to Malmaison.

It was in the old palace of Rambouillet that François I. died, March 13, 1547.

'Une fièvre lente consumait ce monarque, qui usait de château en château sans trouver nulle part de repos ni de soulagement; il fut enfin obligé de s'aliter à Rambouillet, et les progrès d'un ulcère invétéré, qui le tourmentait depuis huit ans, ne laissèrent bientôt plus d'espoir. Ses derniers avis à son fils furent de diminuer les impôts, de conserver pour ministres d'Annebaut et le cardinal de Tournon, de ne point rappeler Montmorenci aux affaires, et de se garder surtout d'y appeler les Guises, 'parce qu'ils tendroient de mettre lui et ses enfants en pourpoint et son peuple en chemise."

'Les paroles du mourant devaient être oubliés avant que son corps fut refroidi : Diane de Poitiers et le Comte d'Aumale étaient là, épiant joyeusement les progrès de l'agonie royale. "Il s'en va, le galand, il s'en va," disait François de Guise.'—*Martin*, '*Hist. de France*.'

Catherine de Medicis and Charles IX. waited at Rambouillet for the issue of the battle of Dreux. Since then it has been chiefly marked by the flight of fallen royalties. Léon Gozlan says that the gate of the château is the funeral arch through which the dynasties of France have passed to the grave. Henri III. fled hither from Paris on the day of the barricades, and 'se coucha tout bottée.' Marie Louise came hither, March 29, 1814, flying from Paris, followed, on the next day, by Joseph Bonaparte. Returning to Rambouillet a month later, the Empress received the visits of the allied sovereigns here, and set out hence for Vienna. In the following year Napoleon came hither after his second abdication, on his way to Rochefort, where he intended to embark for America. At the close of the 'comédie de quinze ans' Charles X. fled hither (July 31, 1830) from S. Cloud, and here he abdicated and the Duc d'Angoulême abandoned his rights, in favour of the Duc de Bordeaux, who was proclaimed as Henri V.

'Le roi Charles X. arriva à Rambouillet; il avait rejoint sur la route Mme la Duchesse de Berry; il était escorté par les gardes du corps et par la gendarmerie d'élite.

'Il fut reçu, non plus avec les démonstrations de joie et les airs de fête qui y accueillaient naguère sa présence, mais en prince malheureux et fugitif. Aucune lumière n'avait été préparée dans la cour d'honneur. La voiture vint se ranger au pied du perron.

'C'était dans ce même château que Napoléon, fuyant de la Malmaison, était venu, lui aussi, passer la première nuit de son éternel exil.

'Le lendemain 1ᵉʳ août, à cinq heures du matin, y arriva Mme la Duchesse d'Angoulême, partie de Vichy l'avant-veille. . . . Elle tourna Paris, traversa Versailles costumée en paysanne, et dans une des petites voitures publiques qui desservaient les environs, traversa les bandes d'insurgés et atteignit enfin Rambouillet en compagnie du Dauphin, qui, averti, était venu au-devant d'elle.

Le roi s'avança jusqu'au perron pour la recevoir ; elle se jeta dans ses bras.

'"Ah ! mon père," s'écria-t-elle, "mon pére, qu'avez-vous fait ? Du moins," ajouta-t-elle, "nous ne nous séparerons plus."'—*Souvenirs du Duc de Broglie.*'

Under Napoleon III. the palace of Rambouillet was made a refuge for the children of officers—'l'Ecole d'Essai des Enfants de Troupe.'

There are pleasant drives and walks in the Forest of Rambouillet. At *S. Hilarion* are ruins of a XIII. c. chapel.

61 k. *Epernon*, on the Guesle, where the pride and injustice of Jean Louis Noganet de la Valette, one of the mignons of Henri III., who made him Duc d'Epernon, gave rise to the distich—

> 'Epernon
> Petite ville sans renom,
> Rivière sans poisson,
> Justice sans raison.'

Scarcely anything remains of the château founded by Amaury II. de Montfort in the middle of the XI. c. At the upper end of the street leading to the church is a good XV. c. house, and on the W. of the place a XIII. c. building called *La Diane.*

9 k. S. is *Gallardon*, with a ruined castle, a cylindrical donjon—*L'Epaule de Gallardon*, founded in the XI. c. by Geoffrey, Vicomte de Châteaudun—and an interesting church, with a mixture of romanesque, gothic, and renaissance architecture. At the W. entrance of the town is a good XV. c. house. The aqueduct of Maintenon is seen on the r. before reaching—

69 k. *Maintenon* (Hotel : *S. Pierre*). The station is 1½ k. from the town. Close to the bridge over the Eure

is the entrance to the château. It was built by Jean Cottereau, *trésorier de finances* under Louis XI., Charles VIII., and François I., and his arms remain over the entrance. Louis XIV. bought it from the Marquis de Villernay to give it to Françoise d'Aubigné, whom he married in 1685. Mme de Maintenon bequeathed Maintenon to the Duc de Noailles, who had married her niece:—

'J'avois plus d'impatience de vous dire des nouvelles de Maintenon que vous n'en sauriez avoir d'en apprendre. J'y ai été trois jours, qui, sans exagération, m'ont paru un moment. C'est une assez belle maison, un peu trop grande pour le train que j'y destine, dans une agréable situation, et qui a de fort beaux droits; enfin j'en suis très satisfaite, et je voudrais y être. Il est vrai que le roi m'a donné le nom de Maintenon.'— *Mme de Maintenon à M. l'Abbé Gobelin*, 15 *Janvier*, 1675.

The picturesque but much restored façade of the château, which faces the entrance gate, has all the richness of the xv. c. In the main building the bedroom of Mme de Maintenon, the ante-chamber where she dined, with her portrait by *Mignard*, and her sedan chair, are shown in the absence of the De Noailles family. Even when the Duke is at Maintenon the portress (r. of entrance) is allowed to take visitors over the buildings on the l. of the court, which look outside like stables, but contain a magnificent gallery, richly adorned with carving and gilding, and hung with portraits of the ancestors of the De Noailles family. At the end it once communicated with a chapel, now disused, outside the precincts of the château, and from its alcove Mme de Maintenon used to hear mass. The inner chapel of the château was built by Jean Cottereau. The garden was designed by Le Nôtre. In the park, the *Avenue Racine* commemorates the long stay of the poet at the château, when he was composing the tragedies of *Esther* and *Athalie* for the young ladies of S. Cyr. A great feature is the ruin of the huge aqueduct constructed by Louis XIV. to convey the waters of the Eure to the fountains of Versailles, on which 30,000 workmen were employed from 1684 to 1688. Gallardon (see above) is 11 k. from Maintenon.

88 k. *Chartres* (Hotel: *du Duc de Chartres; de France*), the capital of the Département d'Eure et Loir, and one of the oldest towns in France. The ancient Autricum, afterwards known as Civitas Carnotum, was, in the x. c., made a countship, which afterwards was bestowed upon younger sons of the French kings. Since Louis XIV. gave it to his brother, Philippe d'Orléans, the title has always been borne by the eldest sons of the Ducs d'Orléans.

The glorious *Cathedral of Notre Dame*, occupying the highest ground in the town, is visible from a great distance over the plains of La Beauce. It is often, and justly, considered to be the most perfectly beautiful church in the world. Tradition tells that it was founded over a cave where Druids had erected a statue '*à la Vierge qui devait enfanter.*' Above this, it is said that the early missionaries, SS. Savinien and Potentien, built a chapel (the earliest church in France dedicated to the Virgin), which was destroyed by Quirinus, who was governor of Autricum in the time of Claudius, and who threw the bodies of his martyrs into its well, called 'Puits des Saints-Forts.' The second church, built under Constantine, was destroyed in the ix. c. In 1020 Bishop Fulbert began a new church, where Adela, daughter of the Conqueror, was married to Stephen of

Blois, Count Palatine of Champagne. This church was destroyed by fire in 1194, with the exception of the crypt and towers. The existing church was a reconstruction with stone from Berchères (8 k. distant), begun by Bishop Regnault de Mouçon, and consecrated in the presence of S. Louis in 1260. The three gables were added early in

CATHEDRAL, CHARTRES.

the XIV. c., the Chapelle de S. Piat in 1349, and the Chapelle de Vendôme in 1412. The spire of the tower on the r. (Clocher Vieux) is of the early church of the XII. c.; that on the l. (Clocher Neuf) was built by Jean Texier, called Jean de Beauce, in 1505-14. The splendid oak vaulting called *le forêt*, supporting a leaden roof, was destroyed by a fire, which melted the bells, in June 1836, and has been replaced by a roof of cast iron and copper.

The cathedral—perhaps the most beautiful in existence [1] —is a Latin cross. Its W. façade has a triple portal, above which are three windows, surmounted by a splendid rose of the XIII. c., an open balustrade, a gallery with sixteen statues of kings, and a gable with a statue of the Virgin between angels, and, above all, Christ in benediction. The lower sculptures are XII. c., the upper XIII. c. and XIV. c. The greater part of the seven hundred and nineteen statues and statuettes of the portals refer to the life of Christ. Those in the tympanum and vaulting of the r. portal are in honour of the Virgin. The vaulting of the l. portal has the signs of the Zodiac and an allegorical representation of the twelve months. The sculptured name of 'Rogerus' is probably that of the architect. On the r. is the noble *Clocher Vieux*.

'On est d'abord frappé de l'unité, de la grandeur, qui regnent dans l'ensemble. Partant du soubassement, on arrive au sommet de la flèche, sans brusque arrêt, sans que rien vienne interrompre la forme générale de l'édifice. Ce clocher, dont le base est pleine, massive, et sans ornement, se transforme, à mésure qu'il s'élance, en une flèche aiguë à huit pans, percés de lucarnes, sans qu'il soit possible de dire où cesse la construction massive et où commence la construction légère.'—*Viollet le Duc.*

The *Clocher Neuf*, with a rich flamboyant spire, is only of the same date as the Clocher Vieux as far the Galerie des Rois. It can be ascended by 378 steps.

The great magnificence of Chartres is chiefly shown in the portals of the transept, which present the most splendid specimens of XIII. c. decoration in France. The N. façade

---

[1] Which Lowell spoke of as 'the most wonderful thing in France,' and which suggested his poem of 'The Cathedral.'

has a projecting porch with three gothic arches to the front, and is decorated with no less than seven hundred statues and statuettes, some of them of the greatest beauty, and, with the whole porch, still (1895) in unrestored splendour.

'C'est sur le front altier de la cathédrale de Chartres qu'est écrit le mot de l'art nouveau, le mot de ce grand douzième siècle, trop peu répété par les âges qui ont suivi. A la baie de gauche du porche septentrional, entre les voussures qui encadrent le tympan de la porte, quatorze *Vertus* sous debout, échelonnées de la base à la pointe de l'ogive : à côté de la *Force* ou *Vertu* par excellence (*Virtus*), mère de toutes les autres Vertus, la première des treize sœurs ; auréolée en signe de sainteté, couronnée en signe de souveraine indépendance, semble montrer de son bras levé son nom gravé sur la pierre. Ce nom est : *Libertas*.'—*Henri Martin*, '*Hist. de France*.'

'Les porches nord et sud plantés devant les portes du transept de la cathédrale de Chartres passent, à juste titres, pour des chefs d'oeuvre. Leur plan, leur structure, leur ornementation, la statuaire qui les couvre, sont des sujets d'étude inépuisables, et leur ensemble présente cette harmonie complète si rare dans les œuvres d'architecture. Celui du nord, plus riche de détails, plus complet comme entente de la sculpture, plus original peut-être comme composition, produirait plus d'effet, s'il était, ainsi qui celui du sud, élevé sur un grand enmarchement et exposé tout le jour aux rayons du soleil. Dans l'origine, ces deux porches étaient peints et dorés ; leur aspect, alors, devait être merveilleux. C'est lorsqu'on examine dans leur ensemble et leurs détails ces compositions claires, profondément étudiées, d'une exécution irréprochable, qu'on peut se demander si depuis lors nous n'avons pas désappris au lieu d'apprendre.

'La somme d'intelligence, de savoir, de connaissance des effets, d'expérience pratique, dépensée dans ces deux porches de Notre-Dame de Chartres, suffirait pour établir la gloire de toute une génération d'artistes ; et ce qu'on ne saurait trop admirer dans ces oeuvres, c'est combien alors les arts de l'architecture et de la sculpture avaient su faire une alliance intime, combien ils se tenaient étroitement unis.'—*Viollet le Duc*.

Above the N. porch the façade has a balustrade serving as base to a gallery of five windows, a great rose with eight niches filled with statues, a covered gallery, a balustrade of open-work, and finally a pointed gable decorated with a statue under a canopy. As far as the covered gallery this façade dates from XIII. c., above it from XIV. c. The S.

NORTH PORCH, CHARTRES.

façade has almost the same disposition, and each façade is flanked by two square towers.

'La nef est courte comparativement au chœur; c'est probablement pour lui donner deux travées de plus, que l'ancien porche de la façade fut supprimé et les portes avancées au nu du mur extérieur des tours. Voulant conserver, pour bâtir le chœur, la crypte qui lui sert de fondations, et les deux belles tours occidentales, il n'était pas possible de donner à l'église une plus grande longueur.'—*Viollet le Duc.*

The interior is a treasure-house of architectural loveliness, pictorially enriched by the sparkle of its ancient glass. It consists of a central nave, with side aisles which begin from the two great towers; a wide transept with aisles, and a vast choir, with double ambulatory and radiatory chapels. The choir was formerly separated from the nave by a magnificent XIII. c. rood-loft, destroyed by the canons in 1763. The inner side of the splendid clôture was mutilated at the same time; but the exterior, begun in 1514 from designs of Jean de Beauce, architect of the Clocher Neuf, remains intact, covered with groups of sculpture which were not finished till the beginning of the XVIII. c. The first four groups, beginning from the transept—the Apparition of the Angel to Joachim and to Anna, the Meeting of Joachim and Anna, and the Birth of the Virgin—are the work of Jean Soulas, of Paris; and many of the other sculptors' names have been discovered. Between the eighth and ninth group two angels sustain the dial of a very complicated and ingenious clock, which has a staircase enclosed in a little renaissance tourelle. Between the twentieth and twenty-first group formerly stood an altar surmounted by reliquaries. In the stylobate of the clôture are twenty-five medallions containing subjects from sacred or profane story, or from the history of Chartres. Behind the altar, an armoire hollowed out of the wall of the sanctuary contains the treasure which was formerly one of the richest in Christendom, but a modern shrine now only encloses 'the veil of the Virgin' (called at Chartres *La Santa Camisia*) said to have been sent to Charlemagne by the empress Irene, and given to the cathedral by Charles le Chauve, *c.* 876, since which it has been looked upon as the palladium of the town. It consists of two fragments of white silk, enveloped in another piece of stuff, which is supposed to have been a veil of the empress Irene. At the entrance of the N. choir-aisle is the famous black *Vierge du Pilier*, a much venerated xv. c. statue. Between the chapel of the chevet and that of the Sacré-Coeur, is a staircase leading to the xiv. c. *Chapelle de S. Piat*, beneath which is the ancient chapter-house.

Against the S. aisle is the *Chapelle de Vendôme*, built 1412. The keystone of its vaulting bears the arms of the founder, Louis de Bourbon, Comte de Vendôme. An armoire contains the relics of S. Piat and of S. Taurinus, bishop of Evreux. The former is invoked for rain, the latter for fine weather.

A hundred and twenty-five windows are filled with splendid stained glass of xiii. c., xiv. c., xv. c. and xvi. c., the upper windows having been, for the most part, given by S. Louis, S. Ferdinand, Blanche of Castille, and the canons of Chartres; the lower by the corporations and guilds of the town. Simon de Montfort is amongst the figures in the glass of the choir. The great western rose-window represents the Last Judgment. In the pavement of the nave is a labyrinth formed by eleven bands of white stone let into the blue.

The *Crypt* (open from 6 to 9 a.m.), built in the xi. c. by Bishop Fulbert, is the largest in France. It is a kind of gallery under the aisles of the nave and choir, with four narrower galleries (constructed after the fire of 1194) under the aisles of the transept. It is reached by six staircases, under the towers or the porches of the transept. The principal entrance is a little E. of the S. porch. Turning

l. from hence down the S. gallery of the crypt, we find, against the l. wall, a Gallo-Roman relief. In the *Chapelle S. Martin* are preserved the remains of the noble *jubé* of the cathedral and the empty tomb of S. Calétric (557), bishop of Chartres. The opposite *Chapelle SS. Clément et Denis* contains remains of a XII. c. and XIII. c. fresco. Near the *Chapelle S. Nicolas* is a curious piscina surmounted by a XIII. c. fresco of the Nativity, and beyond this a monolith font of the XII. c.

Returning to the door by which we entered, and turning towards the apse, we find on r. a succession of chapels. Opposite that of S. Véronique is the entrance of a second crypt, the ancient *Martyrium*, now used as a chapel dedicated to S. Lubin, a simple shepherd, raised to the see of Chartres for his eminent virtues. Reaching the great N. gallery by a narrow, winding passage, the *Chapelle de Notre Dame sous Terre* occupies the site of the cave where Druids are said to have venerated 'the Virgin who gave birth to a child.' The statue is a reproduction of the primitive image which is believed to have existed till the Revolution. The crypt may be left by the stair near the N. transept porch.

To the W., between the cathedral and the Bishop's gardens, is the XIII. c. *Sacristy*; a vaulted passage, lighted by a XIV. c. window, unites it to the church. The *Evêché*, of brick, was built in XVII. c., chiefly at the expense of Mme de Maintenon.

The ancient abbey church of *S.-Père-en-Vallée*, or *S. Pierre*, dating from XI. c. to XIII c., is a three-aisled basilica, having a long choir terminating in a semicircular apse, with rectangular chapels on either side. The church has admirable stained glass of XIII. c., XIV. c. and XV. c.

In the apsidal chapel are enamel pictures of the apostles, executed 1545-47 by *Léonard Limousin* for François I., from designs of Michel Rochetel. Opening from the r. aisle is the *Chapelle de Notre Dame des Sept Douleurs*, containing a tablet epitaph (1037) in memory of Robert, son of Richard I., Duke of Normandy, and himself Comte d'Evreux and Archbishop of Rouen.

The XVI. c. church of *S. Aignan* has a crypt, reconstructed in XV. c. or XVI. c. *S. Martin du Val*, now the chapel of the *Hôpital S. Brice*, is a remnant of a basilica dating before the X. c., and is very curious and interesting. The capitals, both in the church and crypt, are very remarkable. A number of tombs of the Merovingian period have been found beneath the soil. The collegiate church of *S. André*, in the lower town, on the banks of the Eure, is partly used as a warehouse. The church was begun c. 1108, but the crypts, under its side aisles, are probably of much earlier date.

'S. André présente sur sa façade comme un abrégé de l'histoire de l'architecture au moyen-âge. Une porte romane, flanquée d'élégantes colonnettes, soutenant une archivolte richement ornée, est surmontée de trois fenêtres ogivales entourées de tores épais. Ces fenêtres représenteront le gothique primitif, s'élevant sur une base romane. Au-dessus, dans le fronton, l'époque de la décadence et du dernier éclat du style gothique, se montre dans une espèce de rose, ou plutôt une ouverture triangulaire à côtes courbes, remplie de meneaux flamboyans.'— *Prosper Mérimée.*

The only one remaining of the seven gates of Chartres is the *Porte Guillaume*, a magnificent specimen of the military architecture of the XIV. c. Outside this gate, and turning l. by the Boulevard des Fossés, we obtain one of the best views of the cathedral. N. of the cathedral is the *Maison de Loëns*, over a fine XIII. c. crypt. Here the cathedral chapter administered justice. The *Hôtel de Ville*, a brick XVII. c. building, contains the *Musée*. In the Place de la Poissonnerie is the *Maison du Saumon*, a fine XV. c. timber building. In the 'Tertre du Petit Cerf are two XV. c. houses. At 52, Rue du Grand Cerf, is the XVI. c. *Maison de Claude Huvé*, with an inscription over the portal commemorating its founder. At the corner of the Rue des Changes and Rue du Cloître Notre Dame is a XIII. c. house. A little N. of the town is *Lèves*, with remains of a IX. c. monastery, and a cavern which tradition declares to have been a school of the Druids. The church of *Berchères l'Evêque*, a few miles S., is XII. c.

[For the line from Chartres to (43 k.) Dreux see ch. iv.]

[For the line to Paris by Auneau and Dourdan, see *South-Western France*.]

[A line runs S.E. to (76 k.) Orleans, passing (56 k.) *Patay*, where Jeanne Darc gained a victory over the English, June 18, 1429.]

[Two lines lead S.W. to Châteaudun (see *South-Western France*): that (59 k.) by Voves, and that (74 k.) by (25 k.) *Illiers*, with ruins of a once famous castle, and (38 k.) the once fortified town of *Brou*.]

99 k. *S. Aubin—S. Luperce*. Near this are remains of a Gallo-Roman aqueduct 26 k. in length, which served the town of the Carnutes.

106 k. *Courville*. In the XVI. c. church is a fine canopied altar.

At 8½ k., on the road to Illiers, is the *Château de Villebon* (Marquis de Pontois), built by Guillaume d'Estouteville, Grand Master of Woods and Forests, who died in 1449. It is a quadrangular mass of moated building, with seven machicolated towers. The courtyard has four octangular stair-turrets at the angles. The windows are adorned with sculpture. The apartments have a good deal of XVI. c. furniture. The room remains in which Maximilien de Bethune, Duc de Sully, died,[1] and that of Henri IV., with his bed and writing-table.

114 k. *Pontgouin.* 1 k. r. is the church of *S. Lubin*, of XIII. c., enlarged in XVI. c. by Louis Guillard, bishop of Chartres. Towers remain of his episcopal palace.

124 k. *La Loupe*, has small remains of its château, which belonged to the Duc de la Ferté, whose duchess was a celebrated beauty of the court of Louis XIV.

On the road to Longui is a pollard oak of enormous size, with a statue of the Madonna in its branches. 8 k. N. is the moated *Château de Manou*, which belonged in the XIII. c. to Blanche of Castille. A diligence leads to (25 k.) La Ferté Vidame by (12 k.) *Senonches*, which has a church and castle of XII. c.

Leaving La Loupe, the line passes to the l. *Vaupillon*, where nothing remains of a splendid château built at the end of XVI. c. for Henriette d'Entragues. The mound and entrenchments of an earlier castle exist.

141 k. *Condé sur Huisne.*

[A line of 29 k. leads N.W. to Mortagne (see ch. iv.), passing (22 k.) *Mauves*, where nothing remains of a splendid château built by Marguerite de Lorraine 1502-5.]

149 k. *Nogent le Rotrou* (Hotel: *du Dauphin*), capital of the ancient province of Perche, beautifully situated on the

---

[1] One of his ancestors had married a daughter of Guillaume d'Estouteville, in 1450.

Huisne, and a very picturesque place. It is overlooked by the remains of a castle, built in the XI. c. by Geoffroi II., Comte du Perche, grandson of Rotrou I., Comte de Mortagne, on the site of an earlier fortress (Castrum Nogioni) destroyed by the Normans. It is called the *Château de S. Jean*, from a church which Geoffroi II. built near his castle. Nogent was long a residence of the house of Condé, having been made a duchy in 1557, in favour of Louis de Bourbon, Prince de Condé, uncle of Henri IV., killed in the battle of Jarnac. His second wife, Françoise d'Orléans, gave birth here to Charles de Bourbon, Comte de Soissons. In 1624 the seigneury passed to the famous Sully, whose heirs alienated it in 1770. The château (M. des Murs) is shown to strangers who ask permission. Its most ancient part is the keep of 1003-30. The adjoining gate, flanked by machicolated towers, is of XV. c., but the corridor which follows is contemporary with the keep.

The church of *S. Hilaire*, founded x. c., was rebuilt XIII. c. and XVI. c., and its tower is of 1560. *Notre Dame* (near the modern Hôtel de Ville) was formerly the chapel of the Hospital. The W. door is an interesting specimen of early gothic; the triple nave is XIV. c. and XV. c., the rectangular choir XIII. c. Close to the church, in the Rue de Sully, is the entrance of the *Hôtel Dieu*, the ancient hospital of S. Jacques de l'Aumône, founded in 1190 by Comte Rotrou IV. The buildings are chiefly modern. On the r. of the court, against the wall of Notre Dame, is a hexagonal chapel containing the tomb of the Duc and Duchesse de Sully (somewhat mutilated at the Revolution), bearing their kneeling statues. On the figure of Sully is the name of the sculptor, 'B. Bovdin. F. 1642.' Against the wall is the epitaph of Sully and Rachel de Cochefilet; their ashes were dispersed in 1793.

Near the apse of *S. Laurent* (XV. c. and XVI. c.) a vaulted gothic passage, the ancient entrance of the *Prieuré de S. Denis*, leads to the remains of that convent, founded in 1029 by Geoffroi II. The ruined church is chiefly XIII. c., with three chapels added XV. c.

Nogent has several old houses of XV. c. and XVI. c., one of the finest being 47, Rue S. Laurent. On the Route de Dreux is the church of *Margon*, of XI. c. and XV. c., beautifully situated. Nurses for Parisian mothers abound in the environs of Nogent.

The church of *Bazoche-Gouet*, some miles S., is of XIII. c.

170 k. *La Ferté-Bernard* (Hotels: *de l'Ouest*, at S. Antoine; *S. Jean*). The station is in the village of S. Antoine, 1 k. from the town. La Ferté, founded by a bishop of Le Mans in the XI. c., owes its second name of Bernard to a family which possessed it till the XIV. c., when Bernard de la Ferté sold the seigneury to the Comte du Maine, afterwards Philippe VI. His son Jean ceded it to Ingelger, Sire d'Amboise, from whom it passed to the family of Craon, then to the Duc d'Orléans, brother of Charles VI., Louis II. d'Anjou, and Louis III. (1417), to King René, to the House of Lorraine, and finally to Cardinal Richelieu, in whose family it remained till the Revolution. Robert Garnier, the dramatic poet, was a native of La Ferté.

The church of *Notre-Dame-des-Marais* is a very fine specimen of flamboyant gothic. The nave, transept, and tower are of 1450—1500; the l. aisle of the choir of 1500-20, the three apsidal chapels 1520-36, except the vaulting of

1536-44, which has the medallions and little columns of the Renaissance. The pendant of the chapel of the chevet ends in a crown, in the centre of which is seen God the Father borne on the clouds. The lower galleries of the S. façade bear sculptures in which the king of France and his peers are introduced. The upper (XVI. c.) galleries of the choir form the anthem 'Ave, Regina Coelorum.' The beautiful glass of the choir (by François Delalande, Robert and Jean Courtois) is of 1498—1606. The bracket which supports the organ is a very refined work of Évrard Baudot, 1501.

The *Hôtel de Ville* has been established, since 1703, over a fine XV. c. gateway, the only portion of the fortifications remaining. The *Halles* were built by Claude de Lorraine, Duc de Guise, in 1536. In the suburb of *Cherré* was the abbey of *La Pelice*, founded by Bernard de la Ferté in the XII. c.; the church is XV. c.

179 k. *Sceaux* (3 k.) has remains of fortifications, and a XIII. c. church. To the l. of the line, near Duneau, are several dolmens and a menhir.

187 k. *Connerré*. The church of *S. Jacques* is romanesque, with a XVI. c. spire. The presbytery was an ancient priory.

[A line leads N.W. to Mamers, passing—

17 k. *Bonnétable*. The picturesque château, with its six great machicolated towers, was built by Jean d'Harcourt in 1478.

45 k. *Mamers* (Hotel: *d'Espagne*), a town built around two squares, one containing the Halles, S. Nicolas and the theatre, the other the library, college, prison and gendarmerie (in the buildings of the former Convent of the Visitation). The church of *Notre Dame* is XV. c., *S. Nicolas* XV. c. and XVI. c.

12 k. distant is the moated *Château de la Tournerie*, in the

midst of marshy meadows, with buildings of late XVI. c., and with mythological painted decorations of the same date.

A line connects Mamers with (37 k.) Mortagne (see ch. iv.).]

[A line runs S.E. to (52 k.) *Le Pont de Braye*, passing—

32 k. *S. Calais*, which rose around an abbey founded in the VI. c. by S. Calais, a monk of Auvergne. This abbey, rebuilt in the XVI. c. by Jean Ronsard, uncle of the famous poet, was entirely destroyed at the Revolution. The church, of different dates from XIII. c. to XVI. c., has a stone XVII. c. spire. On the hill above the town are remains of an XI. c. castle.

44 k. *Bessé*. A little N.W. of the town is the restored *Château de Courtanvaux*, chiefly XIV. c. and XV. c.]

193 k. *Pont-de-Gennes*, named from an ancient bridge over the Huisne, which replaces one built by the Romans. The church of S. Gilles is XIII. c. 1 k. W. is *Montfort le Rotrou*, where Rotrou, Comte de Perche, built a castle in the XII. c. A modern château has been erected by the Marquis de Nicolaï.

203 k. *Yvré-l'Évêque* owes its name to a château which the bishops of Mans possessed here from the XII. c. to the Revolution. 3½ k. S.W. are the ruins of the Abbey of *Epau* (Pietatis Dei), founded in 1229 by Berengaria, widow of Richard Coeur de Lion, for monks of Citeaux. The first monastic church was destroyed in 1365 by the inhabitants of Mans, for fear it should be fortified by the English; but the church was rebuilt in XV. c., and still exists, though the other monastic buildings have perished.

211 k. *Le Mans* (Hotels: *Grand*—good; *du Dauphin; des Princes*), on rising ground above the Sarthe, the ancient capital of Maine and now capital of the Département de la Sarthe. It occupies the site of the Gallic oppidum Suindinum, a town of the Cenomanes,

which was fortified by the Romans. Palgrave says S. Dionysius was its first bishop, and was visited here by S. Clement, the immediate successor of S. Peter. But S. Julien, who preached Christianity here in the IV. c., is generally supposed to have become the first bishop. In 937 Hugues Capet made the Comtes du Maine hereditary, but in the XI. c. William the Conqueror took Mans. The frequent revolts of the inhabitants afterwards led him to dismantle the town and to build a strong fortress for their repression. Mans suffered greatly in the wars of Philippe-Auguste and Richard Coeur de Lion, and was afterwards an appanage of Queen Berengaria, and of Marguerite, wife of S. Louis. Comte de Maine was a royal title till Louis XIV. gave it to the elder of his sons by Mme de Montespan. The town suffered greatly in the wars of La Vendée; and there (Jan. 11, 1871) the Prussians gained the victory which rendered the defence of Paris hopeless.

The ancient walls are destroyed, and the massive portal through which Duke William of Normandy made his 'joyeuse entrée' after his conquest of Maine, and near which he built a castle, is now reduced to shapeless fragments of wall.

The principal hotels are situated in the Place de la République, which also contains the *Palais de Justice*, occupying part of an old (XVII. c.) convent of the Visitation. In the centre of the square is a fine bronze statue by *Croizy* of General Chanzy, who led the French forces in the battle of Le Mans. Hence the Rue Dumas, the Rue Marchande and (r.) the Rue S. Dominique lead to the Place des Jacobins, where we find all the principal objects of interest.

The *Cathedral of S. Julien*, founded in the IV. c. and rebuilt in the VI. c. by S. Innocent, was again rebuilt in 834 by S. Aldric. In 1060 the famous architect-bishop Vulgrin began a new edifice, dedicated *c.* 1095, but altered in 1120 by Hildebert, who added two lofty towers. Soon after, it was greatly injured by fire, but was consecrated in 1158. The existing nave belongs to this building of XI. c. and XII. c., but the vast choir was an addition of 1217-54; only the transept and tower belong to the XV. c. Part of the ancient rampart was destroyed for the sake of the apse.

The W. façade belongs to the XI. c., except the dividing buttresses and the gables. Its great window retains much ancient glass, relating to the story of S. Julien. The sumptuous side door, of XII. c., ornamented with statues like those of Chartres, is preceded by a porch.

'The capitals are executed in the most elegant and freest Corinthian style; even the coping stones are covered with the most graceful branch-work, and the shafts of the columns on which the figures stand, as at Chartres, are rich with varied designs. All the rest is devoted to isolated works of sculpture. On the capitals there stand ten stiff columnar figures in antique drapery, variously arranged, but exhibiting throughout the same parallel folds and with heads and limbs stiff and constrained. Yet even here, in the slender proportions, and still more in the type of the heads, the strong presentment of a new life is perceptible, though still too dependent on the architecture. We recognise St. Peter and St. Paul and other saints, and finally kings and queens, all full of youth, and, in spite of the severe style of conception, imbued with a breath of grace and feeling. In a small colonnade, above the door, are seated the twelve apostles—short, heavy, stunted figures. In the arched compartment above, solemn and severe, is the enthroned figure of Christ, with the four symbols of the Evangelists, again displaying violent gestures—a recurring trait of the plastic art of the period, which, in its naïve way, endeavoured by vehement action to indicate the divine inspiration of the Evangelists. Lastly, all the four archivolts surrounding the tympanum are covered with sculptures; in the centre angels, swinging vessels of incense, form a circle round the figure of the Redeemer; in the outer circles the whole history of the Life of Christ is depicted in distinct and simple relief, and in a quaint and lifelike manner.'—*Lübke.*

In the *Interior*, the nave has the peculiarity of having five bays in the central and ten in the side aisles, which are of extreme simplicity. The transept is much loftier than the nave. The lower portions are of the XII. c. The N. wall has a magnificent rose-window, the compartments of which are slightly flamboyant, whilst its glass contains 124 subjects, some of them of great historical interest. At the end of the S. transept is the only tower of the cathedral, romanesque on the ground and first floors, but of the XV. c. and XVI. c. above, with a modern dome. The choir (1217) is of the very best period of gothic architecture, and is surrounded by a double aisle and thirteen radiating chapels.

'En passant de la nef dans le choeur, l'impression qu'on éprouve c'est qu'on quitte le temple d'une religion ancienne, pour entrer dans celui d'une religion nouvelle. Ces chapiteaux couverts de monstres, d'animaux fantastiques, de masques hideux, semblent les ornements d'un culte barbare, tandis que ces feuillages variés de mille manières, ces vitraux aux couleurs harmonieuses, donnent l'idée d'une croyance douce et bienveillante.'—*Prosper Mérimée.*

The glorious windows of the choir are filled with magnificent glass of XIV. c. and XV. c. The windows of the side aisle are occupied by the legends of the saints—Evron, Calais, Théophile, Eustache—especially venerated at Mans.

In one of these windows is a curious portrait, inscribed 'Senebaldus,' of Pope Innocent IV. (Sinibaldo Fieschi). The sixth (triangular) window represents a Sire de Pirmil, the seventh probably the Sire de la Guierche, governor of Maine under S. Louis. The clerestory windows are occupied by great figures of S. Matthew, S. Andrew, S. Luke, David, Isaac, Moses, then the Apostles, and finally S. Bertram, founder of the Abbey of La Couture—these windows being the gift of an abbot of La Couture of the family of Cormes. The series of apostles is continued in the fourth great window, signed 'Odon de Coulongé,' with the inscription 'La Verrine des Drapiers, and the members of that corporation are represented in it. Then, in the fifth lancet, are S. Paul and Aaron, signed for the furriers of Mans; the sixth, representing SS. Stephen, Vincent, Gervais and Protais, was given by the innkeepers and publicans. The seventh, or apsidal window, contains the Madonna and Child, and the Crucifixion, beneath which is the prayer of Bishop Geoffroy de Loudon (1254), offering the window to God; his arms are repeated in the border. The eighth great window, signed, represents the architects of the cathedral. With the ninth window begins a series of the sainted bishops of Mans, characterised by the nimbi round their heads and inscriptions beneath. The tenth window is inscribed 'La Verrière Ecles.,' and was given by the clergy of the church. The very curious eleventh window commemorates the players at tric-trac, who consecrated their gains to it. The thirteenth, signed by the bakers of Mans, represents its donors at work. All these windows are of the middle of the XIII. c. The remains of glass of XI. c. are the most ancient known.

'Si l'on ajoute que les vignerons du Mans se sont fait peindre au bas d'une verrière du bas côté, on sera frappé de la puissance et de la piété des corporations de métiers au moyen-âge, et du petit nombre de dons emanés au contraire des personnages de la noblesse et de la bourgeoisie.'—*M. E. Hucher*.

The first choir chapel on r. contains a curious (early XVII. c.) terra cotta S. Sepulcre, restored from injuries received from a mad workman. The double (XIV. c.) door leading to the Psallette, with a figure of S. Julien in the tympanum; and the door of the sacristy, formed from fragments of a destroyed *jubé*, erected by the Cardinal de Luxembourg in 1620, deserve notice. In the l. aisle are XVI. c. tapestries representing the legends of S. Julien and SS. Gervais and Protais. In the baptistery (first choir chapel on l.) are the tombs of Charles, Comte du Maine, 1472 (renaissance), and Guillaume de Langey du Bellay, viceroy of Piedmont under François I., and brother of Cardinal du Bellay, Bishop of Mans, 1543.[1]

'La pose de la statue, les ornements de l'entablement, et les bas-reliefs qui couvrent le soubassement du sarcophage, offrent des modèles qu'on ne saurait trop étudier. Jamais, que je sache, on n'a surpassé les maîtres de la renaissance dans la composition de ces monuments.'—*Prosper Merimée*.

In the r. transept, removed from the choir, is the very interesting XIII. c. tomb of Queen Berengaria of England, daughter of Sancho VI. of Navarre, and wife of Richard Coeur de Lion (celebrated in Scott's *Talisman*), to whom she was married at Limasol by his chaplain Nicolas, afterwards Bishop of Le Mans. After Richard's death she

---

[1] This monument is sometimes ascribed to Germain Pilon.

lived much at Le Mans, which was part of her dower. The statue is one of the most lifelike of its period, with open eyes.

'The drapery flows down in wide folds, the noble head is antiquely grand, the hands are holding a small casket, and the feet rest on a dog, the emblem of fidelity.'—*Lübke*.

Against the first pillar on l. of the nave formerly stood the tomb of Geoffroi Plantagenet, Comte du Maine et d'Anjou, son-in-law of Henry I. and father of Henry II. of England. This interesting monument was entirely destroyed by the Huguenots in 1562, except the enamelled portrait attached to the second pillar after the destruction of the tomb. Having been taken down for security in the Revolution, it is now preserved in the Musée, for which it was purchased from the collection of an amateur.

At the S.W. angle of the cathedral is a large *Peulven*, $4\frac{1}{2}$ mètres in height, leaning against the façade.

'Ce peulven rappelle les âges de la Gaule où s'opérait la transition entre l'antique religion et la religion nouvelle.'

Opposite the W. end of the cathedral is the *Hôtel de la Grabatoire*, a fine renaissance building.

The magnificent church of *Notre Dame de la Couture* (de Cultura Dei), reached by the Rue de la Préfecture (l. of the way to the station), belonged to an ancient abbey founded by S. Bertrand in the VII. c. Its façade and portal, flanked by two low towers, are a splendid work of the XIII. c. At the sides of the entrance are six noble statues of apostles; the tympanum has the Last Judgment and Weighing of the Souls. The outer arch presents a curious collection of crockets, some of them—of animals—very characteristic. The interior is spoilt by restoration. The wide nave is single, but the narrow choir, raised high by steps, has an ambulatory with chapels, and with its little crypt may be attributed to a rebuilding by Hugues I. in 995, after the church had been destroyed by the Normans. There are several good pictures here, the best being a Burial of Christ by *Philippe de Champaigne*. In the sacristy is preserved the *Suaire de S. Bertrand*.

Between La Couture and the Préfecture is the entrance to the *Musée*, only open between 12 and 4. It is worth visiting, for the sake of the precious XII. c. enamelled portrait of Geoffrey Plantagenet, Comte du Maine, son-in-law of Henry I. of England, which formerly stood above the tomb of Geoffrey in the cathedral. The portrait is of the utmost interest as a representation of costume, as well as from its historic associations. The Musée has an important collection of prehistoric antiquities. The canopy which covered the coffin of Queen Berengaria is a historic relic.

Notre Dame du Pré, on the r. bank of the Sarthe, belonged to a Benedictine convent, founded in XI. c. by one Lezeline, on the site of an oratory of S. Julien, and altered XII. c. It may be considered as a miniature of the cathedral before its last restoration, and dates from the XI. c. and XII. c., except a great part of the vaulting renewed in XVII. c. In the N. aisle is a XVI. c. relief, representing the translation of the relics of S. Julien from Notre Dame du Pré to the Cathedral. The crypt is XI. c.

The little church of *S. Pavin aux Champs* dates from XI. c., and contains a sarcophagus, supposed to be that (VI. c.) of its patron saint.

The church of *S. Pierre de la Cour* (XII. c. and XIII. c.), now used as a school, was the Sainte Chapelle of the Comtes du Maine, and was originally built by Hugues I. in 969.

The church of the *Visitation* was built 1737, by Mathurin Ribaillier, from designs of Soufflot.

The *Église de la Mission*, now used as a school of cavalry, was built c. 1180 by Henry II., King of England and Comte du Maine, to serve as a hospital, and was only turned into a church in 1397. In the court of the barrack may be seen the fine XIII. c. portal of the Confrérie de Coëffort, to whom the hospital was granted in 1234.

The *Hôtel de Ville* occupies the site of the palace of the Comtes du Maine, destroyed in 1617.

In domestic architecture we may notice: No. 1, Place S. Michel, as the house of Scarron, who bore the honorary title of Canon of Mans; No. 11, Grande Rue, called sometimes the house of Queen Berengaria, sometimes of Queen Blanche, but xv. c.; the interior has a fine chimney-piece with reliefs; No. 72, Grande Rue, of xvi. c.; No. 17, Rue Dorée, a fine renaissance hotel; and remains of buildings of the xi. c. on the N. and W. of the cathedral. In the Rue Bouquet is a xv. c. statue of the Madeleine with an xviii. c. grille.

At the end of the Place des Jacobins are remains of the Gallo-Roman walls of iii. c. The three aqueducts which brought water to the Roman city are still traceable in different cellars. Nothing remains now of an amphitheatre discovered in the last century.

An excursion may be made to *Alluyes*, 6 k. from Bonneval, on the line to Tours. Here the château is a remarkable specimen of military architecture, with the Loire as a moat. There are remains of a XIII. c. chapel, retouched in XV. c.

'Les tours sont petites et rapprochées ; mais, c'est surtout le donjon, qui, par sa conservation et sa structure, mérite d'être étudié avec soin. Suivant un usage presque général, il s'élève dans un angle des remparts, sans pourtant communiquer avec ceux-ci ; et quoique tangent à l'enceinte du château, il forme une fortification distincte, et peut s'isoler au besoin. C'est une grosse tour circulaire à deux étages, terminée par une plateforme, et plus de deux fois plus haute que les remparts. Elle pouvait contribuer à leur défense, et s'ils tombaient au pouvoir de l'ennemi, soutenir encore un siège particulier.'

Prosper Merimée.

At *Bonneval* itself very little remains of its once important abbey ; but its church, a three-aisled parallelogram of XIII. c., is very interesting.

[A line runs N. to (167 k.) Caen, by—
20 k. *Montbizot.* 5 k. N.E. is *Ballon,* with picturesque ruins of a fine XV. c. castle. *S. Mars-sous-Ballon* (1 k. E.) has a fine XI. c. church. The *Château de Thouars* (2 k. N.) has a romanesque chapel. 6 k. S.E. of Ballon is the ruined *Château de Baigneux.*

30 k. *Vivoin-Beaumont.* *Vivoin* (1 k. E.) has a very fine XIII. c. church. A house, formerly a hospital, has a XII. c. portal. The little town of *Beaumont-le-Vicomte* (1 k. W.) is pleasantly situated above the Sarthe. It has small remains of a X. c. castle and an XI. c. church, and the little promenade called *La Motte à Madame.*

36 k. *Fresnay le Viscomte,* a picturesque old town upon the Sarthe. Its church of *Notre Dame,* a curious specimen of transition, has remarkable sculptured doors of XVI. c. The windows, as well as the portal, are surrounded with quaint sculpture. Above the centre of the nave rises a great tower, with a slated spire. The church is said to occupy the site of an XI. c. building, due to Bertha, the excommunicated wife of King Robert, who fixed her residence at *Montreuil le Chétif,* 6 k. S.W. of Fresnay. In this village a small XV. c. château

still preserves the name of *La Berthérie*. Common lands in this district are known as *Berthonn*, or *Grands et petits Berçons*, and are supposed to have been given by the queen to the villages which own them.

Only the gateway remains of the old *Château*, but its *Chapel*, completely subterranean, still exists at the S. extremity of the Place d'Armes, and appears to be of early XIII. c. In the town are two XIII. c. houses, and some XV. c. buildings of the old priory of *S. Léonard*.

47 k. *Bourg-le-Roi* has ruins of a castle built by William Rufus, *c.* 1100.

56 k. *Alençon*. For this town and the rest of the route see ch. iv.].

[For the route to Vendôme see p. 185, and *South-Western France*, ch. i.]

[For the line to (99 k.) Tours see *South-Western France*, ch. i.]

[For the nearest line to (50 k.) La Flèche see later.]

[A line leads to (71 k.) La Flèche by—

29 k. *Mayet*. The church of *S. Martin* is XII. c. to XVI. c. The *Château du Fort des Salles* was besieged by William Rufus. 6 k. E. are ruins of the *Château de Haute Perche*, and 5 k. S.W. of this the ruined *Château de Sarceau*. 4 k. W. is *La Lande de Rigalet*, where Du Guesclin gained a bloody victory over the English, commemorated in an obelisk called *La Croix Brette*.

38 k. *Aubigné*. The XII c. church has an apse of XVII c.

50 k. *Le Lude* (Hotel: *du Boeuf*) has a splendid château (Marquis de Talhouët), begun by Jean de Daillon, chamberlain of Louis XI., in 1457, and finished twenty years later. The buildings, of early renaissance, replace a feudal castle, and have been added to in the XVIII. c. The windows and machicolations are very richly decorated. In the interior the *Salle des Fêtes* is ornamented in the style of Louis XIII. The room in which Henri IV. and Louis XIII. slept retains its XVI. c. furniture. The N. tower has been rebuilt, and a gallery and staircase added under M. Delarue. The romanesque church of Lude has XVI. c. chapels.]

[For the line from Le Mans to (137 k.) Angers by Sablé (with the interesting excursion to Solesmes) see *South-Western France*, ch. i.]

Leaving Le Mans for Brest, we pass—

223 k. *La Milesse.* 7 k. S. is *Lavardin*, with a XIII. c. church, a ruined castle, and *Les Caves des Vierges*, excavated by Charles VII. during the siege of Mans by the English—'pour mettre les filles d'honneur en sûreté.'

232 k. *Domfront-en-Champagne*, mentioned in the *Roman Comique* of Scarron. The church is dedicated to S. Front, apostle of Maine in the VI. c.

247 k. *Sille-le-Guillaume*, with striking ruins of a castle besieged and taken by William the Conqueror at the end of the XI. c. It was taken by the Earl of Richmond in 1422, and afterwards besieged by the Earl of Arundel, when it was delivered by Gilles de Retz (le Barbe-Bleue). Falling again into the hands of the English in 1432, it was retaken by Ambroise de Loré, but, as soon as he left, again captured by Arundel. The (XV. c.) ruins have several low towers and an immense donjon, cylindrical externally and polygonal internally. Near the castle stands the formerly collegiate church of *Notre Dame*, founded by the early barons of Sille. It has a rich XIII. c. portal. On the S. is a XII. c. gable, beneath which is the entrance to the crypt. The *Hospital* occupies a convent of Minimes, founded 1623.

8 k. N. of Sille is the church (XI. c. and XVI. c.) of *Mont-S.-Jean*, containing the tomb of the Marquis de Dreux-Brezé, 1829.

[A line leads N.E. from Sille to join the line from Le Mans to Caen, at Fresnay-sur-Sarthe: see p. 194.]

[A line leads S.W. from Sille to (50 k.) Sablé, by—
26 k. *Loué*, with the curious xv. c. *Château de la Coulaine*, on the Vègre. ·
38 k. *Poillé*, near which is the handsome but dilapidated *Château de Verdelle*, of the Renaissance.]

253 k. *Rouessé-Vassé.* Vassé, in the valley of the Vègre, has a xii. c. church, founded by the family celebrated in the proverb— ·

> ' Richesse de Bouillé,
> Noblesse de Vassé.'

The château of Vassé, of which there are considerable remains, was rebuilt in 1585 by Jean Grognet, Sieur de Vassé, whose grandson obtained the marquisate of Vassé under Louis XIV.

4 k. N. is the ruined castle of *Courtalieru*, and 5 k. farther N. the *Château du Puits*.

261 k. *Voutré.* The line now skirts, to the r., the granite *Chaîne des Coëvrons*, then leaves to r. *Assé le Béranger*, which has a church and château of xi. c., and a miraculous spring, which is said to have gushed forth at the prayer of S. Thuribe. 5 k. hence is the renaissance *Château de Foulletourte*.

270 k. *Évron* (Hotel: *de l'Écu*), a picturesque town, with many old houses and xvi. c. *halles*. Tradition tells that a pilgrim from Palestine brought back with him in 648 a phial containing some drops of the milk of the Blessed Virgin. Lying down to sleep in the forest by the side of a fountain, he hung up his relic on the branch of a neighbouring thorn-bush. When he awoke the bush had grown so much that he could no longer reach the phial, and it continued growing before his eyes. He tried to cut down

the tree, but his hatchet remained fixed in the trunk. The excitement of the spectators summoned S. Hadouin, bishop of Mans, who knelt before the relic, when the tree again became a bush. Then Hadouin saw that it was the will of the Virgin to be honoured in that place. He built a church, in which he enclosed the fountain, the thorn-bush, and the relic, and founded a congregation of monks to watch over the precious deposit. Of late years the fountain, which was in the choir, has been covered up, to hinder the superstitious practices of women deprived of milk. The story of the pilgrim is represented on the glass of the choir and sculptured on the walls and woodwork of the church.

The monastery was destroyed by the Normans in the IX. c., but rebuilt in 981 by Thibault, Comte de Blois. In the existing (fortified) church nothing remains of this date. Two-thirds of the nave, the W. towers and the chapel of S. Crépin are XII. c., when they were built by Guy de Laval, one of the bravest of the companions of Richard Coeur de Lion. In the XIV. c., at the best period of gothic architecture, the choir was added by Geoffrey de Loudon. The S. façade is of exceeding richness; an immense window fills all the wall of transept on this side. In the interior four great pillars, composed of groups of columns, support the vaulting of the transept, but the arcades of the choir are of exquisite lightness. The stalls of the monks are decorated in the ionic style, and the Abbot's seat has a Virgin and Child of the XIII. c. The *Chapelle S. Crépin* is of the XII. c., and has a most picturesque portal. It consists of a nave of four bays with a pentagonal apse. Traces of its ancient colouring remain, especially in the apse, where is a Christ in benediction, with the symbols of the Evangelists.

The monastic buildings are now occupied by the Maison Mère of the Soeurs de Charité.

An excursion should be made to *S. Suzanne* (7 k. S.E.), a curious old town, most picturesquely situated, which was a Vicomté in the Middle Ages, and was only reunited to the crown under Henri IV. The town is surrounded by walls, with round towers and square bastions at intervals. In the early part of the constructions, the stones are fixed in glazed mortar. A second range—a triangle—of fortifications encloses the castle. The entrance is flanked by two towers, near which rises a donjon of the XII. c. At the hamlet of *Erves* (2 k. N.E.) are several dolmens and two entrenched enclosures known as *Les Camps des Anglais*, and probably occupied by them when S. Suzanne was besieged by the Earl of Salisbury in 1424.

4 k. S. of Évron is *Châtres*, with the ruins of the XVI. c. *Château de Montécler*, which retains its ancient drawbridge, under a square tower, pierced by loopholes, and surmounted by a dome.

[A line leads N. to Domfront by—

4 k. *Mézangers*, overlooked by the XVI. c. *Château du Roches*, with its pinnacled turrets and richly sculptured windows. It contains a beautiful renaissance gallery.

14 k. *Jublains*, on the site of Noviodunum, an ancient city of the Aulerces-Diablintes, fortified by the Romans. It was destroyed in IV. c. by the Saxons and in IX. c. by the Normans, after which it never recovered, and its inhabitants took refuge in the neighbouring towns. The foundations and size of the old town are still perceptible. To the S.W. is the vast *Castellum*, of which the walls are still 5 mèt. high and 3 mèt. thick; they are of small masonry intercepted by bands of brick and resting upon great blocks of granite. A round tower defends each of the four angles, and five other towers are disposed on the side walls. By a wide breach one enters a second inclosure, formed by an earthen rampart rounded at the angles, and defending a central fortress, flanked at the angles by four square towers. The ancient *Theatre* has been cleared out. To the N. of it are remains of *Baths*, upon part of which stands the existing church. The road which leads from the church to the theatre is the

ancient Roman road from Jublains to Angers. Beneath it is a Gallo-Roman canal. Farther N. of the theatre is the *Tonnelle*, a wooded mound. Farther still, quite at the extremity of the town, traces of a *Temple* have been found, supposed to have been dedicated to Fortune.

20 k. *Aron* has a XIV. c. round tower. Near *L'étang de Beaucoudray* is the huge block of granite called *La Chaise au Diable*, supposed to have been a Druidical altar.

25 k. *Mayenne* (Hotels: *de l'Europe; Grand Guillot*), an ancient town, much modernised of late years, occupying the slope of two hills on either side of the Mayenne. Founded by Juhel, son of Geoffroy du Maine, in XI. c., it underwent a famous siege by William the Conqueror in 1064, and was taken by the stratagem of firing the old wooden houses by burning materials thrown over the walls.

In 1424 Mayenne was besieged and taken by the English under the Earl of Salisbury. It was the native place of Ambroise de Loré, the brave defender of Maine against the English, and of Cardinal de Cheverus, first Bishop of Boston in the United States.

The church of *Notre Dame*, of peculiar and varied outline, was founded 1110. The pillars and arcades of the nave are XII. c. The choir is a beautiful specimen of transition. On the opposite side of the river the church of *S. Martin* (in the faubourg of the name) belongs to an ancient priory of the Abbey of Marmoutiers. It is a romanesque edifice, forming a Latin cross, with a tower in the centre, ambulatories around the choir, and apsidal chapel. This church possesses a chalice which belonged to Bossuet. The XIII. c. *Château* (which occupies the site of that of Geoffroy de Mayenne, surrendered on the day after the Conqueror took the town) has five towers towards the river and three towards the N., and now serves as a prison. On the *Place Cheverus* is a bronze statue (1844), by David d'Angers, of Cardinal Cheverus, who died Archbishop of Bordeaux in 1836.

5 k. N.W. is the Cistercian abbey of *Fontaine-Daniel*, founded by Juhel III. in 1204, and now a manufactory. The chapter-house, kitchens, and hall called *La Cacaudière*, are of the time of the foundation; the rest is XVII. c.

[For the line from Mayenne to Domfront see ch. iv.]

LAVAL.

[A line turns W. from Mayenne to (54 k.) Fougères (see later) by—

30 k. *Ernée*, on the river of the same name. Its château, founded by the Seigneurs de Mayenne, belonged, in XVI. c., to the house of Lorraine. Henri de Lorraine, wounded at the siege of Montauban, died there in 1654. A little later, Ernée passed into the hands of Cardinal Mazarin, and was brought by the marriage of his niece, Hortense Mancini, to the Duc de la Meilleraye. Ernée fell into the hands of the Vendéens in 1793. On the hill above the river is the XVI. c. *Château de Panard.*]

282 k. *Montsurs.* In its ruined castle, burnt by the English in 1430, was born André de Laval, Sire de Lohéac, one of the bravest companions of Jeanne Darc. 3 k. N. is the *Château de la Roche-Pichemer*, in a striking position.

289 k. *La Chapelle Anthenaise.* From many trains it is necessary to change here for—

301 k. *Laval* (Hotels: *de Paris; de l'Ouest; de France*). Capital of the Département de la Mayenne. Laval-Guyon (Vallon-Guidonis) is said to take its name from its founder, Count Guy. Of its early lords, Hamon de Laval followed the Conqueror to England in 1066, and Guy IV. became a Crusader in 1096. Emma de Laval brought the seigneury by marriage to the house of Montmorency in 1221, and her descendant Anne de Laval, in 1404, to the house of Montfort, from which it passed successively to the families of Rieux, Coligny, and La Trémouille. In the XV. c. it was bravely defended by Anne de Laval against the English, but eventually taken by Talbot in 1428, though retaken in the following year. At the beginning of the Revolution, Laval belonged to Antoine-Philippe de la Trémouille, Prince de Talmont, who afterwards became general of the Vendean cavalry.

In 1792 the Vendean army took the town, and it was twice the headquarters of La Rochejaquelein. The Prince de Talmont was seized by the royalists and executed at the age of twenty-eight before the gate of the château of Laval, which had been the home of his family for nine centuries. It was in the neighbourhood of Laval that the brothers

LAVAL.

Jean Pierre, François, and René Cottereau first organised the bands of the *Chouans*, which played such a conspicuous part in the wars of La Vendée.

A single wide street (the road from Paris to Brest) penetrates, under many names, the ancient town of Laval, which is being rapidly modernised. From the bridges there is a picturesque view of the château and the quays, extending to the church of Avesnières. The older buildings of the town occupy the S. hill, on the summit of which stands the *Church of La Trinité*, which has been a *Cathedral* since 1855. Its earlier portions (part of the transept and tower) date from the beginning of XII. c., the rest of the transept and the nave (of two square bays) having been finished by Guillaume de Passavant, Bishop of Mans in 1185. The vaulting is domical, in the Angevine manner. The three-aisled choir is XVI. c., and its vaulting has pendants. In the W. wall is a shallow apse, the principal entrance from the XII. c. having been at the E. end of the church. The N. portal, begun in 1575, was not finished till 1597, and is flanked by corinthian columns. The tomb of Guillaume Ouvroin, Bishop of Rennes, 1347, with a fine statue, is in the nave. Behind the high altar is the tomb of Bishop Louis Bougaud, 1888. Close to the cathedral is the *Porte Beucheresse*, flanked by two towers.

The Church of *S. Vénérand* (Rue Pont de Mayenne) was built by Guy XV. in the XV. c. *Notre Dame des Cordeliers* (Rue de Bretagne) was the (XIV. c. and XV. c.) chapel of a convent, founded in 1397 by Guy XII., whose wife was the widow of Bertrand du Guesclin.

The *Château* (now used as a prison), surrounded by high black walls, has a circular XII. c. donjon at its S. angle.

'La façade du château, fort irrégulière, se compose d'une suite de frontons accolés, contenant chacun deux fenêtres, l'une au-dessus de l'autre, l'inférieur appuyée sur une espèce de console. On le voit, c'est encore la disposition ordinaire des maisons du quinzième siècle, mais l'ornementation n'est plus gothique. Au lieu d'ogives, ce sont des ouvertures carrées; des pilastres, des arabesques, des moulures, dans le goût classique, remplacent les feuillages frisés, les crochets, les festons de pierre du siècle précédent. Ces arabesques, sont d'ailleurs exécutés avec une rare perfection, et leur composition est des plus gracieuses qui se puissent voir.'—*Prosper Merimée.*

The inner court has a fine renaissance façade erected by Guy XVI., governor of Brittany in 1525. The XI. c. chapel, divided by romanesque columns with heavy capitals, has been restored for the use of the prisoners. The court, donjon, and chapel are shown from 7 a.m. to 7 p.m.

At 2 k., following the Route du Changé, is (in a garden, but reached through a courtyard) the curious little church of *Price*, of early XI. c. The chains of brick introduced in its masonry indicate that it was constructed on the ruins of a chapel of Merovingian date. It contains a calendar of the XIII. c., and two tombs of the same date.

On the other side of Laval, following the quay on r., beyond the bridge, is the church of *Notre Dame d'Avenières*, said to have been built by Guy V. de Laval in fulfilment of a vow in 1140, when his horse fell into the river in crossing the old bridge, and he was nearly drowned. The ambulatory and the five chapels of the choir, with the walls of the transept and nave, belong to the primitive construction; most of the upper vaults are of late XII. c , and a great part of the two first bays of the nave and the tower are early renaissance. The rich stone spire is of 1534. Great numbers of pilgrims resort hither to invoke a much venerated image of the Virgin, said to have been found by Guy in an old oak.

[A line leads from Laval to (40 k.) Angers, or (166 k.) Nantes, by—

22 k. *Meslay*. 13 k. E. is *Saulges*, where the church contains a XV. c. bas-relief of Christ on the Cross between SS. Julien and John Baptist. Near it is a *Chapelle de S. Cénéré*. Another oratory, *Le Chapiteau de S. Cénéré*, stands near a fountain, which he is said to have caused miraculously to gush forth. It owes its name to a dome resembling an immense capital. 1 k. from Saulges, in the valley of the Erve, is the labyrinthine cavern

of *Margot*, where a vast number of ancient flint weapons has been found.

40 k. Château Gontier. See ch. vii.]

Passing a viaduct, the line leaves to the l. *S. Berthevin*, with a picturesque rocky valley containing the natural *Chaire de S. Berthevin*, where that early missionary is said to have preached.

310 k. *Le Genest.*

Turning l. from the station, and following the line W. for some distance, we reach (2½ k.) the road from Ollivet to Loiron. Following this l. for a short distance, and then turning r, we reach (4 k.) the famous *Abbey of Clermont*, now the property of M. Lonain de S. Martin, who allows it to be visited on application. The monastery was founded in 1150 by Guy V. de Laval, for monks of Citeaux, and was greatly enriched, in 1230, by Emma de Laval, widow of Mathieu de Montmorency. The XII. c. church, of Cistercian simplicity, has a triple nave, square chapels at the transept, and a choir without aisles or apse. The upper windows, vaulting, and spire, are additions of the XVII. c., at which time a great part of the S. aisle was destroyed. On the l. of the choir is the noble tomb of Béatrix de Bretagne, 1401, adorned with six statues of apostles, and on the r. that of Guy XII. or Guy XIII., also ornamented with statuettes. In the chapels of the N. transept are the tomb of Roberte de Montjean and the gravestone of a XVI. c. abbot. At the N. angle of the choir and transept an inscription commemorates an altar erected there by Guy de Montjean in 1417. The cloister and most of the monastic buildings only date from XVII. c. or XVIII. c.; the abbot's house is XV. c.

318 k. *Port Brillet.* The abbey of Clermont is only 3½ k. distant.

5 k. r. is *S. Ouen des Toits*, with the *Closerie des Poiriers*, the parental home of the brothers Cottereau, organisers of the 'Chouannerie.' Of these, Jean Chouan fell in the neighbouring *Bois de Misedon* (a great royalist refuge), July 28, 1794; Pierre

died on the scaffold at Laval; François died of his wounds in the wood of Misedon, and Réné alone survived, to receive—at the Restoration—the trifling annual pension of 400 frs., insufficient for the support—at the Closerie des Poiriers—of his seventeen children, mostly born in the caves of the Bois de Misedon. The mother of this brave family of royalists was run over by a waggon in the flight from Mans, and their two sisters were guillotined at Laval. The little renaissance *Château* of S. Ouen is attributed to Anne of Brittany.

336 k. *Vitré* (Hotels: *des Voyageurs*—close to the station, good, clean and comfortable; *de France*). The town has been greatly injured of late years by the wanton destruction of its ancient gateways and ramparts, its principal ornaments; still it is a picturesque and interesting place. Vitré was an ancient barony, and was brought to the house of Laval by the marriage of its heiress, Philippette, with Guy IX. in 1295, passing afterwards with Laval to the families of Rieux, Coligny, and La Trémouille, the last of whom held it till the Revolution. By the Rieux and Coligny, Protestantism was introduced into Vitré, which became a great Huguenot centre in the XVI. c. and XVII. c. The states of Brittany, alternately presided over by the Barons de Vitré and Barons de Léon, frequently held their meetings at Vitré.

The streets, which abound in curious old houses, cluster round the church of *Notre Dame*, formerly a priory of the Abbey of S. Melaine at Rennes (XV. c. and XVI. c.), with a portal of 1578. The church was built in the decadence of gothic art, but against one of the buttresses on the r. is a beautiful XVI. c. external pulpit, supposed to have been made for the use of a public disputant with the Calvinist preachers. In the first chapel l. of nave is the tomb of Pierre Hubert, 1498. In the chapel of the Virgin is that of Marie de Retz, wife of André de Laval, Maréchal of France, 1457, and a curious enamelled triptych with thirty-two beautiful little pictures and a rhyming inscription saying that it was given by Jean Bricier, 1544.

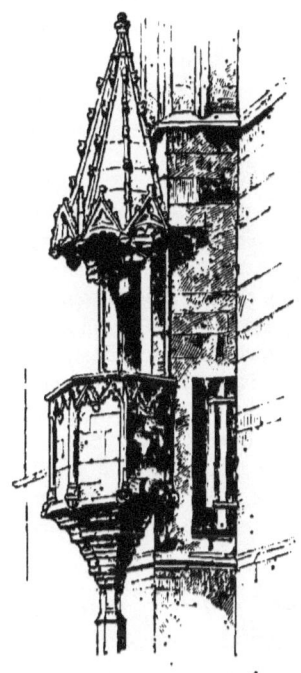

OUTSIDE PULPIT, VITRÉ.

The (rebuilt) church of *S. Croix* (in the faubourg of the name) belonged to an ancient priory of the Abbey of Marmoutiers, founded 1076 by Robert de Vitré. The xv. c. chapel of *Hôpital S. Nicolas* contains the tomb of Robert de Grasmenil, Canon of the Madeleine, 1500.

The *Château* (which can only be seen by permission) was founded at the end of xi. c., but rebuilt in xiv. c. and xv. c., at the best period of Breton military architecture. Its portal, flanked by machicolated towers, and overlooked by tourelles with conical roofs, is known as *Les Chatelets*. It is united by lofty curtain walls to a series of embattled towers, of which the principal are the Donjon (l.), the tours d'Argenterie, Plombée, de la Madeleine, and S. Lazare. The interior, used as a prison, has recently been so mutilated as to have lost almost all interest, except in a single detail.

'Du seizième siècle date une charmante construction, dont la destination n'est pas bien connue, isolée maintenant entre des ruines du moyen-âge et une prison moderne. C'est une espèce de tourelle ou de tribune ronde, finissant en console avec un petit dôme au-dessus, et percée de fenêtres dont les chambranles sont malheureusement très détériorés. On ne peut sans l'avoir vue se faire une idée de la richesse de son ornementation. L'élégance des motifs, l'habileté de l'exécution ne laissent rien à désirer. Autour de la console on lit ces mots : "Post tenebras spero lucem." A l'époque de cette construction, la famille de la Trémouille appartenait sans doute à la religion réformée, et cette devise a pu faire croire que la tribune a servi de chaire à prêcher.'—*Prosper Mérimée.*

No. 7, *Rue Notre Dame,* is an interesting renaissance house, with an admirable wooden staircase in its court. *No.* 40, *Rue Poterie,* has a fine renaissance chimneypiece.

6 k. S., reached by a pretty drive through woods, is the xv. c. *Château des Rochers,* which remains externally much the same as when it was inhabited by Mme de Sévigné. It came to the family in 1410, by the marriage of Anne de Mathefelon, Dame des Rochers, with Guillaume de Sévigné, Chamberlain of Jean V., Duc de Bretagne. After the death of Pauline de Grignan, Madame de Simiane, granddaughter and last descendant of Mme de Sevigné,

Les Rochers was sold (1714) to the family of Netumières, who have ever since inhabited it. The chief objects of interest are shown with great kindness and liberality.

The position is beautiful, overlooking a wide country view. From the road a sudden turn to the l. leads to a little lawn, on one side of which are the residential buildings of the château, on the other the stables and farm. The former are still exceedingly picturesque, with a high central tower and girouettes, though somewhat spoilt by plaster. From the latter comes the

LES ROCHERS.

concierge with her keys, and takes visitors first to the domed chapel, a detached building, retaining all the old fittings of Mme de Sévigné's time, with the arm-chairs used by herself and her guests. Over the altar is a picture of the Annunciation (Carlo Maratta?) which she mentions in one of her letters. Through the delightful garden, which retains the clipped lime avenues planted by Mme de Sévigné, and which is fragrant in summer from the blossoms of thirty magnificent orange trees, also of her time, visitors are taken to her chamber—a most attractive room, where she wrote, with her glass door opening on the garden terrace. The yellow satin coverlet and chairs are exquisitely worked by Mme de Grignan. A full-length portrait in the room, by *Mignard*, represents Mme de Sévigné in her youth. Other portraits of her daughter, granddaughter, etc., are probably copies. The little candlesticks and toilet service are those used by Mme de Sévigné.

This room alone is unaltered from the Sévigné time. The rest of the house is not shown. All relics of the former owners are treated with the greatest care by the present owners, who have collected portraits of the husband of the authoress, Henri de Sévigné; their son, Charles de Sévigné, celebrated for his intrigues with Ninon de l'Enclos; their daughter, Françoise Marguerite de Sévigné, Comtesse de Grignan; the Baron de Rabutin-Chantal, husband of Marie de Coulanges and father of Mme de Sévigné; Christophe de la Tour de Coulanges, Abbé de Livry—'le bien bon'—uncle of Mme de Sévigné; Mme de Coulanges; the Marquise de Lambert, widow of the Marquis de Locmaria, who danced the famous passe-pieds so admired by Mme de Sévigné; and Charles Albert d'Ailly, Duc de Chaulnes, governor of Brittany in 1670.

'Aux Rochers, 18 *Sept.*, 1689.—Voulez-vous savoir notre vie, ma chère enfant?—la voici : nous nous levons à huit heures, la messe à neuf; le temps fait qu'on se promène, ou qu'on ne se promène pas, souvent chacun de son côté; on dîne fort bien; il vient un voisin, on parle de nouvelles ; nous travaillons l'après-dînée, ma belle-fille à cent sortes des choses, moi à deux bandes de tapisserie ; à cinq heures on se sépare, on se promène, ou seule, ou en compagnie, on se rencontre à une place fort belle, on a un livre, ou prie-Dieu, on rêve à sa chère fille, on fait des châteaux en Espagne, en Provence, tantôt gais, tantôt tristes. Mon fils nous lit des livres très-agréables et fort bons ; nous en avons de dévotion, les autres d'histoire ; cela nous amuse et nous occupe; nous raisonnons sur ce que nous avons lu : mon fils est indefatigable; il lit cinq heures de suite, si l'on veut. Recevoir des lettres, y faire réponse, tient une grande place dans notre vie, principalement pour moi. Nous avons eu du monde, nous en aurons encore, nous n'en souhaitons point ; quand il y en a, on est bien aise. Mon fils a des ouvriers, il a fait *parer*, comme on dit ici, ses grandes allées ; vraiment elles sont belles ; il fait sabler son parterre. Enfin, ma fille, c'est une chose étrange comme avec cette vie toute insipide et quasi triste, les jours courent et nous échappent ; et Dieu sait ce qui nous échappe en même temps ; ah ! *ne parlons pas de cela* ; j'y pense pourtant, et il le faut. Nous soupons à huit heures ; Sévigné lit après souper, mais des livres gais, de peur de dormir ; ils s'en vont à dix heures ; je ne me couche guère que vers minuit ; voilà quelle est à peu près la règle de notre couvent ; il y a sur la porte, *sainte liberté*, ou *fait ce que tu voudras*.'

Much mutilated now is the park which Mme de Sévigné was so proud of making, and most of her trees have disappeared.

'Pour nous, ce sont des châtaignes qui sont notre ornement ; j'en avois l'autre jour trois ou quatre paniers autour de moi ; j'en fis bouillir, j'en fis rôtir, j'en mis dans ma poche ; on en sert dans le plat, on marche dessus ; c'est la Bretagne dans son triomphe.'—*Mme de Sévigné*, 1671.

4 k. S. of Les Rochers is *Argentré*, with the old XV. c. manor called *Le Château du Plessis*, which was the abode of the Demoiselle du Plessis, often mentioned by Mme de Sévigné. E. of Argentré, in the forest of *Pertre*, are druidic remains.

[A line runs N.W. from Vitré to (79 k.) Pontorson, passing—

19 k. *Châtillon en Vendelais*. The line runs between a large lake in a wooded flat, and a hill crowned with remains of a XIV. c. castle demolished by Richelieu.

25 k. *Dompierre du Chemin*. Visible from the railway on r. is a gorge, watered by the Cantache, between two rocks—*Les Rochers du Saut Roland*. Legend tells that the Paladin Roland, mounted upon his charger, three times leapt from one to the other ; the first time invoking the name of God, the second time that of the Virgin, but the third time that of the lady of his earthly love,—and then the horse slipped upon the rock on

which he landed, and which ever since bears the impress of his hoofs, and horse and rider were precipitated into the abyss.

3¾ k. *Fougères* (Hotels: *des Voyageurs*—best; *S. Jacques*, with an old courtyard surrounded by galleries—very indifferent). Those who only approach from Vitré and see it from the station have no idea of the peculiarities of this very singular place, and its striking position. But it is not worth staying at except between two trains.

From the station a straight road ascends to a square with an equestrian statue of the Comte de Lariboisière by Recipon. Close by is the xv. c. and xvi. c. church of *S. Léonard*, and behind this an attractive little public garden, with views over the plains on one side and into the gorge with the château on the other. The description of Balzac would lead one to expect far too much, yet is worth reading on the spot.

'Pour donner une idée de l'aspect que présente le rocher de Fougères vu de la Promenade, on peut le comparer à l'une de ces immense tours en dehors desquelles les architectes sarrasins ont fait tourner d'étage en étage de larges balcons joint entre eux par des escaliers en spirale. En effet, cette roche est terminée par une église gothique dont les petites flèches, le clocher, les arcs-boutants en rendent presque parfaite sa forme de pain de sucre. Devant le porte de cette église, dediće à S. Léonard, se trouve une petite place irrégulière dont les terres sont soutenues par un mur exhaussé en forme de balustrade, et qui communique par une rampe à la Promenade. Semblable à une seconde corniche, cette esplanade se développe circulairement autour du rocher, à quelques toises en dessous de la place S. Léonard, et offre un large terrain planté d'arbres, qui vient aboutir aux fortifications de la ville. Puis, à dix toises des murailles et des roches qui supportent cette terrasse, due à une heureuse disposition des schistes et à une patiente industrie, il existe un chemin tournant nommé *l'escalier de la Reine*, pratiqué dans le roc, et qui conduit à un pont bâti sur le Nançon par Anne de Bretagne. Enfin, sous ce chemin, qui figure une troisième corniche, des jardins descendent de terrasse en terrasse jusqu'à la rivière, et ressemblent à des gradins chargés de lierre.

' Parallèlement à la Promenade, de hautes roches, qui prennent le nom du faubourg de la ville où elles s'élèvent, et qu'on appelle les montagnes de S. Sulpice, s'étendent le long de la rivière et s'abaissent en pentes douces dans la grande vallée où elles décrivent un brusque contour vers le nord. Ces roches droites, incultes et sombres, semblent toucher aux schistes de la Promenade ; en quelques endroits, elles en sont à une portée de fusil, et garantissent contre les vents du nord une étroite vallée, profonde de cent toises, où le Nançon se partage en trois bras qui arrosent une prairie chargée de fabriques et délicieusement plantée.

' Vers le sud, à l'endroit où finit la ville proprement dite, et où commence le faubourg S. Léonard, le rocher de Fougères fait un pli, s'adoucit, diminue de hauteur, et tourne dans la grande vallée en suivant la rivière, qu'il serre ainsi contre les montagnes de S. Sulpice, en formant un col d'où elle échappe en deux ruisseaux vers la Couësnon, où elle va se jeter. Ce joli groupe de collines rocailleuses est appelé le *Nid-aux-Crocs*, la vallée qu'elles dessinent se nom le val *de Gibarry*, et ses grasses prairies fournissent une grande partie du beurre connu des gourmets sous le nom de beurre de la Prée-Valaye.

' À l'endroit où la Promenade aboutit aux fortifications s'élève une tour nommée *la tour du Papegaut*. À partir de cette construction carrée, règne tantôt une muraille, tantôt le roc quand il offre des tables droites ; et la partie de la ville assise sur cette haute base inexpugnable décrit une vaste demi-lune, au bout de laquelle les roches s'inclinent et se creusent pour laisser passage au Nançon. Là est située la porte qui mène au faubourg de S. Sulpice, dont le nom est commun à la porte et au faubourg. Puis, sur un mamelon de granit qui domine trois vallons dans lesquelles se réunissent plusieurs routes, surgissent les vieux créneaux et les tours féodales du château de Fougères, l'une des plus immenses constructions faites par les ducs de Bretagne, murailles hautes de quinze toises, épaisses de quinze pieds ; fortifiée à l'est par un étang d'où sort le Nançon, qui coule dans ses fossés et fait tourner des moulins entre la porte S. Sulpice et les ponts-levis de la forteresse ; défendue à l'ouest par la raideur des blocs de granit sur lesquels elle repose.

' Ainsi, depuis la Promenade jusqu'à ce magnifique débris

du moyen-âge, enveloppé de ses manteaux de lierre, paré de ses tours carrées ou rondes, où peut loger dans chacune un régiment entier, le château, la ville et son rocher, protegés par des murailles à pans droits, ou par des escarpements taillés à pic, forment un vaste fer à cheval garni de précipices sur lesquels, à l'aide du temps, les Bretons ont tracé quelques étroits sentiers. Çà et là, des blocs s'avancent comme des ornements. Ici les eaux suintent par des cassures d'où sortent des arbres rachitiques. Plus loin, quelques tables de granit, moins droites que les autres, nourrissent de la verdure qui attire les chèvres. Puis, partout des bruyères, venues entre plusieurs fentes humides, tapissent de leurs guirlandes roses de noires anfractuosités. Au fond de cet immense entonnoir, la petite rivière serpente dans une prairie toujours fraîche et mollement posée comme un tapis.

'Au pied du château, et entre plusieurs masses de granit, s'élève l'église dediée à S. Sulpice, qui donne son nom à un faubourg situé par delà le Nançon. Le faubourg, comme jeté au fond d'un abîme, et son église dont le clocher pointu n'arrive pas à la hauteur des roches qui semblent près de tomber sur elle et sur les chaumières qui l'entourent, sont pittoresquement baignés par quelques affluents du Nançon, ombragée par des arbres et décorés par des jardins; ils coupent irrégulièrement la demi-lune que décrivent la Promenade, la ville, et le château, et produisent, par leurs détails, de naïves oppositions avec les graves spectacles de l'amphithéâtre, auquel ils font face. Enfin Fougères tout entier, ses faubourgs et ses églises, les montagnes même de S. Sulpice, sont encadrés par les hauteurs de Rillé, qui font partie de l'enceinte générale de la grande vallée de Couësnon.'—'*Les Chouans.*'

All the interest of Fougères is on the side towards the ravine. The castle, with its thirteen towers—Coigny, Cadran, Surienne, Guibé, Mélusine, Gobelin, etc.—has many interesting points. The donjon was demolished in 1630. Below it, a very picturesque gateway—*Porte S. Sulpice*—crosses the road near the xv. c. church of *S. Sulpice*, which contains the old statue of Notre Dame des Marais, said to have been dug up in a marsh when the Seigneur de Fougères was laying the foundation of the town. Many houses in the town are pierced by porticoes, admitting the footway, and girt by heavy pillars.

LA GUERCHE.   215

In the forest of Fougères are the dolmen called *La Pierre du Trésor*, and some remains of a convent of Cordeliers.

[A line leads N.E. to (49 k.) Mortain, passing, at 20 k., *Louvigné du Désert*, 1 k. from which is the *Château de Monthorin*, of the time of Louis XIII. In the chapel are preserved the hearts of General de Lariboisière (1812) and his son, killed in the battle of the Moskowa. The tombs of Raoul II. de Fougères (1194) from the Abbey of Savigny, and of Françoise de Foix from the Trinitarians of Châteaubriant, are preserved here.]

68 k. *Antrain* (*inter amnes*) between the Coësnon and the Oysance. The church is transition. 5 k. N.E. is the modern *Château de la Rouerie*, a place which gave a name to Armand Tuffin de la Rouerie, the famous Breton chief of 1792.

[A line runs S. from Vitré to (56 k.) Châteaubriant by—

25 k. *La Guerche* ('guerc'h' is Breton for virgin) built round a castle and chapel of the Virgin, founded x. c. Bertrand and Olivier du Guesclin were its seigneurs in the XIV. c. The château was demolished in 1739. The ancient collegiate church, founded 1206, has an apse of XIII. c., and contains good renaissance stall-work. At 11 k. is the ruined castle of *Marcillé-Robert*, and, at 17 k., *Essé*, where, near the farm of *Rouvrai*, is the curious *Allée Couverte*, called *La Roche aux Fées*, consisting of forty-two blocks of stone, 2 mèt. high, and the whole 22 mèt. in length.

5 k. off the line is *Arbrissel*, the native place of Robert d'Arbrissel, who founded the abbey of Fontevrault.

For Châteaubriant and the rest of the line see *South-Western France*.]

346 k. *Les Lacs*. To l. is *S. Didïer*, where the saint lived in the woods as a hermit at a spot which is still a great point of pilgrimage.

363 k. *Noyal Acigné*.

8 k. S. is *Châteaugiron*, with a ruined castle above the Yaine, which was taken (June 24, 1592) by the Duc de Mercoeur, who hung its defender, Jean Menager, with all the garrison, opposite its great tower, on a tree which thenceforth bore the name of *Le Chêne des Pendus*.

374 k. *Rennes* (Hotels: *Grande*, joining the cathedral; *de France*—clean, otherwise very indifferent), the ancient capital of Brittany, now the capital of the Département d'Ille et Vilaine. The name Rennes (as well as Fougères) means 'fern.' The town was, in great measure, rebuilt after a fire which lasted seven days in 1720; but the *ville basse* retains something of ancient character, though no picturesqueness. The original name of Rennes was Condate, a Gaulish word signifying 'confluent,' expressing its position at the confluence of the Ille and Vilaine. It was the capital of the Redones or Riedones. Numerous relics discovered attest the importance of the town in Roman times. Geoffroy, Comte de Rennes, was the first who assumed the title of Duke of Brittany. His heiress, Constance, married (1182) Geoffrey Plantagenet, one of the sons of Henry II. of England, who convoked the first parliament at Rennes. When his son, Arthur, Duke of Brittany, was murdered by his uncle King John (1203), his sister, Alix, brought Brittany by marriage to Pierre de Dreux, great-grandson of Louis le Gros of France, from whom all the dukes of Brittany descended, till the double marriage of the Duchess Anne with Charles VIII. and afterwards with Louis XII. Each duke came to Rennes to take his oath to the clergy, nobles, and people of Brittany, and to be crowned with the ducal circlet in the cathedral, till the coronation here in 1532 of Francis, Dauphin of France, eldest son of Francis I.

The ancient capital of Brittany has now the distinction of being the dullest, as it is almost the ugliest, town in France. Its wide, featureless streets not only contain no object of interest, but are the climax of monotonous stagnation. There is never any life or movement in Rennes, and there is nothing whatever worth seeing.

The first church in the city of the Redones is said to have been originally a temple of Thetis, which the missionary S. Maximin consecrated under the name of Notre Dame de la Cité. In the IV. c. the Bishop, S. Lunaire transferred it to the present site, where it has since been frequently rebuilt. The present *Cathedral of S. Pierre* (1787—1844) is an Ionic building, much gilt within. The last chapel on the r. has a curious retable. Five bishops of Rennes have been canonised—Melaine (530, first bishop, buried here), Riotisme, Didier (VI. c. or VII. c.), Moderan (730), and Amand. Opposite the W. façade of the cathedral an alley leads to a court whence the ancient *Porte Mordelaise* may be seen imbedded in houses. This was the gate by which the dukes of Brittany made their triumphal entry. Here also every newly-appointed bishop was met by the Baron de Vitré, who held his stirrup as he descended from his horse, and received the horse itself with its equipments as the price of this service. The bishop was borne thence to the cathedral in a chair carried by the seigneurs of Vitré, Aubigné, Châteaugiron, and Guerche, who were permitted, as a reward, to divide all the plate used at the installation banquet. Built into the Porte Mordelaise is a fragment of a Roman inscription referring to the Emperor Gordian III., 238.

The only romanesque bit of architecture in Rennes is a XII. c. porch in the dull church of *S. Melaine*, belonging to a monastery founded VI. c.

The animation which commerce imparts is almost unknown in the capital of Brittany.

'The Breton adheres to his old notion of riches: he makes money if he can, but by close parsimony; he hoards, but he does not invest. The natives are still too poetical for the joys of business. In this, as in many other things, Brittany is a specimen of the Old World; it is still in its poetical phase.'—*Dean Church.*

3 k. S.W. of the town (following the Vilaine from the Pont de Salle-Verte) is the *Château de la Prévalaye,* where Henri IV. slept in 1598. It is of little interest. A tourist may return to Rennes by the farm of *S. Foix,* where an oak is shown as that beneath which the king danced with the peasant beauties of the district. Prévalaye gives its name to the excellent butter of L'Ille-et-Vilaine.

[For the line N. from Rennes to Dol and S. Malo see ch. vi.]

[A road leads N.W. from Rennes to (52 k.) Dinan by (24 k.) *Hédé,* which has a XII. c. church and a ruined castle, which was besieged by Henry II. of England in 1168.

Another road leads to (54 k.) Dinan by—

26 k. (1 k. r. of the road) *Iffs,* which has a beautiful cruciform XV. c. church, with nine stained windows of exceptional merit. 1 k. N. of the church is the *Château de Montmuran.* The original castle, built by Donoal, Sire de Tinténiac in 1036, was destroyed by Henry II. in 1168. The descendants of the house of Tinténiac rebuilt the château, and Du Guesclin was knighted in its chapel, where also he was married to Jeanne de Laval, granddaughter of the Dame de Montmuran, whose château he had defended. Only two towers of the old castle remain, united by modern buildings; the chapel has been rebuilt.

32 k. *Bécherel* retains a XVI. c. gateway of its ancient fortifications. 1 k. W. is the *Château de Caradeuc,* made a marquisate for the procurator-general La Chalotais in 1776. It now belongs to his great-granddaughter, who has married the Comte de Falloux.]

[A road leads N.E. to (48 k.) Fougères by—

28 k. *S. Aubin-du-Cormier,* with ruins of a castle built by Pierre de Dreux, Duke of Brittany, in 1223, to defend his duchy on the side of Normandy and Maine. The château was taken by the French in 1487. In the following year the battle which

gave a first blow to the independence of Brittany was fought close by, at the spot called *La Rencontre*. The prisoners, who included the Prince of Orange and the Duke of Orleans, afterwards Louis XII., were taken to S. Aubin, where a cellar is shown (in the Hôtel du Commerce) as having been the prison of the future King of France.

13 k. from S. Aubin is the renaissance *Château de Bouessay*.]

[A line leads S.E. from Rennes to (61 k.) Châteaubriant by—

10 k. *Vern*. 5 k. W. is *Noyal-sur-Seiche*, where the cemetery has a fine gothic cross. 6 k. is *Chatillon-sur-Seiche*, where the crypt of the church contains the miraculous chain of S. Léonard, with which the sick are touched, and which, with a statue of the saint, attracts a great number of pilgrims.

13 k. *S. Armel*. The tomb of the saint is shown in the church, and on the banks of the Seiche his hermitage, and a spring which he called forth by sticking his staff into the ground.

17 k. *Corps-Nuds*. The xv. c. church has a more ancient chapel, *des Trois Maries*—a place of pilgrimage. The *Château de Châtelier* (2 k. S.), burnt during the Ligue, was rebuilt in 1632.]

[A line leads S.W. from Rennes to (152 k.) Nantes, across Brittany. After the rich vegetation of Normandy the country often appears bare and cold. Women work everywhere in the fields. The Breton story goes, that a husband, returning soaked, found his wife comfortably seated by the fire. 'As you are wet through,' she said, 'you cannot be wetter, so fetch me two buckets of water from the well.' The husband went obediently, but returning with the first bucket and finding his wife in the same place, poured the water over her, saying, 'Now you are as wet as I am, so you may fetch your other bucketful for yourself, for you cannot be wetter.' We pass—

10 k. *Bruz*. 2 k. W. is the handsome xviii. c. *Château de Blossac*.

21 k. *Guichen-Bourg des Comptes*. 9 k. S.W. is *Guignen*, which has a very fine romanesque church, chiefly xii. c., containing the striking tomb of Jean de S. Amadour, Viscomte de Guignen, 1538, knighted by Charles VIII. at the battle of Fornoue, and

who served four kings of France and fought in thirteen battles. Under the choir is a curious crypt, half filled with water.

37 k. *Messac.* The country is full of megalithic remains, especially (18 k. S.) at *Cojous,* near *S. Juste.*

48 k. *Fougeray-Langon.* The church of *Langon* has two romanesque apsides. Overshadowed by a great yew-tree is the curious *Chapelle S. Agathe,* a great point of pilgrimage, and regarded as having been once a temple of Venus.

'La chapelle de Langon, construite en petit appareil, dont les pièces présentent des cubes de 9 à 11 centimètres de haut et de large, incrustés dans un mortier fort épais. Des assises horizontales de briques, séparées elles-mêmes par du ciment, règnent à differentes hauteurs, dans l'élévation du mur.

'Les restes des murs anciens s'étendent sur chaque face latérale, depuis l'extrémité ouest dans une longueur d'environ 5 mètres et dans la plus grande partie de la façade occidentale.

'L'abside conserve des traces de l'appareil primitif; sur la voûte en cul-de-four de cette abside, un enduit assez épais a été décoré de peintures, aujourd'hui très détériorés, mais qui doivent être fort anciennes.'—*De Caumont.*

52 k. *Beslé.* Opposite the station, on the r. bank of the Vilaine, is the village of *Brain,* near which, at the hamlet of *Placet,* was born S. Melaine, bishop of Rennes in VI. c., who is commemorated by a chapel and statue.

71 k. Redon. For this and the rest of the route see *South-Western France.*]

386 k. *L'Hermitage-Mordelles. L'Hermitage* takes its name from the oratory and fountain of S. Avit, abbot of Mercy in VI. c. The tradition that he enabled a dumb child to speak here, causes sick children to be brought here every Whit-Monday in great numbers. The church, partly romanesque, has tombstones of the Seigneurs Du Boberil, whose moated château still remains in the neighbourhood.

396 k. *Montfort-sur-Meu.* This town was founded in

XI. c. by Raoul, Sire de Gaël, who took the name of Montfort, preserved by his descendants, and who accompanied William the Conqueror to England. Some years later he conspired to dethrone William, and nearly succeeded, but was outwitted. Afterwards, joining the Crusades in 1096, he died at the siege of Nicea. After the marriage of Guy XIV., Comte de Laval and Sire de Montfort, with Françoise de Dinan, Dame de Chateaubriant, the family abandoned their residence here for Laval, Vitré, and Chateaubriant. Montfort passed, with the rest of the property of the house of Laval, to the successive families of Rieux, Coligny, and La Trémouille, and under François de Coligny became a Huguenot centre, though in 1417 it had been celebrated for the preachings of S. Vincent Ferrer. The church of *S. Jean Baptiste* has reliefs representing the miracle which long gave the place the name of *Montfort la Cane*, and which dates from the XIV. c.

'Certain seigneur avait renfermé une jeune fille d'une grande beauté dans son château de Montfort. A travers une lucarne, elle apercevait l'église de S. Nicolas; elle pria le saint avec des yeux pleines de larmes, et elle fut miraculeusement transportée hors du château. Mais elle tomba entre les mains des serviteurs du félon, qui voulurent en user comme ils supposaient que l'avait fait leur maître. La pauvre fille éperdue, regardant de tous cotés pour chercher du secours, n'aperçut que des canes sauvages sur l'étang du château.

'Renouvelant sa prière à S. Nicolas, elle le supplia de permettre à ces animaux d'être temoins de son innocence, afin que, si elle devait perdre la vie sans pouvoir accomplir son voeu à S. Nicolas, les oiseaux le remplissent eux-mêmes à leur façon, en son nom et pour sa personne. Par la permission divine, elle échappa des mains des soldats sans aucune offense, mais elle mourut dans l'année. Or, voici qu'à la fête de la translation des reliques de S. Nicolas, le 9 de mai, une cane sauvage, accompagnée de ses petits cannetons, vint à l'église de S. Nicolas. Elle y entra et voltigea devant l'image du bienheureux libérateur, pour l'applaudir par le battement de ses ailes ; après quoi elle retourna à l'étang, ayant laissé un de ses petits en offrande. Quelque temps après, le canneton s'en retourna sans qu'on s'en aperçut.

' Pendant 300 ans et plus, la cane, toujours la même cane, est revenue à jour fixe, avec sa couvée, dans l'église du grand S. Nicolas de Montfort, sans qu'on put jamais savoir ce qu'elle devenait la reste de l'année.'—*Châteaubriand,* ' *Mémoires d'outre Tombe.*'

Only the W. façade remains (S.E. of the town) of the ancient *Abbey of S. Jacques*, founded by Raoul II. de Montfort in 1152. The *Hospital of S. Lazare* (2 k. S.), established for crusaders who brought back leprosy from the East, is now a farm ; but the chapel exists, and contains a curious XIV. c. tomb.

S.W., on the edge of the forest of Coulon, is the overthrown menhir called *Grès de S. Méen,* overshadowed by a great beech.

406 k. *Montauban*. 1½ k. N. of the town is its ruined (XIV. c.) castle, a quadrangular building with towers at the angles.

411 k. *La Brohinière.*

[A line runs S. to (79 k.) Questembert (on the main line between Redon and Vannes) by—

7 k. *S. Méen*, once famous for its abbey (founded in 600 by S. Méen), on a site now occupied by a seminary. The church contains the XIII. c. tomb of S. Méen, a famous Breton saint and abbot, who died in 617, and that (XV. c.) of Abbot Robert de Coëtlogon. An earlier tomb of S. Méen—a granite trough—is seen outside the church.

14 k. *Mauron* has several renaissance houses. 2 k. E. is the church of *S. Lery*, with the XV. c. tomb of the saint, an abbot of the VII. c., and sculptures representing his death and the transla-

tion of his relics. The tomb is inscribed 'Là fut mis le corps de Monsieur S. Léry.'

21 k. *Néant.* The church contains the tomb of the Bienheureuse Anne Toussainte de Volvire, 1694. 4 k. N. are the ruins of the castle of *Bois-de-la-Roche.*

42 k. *Ploërmel*[1] (Hotel: *de France*). Derives its name (Plou-Armel) from the hermit S. Armel, who lived there in the VI. c. The church of *S. Armel*, rebuilt 1511—1602, with a tower of 1740, has beautiful flamboyant windows, and the side-façade is of great richness. Of its numerous external sculptures, many are from sacred history; but many are comic, such as the sow playing the bagpipes, the wife pulling off her husband's nightcap, a barber sewing up his scold-wife's mouth, etc. The stained glass in the church (1533—1602) is magnificent. It also contains the recumbent marble statues of Dukes Jean II., 1305, and Jean III., 1341, brought from the Carmelite church, which was destroyed in 1793. The granite statues of Philippe de Montauban, Sieur du Bois de la Roche, and chancellor of Anne of Brittany, 1514, and his wife Anne de Chastellier, and those of a Seigneur and Dame du Crévy, still remain in the cloister of the monastery. The three gates of the town have been destroyed, but part of the machicolated walls remains. 2 k. l. is the *Château de Malville,* where the chapel has good stained windows of 1520. A number of dolmens and menhirs may be seen in the neighbourhood. It is this district which is especially connected with the story of Merlin.

'La forêt de Brocelinde, et de Paimpoul ou de Brécilien, se trouve située dans le commune de Concoret, arrondissement de Ploërmel ; elle est célébré dans les romans de la table ronde. C'est là que l'on rencontre la *fontaine de Baranton, le Val sans retour, la tombe de Merlin.* On sait que ce magicien se trouve encore dans cette forêt, où il est retenu par les enchantements de Viviane à l'ombre d'un bois d'aubépine. Viviane avait essayé

---

[1] 'The people of S. Armel.' The origin of Breton names is very simple, beginning in general by such radicals as: *aber* (harbour—Aber Ildut); *conc* (port—Concarneau); *car, caër, ker* (fortress, manor—Carhaix); *coat, coët* (wood—Coëtlogon); *lan* (consecrated land—Landerneau); *loc* (hermitage—Locmariaker); *les* (court, jurisdiction—Lesneven); *mené* (mount—Mené-Hom); *mor* (sea—Morlaix); *pen* (head—Penmarc'h); *plé, plo, pleu, plou* (people, tribe —Ploërmel); *ros* (hillside—Rostrenen).

sur Merlin le charme qu'elle avait appris de lui-même, sans croire qu'il pût opérer ; elle se desespéra quand elle vit qui celui qu'elle adorait était à jamais perdu pour elle. On assure que Messire Gauvain et quelques chevaliers de la table ronde cherchèrent partout Merlin, mais en vain. Gauvain seul l'entendit dans le forêt de Brocelinde, mais ne put le voir.'—*E. Souvestre,* '*Les Derniers Bretons.*'

It is 11 k. (omnibus from station 1 fr. 50 c.) from Ploërmel to Josselin. We pass the lake called *L'Étang du Duc.* Halfway, at the spot called *Mi-voie,* opposite a little inn, the road passes on l. a pyramid, marking the site of the famous *Combat des Trente* (March 27, 1351), an extraordinary patriotic duel, in which Jean de Beaumanoir, who was holding the castle of Josselin for the Comtesse de Penthièvre, gained a complete victory over the English captain, Richard Bembro[2]—each of the captains being accompanied by twenty-nine champions. Bembro was among the slain.

'Il n'est pas de grande bataille livrée sur le sol de la France qui ait plus vivement frappé l'imagination populaire que cette lutte à mort entre trente champions de races ennemies.'—*Elisée Reclus.*

'Ce beau duel, qui dura dix heures, et où l'on entendit ces étonnántes paroles qui seraient dans toutes les rhétoriques si elles eussent été dites en latin—" Bois ton sang, Beaumanoir, et tu n'auras plus soif." '—*Emile Souvestre.*

Josselin (Hotel : *de France*—an unusually good, clean country inn, with excellent cuisine), is one of the places which no tourist in Brittany should miss. The attractive little town, with many picturesque houses, clusters round the very fine early xv. c. church of *Notre Dame.* Legend tells that the attention of a poor peasant was attracted to a thorn tree, by seeing that its foliage was always impervious to the severities of winter, and that he then found a luminous image of the Virgin amongst its branches. On the site of the tree, and to contain the miracle-working statue of Notre Dame du Roncier, the church was built. A legend tells that a peculiar form of barking-epilepsy, which long afflicted certain families of the district—*les familles d'aboyeuses*—was a

' Bamborough.

curse brought by some pitiless washerwomen, who refused a cup of water to the Vierge du Roncier when she asked for it dressed in the rags of a beggar-woman. The victims of the barking malady are brought to the church on the feast of Pentecost, and have their lips touched by relics, supposed to be remnants of the miraculous statue, which was burnt in the little square of the town in 1793.

The most interesting parts of the church are the choir and the central square, built in 1400 by the famous Connétable Olivier de Clisson, whose tomb, as founder, originally occupied the centre of the choir. This noble monument, mutilated and battered in the Revolution, was removed in 1858, and is now at the end of the S. aisle. It bears the effigy of the Constable—'the butcher of the English'—and that of his wife, Marguerite de Rohan, an interesting example of XIV. c. costume. Statuettes of monks surround the tomb.

The magnificent *Château de Josselin*—the Warwick Castle of France—occupies a perpendicular rock above the river Oust, and has been an important fortress from the XII. c., when it underwent a siege from Henry II. of England. Its counts exercised sovereign rights over their domain of Porhoët, of which Josselin was the capital, and merging eventually through the house of Fougères in that of Lusignan, gave kings to Cyprus, Armenia, and Jerusalem. In the XIV. c. the countship of Porhoët was confiscated by Philippe le Bel, and, in 1370, Pierre de Valois, Comte d'Alençon, sold it to the Connétable de Clisson, by whom the castle was much enlarged, and whose daughter brought it by marriage to the house of Rohan, which still possesses it.

Strangers are most kindly admitted to visit the château (Duc de Rohan), even when the duke (who as Prince de Léon, the intimate friend of the Duc d'Orléans, became well known at the time of his imprisonment) is residing there. It is approached by a gateway at the foot of the hill on the Ploërmel road. Formerly it was protected by a moat, and remains exist of two towers which guarded the drawbridge, and were pulled down in 1766. The grounds are as well kept as those of a great house in England, though they owe most of their charm to their exquisite position, with embrasures of terrace wall at a great height above the Oust. Whilst the front towards the river presents the severest type of mediæval military architecture, the inner walls towards the garden are covered with the most elaborate ornamentation. The buildings on this side are only one story high, unless we regard the high roof, with two splendid *lucarnes*, two stories high, with pinnacles and flying buttresses.

'Qu'on se figure une suite de frontons aigus se détachant du toit, dont le faîte est une ligne parallèle à celle de la façade, au-dessous, des chambranles très ornés encadrant deux fenêtres,

JOSSELIN.

l'une au-dessus de l'autre. Entre deux chambranles, on voit une galerie à laquelle le toit vient aboutir. Sa balustrade, travaillée à jour, est un chef-d'oeuvre de patience et de légèreté. La devise "A PLUS" s'y trouve répétée de vingt manières différentes, découpée en lettres fantastiques, avec une étonnante variété.'— *Prosper Merimée.*

Olivier de Clisson died in the château. One room contains a number of precious autographs and family memorials. The salle-à-manger and saloon both have noble chimneypieces, though only the former is ancient. Other rooms are hung with historic portraits, and all are well worth seeing, as belonging to what is so rare—the well-preserved residence of a great French noble.

The views of the castle from the bank of the river (which abounds in trout) are very attractive to artists. The inner façade has shown the domestic, this gives the fortress character of a great palace-château.

'Les nobles, ainsi que les prêtres, sont chers à la Bretagne, à la Vendée, comme dépenseurs des idées, des habitudes anciennes. La noblesse innombrable et pauvre de la Bretagne était plus rapprochée du laboureur. Il y avait là aussi quelque chose des habitudes de clan. Une foule de familles de paysans se regardaient comme nobles ; quelques-uns se croyaient descendus d'Arthur ou de la fée Morgane, et plantaient, dit-on, des épées pour limites de leurs champs. Ils s'asseyaient et se couvraient devant leur seigneur en signe d'indépendance. Dans plusieurs parties de la province, le servage était inconnu : les domaniers et quevasiers, quelque dure que fut leur condition, étaient libres de leur corps, si leur terre était servi. Devant le plus fière des Rohan, ils se seraient redressés en disant, comme ils font, d'un ton si grave : *Me zo deuzar armorig ;* et moi aussi, je suis Breton. Un mot profond vient d'être dit sur la Vendée, et il s'applique aussi à la Bretagne : *Ces populations sont au fond républicaines* ; républicanisme social, non politique.'—*Michelet.*

It is a pleasant walk along the river to the shrine of *S. Gobrien*, to whom patients afflicted with boils or tumours make votive offerings of little heaps of iron nails—*clous.*

It is a drive of about 37 k. in the direction of Pontivy to *Rohan*,[1] where little more than its site remains of the château of the greatest nobles in Brittany. The chapel of *Notre Dame de Bonne Rencontre* was built by Duke Jean II.

51 k. *Roc S. André la Chapelle.* The church of *La Chapelle* has an old processional cross. At the hamlet of *Ville-au-Voyer*

---

[1] In Brittany pigs are known as *mab-rohan*, sons of Rohan, no one knows why.

(4 k. N.E.), on an eminence, is the curious dolmen called *La Maison Trouée*, surrounded with a circle of menhirs.

58 k. *Malestroit*, a picturesque and curious little town, which has given its name to a famous family which bore as its device '*Quae numerat nummos, non male stricta domus.*' The (XII. c. and XV. c.) church of *S. Gilles* has a curious porch decorated with the emblems of the Evangelists. The (XII. c. and XV. c.) *Chapelle de la Madeleine* contains some fine old glass, telling the story of the Magdalen. Some timber houses are XV. c. and XVI. c.

428 k. *Broons*. The birthplace of Du Guesclin was the *Château de la Motte-Broons*, of which the site is marked by a pillar, erected in 1840.

439 k. *Plénée-Jugon*. 4½ k. is the ruined *Château de la Moussaye*, of XVI. c. 7 k. are the ruins of the Cistercian Abbey of *Boquen*, including the (XIV. c.) choir of the church where was buried the body of Prince Gilles de Bretagne, smothered in the castle of Hardouinaye, in which his brother, the duke, had imprisoned him. The wooden effigy of the prince, placed upon his grave by the Abbot of Boquen, is now in the Musée de S. Brieuc.

455 k. *Lamballe* (Hotel : *de France*) is a place soon visited. From the XI. c. it was possessed by the family of Penthièvre ; the last remains of the family property (having come to the house of Orleans through the wife of Philippe Egalité, sister-in-law of the friend of Marie Antoinette) were only sold to the town in 1866.

The fine church of *Notre Dame*, on a height, formerly the chapel of the château, was made collegiate by Duke Jean V. in 1485. The nave is XIII. c. with two XII. c. portals. The interior, of grey granite, has much beauty. The central tower is supported by stately columns. The narrow and lofty nave has wide and low side aisles. The

S. aisle ends in a delicately sculptured organ-loft, reached by a winding stair. The choir, rebuilt by Charles de Blois in 1371, has much fine glass. The chapels on the r. are only separated by open mullions of very graceful effect.

In the northern suburb is the quaint church of *S. Martin*, belonging to a priory of the Abbey of Marmoutiers, and founded by Geoffrey I., Comte de Lamballe, in 1083. The S. portal is x. c., and has a curious timber porch; the rest of the church is xv. c. and xvi. c. The church of *Les Augustins*, or *Ave Maria*, now used as a warehouse, has a xv. c. portal surmounted by a flamboyant window.

15 k. N. is the sea-bathing place of *Pléneuf* (Hotels: *Guignan; de la Marine*), and 9 k. E. of this *Erquy* (Hotel: *Garnier*), with a small harbour.

[For the line to Dinan, Dol, Avranches, etc., see ch. vi.]

465 k. *Yffiniac*. 4 k. N. is *Hillion*, on the sea-shore; 4 k. S. the pilgrimage chapel of *Les Sept Saints*.

475 k. *S. Brieuc* (Hotels: *Croix Blanche; de l' Univers;* buffet at station). This clean but exceedingly dull town takes its name from a British missionary of the v. c., a pupil of S. Germain, who built an oratory of Notre Dame near a fountain in the valley of the Gouët. The place was celebrated in the annals of the Vendéen war from the rescue of the royalists under sentence of death in the prisons by a brave attack of the Chouans, Oct. 26, 1799. The inhabitants are called 'Les Briochins.'

'S. Brieuc est une vieille cité replâtrée qui a fait nouvelle peau. Des l'entrée, on respire la préfecture; on se trouve nez à nez avec la civilisation, symbolisée par une prison et une caserne neuves. On a même bâti quelques lignes de hautes murailles qui sont percées de rectangles vitrés, et que l'on appelle des façades; ce sont les *beaux* quartiers de la ville. Il y a, en outre, deux promenades bien taillées au ciseau, avec une statue de tuffeau à chaque bout.'—*Emile Souvestre.*

The *Cathedral of S. Etienne* was begun by the Bishop S. Guillaume Pinchon early in the XIII. c. and continued in the XIV. c., when the keystones of the choir vaulting were sculptured with the arms of Guy de Montfort. It is a low, heavy building, with stumpy towers. The two principal portals are XIII. c. In the interior of the nave only the walls of the two aisles and the S. chapel are of the middle ages. The choir has numerous romanesque capitals, from an earlier building. In the S. transept is the tomb of S. Guillaume Pinchon (1234), with ever-burning lamps. In niches of the wall (*enfeux*) are other tombs of bishops, including Bishop André le Porc de la Porte (1632). At the entrance of the choir is Bishop Fretat de Boissieux (1720); the black marble tomb of the constitutional Bishop Jacob (1801); at the back of the choir, Bishop Caffarelli (1815), and Bishop de Boisgelin (1633); in S. transept, Bishop le Groing de la Romagère (1841), Bishop le Mée (1858), and Bishop Martial (1863).

Every second house in the old part of S. Brieuc would seem to have been monastic. There are several fine old timber houses. James II. of England is said to have lodged in the renaissance house called the *L'Hôtel des ducs de Bourgogne,* in the Rue Fadel, in 1689, when he came to S. Brieuc to review his disembarked troops. The modern church of *Notre Dame de la Fontaine* marks the site of the V. C. oratory.

3½ k. (by the r. bank of the Gouët) is the *Tour de Cesson,* built by Jean IV. in 1395, formerly a very curious specimen of the military architecture of its time, but half blown up by Henri IV.

NOTRE DAME DE LA COUR. 231

[A road runs N.W. from S. Brieuc to (44 k.) Paimpol by (13 k.) *Binic*, a small seaport at the mouth of the Ic.

18 k. *Portrieux* (Hotel: *de la Plage*) a small seaport and bathing-place.

19 k. *S. Quay*, a bathing-place named from a monk of the VI. c.

28 k. *Plouha*. 4 k. W. is the chapel of *Kermaria-an-Isquit*, which existed in XIII. c., and which (modernised) has always been a famous place of pilgrimage. A curious mural painting represents the Dance of Death.

33 k. *Lanloup*. The *Manoir de la Noé Verte* is XV. c. The little port of *Bréhec-en-Plouha* was the landing-place of S. Brieuc and his missionary companions.

41 k. On the r. are the ruins of the abbey of *Beauport:* see later.

Another route from S. Brieuc to (44 k.) Paimpol passes—

16 k. *La Pinte Blanche*. A short distance hence on the road to Lantic is the interesting church of *Notre Dame de la Cour*, begun by Duke Jean V. (1420-22). A fine flamboyant window has splendid XV. c. glass representing the life of the Virgin. In front of the choir is the tomb of Guillaume de Rosmadec, Seigneur de Buhen (1640). The fête of Notre Dame, on August 10, is well worth seeing. Vast multitudes of pilgrims arrive by land with bare feet and lighted candles; but numbers also arrive by sea, who, never speaking or noticing any of their friends or relations on landing, begin at once to sing the litanies of the Virgin as they join a procession to Notre Dame.

25 k. *Lanvollon*, named from S. Vollon, who founded a monastery here in the VII. c. The church is dedicated to S. Brandan, an Irish bishop in the VI. c. The *Hôtel Keralry* is a fine timber mansion, with renaissance sculptures of 1559. *Le Puits de S. Turiaff* commemorates the birth here of S. Turiaff, Archbishop of Dol in the VIII. c.

30 k. *La Tournée*. A little farther is seen the ruined (XII. c.) *Château de Coëlmen*, then (1½ k.) the XVI. c. *Chapelle S. Jacques*, with good flamboyant windows, and a fountain near it, surmounted by a statue of S. James. To the l. is the *Château de Boisgelin*, which has belonged to the family of that name since the XIII. c., and (1½ k.) the very curious building known as

Le Temple de Lanleff (see later). This is 'La Bretagne bretonnante,' *i.e.*, where only Breton is spoken, and a traveller may find some difficulty in making himself understood.]

[A line runs S. from S. Brieuc to Auray by—

8 k. *S. Julien de la Côte.* 2 k. N.E., in the district of Plédran, is the curious *Camp de Péran* or *des Pierres brûlées*. It is an irregular enclosure of 134 mèt., near the Roman road called *Le Chemin de Noë*. The two walls used in the construction of its rampart are separated by a mass of scoria and burnt material, which local tradition asserts to have taken seven years in consuming. The number of Roman objects found in the ruins prove the date of the camp to have been later than the Roman occupation, and it is now generally believed that the fire was employed as a means of consolidating an artificial rock impervious to time; for granite, which is not to be found in this district, and which, when burnt, furnishes a strong vitrified material, was evidently brought hither to be used. Walls of this kind are to be seen at S. Susanne, in Maine. In the neighbourhood of the Camp de Péran are the *Chapelle du Créha*, an ancient commanderie of the Knights of Malta; *La Chapelle S. Nicolas*, of xv. c., with a sculptured *jubé;* and *La Grotte aux Fées*, a Druidical monument surrounded by old oaks.

18 k. *Quintin* (Hotel: *de la Grande Maison*) founded in the XIII. c. by the crusader Geoffroy de Penthièvre, and picturesquely situated above the Gouët. The (rebuilt) church of *Notre Dame* contains the relics of S. Thurian, and a fragment of the girdle of the Virgin, brought back by the Crusaders in 1248. It used to be carried to women in childbirth—'pour en estre ceintes avec révérence et obtenir un facile et heureux accouchement.' Near the entrance of the town from the station is a pavillon of the *Château*, rebuilt by Amaury de Gouyon, in 1662, on the site of a castle demolished in the wars of the Ligue. Later buildings of the XVIII. c. are due to the Vicomte de Choiseul, and contain a number of interesting portraits of the family of De Lorges, etc., and pictures illustrative of the glory of Mme de Pompadour, prepared to flatter her during a visit to the Duc de Lorges. The *Porte Neuve* is XIV. c. or XV. c., and several old houses are interesting.

[A road (diligence) leads S.W. to—

15 k. *Corlay* (Hotel: *Thierry*), which had its origin in a XII. c. castle belonging to the family of Rohan, demolished by order of Henri IV. in 1485. It remains as a striking ruin, with a great tower (Le Prison), round externally and quadrangular within. The church (XV. c. and XVI. c.) has a handsome portal of 1575. The *Chapelle S. Anne* is XV. c. and XVI. c. A number of megalithic remains (menhirs, etc.) exist in the neighbourhood of Corlay. 11½ k. on the road to Guingamp are the ruins of the Cistercian Abbey of *Coëlmalouen*, founded 1142 by Alain le Noir, Comte de Penthièvre. 12 k. hence, by a side road, is the interesting church of *Bourbriac*, chiefly XV. c., but with portions of romanesque, and a noble tower of 1501. It contains the tomb of S. Briac.

23 k. *S. Nicolas de Pélem*, has a XV. c. church with fine glass.

39 k. *Rostrenen*, has a number of old houses and a (restored) church founded in 1295 by Pierre de Rostrenen. Its modern name of *Notre Dame du Roncier* refers to the belief that its miraculous statue of the Virgin was discovered in a thorn bush. It has a pilgrimage on August 15.]

The line enters the forest of Lorges, and leaves the *Château de Lorges* to l. before reaching—

28 k. *Ploeuc l'Hermitage*. At *Ploeuc* are a number of large menhirs.

35 k. *Uzel*. The road hence to (19 k.) Corlay, passes (3 k.) the XV. c. *Chapelle S. Jacques*, with interesting glass and wall paintings of the same date.

49 k. *Loudéac* (Hotel: *de France*), important from its cloth manufactories—'toiles de Bretagne.'

72 k. *Pontivy* (Hotels: *Gressen*—recommended ; *de France*), an intensely Breton town, which originated in a monastery founded in the VII. c. by S. Ivy, monk of Lindisfarne. The town, besieged by the insurgent peasants in 1790, was fortified by Napoleon I., who tried to change its name to Napoléonville. The church of *Notre Dame de la Joie* is XV. c. The *Château*, a fine building of 1485, with four huge towers, is now a convent of Sisters of Charity. Only one (XVII. c.) of the four city gates remains. Some houses are XVI. c. and XVII. c.

2 k. S.E. is a fine menhir surmounted by a cross. 7 k. E., in the xv. c. church of *Noyal-Pontivy*, is the granite sarcophagus known as the tomb of S. Mériadec. The forests of this district are still full of wolves.

[A road leads S.E. from Pontivy to—

23 k. *Locminé*, which takes its name (Loc Menec'h—a cell of monks) from a monastery founded by S. Columban in the vi. c. The xvi. c. *Chapelle S. Columban*, which forms an aisle of the church, has the story of the saint in stained glass. S. Columban is the patron of madmen, and maniacs used to be chained in the crypt under his chapel to effect their cure. The road is continued across the wild Landes, sprinkled with menhirs and peulvens, to (51 k.) Vannes.]

[A road leads W. from Pontivy to—
3 k. *Stival*. The xvi. c. church of *S. Mériadec* replaces the hermitage of the saint, afterwards Archbishop of Vannes, in the vii. c. Fine stained glass by 'Jean le Flaman,' 1552, tells the story of the Passion. Frescoes, on either side the choir, tell that of the saint. The chapel is a much frequented point of pilgrimage. The copper bell, called *Bonnet de S. Mériadec*, is said to have belonged to the saint. It is rung over the heads of persons afflicted with deafness. 5 k. N.W. is the *Chapelle S. Morvan*, containing the tomb of the saint. On the territory of Cléguérec are the dolmen of *Bod-er-Moët*, and the gorge of *Stang-en-Ihuern*. A road turns N.W. to (49 k.) *Carhaix*, by (l.) the ruined *Château de Coëtanfao*, built at the end of the xviii. c. in imitation of the Petit Trianon, and the gothic xvi. c. chapel of *Locmaria*.

17 k. A road turns r. to (8 k.) *Guern*, near which is the *Chapelle Notre Dame de Quelven*, with a fine stone spire and good xvi. c. glass.

21 k. *Guéméné sur Scorff*, originated in the castle of Guéméné Guégant, erected by one Guegant in 1022. It was rebuilt in xv. c. by Louis de Rohan, but dismantled under Louis XIII. The old road S.W. from Guéméné to (24 k.) Le Faouet passes (l. 2½ k.) the *Chapelle Notre Dame de Crénénan*, which belonged to the Templars and is covered with xvi. c. frescoes; and (17 k.) *Priziac*, with the ruined *Château de Belair* and the xvi. c. church

of S. Beho (an Irish bishop). 2 k. from Priziac is the XVI. c. *Chapelle S. Nicolas*, with a rich jubé and sculptures of the legend of S. Nicolas.

33 k. *Kernascléden*, famous for its beautiful chapel of *Notre Dame*, built as a Latin cross, 1453, at the same time with S. Fiacre. It is said that, as tools were scarce, angels carried them backwards and forwards between the workmen of the two chapels. The two S. porches are full of exquisite granite sculpture. The S. transept has a grand flamboyant rose-window. On the vaulting of the choir and N. transept are decaying frescoes relating to the life of Christ and the Virgin.

For the rest of the way to Quimper and Quimperlé see ch. vii.]

87 k. *S. Nicolas des Eaux*. The interesting XVI. c. chapel of *S. Nicodème*, in a very pretty spot surrounded by chestnut groves, has a flamboyant spire. Near it are two sacred fountains, one of them, of 1608, adorned with statues of three Jew-saints— S. Nicodème, S. Gamaliel, and S. Abibon—with suppliant figures. On the day of the pardon, the first Saturday in August, all the oxen in the neighbourhood, adorned with ribbons, are brought hither to receive the blessing of S. Nicodème. A young ox is offered to the saint, and the price for which it is sold is used for the poor, especially for farming people who have suffered loss through fire, storm, or disease. The pardon ends in a *feu de joie*, and an angel, flying down from the church tower by machinery, sets light to the bonfire.[1] The neighbouring *Chapelle S. Anne* is XVI. c.

The hamlet of *Castennec* is believed to stand on the site of the Roman station of Sulis.

The line passes the *Chapelle S. Adrien*, with two sacred fountains, frequented by those suffering from intestinal disorders.

103 k. *Baud*. It is from this station that a visit must be paid to the famous Venus of Quinipily. The town of Baud is 5 k. from the station, and the omnibus will set visitors down within $\frac{1}{4}$ k. of Quinipily, which is about $3\frac{1}{2}$ k. distant. Pedestrians must turn r., cross a bridge over the Blavet, ascend a hill, passing

---

[1] This ceremony is well described in the *Through Brittany* of Mrs. Macquoid.

an old cross on l., and when they come to a common, take a path on r. to a mill-pool. Close by is the old château-farm of Quinipily (Chinipily in Breton), where, in an orchard, is the famous idol-statue *La Vénus de Quinipily*. It was brought hither in 1696 from the hamlet of La Gouarde, where it bore the name of *Groac'h er Gouard*—the sorceress of La Garde. It continued to be an object of worship till the end of XVII. c.

THE IDOL OF QUINIPILY.

'La première fois qu'elle se trouve désignée dans un titre historique, c'est à la fin du seizième siècle. L'évêque de Vannes fut informé qu'il existait au village de Bieuzy une statue de femme, qui était pour les habitans du lieu l'objet d'un culte particulier. Ils lui attribuaient le pouvoir de marier les garçons et les filles, et voici de quelle manière il fallait s'y prendre pour mériter le bienveillance de cette étrange divinité. Après une prière, je ne sais laquelle, chacun pratiquait isolément, aux pieds de la statue, une cérémonie quelque peu leste, réputée agréable à une déesse à laquelle on n'attribuait point les fonctions de *Venus genitrix*, puis on se baignait dans une grande cuve en pierre placée devant l'idole. On rapporte vaguement qu'elle se trouvait alors parmi les ruines d'un édifice antique, mais je n'en ai trouvé nulle part de description satisfaisante. A bon droit scandalisé, l'évêque de Nantes requit le seigneur de Lannion de faire cesser ce désordre. Celui-ci, accompagné de ses vassaux, se présente pour enlever l'idole ; mais les gens de Bieuzy prétendaient la garder, d'où ensuivit un combat. La victoire demeura aux assaillans, qui enlevèrent la statue et le portèrent en triomphe au château de Quinipili, appartenant au seigneur de Lannion. Dans cette bataille, sans doute, La Vénus perdit son nez ; c'est la seule mutilation qu'elle ait subie. Bien plus, le seigneur de Lannion lui donna un asile, ce qui semble fort extraordinaire, car, proscrite par l'autorité ecclésiastique, elle semblait condamnée à la destruction. Au contraire, un de ses successeurs la plaça honorablement sur un piédestal, en 1696, offrant ainsi, en quelque sorte, une tentation à la superstition des paysans. Ou ajoute qu'en effet on lui rendit de nouveaux hommages, et l'on m'a même assuré qu'elle en recevait encore quelquefois aujourd'hui. Le château avait été détruit dans la révolution ; au commencement du siècle on découvrit au milieu de ses ruines, sous un hangar envahi par les ronces, deux autres statues représentant des hommes armés de massues. Elles restèrent longtemps oubliées, jusqu'à ce qu'un fermier de Locminé, les ayant achetés, les plaça dans deux niches devant sa maison, sur le bord de la route qui traverse le faubourg de Locminé.'—*Prosper Merimée.*

The Venus, formed from a single granite block, is 6½ feet high. The colour of the stone causes her to be called *grouec'h houarn*—the iron woman. She is standing, with her hands crossed upon her breast. The band on her forehead bears the letters I L T—a puzzle to antiquaries.

The statue is mounted upon a little classic portico, in front of which is a fountain, and the bath till recently used by devotees. It is a very picturesque and attractive spot.

The path may be continued to Baud, 1½ k., through a beautiful beech wood, passing (l.) the oratory chapel of *Notre Dame du*

Roc. The mistletoe, which abounds, having become 'l'herbe de la croix,' has lost none of the powers ascribed to it in pagan times. At the end of the wood a turn l. should be taken, and again l. on reaching the road.

Baud (a tolerable hotel) occupies a very lofty situation, and has two dull churches, side by side, in its square. The pilgrimage chapel of *Notre Dame de la Clarté* and the *Fontaine de la Clarté* are much frequented by those who are suffering from weak eyes. The blessing of cattle and the blessing of horses is carried out here with great ceremony on two festivals in July.

Those who visit Quinipily by an early train from Auray may take a carriage on from Baud to S. Nicodème, and join the return train at S. Nicolas.

115 k. *Pluvigner.* The church is dedicated to S. Guigner or Vener, an Irish prince martyred in v. c. The *Chapelle S. Fiacre* was restored 1640. 2 k. N.W. is the xv. c. *Château de Keronic.*

127 k. Auray.]

Leaving S. Brieuc, the line crosses the valley of the Gouët by the viaduct of *La Méaugon.*

487 k. *Plouvara-Plerneuf.* Near Plerneuf is the fine *Dolmen des Rochers*; at Plouvara the pilgrimage chapel of *Notre Dame de Clarté.*

492 k. *Châtelaudren.* The *Chapelle Notre Dame du Tertre* has a fine retable of 1589, and curious wall-paintings of xv. c. A promenade occupies the site of the castle, connected with the popular Breton legend of the prisoner Azénor.

505 k. *Guingamp* (Hotel: *de l'Ouest*—tolerable), an ancient property of the house of Penthièvre in the valley of the Trieux, and still a very stirring place. The church of *Notre Dame de Bon Secours,* in the principal street, which was the chapel of the Comtes de Penthièvre, was rebuilt XIII. c. to XVI. c. The façade has a double portal, and is

very richly sculptured. On the N. are two beautiful portals with porches; on the central pillar of the first of these is the famous and much revered statue of *Notre Dame de Halgoët* or *de Bon Secours*. The central tower, of XIII. c., has a handsome stone spire. The crushing of part of the church by the fall of the S. tower in 1535 has caused one side of the nave to be renaissance whilst the other is pure gothic. The choir, with two ranges of galleries, was built

MILL OF GUINGAMP.

1462-80; the Chapelle du Trésor by Charles de Blois in 1371. The aisles of the choir are the same height as the choir itself, and (a peculiar feature) the flying buttresses which sustain the principal vaulting are inside the church. Under the choir is a (closed) crypt, in which Jean and Bastien de Luxembourg are buried. In the S. aisle are the vault and tomb of Rolland Phélippes, sieur de Coëtgouréden, seneschal of Charles de Blois, and the tomb of

Pierre Morel, Bishop of Tréguier, 1401. The pardon or pilgrimage of the Bon Secours, one of the most crowded in Brittany, takes place on the Saturday before the first Sunday in July.

'On voit alors les longues files de pélerins s'avancer au milieu des ténèbres, comme un lugubre cortège de fantômes. Chacun des pénitents tient à la main droite un chapelet, à la gauche un cierge allumé, et tous ces visages pâles, à moitié voilés de leurs longs cheveux, ou de leurs coiffes blanches qui, pendant des côtés comme un suaire, passent lentement en psalmodiant une prière latine. Bientôt une voix s'élève au-dessus des autres: c'est le conducteur des pélerins qui chante le cantique de *Madame Marie de Bon Secours.*'—*Emile Souvestre,* '*Les Derniers Bretons.*'

The market-place—*Place du Centre*—is extremely picturesque, with old houses faced with grey slate, fine trees, and a very pretty lead fountain—*La Fontaine du Duc Pierre*—first constructed in xv. c., but renewed in 1743, when the existing leaden ornaments were executed by the sculptor Carlay. A little below, turning l., we find a charming old mill (well worth painting) upon the Trieux.

There are many pretty 'bits' beneath the remains of the old walls, overhung with valerian and clematis. Three towers of the château exist. In the N. of the town the *Chapelle S. Léonard*, chiefly modern, retains the four romanesque pillars which support the spire, from a chapel built by Charles de Blois in 1356. Every May persons suffering from fever come hither to look for snails in the crevices of the walls; they must find them themselves, and having found them, they shut them up in a bag, which they hang round their necks. When cured of their fever, they bury the bag beneath the walls of the chapel, and, if they omit this duty, expect the fever to return.

NOTRE DAME DES GRÂCES. 241

The *Abbaye de S. Croix* (1 k. S.), founded *c.* 1130 by Etienne de Penthièvre, has been converted into a farm; its xv. c. gateway and its early gothic church remain. The abbot's house, built by Abbot Pierre de Kernévénoy in 1530, has a picturesque hexagonal tower, with a tourelle.

NOTRE DAME DES GRÂCES.

2½ k. W., by pretty Devonshire-like lanes, is the *Chapelle de Notre Dame des Grâces*, built by Guy de Bretagne, 1507-21. It has a graceful stone spire, with widely detached pinnacles. Over the doors are very quaint lions with lolling tongues. To the r. of the high altar a shrine of carved wood contains the remains of Charles de Blois, killed in the battle of Auray. The hour-glass stands are very richly carved—a devil drawing a cart full of monks, etc. The *Château de Keranno* was, for a time, the residence of James II. of England. 3 k. N.W. of Guingamp is the XVII. c. *Château de Carnabat.*

[The direct road N.W. to (32 k.) Lannion passes—

10 k. *Pédernec*, overlooked by the hill of Bré, crowned by the *Chapelle de S. Hervé*, which, with its sacred fountain, is a great place of pilgrimage. The *Chapelle de Lorette*, rich in sculpture, was founded (XVI. c.) by the Seigneurs de Kerma-thamam.

14 k. *Bégard* had its origin in the Cistercian abbey founded by Etienne, Comte de Penthièvre, in 1130, which is now a female lunatic asylum. Part of the abbey church remains, and is now parochial. A tomb in the choir is supposed to be that of Alain, Comte de Penthièvre, 1146. The monastic buildings which remain are XVII. c. and XVIII. c. 11½ k. on the road from Bégard to Pontrieux is the XVI. c. *Chapelle de la Trinité*, with paintings of the legend of St. Jorand, of whom it contains the tomb.

21 k. *Cavan.* The church (XVI. c.) has a good spire.

28 k. *Buhulien* has a Calvary of 1679.]

[The direct road which runs N.W. from Guingamp to Tréguier passes—

3 k. *Pabu*, with a church frequented on pilgrimage by epileptics. Just beyond this a road turns r. to (10 k.) *Pommérit le Vicomte*, which has a XIV. c. church with a tall spire. The *Chapelle du Paradis* is XVI. c.

20 k. *Pontrieux*, in the valley of the Trieux.

24 k. *Ploëzal.* 4 k. N.E. is the *Château de la Roche-Jagu*, chiefly XV. c., with picturesque masses of lofty decorated chimneys.

27 k. *Pommerit-Jaudy.* Near this is the ruined *Château du Plessix*, and a moated tumulus near the old *Château de Coat-Nevenez.*

29 k. *La Roche-Derrien*, founded by Derrien, younger son of Eudon, Comte de Penthièvre, on a rock above the Jaudy. Beneath its walls Charles de Blois was defeated, and, after

receiving eighteen wounds, was obliged to give himself up as a prisoner to Tanneguy du Chastel, in 1347. Only small ruins of the castle exist. The church of *S. Catharine de Suède* has a lofty spire: its S. transept, called La Chapelle du Château, is XIV. c. On the r. of the porch is a curious granite bénitier. An old timber house on the Place bears the date 1647. At 2 k., beyond the Jaudy, the modern church of *Langoat* contains the tomb (1370) of S. Pompée, mother of S. Tugdual. The tomb, surrounded by the history of the saint in a series of gothic bas-reliefs, is surmounted by a good marble statue.]

[Tourists may leave the railway at Guingamp, sending on their luggage to Morlaix, and engaging a carriage for two days (45 frs.) to take them to Paimpol and Lannion, arranging to turn aside (inclusive) to the Temple de Lanleff on the way. This excursion, however, has no great attraction, and Paimpol may be more easily visited from Lannion.

There is nothing of special interest till we reach—in a little hollow below a poor village—the curious building known as the *Temple de Lanleff*, which has long puzzled antiquaries. It was formerly considered to be a Roman temple, but is more probably the ruin of a round Templar church of the XII. c. It is not unlike S. Stefano Rotondo at Rome in miniature. It has two circles of wall, the inner pierced by twelve arches. Close by is a spring, of supposed miraculous properties.

33 k. *Paimpol* (Hotel: *Gicquel*—very good) is a very dull little town of no interest. An excursion may be made (6 k.) by land to the Point of *Arcouet*, the nearest for crossing to the *Île Bréhat*; but there is nothing to make it worth while, except the beauty of the inhabitants and the wonderful healthiness of the island.

'La partie de la côte qui a la mieux résisté au choc des vagues se termine à l'ouest de Bréhat par les redoutables "Epées de Tréguier," véritable jetée de cailoux que les vagues ont elles-mêmes construite et sur laquelle tant de navires sont venus se briser; elles guident aujourd'hui le navigateur, grâce au superbe phare des Héhaux, dressé sur un de leurs écueils.'—*Elisée Reclus.*

A pretty walk leads E. from Paimpol to (3 k.) the ruins of the *Abbaye de Beauport*, close to the road on l. The abbey was founded in 1202 by Alain, Comte de Penthièvre. The ruined church—a Latin cross with three aisles—is XIII. c. Parallel with it is a hall of XIII. c. or XIV. c., divided by circular pillars with rich capitals, which communicated on the W. with a great cloister. To the E. is the refectory, another vaulted gothic hall, built by the Abbot Hervé in 1269. Unfortunately these remains are too much shut in by walls to be the least picturesque or beautiful; but in the neighbourhood there are lovely views of the bay, with its yellow seaweed, distant islets, and pines in the foreground.

The road from Paimpol to Tréguier crosses (3 k.) the valley of the Trieux by a lofty suspension bridge, passes through (5 k.) *Lézardrieux*, and crosses the Jaudy before reaching (15 k.) *Tréguier* (Hotel: *de France*—a very good country inn),[1] an interesting little episcopal city, occupying a promontory at the junction of the Jaudy and Guindy, with a creek which runs 9 k. inland from the sea. The town had its origin in the monastery of Trécon, which was founded by S. Tugdual in the VI. c.

The most celebrated of the Trégarrois, Ernest Renan, was born at Tréguier in 1823. His father, master of a small coasting vessel, was drowned when he was three. He carried off all the prizes of his class at the college of Tréguier, and thus attracted the notice of the Abbé Dupanloup, then superior of the little seminary of S. Nicolas du Chardonnet, which he persuaded Renan to enter. Thence he went for four years' more training to the great seminary of S. Sulpice, which he quitted in October 1845, leaving behind him the faith he had hoped to teach.

In the town square is the noble church, formerly *Cathedral*, founded early in the IX. c., but almost entirely rebuilt in 1339.

'Chef d'oeuvre de légèreté, fol essai pour réaliser en granit un idéal impossible.'—*Renan.*

[1] An old Breton song is literally translated—
'Moi, j'aime beaucoup le Léonard,
Celui-là se nourrit avec de la viande grasse.
Le Tregorrois a le goût
Des crêpes et du lait frais tiré;
Mais Cornouillais et Vannetais,
Avec leur blé noir, sont après.'
See '*Le Foyer Breton.*'

It is a Latin cross. The centre and the extremity of each transept has a tower—that on the N. being romanesque, and named *Le Tour de Hasting*, it is supposed, from a great pirate chief. That on the S. (XV. c.) has a lofty spire of 1787, spoilt by its many irregular openings. In the XIV. c. the principal entrance of the church was by the S. porch, now used as a baptistery; above it is a terrace, entered from a kind of external pulpit in the centre of the gable. The W. porch has a fine XIV. c. window above it. Hence one descends fourteen steps into the triple nave of five bays. The choir has four bays, accompanied by chapels, and two square chapels with five-sided apsides at the E. end. Parallel with the N. transept is the *Chapelle du Duc*, built by Jean V. in 1420, and where he was buried in 1451. The stall-work of the choir is of 1648. The two stalls nearest the entrance represent its sainted bishop, S. Tugdual (564),[1] binding with his stole a dragon which desolated the valley of Trécor, and throwing it into the sea; and an angel dividing the waters of a river that S. Yves might pass through on dry land. Many fine, but much mutilated, tombs remain of bishops and knights, and there is a very noble modern monument to S. Yves.

'S. Yves de la Vérité s'aide que les innocents injustement opprimés, les pauvres, les veuves, les orphelins; c'est le grand justicier, le redresseur de torts.'—*Elisée Reclus.*

The immense bénitier is like a cattle-trough.

'La sculpture de bois a été longtemps florissante en Bretagne. Les statues de saints sont d'un réalisme étonnant; pour des imaginations plastiques, elles vivent. Je me souviens d'un brave homme, pas beaucoup plus fou que les autres, qui s'échappait quand il pouvait, le soir. Le matin, on le trouvait dans les églises en bras de chemise, suant sang et eau. Il avait passé la nuit à déclouer les christs en croix et à tirer les flèches du corps des Saint Sebastien.'—*Ernest Renan,*

On the N.E. is a very picturesque and beautiful *Cloister*. The single XII. c. tower is well seen from hence, or from the court-

---

[1] S. Ruelin was another canonised bishop of Tréguier of the VI. c.

yard of the former *Évêché*. The house of Renan is just below the cathedral. On the quay are some quaint old houses.

At 1 k. S. is Minihy,[1] where the fine xv. c. church was once the chapel of the manor of *Kermartin*, where, in 1255, was born S. Yves—the patron of lawyers, who is declared to have nourished two hundred persons with two sous' worth of bread.

> 'Advocatus et non latro
> Res miranda populo.'

He is honoured every May 19 by a procession from the cathedral of Tréguier to the church of Minihy, where his will hangs on the wall and the remains of his breviary are preserved. The manor-house of Kermartin was rebuilt in 1834; the farmers who own it claim to possess the bed of S. Yves.[2]

'Le digne patron des avocats est né dans le *Minihi* de Tréguier, et sa petite église y est entourée d'une grande vénération. Ce défenseur des pauvres, des veuves, des orphelins, est devenu dans le pays le grand justicier, le redresseur de torts. En l'adjurant avec certaines formules, dans sa mystérieuse chapelle de Saint Yves *de la Verité*, contre un ennemi dont on est victime, en lui disant: "Tu étais juste de ton vivant, montre que tu l'es encore," on est sur que l'ennemi mourra dans l'année. Tous les délaissés deviennent ses pupilles. À la mort de mon père, ma mère me conduisit à sa chapelle et le constitua mon tuteur.

'Le mois de mai, où tombait la fête de ce saint excellent, n'était qu'une suite de processions au *Minihi*; les paroisses, précédées de leurs croix processionnelles, se rencontraient sur les chemins, on faisait alors embrasser les croix en signe d'alliance. La veille de la fête, le peuple se réunissait le soir dans l'église, et à minuit, le saint étendait le bras pour bénir l'assistance prosternée. Mais s'il y avait dans la foule un seul incrédule qui levât les yeux pour voir si le miracle était réel, le saint, justement blessé de ce soupçon, ne bougeait pas, et, par la faute du mécréant, personne n'était béni.'—*Ernest Renan*.

Amongst the curious relics of pagan times in the environs of Tréguier is the chapel of *Notre Dame de la Haine*—'heiress

---

[1] Minihy means a consecrated circle, of two or three leagues, near some great abbey or other religious foundation.

[2] S. Yves is invoked to make crust rise.

of some fierce Celtic deity'—where, at night, an injured wife comes to pray for deliverance from the husband she detests, and the son for the death of the father who keeps him out of his inheritance.[1]

At the *Chapelle S. Michel*, Renan says that a white seagull flies nightly round the doors and windows, seeking to penetrate. It is the soul of a priest longing to say a mass he neglected.

'Les environs de la ville de Tréguier présentaient le même caractère religieux et idéal. On y nageait en plein rêve, dans une atmosphère aussi mythologique au moins que celle de Bénarès ou de Jagatnata. L'église de Saint-Michel, du seuil de laquelle on apercevait la pleine mer, avait été détruite par la poudre, et il s'y passait encore des choses merveilleuses. Le jeudi saint, on y conduisait les enfants pour voir les cloches aller à Rome. On nous bandait les yeux, et alors il était beau de voir toutes les pièces du carillon, par ordre de grandeur, de la plus grosse à la plus petite, revêtues de la belle robe de dentelle brodée qu'elles portèrent le jour de leur baptême, traverser l'air pour aller, en bourdonnant gravement, se faire bénir par le pape.—*Ernest Renan.*

'Si le patriotisme de langue s'éveille jamais, le "trécorien," idiome du pays de Tréguier, est celui qui mériterait de devenir le bas-breton litteraire ; c'est de Tréguier que nous viennent le plus de chants, de récits et de proverbes celtiques.'—*Elisée Reclus.*]

[A road runs N. by (2 k.) *Plougniel* (where the modern church has a XV. c. statue of S. Gouesnou and a XIII. c. tomb of a Sieur de Kerousy) to (7 k.) *Plougrescant*, on a promontory surrounded on three sides by the sea. A modern church replaces the XV. c. *Chapelle de S. Gonery*, and contains (in the sacristy), a curious chest, sculptured with the story of S. Gonery, and the fine renaissance tomb of Guillaume de Halgouët, Bishop of Tréguier, 1602. The tomb, constructed in the bishop's lifetime, bears the date 1599.]

It is a pleasant drive of 18 k. from Tréguier to Lannion : see later.

[1] See Elisée Reclus.

[A road leads S.W. from Guingamp to (51 k.) Carhaix by—

9 k. *Moustérus*, where the church was formerly the chapel of the now ruined *Château de l'Îsle*.

15 k. *Kernon*. A road turns l. by (3 k.) *Pont Melvez* (with the chapel of a Commanderie of Knights of Malta) to (6 k.) *Bulat-Pestivien*, with the beautiful xv. c. and xvi. c. *Chapelle de Notre Dame de Bulat*, an exquisite gothic building of granite, with a noble renaissance porch. Beneath the tower (of 1552) is a sacristy, adorned externally with admirable sculptures of skeletons fulfilling the duties of the living, and signed by 'Fouquet Jehannou, maistre de l'oeuvre, 1552.' There is a great pilgrimage to Pestivien for the *pardon* of Sept. 8. 5 k. distant is the *Chapelle de S. Gildas*, containing the tomb of the saint: see later.]

520 k. *Belle Isle—Bégard*. The *Chapelle de Locmaria* has a rich xvi. c. jubé. 3 k. is the fine xv. c. church of *Locquenvel*, with a jubé, of which the sculpture, as well as the stained glass, relates to the story of S. Envel, who was born and died here.

531 k. *Plouaret-Lannion*. The church of *Vieux Marché* (l.) is chiefly xv. c., with a fine renaissance tower. The xvi. c. church of *Plouaret* has a vault, marked by arms, beneath each window. Seven remain of the twenty-four chapels which were formerly scattered over the parish of Plouaret. Near the ruins of *S. Anne de Kerminihy* an immense ash overhangs a consecrated fountain. The *Chapelle des Sept Saints* (5 k.) is placed upon a dolmen, which forms a crypt in which tradition declares that images of the seven sleepers were miraculously found. 7 k. S. is the village of *Plouénez-Moëdec*, 3 k. W. of which (on the road to Brest), near a fine menhir, is the interesting xv. c. *Chapelle de Keramenac'h*, which belonged to the Knights of S. John of Jerusalem. The porch is exceedingly rich, and

over the altar is a curious XVI. c. alabaster retable of most delicate workmanship.

[A line leads N. from Plouaret to Lannion by—
8 k. *Kérauzern*. A station whence the châteaux of Kergrist and Runfao (see later) may be visited.

17 k. *Lannion* (Hotels: *de France*, best situation on quay; *de l'Europe*, with a pleasant garden—both tolerable). In the square are several curious old houses, especially one of slate and timbers painted red. The church of *S. Jean du Baly* replaces the chapel of the château; it has good flamboyant windows. Only a portal remains of the XII. c. church of *Kermaria au Traon*. A cross against one of the houses of the Rue du Tréguier commemorates the heroic death, on that spot, of the knight Geoffroy de Pontblanc, literally hacked to death by the English whilst defending the town against them in 1346.

Crossing a narrow valley, we find a long staircase, bordered by cottages and gardens, leading to the church of *S. Loup de Brélèvenez*, of XII. c., altered in XV. c., with a stone spire of XVI. c. An ossuary and calvary stand on its terrace. The aisles which surround the church are surmounted throughout by a triforium. The crypt dates from XI. c.

Renan recounts delightfully a souvenir of the environs of Lannion during the Revolution :—

'Madame Taupin, dame très pieuse, fut guillotinée. Le jour de l'exécution, ma bonne maman emmena toute la famille hors de Lannion, pour ne point participer au crime qui allait s'y accomplir. On se rendit avant le jour à une chapelle située à une demi-lieue de la ville, dans un endroit désert, et dédiée à Saint Roch. Beaucoup de personnes pieuses s'y rencontrèrent. Un signal devait les avertir du moment où la tête tomberait, pour que tous fussent en prière quand l'âme de la martyre serait présentée par les anges au trône de Dieu.'

Lannion is a wonderful centre for excursions of great interest, and carriages may be obtained there for the day at very reasonable prices.

It is a short drive, keeping to the E. bank of the Léguer, to the ruined *Château de Tonquedec*, situated on a richly wooded height, by a large pool swarming with frogs. There are lovely walks in the beech woods, but the castle itself is too much ruined to have much architectural beauty. It belonged from time immemorial to the Vicomtes de Coëtmer, one of whom,

THE STAIRS OF BRÉLÈVENEZ

Rolland, took part with Clisson against Jean IV., by whom his castle was destroyed, though he rebuilt it after the death of the duke.

'Une première enceinte forme en quelque sorte le corps avancé de la place. Un pont-levis y donnait accès. Le corps de la place était composé de constructions militaires, avec un massif d'habitations développés sur trois des faces du trapèze.

Des salles d'armes encore voûtées et très-belles se remarquent dans cette partie. Venait enfin le donjon, auquel on arrivait de la place par un pont volant qui reposait sur une pile quadrangulaire, dont le sommet était au niveau d'une porte placée au premier étage de la tour. Ce donjon et la tour qui avoisine l'entrée sont hexagones intérieurement et à quatre étages. Les murailles ont trois mètres d'épaisseur dans leur plus grande largeur.

'Le vicomtes de Tonquédec étaient au premier rang dans la noblesse de Bretagne; ils devaient au duc cinq chevaliers d'ost et au parlement général ils prétendaient tenir la première place comme premiers bannerets de la province. Ils avaient des cours dans soixante-une paroisses et trois grandes jurisdictions principales; ils possédaient de nombreux privilèges.'—*De Caumont*.

A delightful walk may be taken from Lannion on the W. bank of the Léguer. At 4 k. is the ruined xv. c. *Château de Coëtirec.* The *Chapelle de Kerfons* (7 k.) is an admirable building of 1559. On the same side of the river is (10 k.) the still inhabited and picturesque *Château de Kergrist,* and (1 k. farther) the chapel and mound of the *Château de Runfao.* Hence, descending a steep path to the river, and crossing it by the *Pont du Châtel,* the pedestrian may reach majestic, melancholy Tonquedec, and return by the route on the other side of the river.

But far the most interesting excursion from Lannion—indeed, the best in Brittany—is that (carriage, 14 fr. for the day) across a wild country, sprinkled with dolmens, to Trégastel, returning by Perros Guirec. The land is fertilised by the seaweed or *maërl* found so abundantly on this coast. As we come in sight of Trégastel, a large dolmen is seen on the r., surmounted by a calvary, and with a very fine view.

Trégastel (10 k.) has a large hotel kept by nuns, who take visitors (of both sexes) *en pension*. Near the shore in summer is a restaurant, where an excellent luncheon may be obtained. It is a perfectly beautiful and delightful place. The moorland country reaches to the silvery sands, sprinkled with gigantic masses of orange rock of the most extraordinary and picturesque forms, and between them the sea rushes up in deep blue and brilliant green waves of indescribable transparency. On a bright summer day the whole scene is one of unspeakable radiance. Delightful little walks wind round the western headland, where more groups of rock appear, as weird and fantastic as the first. An old castle crowns one of them. Endless are the rocky islets. In the distance are *Les Sept Isles*—L'Île Plate, l'Île du Cerf, Rouzic, Melban, Bonneau, la Pierre, and l'Île aux Moines with a lighthouse.

Not far from the coast also is the mysterious island of *Avalon*—the 'Isle of the Blessed'—where, and not at Glastonbury, Breton legend affirms that King Arthur is buried, as he desired, in 'the island valley of Avilion'—

> 'Where falls not hail nor rain nor any snow,
> Nor ever wind blows loudly, but it lies
> Deep-meadow'd, happy, fair, with orchard lawns
> And bowery hollows crowned with summer seas.'

Driving westwards through the narrow ways girt by low stone walls, we reach the harbour of *Ploumanac'h*. We may skirt the sands on foot while the carriage is obliged to go round, and, taking a stony path between cottages and pigstyes, descend into a little bay, where an islet rock, which we can reach at low water, is surmounted by a shrine of S. Guirec, who landed here from Britain in the VI. c. There are two rude statues of the saint, one in stone of XIII. c., the other in wood, into which young girls stick pins when they want to marry. This most romantic little spot is much resorted to for this purpose.

'The little village of Ploumanac'h is a collection of hotels built *pêle-mêle* among the masses of red granite, which are here flung about the shore as if the Titans had been playing at ninepins and had suddenly left off the game. The view from the hill overlooking the village and sea is magnificent; intense blue water smooth as a lake, pale purple islands beyond, and nearer, lying close under our feet, houses and rocks huddled confusedly together, huge fragments here piled one on the top of the other like a child's tower of bricks, there so closely wedged together as if even an earthquake could not separate them. Sometimes an enormous slab would be perched dolmen-like on the narrowest point of columnar supports, looking as if you could tip it over with your finger; at others, you might see a grand monolith standing alone like some solitary menhir; whilst all around, near and afar, the ground was covered with blocks, cones, pyramids, every fantastic form that granite can take, making up an indescribably strange and fantastic scene.'—'*Autumn in Western France*.'

The road ascends a very long steep hill, and descends abruptly upon the bay of *Perros* (Hôtel des Bains), with its long stretch of finest sands, very safe for children, but far less interesting than those of Trégastel.

Another long hill is picturesquely crowned by the fine church of *Notre Dame de Clarté*, a beautiful gothic building of 1350, with a spire. Hence there is a grand view over land and sea. Notre Dame de Clarté is invoked for weak eyes. About 8 k. from Trégastel we reach *Perros Guirec*, where Renan usually spent his summers, and where he died. The church, in a cemetery garden, is full of quaint character, mostly XII. c., with a very deep porch and a renaissance tower. The interior has heavy, rudely-sculptured capitals, and an immense bénitier. It is 10 k. from Perros Guirec to Lannion.]

[Those who drive from Lannion to (36 k.) Morlaix may, by a divergence, visit S. Jean du Doigt on the way; it is, however, as well visited as an excursion from Morlaix. 11 k. from Lannion in this direction is *S. Michel en Grève*, in a bay once covered with forest, but now very bare. The church has a beautiful spire of 1614. 1 k. distant is *Trédrez*, of which S, Yves was rector in the XIII. c. It was in the waste land of the grève that King Arthur (Artus in Breton chronicle) is said to have fought the dragon; but another legend tells that the dragon of the red rock—Roch' Ru—was killed by S. Efflam, an Irish saint who landed near this, at the spot where *La Chapelle S. Efflam*, and his sacred well, are still visited by numbers of pilgrims. The church of *Plestin* (17 k.) contains the XVI. c. tomb of S. Efflam and XV. c. statues of S. Cadoc and S. Herblain. At 25 k. the road reaches *Lanmeur* (Grande Lande), occupying the site of the ancient city *Kerfunteun*. The church of *S. Mélar* has some remains of a rebuilding in the XI. c. of the church of the older city, of which the original crypt remains. It is dedicated to Mélar or Méloir, a Breton prince, put to death by Rivod, Comte de Cornouaille, in 538. His XIV. c. statue represents him with his right hand and left foot cut off, mutilations he received from Rivod to unfit him to ride, and that his conqueror might more easily seize his estates; but God restored them 'comme une patte d'écrevisse.' The crypt, with curiously sculptured capitals, contains the fountain still called Kerfunteun (in Breton 'the village of the fountain'), formerly used for baptism by immersion, which it is believed will overflow on a Trinity Sunday and destroy the church; wherefore, to protect the town, high mass is always celebrated in the chapel on Trinity Sunday. The priory church of *Kernitron* (the place of Our Lady the Virgin) is an interesting rebuilding dating from XII. c. There is a much frequented *pardon* here. Near the village are the menhirs of *Ru-Peulven* and *Kermerchou*, and (2½ k.) the tumulus of *Tossen-ar-Choniflet*. It is from Lanmeur that one must diverge 8 k. to S. Jean du Doigt (see later).

540 k. *Plounérin* has a ruined romanesque church. The *Chapelle du Bon-Voyage* is renaissance.

[The railway leaves to l. the *Chapelle de S. Laurent du Pouldour*, to which there is a famous pilgrimage.

'La nuit du 9 au 10 août de chaque année, une foule de dévots s'y rendent des paroisses environnantes, et, quand ils ont fait sur les genoux le tour du cimetière, ils entrent en rampant dans un fours pratiqué sous l'autel, pour rappeler le supplice du feu infligé à S. Laurent, baisent la pierre de l'âtre et ressortent par l'étroite ouverture qu'assiègent d'autres pèlerins impatients. Puis, après s'être frotté les mains et la figure aux pieds de la statue du saint, ils se dépouillent complètement de leurs vêtements et se plongent à l'envie dans une fontaine sacrée, construite en forme de niche, avec un siège en pierre pour asseoir les baigneurs. L'eau de source, s'échappant avec abondance par un canal supérieur, pour retomber dans le bassin de la fontaine, jaillit en cascade sur leur tête, et chaque baigneur, avant de ceder la place à un autre, prononce ces paroles sacrémentelles : '*Sant Lorans hon préservo hag a lamo diganéomp ar boan izili*' (Que S. Laurent nous préserve et nous guerisse des rhumatismes).

'La vertu de ces ablutions est, comme nous l'avons vu, de préserver ou de guérir des rhumatismes ; quelques-uns des pélerins, moins fervents et plus frileux, se font remplacer par des mendiants qui s'offrent, moyennant une légère rétribution, à recevoir coup à coup plusieurs douches pour le compte d'autrui.

'Au coup de minuit, la foule abandonne la fontaine du Pouldour, pour se porter dans une prairie où commencent, à la clarté de la lune ou à celle des cierges empruntés à la chapelle, des luttes qui durent plusieurs heures. Des vieillards les juges du camp, ont précédé, dans de longs conciliabules, à l'admission des concurrents, à leur classement suivant leur âge. Les hommes mariés sont formellement exclus. Il n'y a point de prix, ou plutôt il n'y en a qu'un digne de la valeur des combattants : on lutte pour l'honneur de la paroisse. Quand les préparatifs sont terminés, d'anciens lutteurs, reduits au rôle de hérauts, crient : *Lice ! lice !* comme on le faisait dans les tournois, et rangent en rond les nombreux spectateurs. Cette opération s'exécute dans un ordre merveilleux ; et cependant l'autorité civile est absente : elle dort. Quant à l'autorité ecclésiastique, elle a, depuis 80 ans, intendit la chapelle, où aucun office religieux n'est célébré, mais cette prohibition n'a pas fait perdre à cette chapelle ses titres à la vénération.

'Quand le soleil se lève, les femmes, qui n'avaient pas encore paru, remplacent les hommes à la fontaine ; seulement leur costume est moins léger que celui de ces derniers ; elles passent derrière une haie pour quitter la chemise, qu'elles y reprennent ensuite ; mais elles conservent leur jupe, et les cheveux épars, la gorge couverte d'un mouchoir sous lequel personne ne songe à jeter des regards indiscrets, elles viennent à leur tour courber la tête sous les flots de l'eau lustrale.'—*Pol de Courcy*, '*La Bretagne contemporaine.*'

563 k. *Morlaix*[1] (Hotels : *de l'Europe*—first rate, a most capital centre for a week of excursions ; *de Provence*). The

[1] From *mor*, sea, and *lès*, high, because of its position above an arm of the sea.

first view of Morlaix—the second town in Finistère—from the railway shows its peculiar character. Its houses fill a very deep hollow between two steep hills; the railway crosses the valley at a great height by a magnificent viaduct; and, through the centre of the hollow, the little stream of the Morlaix trickles into the port (*bassin à flot*), half canal, half estuary, which is navigable for the 11 k. which separates the town from the sea.

'Morlaix, assis au fond de sa vallée, avec sa couronne de jardins et les paisibles caboteurs à voiles roses qui dorment sur son canal.'—*Émile Souvestre.*

The Latin name of the town, Mons Relaxus, came from its fortress, which existed at the time of the Roman occupation. Drennalus, disciple of Joseph of Arimathea, and first bishop of Tréguier, is said to have preached the gospel here A.D. 72. The town and castle were besieged for two months by Henry II. of England. Emile Souvestre, the romantic writer on Brittany, and General Moreau, were natives of Morlaix.

There is little remarkable in the town, though many of its old houses are very quaint and picturesque. The handsome collegiate church of *Notre Dame du Mur*, where a Te Deum was chanted when Mary Queen of Scots arrived at Morlaix as a bride, was demolished in 1805. *S. Mathieu* has a heavy renaissance tower. *S. Melaine*, founded 1150 and rebuilt 1489, is chiefly remarkable for its gargoyles representing the vices of monks, and for its sculptured organ and font-cover. The church of the Dominican convent, now used as a public library, is XIII. c. and XIV. c. In the Rue S. Melaine and Rue de Bourret are a number of fine timber houses of xv. c., xvi. c. and xvii. c. When their little courtyards are covered in and lighted by skylights, they are known as *maisons à lanterne*. No. 12, Rue des Nobles, has a fine sculptured staircase. On an island rock, where the canal of the port enters the sea, is the *Château du Taureau*, built by the merchants of the town in the xiv. c. to defend it against the English, and now a state prison.

The six principal excursions to be made from Morlaix are: S. Pol de Léon and Roscoff, S. Jean du Doigt, Huelgoat and S. Herbot, S. Thégonnec and Guimiliau, Plougastel, and the Folgoët, though the last may be taken on the day of leaving Morlaix.

The district is full of local superstitions.

'Nos laboureurs se meuvent, ils agissent dans un monde réel, quand leur imagination erre sans cesse dans un monde de chimères et de fantômes. L'oiseau qui chante[1] repond à leurs questions, marque les années de leur vie, l'époque de leur mariage. Un bruit fortuit, répeté trois fois, leur prédit un malheur; les hurlemens d'un chien leur annoncent la mort; le mugissement lointain de l'océan, le sifflement des vents entendus dans la nuit, sont la voix du noyé qui demande un tombeau. Des trésors sont gardés par des géans et par des fées. Chaque pays a sa folie, Brétagne les a toutes.

'Dans les cantons environnant Morlaix, on craint des génies nommés *Teus*. Le *Teus-ar-pouliet* se présente sous la forme d'un chien, d'une vache, ou d'un autre animal domestique. Tout l'ouvrage de la maison est exécuté par eux.

'On parle du *Cariquel-an-Ancou* (la brouette de la mort). Elle est couverte d'un drap blanc, des squelettes la conduisent; on entend le bruit de sa roue quand quelqu'un est près d'expirer.

'Sous le château de Morlaix, il existe de petits hommes d'un pied de haut, vivant sous terre, marchant et frappant sur des bassins; ils étalent leur or et le font sécher au soleil, L'homme qui tend la main modestement reçoit d'eux une poignée

---

[1] The cuckoo.

de ce métal ; celui qui vient avec un sac, dans l'intention de le remplir, est éconduit et maltraité.

'Les laveuses, *ar Cannerez nos* (les chanteuses de nuit), qui vous invitent à tordre leurs l'nges, qui vous cassent les bras si vous les aidez de mauvaise grâce, qui vous noient si vous les refusez, vous portent à la charité.'—*Cambry,* '*Voyage dans Le Finistère.*'

[A line runs N. from Morlaix to—
17 k. *Plouénan.* The church has a fine processional cross. Soon S. Pol de Léon appears on the r.

'The country began to run in straight horizontal lines—a moorlike tableland with furze and broom. On turning a corner we caught sight of the sea on our right, and before us rose a tall single spire, and near it a pile with two lower spires of the same kind. It is a stern, hard, rugged town, people and houses clean, but small and stern ; houses all granite, even to the least, and very plain, and there are no very large ones. The single spire is most beautiful, but, like everything else here, there is a severe cast about it. It is granite, and there are many square forms about it ; but it quite shoots up from the dreary, desolate, silent place.'—*Dean Church,* '*Letters.*'

21 k. *S. Pol de Léon* (Hotel: *de France*—tolerable ; *du Cheval Blanc*), a place named from its first missionary Paul-Aurelien, who came from England in 530. S. Pol was the birthplace of the sculptor Michel Colomb. From a great distance its exquisite spires, which give the town the name of *la Ville aux clochers à jour,* are seen rising over the surrounding flats.

'I can remember nothing so unique, so solemn, so melancholy, and so majestic. Far off, rising statelily above wide brown plain, barren shore, and silvery sea, you see the twin spires of S. Pol, and near it, but towering far above, the airy, glorious tower of the Kreizker, so celebrated in Breton legend and song, and so deservedly the boast of the county of Léon. Slowly the distinctive features of the scene are made out—the little town clustered around the gracious cathedral, the gardens and fields stretching to the sea, and the Kreizker crowning all, its light yet solid spire, pierced with star-shaped openings, letting in the day. "Were an angel to come down from heaven," writes a Breton author, " he would alight on the Kreizker before setting foot on Breton soil."'—*Autumn in Western France.*

' De la route de Morlaix l'aspect de la ville est très pittoresque. La haute tour du Kreizker, surmontée d'un flèche élancée, travaillée à jour, la domine, et semble se lier à la cathédrale dont on aperçoit en même temps le toit et les deux clochers. Plus loin, à l'orient de celle-ci, on découvre une autre tour, mince et svelte comme un minaret, qui, bien que fort moderne, se marie assez heureusement à distance avec les clochers gothiques. On dirait que toute la ville n'est qu'une immense église, et il y faut entrer pour reconnaître son erreur.'—*Prosper Mérimée.*

The churches are perfect in the beauty of their proportions. The ancient *Cathedral* of S. Pol,[1] which has the unusual virtue of being entirely mediæval, is XII. c., XIII. c., and XIV. c., having been finished in 1540. The W. façade has a single portal, preceded by a porch, above which is a balustraded terrace. Higher are three lancets, surmounted by a gallery and balustrade. A third balustrade unites the towers, which have splendid stone spires, pierced with roses and adorned with pinnacles. On the S. is the beautiful XIII. c. porch called *Porte des Lépreux*. The low nave, of seven bays, has a triforium and clerestory. In the S. transept is a glorious rose-window. The stalls are of 1512. The local saints, of whom relics are preserved here, include S. Pol Aurelien, *c.* 570; S. Jennenon, 530; S. Joevin, 562; S. Houardon, S. Ternoc, S. Gouesnon, S. Guinger, and S. Goulven. The church contains a fine series of episcopal tombs, from the repose of the XV. c. to the kneeling figures of

[1] S. Pol was born in England in 492, and died at the age of 102 in 594. In much he resembled S. Francis. When birds ravaged the fields of his master, S. Hydultus, he summoned them to follow him to the monastery, where that gentle abbot chid them, and then blessed them, and they never despoiled his fields any more. When the incursions of the sea threatened the monastery of his sister, which was near the shore, he bade the waves retire a thousand paces, and then desired his sister to place a range of pebbles along the new shore; these at once grew into a wall of rocks, which stopped the encroachments of the sea for ever. When a terrible dragon ravaged the promontory, S. Pol ordered a young gentleman of Cleder to accompany him; and when the dragon came forth roaring and vomiting flames, he bade him follow that young man, who led the dragon to a point of rock, whence it was precipitated into the sea. This point is still called Toull-ar-Sarpant. The name of Kergournadac'h—'he who will not fly '—was given to the young man, who has left it to his castle.

the XVIII. c. and XIX. c. Far earlier is that of Conan Mériadec, first sole sovereign of Brittany, the founder of the original church in the IV. c. or V. c. It resembles the Christian sarcophagi at Arles, and is now used as a bénitier near the W. door. This Conan was the father of S. Ursula, celebrated in the pictures of Carpaccio at Venice, and is described as the cruel oppressor of the Druids. Formerly a copper plate, raised three feet from the pavement, was inscribed, 'Hic jacet Conanus, rex Britonum.' In the choir are the tombs of Bishop François Visdelou, 1671, one of the rare monuments of Brittany which have escaped from vandalism, and of the last Bishop, de la Marche, who died in London, 1806. Before the altar of the Bon Secours is the tomb of the blessed Amice Picard, 1599—1652, who is supposed to have lived for eighteen years without other nourishment than the sacrament, and to whom children who have no walking power are brought to obtain the use of their limbs. On the vaulting of a chapel of the S. aisle is a quaint emblematical XVI. c. painting of the Trinity. On the choir screen and tombs are rows of little gable-ended boxes, surmounted by a cross, each containing a skull, and inscribed, 'Ici repose le chef de . . .' There is a dreary little *Public Garden* behind the cathedral.

Notre Dame du Kreizker[1] is said to have been founded in gratitude by a young girl of Léon, who was cured by S. Kirec, Archdeacon of Léon in the VI. c., of a paralysis with which she had been punished for profaning a festival of the Virgin with mundane employments. The church is chiefly XIV. c., with aisles and porches of XV. c. The N. porch is an exquisite specimen of flamboyant gothic; but the great feature is the glorious tower, 'chef d'oeuvre de grâce et de légèreté,'—which Vauban called 'un coup d'audace,'—which rises between the nave and choir.

'Ce ne sont pas des mains d'ouvriers qui ont porté ces pierres dans le ciel : le *vieux Guillaume*[2] a tout fait en une seule nuit. Il voulait se bâtir une église plus belle que toutes celles qui avaient été élevées au vrai Dieu par les hommes ; mais, une fois le coq posé sur le haut de la flèche S. Pol est venu avec de l'eau bénite, il a chassé Satan et il a confisqué son travail. Aussi

---

[1] From *kreis*, the middle of ; *ker*, the town.
[2] A Breton name for the devil—also called 'le loup Guillou.'

dans le pays, appelle-t-on encore Kreis-ker—la tour du diable.'—
Le Foyer Breton.

The four pillars, which so marvellously support the tower,

THE KREISKER, S. POL DE LÉON.

are the only interesting feature of the interior. There is a fine view from the summit of the tower.

'Ce clocher, tant célébré par les dictons et les poésies populaires, est le roi des campagnes du Léonais et l'orgeuil de la Bretagne.'—*Henri Martin.*

Several houses are XIII. c., XIV. c., and XV. c.

Emile Souvestre says that at S. Pol the reverence for children is such that no woman suckles her infant without crossing herself, and if you pass a woman with a child in her arms you must say 'God bless you.' Many of the poems in the *Bargaz Breiz* are in the dialect of Léon. The Léonais detest the Cornouaillais, who have generally got the better of them. One of the proverbs of the latter says: 'Un cornouaillais, vieux et cassé, vainquit trois léonnais, jeunes et robustes.'

The ruined manor of *Kerangouez*, near S. Pol, bears the device, eminently Breton, of '*Mutoudez*' ('be silent'). Near the manor of *Pontplancoët* is a peulven, said to have been hurled by the devil at the cathedral of S. Pol, and, missing its mark, to have fallen here. The *Manoir de Kermor-ruy* (of the Red Sea) was built by a returned crusader. One of the Perfeunteniou, born here, wrote, as general of the Cordeliers, 'Le Point d'Honneur en Matière de Duel.'

Not far from the Kreisker is the *Cemetery*, with its curious calvary and ossuaries.

'An avenue of trees runs up to an extraordinary-looking church, another to a calvary. At intervals, on the outside walls, were arched places in which were skulls and bones,—the skulls sometimes in a sort of box with the name of the person on it. On each side of the avenue to the calvary were shrines with a representation—large wooden or earthenware figures—of a scene of the Passion; and at the end there was a circle, in the midst of which a large crucifix rose against the sky, with two large columns on each side, and two shrines with representations of the Taking Down from the Cross and the Burial. In front was a large space, paved with gravestones. I never saw any representation of this kind which struck me so much. It is no use being sentimental, but the effect of these "stations" among the tombs in a cool evening following a hot day, and among these wild, sad people, with their gloomy customs respecting the dead, was something unlike anything I ever felt. From this place we looked down on a bay; it was quite dusk, the sea a black blue, and the hills a deep blue-grey. The moon rose behind them, first a deep red, then burning copper, then with a strange yellow brilliance all round, reflected dimly on the bay.'—*Dean Church*, '*Letters*.'

'On ne jette plus de fleurs sur les tombeaux. Un petit bénitier, placé sur chaque tombe, aide à chasser les mauvais anges qui troublent les repos des morts. On les veille pendant quelques nuits, pour empêcher les diables à les emporter en enfer. Dans le Léonnais, on dit à ceux qui foulent les tombeaux,
"Quit a ha lesse divan va anaoun :"
mot à mot—
"Retirez-vous de dessus mon trépassé."

CHÂTEAU DE KÉROUZÉRÉ.

On a, dans ces contrées, une profonde vénération pour les morts.'—*Cambry*, '*Voyage dans le Finistère.*'

As in most Breton bone-houses, the skulls are inscribed with the names of those to whom they belonged. 'Cy est le chef de M. . . . .'[1]

[1] Read *A Summer in Brittany*, by T. A. Trollope.

A little W. of S. Pol, in the direction of Plouescat, is the XV. c. and XVI. c. *Château de Kérouzéré*, chiefly built in 1458, but restored in 1602. The tomb of its founder, Jean de Kérouzéré (1460), cup-bearer to Duke Jean V., is in the neighbouring church of *Sibiril*.

20 k. *Roscoff* (Hotel: *des Bains de Mer*—good) is a little town on the sea shore—' petite ville jetée en avant dans la mer comme un navire à l'ancre.'[1] Here Mary Queen of Scots landed at five years old to be affianced to the Dauphin, and founded the chapel of *S. Ninian*, now in ruins. Here also Charles Edward landed as a fugitive after the battle of Culloden. The *Church of Notre Dame de Croaz Baz* (of sculptured friezes) has two quaint renaissance ossuaries. It contains three alabaster reliefs of the Annunciation, Adoration of the Kings, and Scourging of Christ.

'A late and admirable remnant of the gothic style.'—*Lübke.*

The port and harbour, with rocks and a distant lighthouse, are rather pretty: an enormous fig-tree has great local celebrity.

'Roscoff est une petite colonie maritime placée sur l'océan, et qui, lorsqu'on vient de la mer, paraît accrochée au bas du promontoire, comme une coquille marine. D'après sa position, on devrait s'attendre à voir tous les habitants de la commune consacrés au service de la mer; cependant il n'en est rien. Roscoff ne fournit pas plus de marins que les autres points de Finistère, et presque toute sa population s'occupe de la culture des terres, qui sont, dans ces parages, d'une incroyable fertilité. Les légumes les plus délicats y poussent en plein champ, et les Roscovites en font un commerce immense dans toute la Bretagne. Quelque route que vous parcouriez, vous les rencontrez assis sur le brancard de leurs charrettes légères, rapidement emportés par le petit cheval du pays, et chantant une ballade Bretonne.'—*E. Souvestre*, '*Les Derniers Bretons*.'

A little mail-boat (25c.) crosses to the *Isle de Batz* (Enez-Baz, Isle of the Staff—of S. Pol), where S. Pol landed and subdued a terrible dragon, leading him captive by his stole,

[1] Souvestre.

which (l'Etole de S. Pol)—a piece of Byzantine embroidery—is preserved in the church.

'Nul parmi les apôtres monastiques de la Petite-Bretagne ne passe pour avoir exercé sur les animaux les plus féroces un empire plus absolu et plus secourables aux populations que S Pol. Tantôt il fait rentrer pour toujours au fond des forêts un buffle, qui avait renversé et mis en pièces à coup de cornes la cellule qu'un moine avait bâtie auprès de la fontaine où venait boire cet animal. Tantôt il apprivoise et réduit à l'état domestique une laie féroce avec ses marcassins, dont la race fut longtemps reconnue et conservée par les gens du pays. Ici, c'est une ourse énorme qu'il fait reculer jusque dans une fosse où elle se rompt le col. Là, c'est un crocodile ou un serpent de mer qui avait mis en fuite le comte du canton avec tous ses guerriers, mais que Paul oblige à se précipiter dans la mer, sur le point du rivage de la Cornouaille où l'on montre encore un tourbillon qui se nomme *l'Abîme du Serpent*.

'La légende ne s'arrête pas en si beau chemin ; elle ajoute que, voyant le monastère qu'habitait sa soeur, sur le bord de la mer, menacé par les grandes marées, il fit reculer la mer de quatre mille pas, et commanda aux religieuses de borner la nouvelle limite avec des cailloux "lesquels tout à l'instant crurent en grands et hauts rochers pour brider la furie des flots." On comprend assez que l'on interprétait ainsi, sous le toit de chaume du paysan celte, les travaux d'endiguement auxquels avait sans doute présidé l'émigré breton qui fut le premier évêque de Léon.'
—*Montalembert.*

The romanesque church which succeeded the monastery of S. Pol is now ruined and half buried in sand. There is not a tree in the island, all the men are sailors, and the women wear a pretty costume of black, with white linen sleeves and collar, and a white cashmere hood—no colour whatever. A rock on the shore is known as *Roche Moloch*.

Near the hamlet of *Keresta* is a Celtic monument of four dolmens grouped together.]

[One of the pleasantest excursions from Morlaix is that to S. Jean du Doigt. Carriage for the day, 12 frs. *Lanmeur* (see p. 253) may be (12 k.) taken on the way.

S. Jean du Doigt is one of the loveliest spots in Brittany. A dull drive leads to it. Then you descend into a deep green valley, recalling those of Devonshire, and opening to the deep blue sea, with rocky islets covered with seaweed. Against the hillside the grand church spire rises from the rich woods. The little *Hôtel de S. Jean* is clean, and has excellent food—a comfortable and economical resort for artists.

An exquisite gothic lych-gate is the entrance to a churchyard

S. JEAN DU DOIGT.

of marvellous picturesqueness. On one side is a beautiful and vast renaissance *fountain*, said to have been made for Anne of Brittany by an Italian artist.

'La fontaine est la plus élegante, la plus mignarde, la plus aërienne que nous ayons jamais vue. Elle est construite en Kersanton et en plomb. Trois bassins superposés et decorés d'admirables festons et de têtes d'anges d'une exquise delicatesse, sont surmontés d'une figure représentant Saint-Jean, qui confère le baptême à Jésus Christ. Il est impossible de dire quelle est la grâce de cette construction, dont les détails apparaissent à travers une pluie d'eau limpide qui retombe en cascade des trois bassins.'—*Emile Souvestre.*

At the time of the Pardon,[1] crowds of pilgrims always surround the fountain.

THE LYCH GATE, S. JEAN DU DOIGT.

'Son eau, vivifiée par l'index du saint, guérit toutes les maladies, est sans cesse entourée de femmes et d'enfants d'hommes à la barbe grise, qui se lavent les mains, les yeux,

[1] *Les Bretons* of Auguste Brizeux describes a pilgrimage to the pardon of S. Jean du Doigt, where Anna hangs up a waxen heart for the cure of Guenn-Du,

et les genoux. Toutes les parties du corps que le douleur attaque, reçoivent du soulagement par cette liqueur admirable; elle charme l'ennui, dissipe les chagrins; les moly des anciens, le serpent d'Esculape, tout les sécrets de l'Île de Cos, produisaient jadis moins d'effet; et, dans les temps modernes, l'Averne à Rome, Saint Jacques de Compostelle, le tombeau de Mahomet, et Notre Dame de Lorette, donnent moins d'indulgences aux fidèles qui les visitent.'—*Cambry*.

Close by, amongst the grey gravestones, is a tall stone crucifix of great beauty. On the other side of the porch stands a very curious *funeral chapel*, open at the end; and the whole is overlooked by the graceful flamboyant tower surmounted by a lead spire.

The interior of the church has a triple nave, with a chevet ending in a straight wall. The timber ceiling has great refinement of finish. Behind the high altar is preserved the great relic of the place—'the right-hand first finger of S. John the Baptist'—preserved in a casing of silver and crystal. The priest touches with the relic the eyes of those who kneel to receive it, and it is believed to strengthen them.

'On brûlait le corps de S. Jean à Samarie, par ordre de Julien l'Apostat; une pluie miraculeuse permet aux chrétiens d'en dérober quelques reliques; un de ses doigts fut envoyé par eux à Philippe le Juste, patriarche de Jérusalem. Tècle, vierge normande, le transporte dans sa patrie, fait bâtir une église dans laquelle elle le consacre à la vénération publique. Un jeune bas breton, natif de Plougasnou, se passionne pour cette pièce merveilleuse, et forme le projet de l'enlever. Le doigt n'attend pas cette violence, et se place, entre cuir et chair, sous le poignet de son adorateur; sans qu'il se doutât de cette bonne fortune. Ce fut en 1437 que, miraculeusement entraîné vers sa patrie, il se met en marche. Dès la première journée, passant dans une petite ville, les cloches sonnent d'elles-mêmes, les arbres s'inclinent; toute la nature s'emeut et de respect et de plaisir. Il passe pour sorcier; on le saisit, on l'enferme. Le lendemain, qui le croirait? il s'éveille dans son pays dans la commune de Plougasnou, près d'une fontaine qu'on nomme encore *Feunteum ar Ris* (Fontaine du Doigt). Tout s'emeut dans Plougasnou; la chapelle de S. Méridec s'ouvre ; la terre tressaile d'allegresse et se couvre de fleurs nouvelles. À peine notre breton était-il à genoux que le doigt du saint se dégage et va se placer sur l'autel. Il reconnaît l'objet de son adoration ; les cierges s'allument, le peuple se prosterne. Le duc Jean, qui résidait à Vannes, accourt à cette nouvelle ; il arrête d'élever une église à son patron. Que de miracles ! les morts ressuscitent, les sourds entendent, les aveugles voient. Les offrandes des fidèles facilitent la construction du nouveau temple. La première pierre en fut posée par le duc Jean, le premier août 1440. Il ne fut achevé qu'en 1513, par la libéralité de la reine Anne.'—*Cambry*, '*Voyage dans le Finistère.*'

Some of the precious gifts to the church are also exhibited—a glorious golden chalice given by Anne of Brittany, who considered herself cured from illness by a pilgrimage to S. Jean, and another chalice, with beautiful enamels, given by Claude de France (daughter of Anne of Brittany), wife of François I., on the birth of the Dauphin in 1517. A *Hospice*, for the use of pilgrims, stands close to the churchyard.

The surroundings of S. Jean—the deep lanes through woods by the side of clear brooks, the rocks and islets of the sea-shore, the cottages buried in roses and clematis—have a wonderful charm.

'Le Pardon de S. Jean du Doigt offre une physiognomie à part. Il n'est pas très-aisée de bien voir la procession annuelle du 23 juin sans être incommodé par la foule compacte qui encombre les pierres tombales à la sortie de l'église ; mais il est surtout impossible de n'être point assourdi par les glapissements de la plus affreuse réunion de mendiants et d'estropiés que la Bretagne renferme, étalant toute l'horreur de leurs plaies et nasillant sans discontinuer leur interminables complaintes.

'Pour embrasser dans leur ensemble toutes les parties de la fête, il faut monter jusqu'à la plate-forme de la tour, d'où part le *dragon* ou pièce d'artifice qui va allumer sur la montagne voisine le *tantad* ou feu de joie. De ce poste élevé, on domine la foule bigarrée gravissant lentement, au chant des hymnes sacrées, le coteau qui conduit au bûcher, pendant que les pélerins se distribuent l'eau de la *Fontaine du Doigt* pour la boire et pour s'en baigner les yeux. Au moment où le *dragon* communique son feu au bûcher, une décharge générale de mousqueterie se fait entendre, les tambours battent aux champs, la fumée de l'encens s'élève vers le ciel mélée à celle de la poudre, à celle du pétillant feu de lande et de la couronne de fleurs qui le domine, et la voix des prêtres entonne l'hymne du S. Doigt.

'La procession redescend ensuite la montagne, pour rentrer dans l'église, ayant, en tête, des porteurs de lourdes bannières herminées, qui se disputent l'honneur de les faire passer sous l'arc de triomphe du cimetière ; des clameurs s'élèvent de la foule

L'ORATOIRE DE PLOUGAZNOU.

en faveur du Trégonais, du Léonard ou du Cornouaillais qui réussira dans ce tour de force, auquel peu de bras et de reins peuvent aspirer. À la suite des bannières et au milieu d'une flotille de navires pavoisés, portés sur des brancards par des marins, se distingue le vaisseau *la Cordelière*, dont le nom rappelle la plus grande des *nefs* du XVI. c., que la reine Anne avait fait construire au Dourduff, port voisin de S. Jean, et qui eut une fin si glorieuse en abordant *la Régente* d'Angleterre au combat de S. Mathieu, en 1512. De jeunes mousses impriment avec des rubans un mouvement alternatif de roulis et de tangage aux navires, et, à chaque arrêt de la procession, un maître d'équipage donne, par un coup de sifflet, le signal de changer les pièces ; au second coup de sifflet, les bâtiments font feu de tribord et de bâbord, et l'on se remet en marche. La vue se porte ensuite sur le défilé des *Miraclou*. C'est ainsi qu'on désigne les gens guéris dans l'année par l'attouchement du doigt et par l'eau de la fontaine. Vient enfin, derrière les porteurs et porteuses de croix, d'oriflammes et de statues de la Vierge, restes des trésors de S. Jean et de Plougasnou, un nombreux clergé en dalmatiques, portant, sur des brancards, dans des reliquaires d'argent, le chef de S. Mériadec, le bras de S. Maudez ou Mandé, en enfin le *bis sant Jan*, posé sous un petit temple, dans son étui de cristal monté en or. Une mêlée générale s'engage devant la balustrade de l'autel pour se faire *donner le doigt*, c'est à-dire se le faire appliquer sur l'oeil par la main du prêtre.'—*Pol de Courcy.*

On the hill W. of S. Jean is (1 k.) an oratory—*L'Oratoire de Plougaznou*—whither girls who wish to marry within the year resort to offer their hair to the Virgin.]

[A line leads S.E. from Morlaix to Carhaix, passing through a wild district of moorland, brown burns, stunted trees and heather—the whole effect recalling Scotland—before reaching—

33 k. *Huelgoat-Locmaria.*[1] Here an omnibus meets the train and takes travellers for 7 k., passing through a wooded gorge strewn with great rocks, and not unlike Killiecrankie, to—

Huelgoat (Hotel: *de France*, a good country inn, with *pension*), a quiet little town in a moorland district. The principal church, of 1591, contains a very curious lectern sculptured with figures in relief. Turning r. from the hotel, we soon reach a little lake. Thence a path r., by the cross beyond the mill, leads in a few minutes to *Le Rocher Tremblant*, a curious rocking-stone. Below this, by the river, is the strange hole in the rocks known as *Le Ménage de la Vierge.* The whole country is very pretty. *Osmunda regalis* grows abundantly by the banks of the stream.

A carriage (6 fr.) should be taken to (7 k.) *S. Herbot*, a very pretty spot, where the fine XVI. c. *Church of S. Herbot*, with a very beautiful tower, rises amongst the woods. Near the S.

[1] 'The place of Mary.'

porch, with its curious coloured statues of the twelve apostles, are an interesting calvary and ossuary. The interior has much solemn beauty. A very rich screen surrounds the chancel and supports a huge crucifix and images of saints. Within is a bier-like altar-tomb of XV. c., bearing the venerable figure of the hermit S. Herbot. There is much fine stained glass of 1556.

OSSUAIRE DE S. HERBOT.

The Pardon de S. Herbot (in May) is remarkable for the mass of tails of cows and oxen offered on the altar to the patron of horned beasts. The hair thus offered to the church produces an annual revenue of 1500 to 1800 fr. In the neighbourhood are the *Cascade de S. Herbot*, and the *Moulin* and the *Château du Rusquec*, a ruin of the XVI. c.

Near S. Herbot is the dolmen called *Tombeau du Géant*.

It is said that the giant was obliged to be doubled up six times before he could be enclosed here. This is perhaps the only dolmen which the people regard as a sepulchral monument.

At about 22 k. from Huelgoat, on the highest point of the hills of *Arhès*, the *Chapelle S. Michel* may be visited, in a bleak spot, with a very wide view.

45 k. *Carhaix* (Hotel: *de la Tour d'Auvergne*—tolerable), a small, but once important town, occupying the site of Vorganium, capital of the Osismii. In the v. c. it became part of the kingdom of Cornouaille, and the residence of Ahès, second daughter of Grallon, who gave its name of Ker-Ahès—the town of Ahès. The desecrated collegiate church of *S. Trémeur* was built 1529-35. It has a rich flamboyant portal, and a lofty square tower, which once supported one of the loftiest spires in Finistère, now destroyed by lightning. On the lower walls are traces of bullets, evidently left from the siege by Duguesclin in 1363. The xvi. c. doors are sculptured with scenes from the life of S. Trémeur. He is ordained; is martyred; his body kneels before Comorre, Count of Cornouaille, and he picks up his head; an angel guides him to heaven with his head in his hand. In the cemetery are remains of the cross, called from its sculptures ' *La Croix des douze Apôtres.*'

The house is preserved where La Tour d'Auvergne, *premier grenadier de France*, was born in 1743. His statue (1841) adorns the place, and his portrait is in the Hôtel de Ville. Near the town are caverns which local superstition believes to be the abode of demons. The Little Partridge, formerly abundant here, has now become rare.

To the l. of the road to Guingamp, about 8 k. from Carhaix, is *Carnoët*, with the gothic chapel of *S. Gildas*, containing the tomb of its patron saint, a great point for pilgrimage. Near this, at *Lancarnoët*, is a lofty menhir.

A line leads from Carhaix to Loudéac. See p. 233.]

[The road from Carhaix to (61 k.) Quimper passes—

9 k. *Cléden Poher*, with a xvi. c. church and granite calvary.

15 k. *Landeleau*, named from S. Téleau, bishop of Llandaff in the vi. c. His stone sarcophagus—in which S. Yves once slept as a penance—remains in the church, which also contains

the tomb of François du Chastel, Marquis de Mesle, 1612. His château of *Châteaugal* is now transformed into a farm. A well, in the circuit of an ancient camp, is the only remnant of the *Château de Granec*, destroyed at the end of the XVI. c.

24 k. *Châteauneuf du Faou* ('of the oak'), on the Aulne. The famous chapel of *Notre Dame des Portes* occupies the site of an oak in the trunk of which a silver statue of the Virgin was found. It was stolen by a soldier.

'Un bois sacré descende jusqu'au rivage, par une pente de 5 à 600 pieds, sur laquelle on a pratiqué des allées. C'est là que dans les nuits, on voit errer Notre Dame des Portes, en robe blanche, éblouissante de lumière. Le frottement de sa robe de soie se fait entendre au loin dans la campagne; cette apparition annonce des beaux jours, d'amples récoltes, et des succès à ses fidèles adorateurs. On n'ose pas alors approcher de l'enceinte; on s'agenouille, on s'humilie; on chante une hymne en l'honneur de la Vierge; on se retire enfin à reculons, et sans tourner le dos à la déesse. Ainsi nos bons aïeux sortaient jadis des forêts druidiques.'—*Cambry*.

(9 k. from Châteauneuf is *Spézet*, where, on the stream so called, is the *Chapelle du Cran*, built by the Seigneurs de Cranhuel in 1532, and possessing six windows filled with very beautiful stained glass of that date. The altar-piece, bearing the date of 1548, is very interesting.)

The road, after crossing the Aulne at 29 k., ascends the *Montagnes Noires*, passing to the r. *S. Thois*, and then the ruins of the *Château de la Roche*.

42 k. *Édern*. The XVI. c. church contains a statue of the English hermit S. Edern, mounted on the stag which he had tamed, and on which he used to ride. There is some good glass. In the churchyard is a fallen menhir.

44 k. *Briec*, near which are many megalithic remains.]

Leaving Morlaix, the railway reaches—

572 k. *Pleiber-Christ*. The church, chiefly renaissance, has sculptured stalls and a fine procession cross.

S. THÉGONNEC.

There is a public carriage from the station to Huelgoat, crossing the chain of the *Monts d'Arrée*, in the centre of which is (8 k.) *Plounéour-Ménez*, with a XVII. c. church, dedicated to S. Enéour. 4 k. E. of this is the ruined abbey of *Relecq*, founded 1132. One gallery of a (XIII. c.) cloister remains. Pilgrims resorting hither offer white fowls and a measure of wheat.

578 k. *S. Thégonnec.* There is no omnibus at the station, and travellers who wish to visit the famous calvary

THE CALVARY OF S. THEGONNEC.

must walk to the town, 3 k. N. There is a primitive inn, with good food but bad accommodation.

The churchyard of this very quiet little place is entered by a sumptuous renaissance *Gateway* of 1587. On the side entrance, S. Thégonnec, patron of beasts, is represented with the cart, drawn by a cow, which brought the materials of the church. The *Calvary* is much simpler than those of several neighbouring places; the centurion's figures are mounted on horseback on the upper story. Close by is an *Ossuary*, of 1677, consisting of two stories; its crypt contains a coloured wooden Entombment of 1702, of good execution.

On All Souls' Day immense crowds visit these cemeteries.

'Au jour des Morts, le lendemain de la Toussaint, la population entière du Léonais se lève sombre et vêtue de deuil. C'est la véritable fête de famille, l'heure des commémorations, et la journée presque entière se passe en dévotions. Vers le milieu de la nuit, après un repas pris en commun, on se retire; mais les mets sont laissés sur la table; car une superstition touchante fait croire aux Bretons qu'à cette heure ceux qu'ils regrettent se lèvent des cimetières et viennent prendre sous le toit qui les a vus naître, leur repas annuel.'—*Emile Souvestre*, '*Les Derniers Bretons*.'

In the fine XVII. c. *Church* is a richly sculptured bier. The 'costume' of S. Thégonnec—male and female—was always entirely black. The ruined castle of *Penhoat* is XIII. c.

Except in hay-harvest a vehicle may be obtained, but then it is necessary to walk 8 k. to reach *Guimiliau*, a little village celebrated for a magnificent *Calvary* of 1581-8. Its platform is crowded with stone statuettes, encircling the central crucifix and portraying the whole life of Christ in figures wearing XVI. c. costume. Most remarkable are the musicians, who precede the Bearing of the Cross. In a side-scene appear Catel Gollet (Catherine the Lost) hurled by devils into the mouth of a dragon representing hell. This Catherine, having made a false confession, died, but came back in 1560, to reveal her misery in the words—

'Voici ma main, cause de malheur,
Et voici ma langue détestable !
Ma main qui a fait le péché,
Et ma langue qui l'a nié.'

The XVI. c. *Church* is dedicated to Miliau, King of Cornouaille, assassinated in 531 by his brother Rivod, who seized his kingdom. The S. porch, of 1605, is very rich in sculpture. The font, of 1675, has a magnificent cover, and the organ loft and pulpit (1647) deserve notice.

The manor of Guimiliau is connected with the favourite Breton story of its handsome owner Marhek, who eloped with the beautiful daughter of the Marquis de Penmarc'h. He pursued the lovers, and having surprised them at the Château de Lestourd'hu, hanged Marhek from an oak in front of his own manor-house of Guimiliau, and enjoined upon his heirs to renew the oak for ever in memory of his vengeance.

3 k. W. of Guimiliau is *Lampaul*, where the XVI. c. church is approached by a triumphal arch surmounted by a calvary of 1668. The side porch of 1533 bears a statue of S. Pol with his dragon, and the dragon is often repeated in the decorations of the edifice.

590 k. *Landivisiau* (Hotel: *de Commerce*—tolerable). The church of *S. Turlaff* (archbishop of Dol in VIII. c.) has a rich portal of 1552-4 and a tower of 1590. The magnificent S. portal is adorned with delicate renaissance sculpture in Kersanton stone. A tomb commemorates the founder, François Tournemine. In the new cemetery is the curious sculptured façade of an ancient ossuary.

[A road leads N.W. through a wild country to (22 k.) Lesneven: see later.]

[A road leads N.E. to Plouescat by—

6 k. *Bodilis*, with a magnificent renaissance church, very rich in flamboyant decoration, containing a remarkable renaissance baptistery.

12 k. The road passes within sight (l.) of the moated *Château de Kerjean* of 1560—the 'Versailles of Brittany'—a very fine specimen of the Renaissance, with a gothic chapel of the same period. Kerjean was made a marquisate by Louis XIII. The château was built by Louis and Hamon Barbier in the middle of the XVI. c.; before that the lords of Kerjean lived in a little manor which was the scene of an adventure celebrated by Alfred de Musset in 'La Quenouille de Barberine.'

14 k. *S. Vougay*, which has a cemetery-cross of 1677. In the ruined chapel of *S. Jean Kerhan* is a vault containing the tomb of a knight of the time of Louis XIII. The ruined chapel of *Lanven* is built above a fountain once consecrated to Druidical worship. 2 k. E. is *Plouzévédé*, 1 k. N. of which the cemetery containing the *Chapelle de Berven* has a beautiful renaissance portal. The steeple (1575) is composed of a number of domes, one above the other. The cemetery-cross is sculptured with scenes from the Passion. Near the farm of Castel are the remains of *Castel-Coat-ar-Gars*.

18 k. On the l. are the *Château de Maillé* of 1550, and 4 k. W. *Lochrist*—'the place of Christ'—abounding in menhirs. Here, in 401, Fagan, Comte de Léon, vanquished the barbarians at the head of his Bretons, while S. Goulven, on the height, kept his hands, like Moses, lifted up in prayer. The church of *Plouvénez Lochrist* was built on the spot, and repaired in the XII. c., from which much remains. Amongst its old monuments is that of Jean de K'rmavan, bishop of Léon, 1514. This family bore the device of *Dieu Avant*, because when their château de Karman was burnt, during the absence of its lord, he rushed to the spot as soon as he heard of the catastrophe, and before attempting to save anything else broke into the chapel to rescue the sacred vessels, shouting ' Dieu, avant!'

23 k. *Plouescat*, in a country full of megalithic remains. The *Château de Kerlivri* has great towers, a gothic portal, and a donjon : its device is *Youll Doue*—'the will of God.' At 5½ k., on the way to S. Pol de Léon, is *Cléder*, with a *carneillon* or Celtic cemetery. Hence came the young man who helped S. Pol to subdue the dragon.[1] Near this is the *Château de Kermenguy*, inhabited by the family of the same name since 1400, and the ruined *Château de Kergournadec'h*,[2] built *c*. 1630.]

[8 k. from Landivisiau, on the road to S. Pol de Léon, is *Lambader*, where a XIV. c. chapel, rebuilt 1837, retains its side porch and a magnificent wooden *jubé*, given by Marc de Troërin in 1481. To the S. of the chapel is a pilgrimage fountain.]

[1] See p. 259.
[2] The name of the castle, Kergournadec'h, refers to this legend, signifying in Breton the *fearless one*, because its founder was the only man in the parish of Cleder who dared to accompany S. Pol in his expedition against the serpent.

599 k. *La Roche.* A rock on the l. of the railway is crowned by the ruins of the *Château de la Roche-Maurice* (Ro'ch Morvan), founded by Maurice or Morvan, king of the Bretons, Léon, and Cornouaille in 819, and demolished in 1490, during the wars made by Charles VIII. upon Anne of Brittany. Here Breton legend narrates that the chieftain Elorn used to appease a terrible dragon, by giving him one of his servants—selected by lot—to devour every Saturday. At last, only Elorn himself, his wife and daughter, remained. Then, in despair, Elorn threw himself down from his castle into the river Dourdoun, thenceforth called Elorn. But it happened that two Christian knights, returning from the Holy Land, saw him fall, and they drew him safely from the water, and dragged the dragon to Plounéour-Trez— 'the port of the beast'—where they drowned him. The church, of 1559, has a fine stained window and timber *jubé*. The renaissance ossuary has reliefs of the Dance of Death.

604 k. *Landerneau* (Hotels: *de la Univers*—tolerable; *Raould*) had its origin in a village which arose round the cell of S. Ernec, a Breton prince who became a hermit on the banks of the Elven. It has important cloth manufactories, in which many of the workmen are of English origin. The town is chiefly interesting from its curious bridge crossed by a street of old houses with a desecrated flamboyant chapel, which, from the gardens on the farther bank of the river, is an exquisite subject for an artist. The church, of *S. Houardon*, recently removed from its old site, has its tower and renaissance porch rebuilt as before, *S. Thomas de Cantorbèry* (l. of the river) is xvi. c. An excursion may be made to *Sizun*, with its beautiful triumphal arch at the entrance of the churchyard.

7 k. E., near the road to Carhaix, is *La Martyre*, with a fine church dedicated to the Breton king Salomon (*Merzer Salaun*— the martyr Salomon), which dates from XV. c. and XVI. c. The side porch is very rich in sculpture. The churchyard is entered by a triumphal arch surmounted by a flamboyant calvary in Kersanton stone. It was at La Martyre that the Breton gentlemen conspired, in 1718, to remove the regency from Philippe d'Orléans and give it to Philippe V. of Spain.

THE BRIDGE OF LANDERNEAU.

4 k. N., at the top of a long hill, (l.) is the *Chapelle S. Eloi*,[1] on whose festival numbers of horses are brought hither, to the shrine of their special patron, and forced to perform a kind of salutation to the statue of the saint. Then the rider makes the circuit of the chapel three times, and, before leaving, lays before the altar a handful of hair from the mane and tail of his steed.

[1] The monks latinised at pleasure names of Breton saints. Thus, what was originally S. Alar became S. Eloi; S. Gily was turned into S. Gilles; S. Dominoc'h into S. Dominique; S. Derien into S. Adrien.

[From the railway station a tram-line in conjunction with the principal trains gives easy and pleasant communication with—

11 k. *Ploudaniel*, which takes its name from the holy Daniel, whose worship is now replaced here by that of S. Guinien, brother of S. Judicaël, king of La Domnonée in the VII. c.

13 k. *Le Folgoët*. It is 1 k. direct W. to the village (Inn : *Trois-Rois*—very humble), which has risen around the famous pilgrimage church of *Notre Dame du Folgoët*. Here, in the midst of the woods, lived in the middle of the XIV. c., 'like a lonely sparrow,' a poor idiot named Salaun,[1] and day and night, after his manner, by the perpetual repetition of 'Ave Maria,' gave praise to the Virgin. Clothed in rags, and with no home but a hollow tree near a spring, he went daily to beg at the house doors of Lesneven, repeating his ' Ave Maria,' followed by ' *Saloun a zébré bara* ' ('Solomon could eat bread '), took that which was given to him and returned to his hermitage by the spring, into which he dipped his crusts, repeating still his 'Ave Maria.' In the depth of winter he would plunge in the fountain to his chin, till he was half frozen, and then would climb into the tree, and holding two of its branches, would swing himself backwards and forwards, singing 'O Maria !' and so would warm himself; but by his conduct obtained the name of *Le Fol*.

Thus he lived his harmless life for forty years, and then he fell sick, and, refusing to leave his cell, died with the name of Mary upon his lips, and was buried at the foot of his tree by the side of the spring. He was already forgotten, when 'God caused an exquisite lily to spring forth from his grave, a flower of celestial fragrance, and upon each of its leaves was written, in golden letters, "*Ave Maria !*" It flowered for a whole month, during which thousands flocked to see it, and, when it faded, the clergy dug around it to discover whence it took its root, and they found that it proceeded from the mouth of the dead body of Salaun.' The story is told by Jean de Langoućznou, Abbot of Landévennec, one of the witnesses of the miracle. The crowd of pilgrims never ceased around the *tombeau fleur-de-lysé*, and thus

---

[1] In Brittany idiots are still looked upon and spoken of as 'gifts of God,' and, as such, are tenderly regarded and cherished, maintained on the farms without work, and mourned when they die.

it was resolved to build the noblest church in Finistère over the fountain of the poor beggar.

'Vers le milieu du quatorzième siècle, un pauvre idiot vivait dans les bois aux environs de Lesneven. Les seuls mots qu'on lui entendît prononcer étaient une invocation à la Vierge : *O Itron verc'hes Vari!* (" O Madame, vierge Marie "). Avec cette phrase il demandait l'aumône. On ne le connaissait dans le pays que sous le nom du Fou du Bois, *ar fol coat*. Il mourut et fut enterré dans le cimetière du village où il était né. Quelques jours après, un beau lis poussa sur sa fosse, et la racine, dit la légende, sortait de la bouche même du cadavre. Chacun va crier au miracle. On accourt, on examine la fleur. Les dévots lisent dans son calice le nom de Marie. On décide que la Vierge, sa patrone chérie, en faisant croître sur sa tombe la fleur qui lui est consacrée, avait voulue montrer qu'elle avait récompensé la foi du pauvre mendiant. A cette époque, la Bretagne était déchirée par la guerre civile des deux prétendans à la couronne ducale, Jean de Montfort et Charles de Blois. Montfort ayant appris le miracle du lis, touché de dévotion, ou peut-être voulant gagner à son parti les gens de Lesneven, fit vœu de bâtir une chapelle à la Vierge du Fou de bois, s'il triomphait de son rival. Après la bataille d'Auray, devenu seul possesseur de son duché, il posa la première pierre de l'église, au lieu même où le lis avait poussé.'
—*Prosper Mérimée.*

Begun 1364, consecrated 1419, the church of *Folgoët* was made collegiate by Jean V., son of Jean de Montfort, in 1423. The W. end has two towers, separated by a porch. A third tower was built by Queen Anne, *c.* 1505 ; the S. porch is due to Alain de la Rue, Bishop of Léon, by whom the church was consecrated, and bears his statue on its central pillar. Before it are remains of the cross erected by Alain, Cardinal de Coëtivy, who is represented kneeling, with joined hands, upon the pedestal, holding his pilgrim's staff, and with his cardinal's hat upon his shoulders. Behind him stands a bishop, probably his patron S. Alain, and presents him to the Virgin; this work is attributed to Michel Colomb. At the angle of the side aisle and the *Chapelle de la Croix* is the *Portique des douze Apôtres*, covered with sculpture of the most exquisite refinement and delicacy;

but the statues of the apostles, destroyed at the Revolution, are replaced by feeble modern figures. The arms of Brittany and France are represented on one of the key-stones of the vaulting, in allusion to the marriage of Jean V. with Jeanne de France, daughter of Charles VI. On the lintel of the doors are *hermines passantes*, with the device of Brittany: *A ma vie*. On a pinnacle to r. of the porch is a statue of Jean V., bearing his sceptre and the charter of his foundation. On the whole, the architecture

NOTRE DAME DU FOLGOËT.

of the church is not imposing, but the details are of the utmost grace. The windows of the church are chiefly flamboyant, those of the sanctuary and the chapel of the Cross being of great beauty. A little portico shelters the waters of Salaun's fountain, as they issue from the building, from their source under the high altar. All round the E. part of the church is a beautiful frieze of mallow leaves. The exquisite detached foliage of the doors is still happily unrestored.

This is truly one of the 'secluded corners of Norman and Breton towns, where the cathedral stands, with delicate thistles and dog-rose and hawthorn carved in its crumbling grey stone; and plants as delicate as they, stone pinks and long-seeded grasses, grow in the crannies of its buttresses and belfry, round which circle the rooks; the corn fields and apple orchards as near by as the black carved and colonnaded houses of the town; places where art still keeps up its old, familiar, original framework of reality, of nature, of human life.'—*Vernon Lee*, '*Juvenilia*.'

STATUE OF SALAUN, LE FOLGOET.

The great feature of the interior is the magnificent *jubé*, like a lace veil, between the nave and choir. Very interesting also are the five altars, of Kersanton stone, which are contemporary with the building. The most remarkable is decorated with little figures of angels holding shields and phylacteries alternately.

'La pierre employée à cet effet est éminemment propre à la sculpture d'ornemens par sa dureté et la finesse de son grain. Elle ne se polit jamais parfaitement et reste âpre au toucher. Sa couleur est verdâtre, et lorsque l'on voit pour la première fois ces clochetons délicats, ces colonnettes en miniature, véritable travail de bijouterie, on est tenté de les prendre pour des bronzes incrustés. On nomme cette pierre d'après le lieu d'où on la tire, Kersanton, et l'on en fait encore un assez grand usage.'—*Prosper Merimée.*

On a credence table of granite, with a canopy, N. of choir, was placed the statue of the Virgin, formerly venerated by the pilgrims, but a wretched modern image replaces it.

The *Doyenné* is an interesting turreted building, adorned with the arms of Brittany and of the ecclesiastical dignitaries who have inhabited it. The buildings of *La Collégiale* were renewed at the end of XVII. c. 'Notre Dame du Folgoët' is one of the poems of the Barzaz Breis.

15 k. *Lesneven*[1] (Hotels: *des Trois Piliers ; de France*). The name recalls the castle of Even, Comte de Léon in the IX. c., now destroyed, and its ramparts made into gardens.

The storm-beaten district beyond Lesneven seems to have been the especial home of the Breton saints, of one of whom almost every village bears a name. Their exhortations and miracles were especially needed here. The *Peninsula of Pontusral*, which runs into the sea to the N. of Lesneven, is still called the land of the pagans (*ar paganiz*), because its inhabitants persisted in adhering to pagan practices through the middle ages. The inhabitants of this peninsula, 'à face étroite et longue,'[2] also, says Roget de Belloguet, preserved longest the horrible 'droit de bris'; and they were accused of setting up false signal lights on their shores, to profit by the shipwrecks they caused. The wild wastes abound in tumuli, dolmens, menhirs, and 'pierres branlantes.' Near Pontusval are the Druidical remains known as 'Les Danseurs.' It is said that a number of girls, who insisted on continuing to dance as a Christian procession passed, were turned into stone.

21 k. *Plouider.* In the church is a curious ancient statue of S. Didier.

24 k. *Goulven.* The XVI. c. church has a good stone spire.

25 k. *Plounéour-Trez* (see p. 279). Near this, at *La Grève de l'Enchanteur*, is an unusually fine dolmen.

---

[1] From *les*, near, and *even*, a river.
[2] See *Elisée Reclus.*

26 k. *Brignogan* (Hotel: *des Baigneurs*) has a little rocky cove. Amongst the great blocks of granite on the N.W. is the great menhir called *le Men Marz* (' the miraculous stone '), probably an idol in pagan times, and one upon which the first missionaries have left the sign of the cross. An excursion may be made to the *Chapelle S. Pol*, with a XVI. c. calvary.]

[A line leads S. from Landerneau to (338 k.) Nantes by (84 k.) Quimper, passing—

12 k. *Dirinon* (Terre de Nonne), which has a church containing a XIV. c. statue of S. Goulven, and possessing a fine spire of 1588-93. It occupies the site of a chapel erected over the grave of S. Nonne (or S. Melaine), who died here in the beginning of the VI. c. Her tomb bears her statue. The buildings are said to have been commenced on another spot; but the master-mason, seeing that an invisible power perpetually overthrew his work, placed one of the stones destined for the building upon a cart drawn by oxen, who stopped at the spot evidently chosen by the saint. This stone is shown in the *Chapelle S. Nonne* (1577), as well as the tomb of the saint, and her relics are preserved in a gothic reliquary. S. Nonne, so called from her profession, and commemorated in a mystery, was the princess Mélaine, daughter of Brécan, king of Wales, and the Irish princess Dinam (the spotless). She was sister of S. Keine and S. Ninnoc. One day, as she was traversing a forest as a pilgrim, she met the king Kéretic, by whom she had a son called S. Divy, born upon a rock, which became like wax, to form a cradle for the newborn child. The peasants still show the cradle of S. Divy, and the marks left by the knees of S. Nonne, near the Chemin de Daoulas, and they carry thither all babes born with a blue mark between the eyebrows. Children so marked are said to have the *Mal de S. Divy*—*i.e.* to be doomed to an early death, if the saint does not prevent it.

19 k. *Daoulas-Irvillac*—a very interesting place. It is 1½ k. (turning l. from the station—no omnibus), with lovely views over a land-locked bay, to the large village of *Daoulas* (Hotel: *de Brétagne*—very poor), which is said to have originated in the remorse of a seigneur de Faou, who (*c.* 510) murdered two monks at the altar, and was forthwith seized by an evil spirit, from

which he was delivered by the prayers of S. Pol, bishop of Léon. On the spot where his crime was committed he founded a monastery, called in Breton *moustier daou laz*—'the monastery of the double murder.' In the VI. c. this monastery was replaced by an abbey of Augustinian canons, founded (1167-73) by Guyomarc'h, Comte de Léon, and his wife Nobile. The abbey church, at the top of the hill, above the village street, is beautifully situated, and most picturesque in its surroundings of calvary

THE SACRED WELL OF DAOULAS.

and ancient graveyard. The church itself has lost its choir and tower. The W. façade and most of the building are romanesque: to the S. aisle a renaissance porch has been added, bearing the arms of Abbot Jean le Prédour, 1573. The portals within have their vaulting exquisitely decorated with vine leaves, and the pillars of Kersanton stone are spiral. The ruins of the choir and *Chapelle de Faou* contain a vault of the family of Lec'h, and the gravestone of an abbot of 1535. A fine old *Gateway*, containing statues of the twelve apostles, forms the W. approach to the churchyard. The upper story is used as a belfry. On the N., behind the house adjoining, visitors are admitted to the roofless ruins of the *Cloister*, which dates from the foundation of the abbey; of great beauty, though only ten arcades of the E. corridor remain. Their capitals present exquisite specimens of XII. c. sculpture. In the centre of what was the cloister are remains of the monastic lavatory fountain. Two arches on the N. form the entrance to the gardens. A delightful walk leads hence to a hollow, with the *Chapelle S. Anne* of 1667, containing a curious figure of a bishop riding on a stag. Close by is—an architectural gem—a most lovely shrine of the Virgin of 1550, with a miracle-working fountain of great beauty.

29 k. *Hanvec-le-Faou*. The church of *Hanvec* is of 1625: the cemetery cross bears the arms of Kerliver.

7 k. W. is *Faou* (*fagus*, a beech), on a little arm of the sea. 2 k. E. of Faou is the pilgrimage church of *Rumengol*, of 1536. It is dedicated to *Notre Dame de Tout Remède* (Remed oll-Rumengol). The interior is of great richness. Close by is a miraculous fountain under a gothic canopy. On the hill above the church is a pavillon, where mass is said daily during the *pardon*. The fêtes or pardons of Rumengol are March 25 (the Annunciation); Trinity Sunday; August 15 (the Assumption); and Nov. 8 (the Nativity of the Virgin). The pardon of Trinity is the most important.

'La procession sort de l'église avec les bannières, les croix d'argent et les reliques portées sur les brancards par ceux qui en ont acheté le droit. Tous sont vêtus d'aubes ou de chemises blanches, ceint d'un ruban de couleur vive, et portent sur la tête un bonnet de coton blanc. La foule des fidèles se précipite pour toucher ces précieux talismans, que les porteurs tiennent, à cet effet, le plus bas possible : ils sont escortés de gardes, costumés comme eux, et qui frappent du *pen-bas* ceux qui ne s'inclinent pas assez vite. À la suite des reliques on porte assez ordinairement des saints sculptés, placés au bouts de bâton coloriés.

'Le soir, quand les tentes sont repliées, lorsque le silence et la nuit ont repris possession de la plaine que foulait peu auparavant une multitude bruyante, les mendiants se réunissent par groupe auprès des feux d'ajonc qu'ils allument. Alors c'est un spectacle dont aucune parole ne peut rendre la fantastique magie, que celui de ces 300 deguenillés assis autour de leur foyer en plein vent. Par instants, un jet de flamme éclaire ces visages grimaçants, hagards ou stupides, marqués au coin de vice ou des misères humaines ; puis une rafale éteint les feux qui rampent en tournoyant, et l'on n'aperçoit plus que des ombres qui s'agitent dans les ténèbres visibles. Alors tout bruit meurt ; les 300 mendiants, couchés sur la terre, ont oublié leurs peines aussi profondément que s'ils dormaient dans un cercueil.'—*Emile Souvestre.*

It is a very short distance from Le Faou, crossing the mouth of the estuary, to the remains of the famous *Abbey of Landévennec* —"chartreuse des lettres bretonnes"[1]—the oldest and most important monastic establishment, not Druidical, in Finistère,[2] founded by the holy hermit S. Guénolé, who died in 504. Hither King Grallon retired in his old age, and here he was buried in an ancient sarcophagus, which existed till long after the Revolution. It bore the epitaph—much later than itself—

' Hoc in sarcophago jacet inclyta magna propago
Gradlonus magnus Britonum rex ; mitis et agnus
Noster fundator, vitae coelestis amator ;
Illi propitia sit semper virgo Maria.'

The *Church* dates from xi. c. Its three naves terminate in three apses. Under the S. aisle is a crypt, still retaining the niche which contained the tomb of King Grallon. That of S. Guénolé [3] was moved to the Chapelle Notre Dame built by Abbot Jean de Vieux-Châtel, who died in 1522. Close to the E. end of the church is a statue of S. Corentin. The remains of several other abbots were collected here. The principal remnant of monastic buildings is the *Abbot's House*, only dating from 1630. It was formerly known as Le Manoir du Penity. In its court is preserved the tomb of Abbot de Vieux-Châtel. Through the

---

[1] Emile Souvestre.
[2] The other monastic establishments of Finistère were—S. Jacut, S. Melaine, S. Meen, S. Gildas de Rhys, S. Matthieu, S. Sauveur de Redon, Le Chaume. Notre Dame de Tronchel, S. Martin de Vertou, S. Georges, S. Sulpice, S. Pierre de Rille, S. Jean des Près, S. Jacques de Montfort, Daoulas, Beaulieu, Vieuville, S. Aubin des Bois, Mellerai, La Joie, Prières, and Bonrepos.
[3] S. Guénolé was born in the Château de Lesquer, in the parish of Plouguin, in Léonnais.

Bois des Moines we reach the Bois du Folgoët, named from a chapel erected in 1645 to the idiot Salaun (see p. 281).

54 k. *Châteaulin* (Hotel: *de la Grande Maison*), formerly Castel-Nin, picturesquely situated on the Aulne, where S. Idunet had a hermitage in the IX. c. The church of *Notre Dame* (XV. c. and XVI. c.) was the chapel of the château. Its churchyard has a sculptured cross and gothic ossuary. An ivy-covered wall, on the hill above the church) is the only remnant of the castle said to have been built by Alain Debré, grandson of King Salomon, who died in 907, but really built by Budic Castellin, Comte de Cornouaille, in the XI. c. The slate quarries of Châteaulin are celebrated. 3 k. distant is its port—*Port Launay*.

(A road leads N.W. from Châteaulin, passing (11 k.) the height of *Méné-Hom*, crowned by the XVI. c. *Chapelle S. Côme*, to—

33 k. *Crozon* (Hotel: *des Grottes*) in the centre of a wild, bare, storm-beaten peninsula, full of megalithic remains. 1 k. S. is the *Anse de Morgat*, with curious sea-caverns, especially the *Grotte de l'Autel* and *Grotte de S. Marine*. A fissure in the vaulting of the latter is called *La Cheminée du Diable*. Near this, above the village of Kermel, are the *Alignements de Kercolleoc'h*, commonly called La Maison du Curé, several ranges of peulvens, and a kind of square enclosure (temple?) formed by blocks crowned with menhirs. 3 k. farther S. is a dolmen, 1 k. S. of the *Chapelle S. Hernot*, a tumulus surrounded by a little entrenchment. 8 k. from Crozon is the *Anse de Dinant*, with a curious island rock connected with the mainland by a natural bridge of two arches, and known as the *Château de Dinant*, from its embattled forms. It is 8 k. from Crozon to *Camaret*, 2 k. E. of which is the *Pointe de Toulinguet*.

'La pointe de Toulinguet est la plus curieuse de toute la Bretagne. La parole s'épuise à raconter tant de sauvages merveilles, et l'on renonce malgré soi à les peindre. Il faut avoir vu ces hauts caps de granit tapissés d'une rare bruyère, que parsement de loin en loin quelques gazons marins et quelques roses pimprenelles, ces vieux forts qui decoupent sur le gris du ciel leurs murs jaunes, et où dorment couchés dans l'erbe les canons sans affûts ; ces flots dont l'éternelle écume brodé la robe bleue de la mer; il faut avoir entendu, pendant plusieurs heures, les gemissements tristes de la rafale sur les dunes, avoir été étourdi par les hurlements des vagues ; il faut avoir éprouvé par soi-même quelles choses passent devant les yeux et étonnent les oreilles sur ces dernières limites du vieux monde, pour que des mots puissent rappeler quelques traits de cet inexprimable spectacle.'—*Emile Souvestre*, '*En Bretagne*.'

2 k. N.E. of Camaret is the *Presqu'île de Roscanvel*.

'C'est le Gibraltar de la France, comme le goulet·en est des Dardanelles. Aussi cette position a-t-elle, de tout temps, été convoitée par les ennemis de la France. Les Espagnols, auxiliaires de la Ligue, s'y établirent en 1594, et construisirent à la pointe de la presqu'île, qui a conservé depuis le nom de Pointe des Espagnols, un fort qu'ils auraient rendu inexpugnable, si le Maréchal d'Aumont n'eût réussi à les en déloger, après un siège meutrier. Les Anglais, alliés d'Henri IV. en cette circonstance, apprécièrent la situation de la presqu'île, et tentèrent de l'occuper en 1694. Vauban, qui avait pressenti leur projet, prit toutes les mesures propres à le faire échouer. Aussi, quand ils voulurent debarquer, le 18 juin, dans la baie de Camaret, furent-ils repoussés par les troupes que commandait le marquis de Langeron, troupes composées en partie de milices gardes-côtes. Les vaisseaux anglais, commandés par l'amiral Berkley (Berkeley), s'éloignèrent en desordre après avoir essuyé de grandes pertes, et le lieutenant-general Talmash (Tollemache) commandant les troupes de débarquement, mourut de ses blessures peu de jours après sa rentrée en Angleterre.')

[The road E. from Châteaulin to (49 k.) Carhaix passes (11 k.) *Pleyben*, which has a fine church of mingled gothic and renaissance. At the base of the lofty tower is a beautiful porch (1588-91) with statues of the apostles. The flamboyant windows of the choir are of great elegance. Attached to the chevet is the renaissance domed sacristy. In the churchyard is an ossuary. But that which gives Pleyben real importance is its *Calvary* of 1650, decorated with numerous statues representing the history of our Saviour. It is perhaps less magnificent than that of the Plougastel, and of the same character, but exceedingly curious and interesting.]

[14 k. S.W. of Châteaulin, on the way to Locronan, is the great pilgrimage *Chapelle du Kergoat*, of mingled renaissance and gothic, with fine stained glass, and a good cemetery cross.]

There are very beautiful views from the railway before reaching—

84 k. Quimper. See ch. vii.]

Leaving Landerneau, the line passes beneath the ruined church of *Beuzit-Conogan*, which contains the fine XVI. c. tomb of Troilus de Mondragon. After entering the forest of Landerneau, it crosses the avenue of the *Château de la Joyeuse-Garde*, celebrated in the story of King Arthur. Only a gothic vault and XII. c. gateway remain.[1]

'Le château de la Joyeuse Garde est célèbre dans les romans de la Table ronde. Tous les personnages de ces romans, Tristan le Léonnais, la belle Yseult, le roi Artus, Lancelot, l'habitèrent. Les romans de la Table ronde furent eux-mêmes écrits en celto-breton, avant de l'être en langue romane; ce ne fut que vers le douzième siècle qu'on les traduisit. Il est donc constant que la chevalerie prit naissance en Bretagne, et y brilla de tout son éclat; que les premiers poèmes chevaleresques furent écrits en langue celtique. Les monuments, les traditions, les noms, les indications des plus anciens auteurs s'accordent pour faire de la Bretagne la patrie de tout ce monde chevaleresque et féerique dont, plus tard, le Tasse et l'Arioste tirèrent tant de parti.'—*Emile Souvestre.*

The bay of Kerhuon is crossed by a viaduct.

615 k. *Kerhuon.*

The famous *Calvary* of Plougastel is 3½ k. walk from Kerhuon. It is about 1 k. to the ferry—a sailing boat—over the broad estuary of the Elorn, by which (with beautiful views towards Brest) we reach the peninsula of *Plougastel-Daoulas.*

[1] Only the ruins of the Joyeuse Garde, those of Roche Maurice, and the foundations of the halles and prisons of Landerneau, remain to the house of Rohan of all their principality of Léon.

Near the landing-place is the *Chapelle de S. Languy*, with a statue of the saint, invoked for maladies of children. 15 min. farther, on the shore, is the *Fontaine de S. Languy*, into which peasants plunge the linen of their sickly children; the fountain is covered at high tide, being half salt. The wild district is covered with large blocks of stone, which the peasants believe to have come from Léon. The legend tells that a Druid who was received well at Léon and ill by the Cornouaillais, avenged himself by scattering the stones of Léon over Cornouaille, from

THE CALVARY OF PLOUGASTEL.

Plougastel to Huelgoat. A steep path ascending behind a group of these rocks leads from the ferry to the village of *Plougastel* —a miserable village with a very poor inn. In the churchyard is a splendid and almost unique calvary erected by a nobleman (1602-4) after the pestilence of 1598. Its sculptor's name (A. Corr) is preserved. It has a massive terrace pierced by arches, and adorned with a rich frieze representing the Life of Christ. Above are the Saviour and the two thieves, and below the story of the Passion is told in as many as two hundred statuettes of wonderful originality, full of life, vigour, and passion, carved in green Kersanton stone. In the Triumphal Entry into Jerusalem, the Saviour is preceded by peasants in Breton costume, playing the national instruments of Brittany. 3 k. E. are the *Chapelle de la Fontaine Blanche* and its fountain, frequented by the parents of feeble children. On the l. bank of the river is the pilgrimage *Chapelle de S. Jean de Plougastel*, celebrated for the 'pardon des oiseaux,' to which all the peasants in the neighbourhood bring different birds in cages.

The S. side of the promontory of Plougastel—'le Montmorency Bretagne'—is almost entirely covered by strawberry gardens. A 'Liqueur des Quatre Fruits,' also called 'Vin de Plougastel,' is obtained from hence.

Of all isolated sea-coast populations that of Plougastel is the most curious. Till recently the men all wore Phrygian caps, the women a headdress like that of the goddess Isis; country people call them 'Les Galiléens': and they have always been a colony, living apart like Jews, intermarrying with each other and keeping up all old customs. They are said to be emigrants from the Troad. The very beautiful costume of the women of Plougastel has become nearly extinct in the last few years.

'If the weather is wet—and more rain is said to fall in Finistère than in any other part of France—wait; if you are bored to death in your hotel, put up with it; if your time is limited, relinquish everything else, but on no account omit Plougastel.'—*'Autumn in Western France.'*

Passing *Le Rody*, we have a view of the *Anse de S. Marc*, then of the harbour of Brest, before reaching the Sea Queen of the West.

623 k. *Brest* (Hotels: *des Voyageurs; Grand*—very good; *de la Bourse*), the capital of the Département du Finistère, but a place of no interest to tourists.

'Le grand port militaire, la pensée de Richelieu, la main de Louis XIV.; fort, arsenal et bagne, canons et vaisseaux, armées et millions, la force de la France entassée au bout de la France: tout cela dans un port serré, où l'on étouffe entre deux montagnes chargées d'immenses constructions. Quand vous parcourez ce port, c'est comme si vous passiez dans une petite barque entre deux vaisseaux de haut bord ; il semble que ces lourdes masses vont venir à vous et que vous allez être pris entre elles. L'impression générale est grande, mais pénible. C'est un prodigieux tour de force, un défi porté à l'Angleterre et à la nature. J'y sens partout l'effort, et l'air du bagne et la chaîne du forçat. C'est justement à cette pointe, où la mer, échappée du détroit de la Manche, vient briser avec tant de fureur, que nous avons placé le grand dépôt de notre marine. Certes, il est bien gardé. J'y ai vu mille canons. L'on n'y entrera pas ; mais l'on n'en sort pas comme on veut. Plus d'un vaisseau a péri à la passe de Brest. Toute cette côte est un cimetière. Il s'y perd soixante embarcations chaque hiver. La mer est anglaise d'inclination ; elle n'aime pas la France ; elle brise nos vaisseaux ; elle ensable nos ports.'—*Michelet.*

A very small portion of the *Château* is older than the XII. c., and the greater portion is of the XIII. c., altered by Vauban, who destroyed the conical roofs of the towers, replacing them by platforms for cannon. The most ancient portions are the Tour de César (XIII. c.) and Tour d'Azenor, so called because Azenor, daughter of a Comte de Léon, is said to have been imprisoned there.

The church of *S. Louis*, begun 1688 and only recently finished, contains a monument to Louis Ducouëdic, who died of wounds received in a naval engagement with the English, Oct. 6, 1799.

'Excepté les fortifications du château, tout est moderne à Brest ; Louis XIV. et Vauban y ont tout fait. Il me semble que les environs de Brest peuvent donner une idée de la France sous le grand roi. Des chaumières misérables et des églises bâties avec soin, mais d'un goût detestable ; çà et là quelques grands manoirs mal tenus, rarement visités par leurs propriétaires ; en un mot, l'apparence du luxe voisine de celle de misère. Le costume des paysans n'a pas changé, je crois, depuis que Vauban le leur apporta. Ils ont un habit noir à grandes basques, avec de larges culottes plissées et un chapeau à grands bords. En tout point ils rappellent les costumes des bourgeois de Vander Meulen.'—*Prosper Merimée.*

It is a lovely excursion from Brest to Plougastel.

[A road leads W. from Brest, by *Kerangoff*, celebrated for its pardons, and the *Anse de Bertheaume* to (22 k.) *Le Conquet*, a small bathing-place on the extreme western point of Brittany. On the neighbouring promontory of *Kermoran* is a lighthouse. A road, diverging 18 k. from Brest, leads (l.) to (23 k.) *S. Mathieu*, the W. point of Finistère, called by the Bretons *Loc-Mazé Pen-ar-Bed* ('the cell of S. Matthew at the end of the earth'). Here monks, under the guidance of S. Tanguy, built a monastery in the VI. c., choosing the site because the head of S. Matthew (also claimed by Rome) is supposed to have been landed there by sailors of Léon coming from Ethiopia. The abbey church, at *Fine Terre* or *Bout du Monde*, of the XII. c., is now a very imposing ruin; beside it is a lighthouse.

'C'est sur la pointe de Saint Mathieu que les amis, les mères, les amantes tendent les bras, présentent leurs enfans, fondent en larmes au départ des vaisseaux qui sortent pour la guerre ou pour les courses éloignées. C'est là qu'on les attend, qu'on les salue, quand une flamme bienfaisante ou le canon annonce leur retour; on les appelle, on les suit le long du rivage, on ne peut les perdre de vue; impatience, cris d'allégresse, mouchoirs agités dans les airs, marche précipitée, inquiétude, battements de coeur, convulsions, tout genre de sentiment, d'émotions d'amour, d'amitié, de frayeur, tout mouvement que le coeur détermine, se manifestent sur ce rocher aride et sur ces routes momentanément animées.'—*Cambry*, '*Voyage dans le Finistère.*']

[A steamer leaves Brest twice a week for (28 k.) the *Île d'Ouessant*, the Uxantos of Pliny, the l'Enez-Heussa of the Bretons, where S. Pol Aurélien preached the gospel in the VI. c., but where idolatry existed as late as the XVII. c. Ouessant—the home of winds and tempests—is the largest island of a group the characteristics and dangers of which are summed up in the proverb, 'Celui qui voit Belle-île voit son île; celui qui voit Groix voit sa joie: celui qui voit Ouessant voit son sang.' It is Ouessant, separated from the rest of the islands by the *Passage du Fromveur*, that mariners dread, but its natives are famous for their courage in rescuing the shipwrecked, and their hospitality to them when saved.

'Un ouessantin mourait-il dans le cours d'un voyage, on portait aussitôt une croix dans sa maison; le clergé allait prendre cette croix, avec les cérémonies funèbres accoutumées, et on en faisait l'inhumation. Je n'ai pas besoin d'ajouter que ce simulacre d'enterrement était payé comme un enterrement véritable.

'La jeune fille qui se proposait pour épouse à un jeune garçon restait dans la famille de celui-ci, s'il acceptait, et vivait avec lui dès ce moment (sans faire chambre commune toutefois) jusqu'au terme fixé d'avance pour ce noviciat matrimoniel. Ce terme arrivé, si les deux jeunes gens ne se convenaient pas, la fille rentrait sous le toit paternel sans que sa réputation ne souffrit nullement.

'Cet usage, il y a cent ans, avait encore quelque chose de plus bizarre. Le jeune homme, prévenu des desseins qu'une jeune fille pouvait avoir sur lui, se tenait au lit: la jeune fille lui présentait un morceau de lard. S'il en goûtait, l'adoption était censée faite; dans le cas contraire, l'exclusion était sans retour. Cet usage existe encore en Norvége.'—*Emile Souvestre.*

A little S. is the *Île Molène*, a very poverty-stricken place, and still farther S. the *Île Béniguet*, where some tombs are pointed out as those of Druid priests and priestesses.

[It is 26 k. N.W. from Brest to Ploudalmézeau. At 6 k. on l. is the *Château de Keroual*, which was the birthplace, in 1649, of Louise-Renée de Penancoët de Keroual, afterwards Duchess of Portsmouth and mistress of Charles II., who, after the death of the king, returned to reside here, and embellished her château with mythological paintings, which still exist.

13 k. *S. Renan*, a town built round the site of the hermitage of the Irish hermit S. Renan. It has a ruined XIII. c. portal of a church.

'Entre tous les saints de la Bretagne il n'y en a pas de plus original. Il habitait la Cornouaille, près de la petite ville qui porte son nom. C'était un esprit de la terre plus qu'un saint. Sa puissance sur les éléments était effrayante. Son caractère était violent et un peu bizarre ; on ne savait jamais d'avance ce qu'il ferait, ce qu'il voudrait. On le respectait ; mais cette obstination à marcher seul dans sa voie inspirait une certaine crainte ; si bien que, le jour où on le trouva mort sur le sol de sa cabane, la terreur fut grande alentour. Le premier qui, en passant, regarda par la fenêtre ouverte et le vît étendu par terre, s'enfuit à toutes jambes. Pendant sa vie, il avait été si volontaire, si particulier, que nul ne se flattait de pouvoir deviner ce qu'il désirait que l'on fît de son corps. Si l'on ne tombait pas juste, on craignait une peste, quelque engloutissement de ville, un pays tout entier changé en marais, tel ou tel de ces fléaux dont il disposait de son vivant. Le mener à l'église de tout le monde eût été chose peu sûre. Il semblait parfois l'avoir en aversion. Il eût été capable de se revolter, de faire un scandale. Tous les chefs étaient assemblés dans la cellule, autour du grand corps noir, gisant à terre, quand l'un d'eux ouvrit un sage avis : "De son vivant, nous l'avons jamais pu le comprendre ; il était plus facile de dessiner la voie de l'hirondelle au ciel que de suivre la trace de ses pensées ; mort, qu'il fasse encore à sa tête. Abattons quelques arbres ; faisons un chariot, où nous attellerons quatre boeufs. Il saura bien les conduire à l'endroit où il vent qu'on l'enterre." Tous approuvèrent. On ajusta les poutres, on fit les roues avec des tambours pleins, sciés dans l'épaisseur des gros chênes, et on posa le saint dessus.

'Les boeufs, conduits par la main invisible de Renan, marchèrent droit devant eux, au plus épais de la forêt. Les arbres s'inclinaient ou se brisaient sous leurs pas avec des craquements effroyables. Arrivé enfin au centre de la forêt, à l'endroit où étaient les plus grands chênes, le chariot s'arrêta. On comprit ; on enterra le saint, et on bâtit son église en ce lieu.'—*Ernest Renan.*

'Là, sous vos pieds, dorment plusieurs générations ; cette lande immense fut *la cité des morts* : elle a conservé encore le nom sonore et triste de *Ker-gloas* (le lieu de la douleur). Le menhir immense est peut-être la tombe de quelque chef celtique fameux dans sa tribu, et dont on voulut immortaliser le souvenir ; peut-être aussi était-ce un de ces *ir-mensuls* (longues pierres du soleil) qu'adoraient nos pères. Fidèles à la tradition, les habitants de ces côtes ont conservé encore pour ce monument une sorte de respect craintif, et des pratiques superstitieuses sont restés en usage dans le pays. Souvent, à la nuit tombante, vous voyez deux jeunes époux se diriger vers la pierre mystèrieuse, se dépouiller de leurs vêtemens, et appuyer leurs poitrines aux bosselures qui se relieffent sur les deux faces du menhir. Après s'y être frottés quelque temps, ils reprennent leur vêtemens et s'en retournent joyeux, l'époux sûr de n'avoir que des fils, et l'épouse heureuse de penser que son mari lui sera soumis.'— *Emile Souvestre.*

9 k. to the W. is *Plouarzel*, with the most important menhir in Finistère—*le Menhir de Kerveac'htou* (28 ft. high and 19 ft. round). Near this is the old manor-house of *Kergadion*, with a ruined portal between towers. In this district is the ruined *Château de Pont ar Chastel* (castle bridge), with four corner towers. Here lived that Thibault du Pont who fought under Duguesclin, armed with a sword five feet long and weighing twelve livres. The pilgrimage *Chapelle du Trézien* (3 k. W.) has a porch bearing the arms of Chastel. Near this also is the ruined *Château de Kergroadez*, known as the *Château de Roquelaure*, dating only from the XVI. c., but on the site of an earlier building. Thence by the *Château Kerveac'htou*—passing the mill of Chanan, where, near the river, S. Renan has left the mark of his foot upon a rock—a cross-road leads l. to Plouarzel.

Continuing the road to Ploudalmézeau, is—

18 k. *Lanrivoaré*, named from the early missionary S. Rivoaré. Here is the *Cimetière des Sept mille saints*, where the Christian population of the district is said to have received burial after a massacre by pagan neighbours. This cemetery, in which no one has been buried since, is surrounded by arcades, of which the faithful make the circuit upon their knees on the day of the pardon. Seven round stones upon the steps of a cross are shown as bread changed into stone by S. Hervé,[1] who was nephew of S. Rivoaré, to punish a baker who had harshly refused him

---

[1] The name of Landhuvarne commemorates S. Hervé.

alms. Against the same cross rests the trunk of a tree, shreds of which are carried away as a preservative against fire in a dwelling.

From Lanrivoaré one may explore the banks of the river or fiord of *Aber-Ildut*, the ancient Gillidon, where Conan Mériadec landed from England. There are still remains of the *Château de Mériadec*.

L. of the road, after leaving Lanrivoaré, is (2 k.) the church of *Plourin*, containing fine XIV. c. tombs of the Seigneurs de Kergroadez.

'C'est dans le pays de Léon que se passa la scène des trois fermiers. M. de Kergroadez devait cent mille écus; ses fermiers, instruits du désordre de ses affaires, lui fournissent cette somme, gèrent ses terres pendante quarante ans, lui laissent la moitié de ses revenus, et font présent à son épouse de huit beaux chevaux de carrosse, afin (dit un acte qui subsistait en 1788) que madame puisse venir à la paroisse d'une manière convenable.'— *Cambry*.

26 k. *Ploudalmézeau*, in a district full of menhirs, tombelles, dolmens, etc. 4 k. N.W. is the XV. c. church of *Kersaint*, built by Tanneguy du Châtel and his first wife Louise de Pont l'Abbé. It contains the tomb of S. Haude. At the W. entrance of the bay of Porzal are the ruins of the *Château de Trémazan*, from which the family of Tanneguy du Châtel emanated.]

[A road leads N.W. from Brest to Lannilis, passing the *Fountain of S. Trouberon*, formerly adored by the Celts, now under the protection of the Virgin.

4 k. *Pontanézen*, 2 k. r. of which is the ruined *Château de Mesléan*, with fortified towers.

8 k. *Gouesnou*, which has a fine church of 1552, with a stone spire. There are remarkable gargouilles representing dragons, and a cemetery cross. In the *Chapelle S. Mémor*, at the entrance of the village, is one of the pierced stones adored by the Celts, and of which they sought cures. It was moved by a priest from a field to which the maimed still resorted to place their maimed limbs in its hole. Now, it is asserted that the virtues of the stone are due to S. Gouesnou, who, as a penance,

kept his arm motionless in its hole for several hours daily. There is a famous pardon at Gouesnou.

'On trouve encore à Gouesnou la pierre où le patron du bourg se coucha sur le refus qui lui fut fait d'un asile. Hommes et femmes, le jour du pardon, s'y étendent et s'y frottent. Sa vertu est de guérir les douleurs. Une fontaine près de l'église a le privilège de guerir les maladies cutanées; il suffit d'y plonger le membre malade.'—*Emile Souvestre.*

(Here the road to Lesneven turns off to r., passing (15 k. from Brest) *Plabennec,* with the ruined *Château de Lesquelen.* Near *La croix des trois Recteurs,* at the meeting of Plabennec, Ploudaniel, and Kersaint Plabennec, is a rock, inscribed in unknown characters, supposed to indicate a hidden treasure. Near *Kersaint Plabennec* are remains of the tower whither S. Thénénan retired to escape the persecution of the pagans: the moated ruins are said to date from the VII. c.)

15 k. *Bourg Blanc,* on an affluent of the river *L'aber Bénoît* (from Benonic, father of Lancelot du Lac). 18 k., 3½ r. of the road, is *Plouvien,* where the XVI. c. *Château du Bois des Anges* commemorates the legend of a lady who fled from the cruelties of a jealous husband into the thick woods, where God took care of her, and the angels comforted her by their songs, and every night the shepherds of the surrounding country heard celestial music, yet none dared to enter the woods. But one day Count Even penetrated them, as he was hunting wild beasts, and in the thickets found the injured wife and fell in love with her. She fled from his addresses. He pursued her, but as he was about to seize her, two angels appeared and covered her with their wings. Then a celestial voice told him that the lady was none other than the lost wife of Siffroi, who had concealed herself for four years in the woods, and Even took her back to her husband and testified to her innocence. The château was built in honour of her reunion with Siffroi.

'Le paysan qui passe devant ses ruines se signe encore en souvenir de la sainte femme qui l'habita; et le soir les pâtres attardés croient souvent entendre sortir de ces bocages des chants étranges qui inspirent à la fois de la joie et de la terreur, comme le son de voix venant d'un autre monde.'—*Cambry.*

Only 1 k. S.W. from Plouvien is the interesting *Chapelle de S. Jaoua,* an Irish saint, whose mother was the sister of S. Pol Aurelien, first bishop of Léon, and who was nominated to the parish of Braspartz by S. Judulus, Abbot of Landevennec. Soon afterwards, at a meeting of all the abbots of Cornouaille, S. Judulus and S. Tadec were murdered by the pagans at the moment of repeating 'nobis quoque peccatoribus.' In punishment for this, the pagan prince was possessed by demons, and a dragon was sent to ravage his country. S. Pol and S. Jaoua were at length moved by pity to bind the dragon, and to heal the prince on his promising to build a church (Daoulas) on the site of his two murders.

'.S. Pol et Jaoua s'en allèrent ensuite en Léon, traînant après eux le dragon. Un paysan vint dire que le serpent avait laissé dans sa tannière un faou bientôt aussi redoutable que lui. S. Pol délia alors la bête, lui commanda de la part de Dieu d'aller chercher son faou, sans faire de mal à personne, et le serpent obéit; en mémoire de quoi le bois situé entre Land-Pol et Gui-milliau, dans lequel S. Paul détacha le dragon, s'appelle encore *Coat-ar-Sarpent.* Il conduisit ensuite ces deux dragons à l'île de Batz, et les attacha à son bâton, où ils restèrent jusqu'à ce qu'ils ne fussent morts de faim. Pour ce que S. Pol avait ainsi donné pour barrière à deux bêtes furieuses un simple bourdon, fut appelée cette île, *Île du Bâton* (Enez Batz).'— *Emile Souvestre.*

S. Jaoua died in his presbytery at Braspartz. His body was laid on a cart drawn by two oxen, who drew it to the spot Porz-au-Chraz, where the cart broke down. There a cross was erected. A little farther the cart broke down a second time, and could not be mended. Here the saint was buried. His chapel was rebuilt in the XVI. c. The saint's tomb is a sarcophagus of that date, surrounded by gothic arcades, and bearing the figure of S. Jaoua, in episcopal costume.

25 k. *Lannilis* (the land of the Church), celebrated in Brittany for the legend of the Groac'h de l'Ille du Lok. The country is rich.

'Là, il y a toujours eu, outre les fourrages et les blés, des vergers qui donnent des pommes plus douces que le miel de Sizun, et des pruniers dont toutes les fleurs deviennent des fruits. Pour ce qui est des jeunes filles à marier, elles sont toutes sages et ménagéres, à ce que disent leurs parents.'—*Emile Souvestre*.

Lannilis is picturesquely situated. In the cemetery is the XVI. c. tomb of François de Coum. The chapel of *S. Tariac* contains the curious XVI. c. tomb of Olivier Richard, doctor of theology.

Descending the river of Aber Vrac'h, you come to *Plouguerneau*, supposed to occupy the site of Tolente.

'Descendez sur cette grève que la mer vient d'abandonner, et arrêtez-vous. Vous foulez ici l'une des plus opulentes villes de l'Armorique. Cette plaine qui s'étend sous vos yeux belle et unie fut autrefois couverte d'édifices. Le murmure du peuple, les cris des marchands, le bruit des chariots, les appels des marins ont retenti sur cette plage ou la mer seule fait entendre maintenant son murmure monotone et solennel. Sous ce linceul de sable dorment les débris de la Tyr armoricaine; ce fut la ville du détroit de Hent (Tolente), dont les vaisseaux couvraient autrefois l'océan. Les normands y débarquèrent un jour, le fer et le feu à la main, et quand ils repartirent la riche cité n'était plus qu'une ruine. Depuis la mer, comme jalouse de cacher les crimes de ses favoris, a étendu ses vagues sur la ville détruite, et en a effacé jusqu'aux moindres traces.'—*Emile Souvestre*.

In the church of *Landèda*, on the other side of the Aber Vrac'h, are the curious tomb of Simon de Tromenec, and the mummy of a holy centenarian.

CHAPTER VI

BAYEUX TO LAMBALLE BY S. LÔ, COUTANCES, AVRANCHES, MONT S. MICHEL, DOL, S. MALO, AND DINAN.

SEE ch. iii. for the line from Bayeux to—

27 k. Lison, whence the line to Brittany diverges to the S.W. from that to Cherbourg.

46 k. *S. Lô* (Hotels: *du Cheval Blanc*—tolerable, but primitive; *de Normandie*), capital of the Département de la Manche, the ancient Briovira, received its present name from a sainted bishop. The picturesque little town has clean wide streets, and a central hill, with a terrace overlooking the valley of the Vire. Here, facing the marketplace, rises the magnificent xv. c. and xvi. c. church of *Notre Dame*, finer than many cathedrals, and very beautiful in colour. It has two noble W. towers with spires. On the N.E. is the celebrated outside xv. c. pulpit, whence the bishop used to deliver his edicts, temporal and spiritual, and which Prout and so many other artists have painted. The statue called *La Vierge du Pilier* is a great object of worship. Opposite the cathedral is the beautiful old timber house known as *la Maison de Dieu*.

The church of *S. Croix* was rebuilt in 1860 on the site of a church attributed to Charlemagne. The abbey buildings have two fine gothic windows surmounted by a turret, supposed to have served as a lanthorn.

(A line leads S.E. from S. Lô to (50 k.) Vire (see ch. iv.) by—

OUTSIDE PULPIT, S. LO.

18 k. *Torigni sur Vire*, with a fine XVI. c. château built by Jacques de Matignon, first Comte de Tórigni. It is now used as an *Hôtel de Ville*, and contains some tolerable portraits.)

A crown of grey towers and spires rises above a hill on the r. as we approach—

74 k. *Coutances* (Hotels: *d'Angleterre*—very good; *des*

20

Trois Rois). The ancient Cosedia probably received its second name of Constantia from Constantius Chlorus, and gave a name to the Cotentin. It is when seen from a distance that Coutances excels. From the opposite hill— the first which is crossed on the way to Hambye—the view is magnificent of the cathedral, throned above the grey town with its verdant ramparts. As you approach nearer, the cathedral is ill seen. The E. end is enclosed in the bishop's garden, and the rest of the building, except the W. front, is hemmed in by commonplace houses. The streets of Coutances are not picturesque.

The magnificent cathedral of *Notre Dame de Coutances* was engrafted, in XIII. c., chiefly during the episcopate of Hugues de Morville (1208-38) upon a church of the XI. c., of which some traces remain in the lower part of the W. towers. The portals and arcades are remarkable for their exquisite foliage sculpture. In addition to the two great towers and spires of the W. front are two smaller spires, increasing the breadth and dignity of outline. The beauty of the central tower has been copied in many neighbouring churches.

In the interior is much fine glass of XIII. c., XIV. c., XV. c., and XVI. c. There are several incised gravestones of bishops.

The church of *S. Pierre* is a mixture of flamboyant and renaissance (XV. c. and XVI. c.), but very stately. It copies many features of the cathedral, and, being placed on a lower level, combines well with it in all distant views. *S. Nicolas* is XVII. c. and XVIII. c. The *Aqueduct*, constructed 1232, was restored in XVI. c.

The neighbourhood of Coutances abounds in beautiful

walks. Many are the deep-cut lanes like those of Devonshire, fringed with fern and abounding in wild flowers.

It is a pleasant drive of 22 k. to *Hambye* (carriage 14 fr.), a lovely spot on the Sienne, a clear trout river winding between wooded hills. An important Benedictine abbey was founded here in 1145 by Guillaume Pesnel. The principal remains are those of a noble church dating from

ABBEY OF HAMBYE.

XII. c., but restored XV. c., something like the ruins of Furness on a smaller scale. The abbey belongs to the bishops of Coutances. A castle was founded here in the XIV. c. From the summit of the last hill which is crossed between Coutances and Hambye there is a fine view towards the Jersey coast.

[10 k. is the little sea-bathing place of *Montmartin sur Mer*, 2 k. S.W. of which is *Hauteville-sur-Mer*, whence came the conquerors of Apulia and Sicily, and 3 k. N.W. of which is

Regneville, with some remains of a castle built by Charles le Mauvais.]

[A road leads S.W. to (29 k.) Granville, by—

18 k. *Bréhal*, 2 k. from which is *Chantéloup*, with a noble and picturesque renaissance château. The church has a nave of XI. c. or XII. c. The family of Canteloupe, migrating to England with the Conqueror, held great domains in Dorsetshire, and in Warwickshire the parish of Aston-Canteloupe.]

The railway now runs through a richly-wooded country, the cider orchards giving it the appearance of an immense garden.

81 k. *Orval-Hyenville*. The church (2 k. N.) of Orval has a nave and tower of XII. c. and choir of XV. c.

102 k. *Folligny*, on the line from Paris to Granville (see ch. iv.).

107 k. *La Haye Pesnel*. Outside the town are the rude remains of a castle, called *Château Ganne*, because one of its lords (Foulques) took part with the English during the regency of Queen Blanche. 2½ k. S.W. are the remains of the *Abbey of Luzerne*, founded XII. c. The ruins are chiefly XIV. c. The granite church is late romanesque and early pointed, with a noble central tower, having three long pointed windows on each face.

120 k. *Avranches* (Hotels: *d'Angleterre*—very good; *de Londres; de Bretagne*). The station is at the foot of the hill on which the town is built, being the highest steep in Normandy. It has been an episcopal see from the VI. c. At the time of the invasion of England it was the domain of Richard Goy, who married Emma, half-sister of the Conqueror, and whose son was Hugh Lupus, first Earl Palatine of Chester. Lanfranc, then only known as a learned professor from Pavia, founded a college here.

Avranches is one of the places in France most frequented by English, but has few attractions beyond its good air and the beautiful view from its gardens. The modern streets have no interest. The remains of a xv. c. Evêché are used for a *Musée*. The garden of a former Capuchin convent is now one of the most beautiful small *Public Gardens* in Europe. From its shady terraces one overlooks the whole bay of Mont S. Michel, entrancing in the soft beauty of its opaline colouring, with its glorious castellated rock, and the lonely islet of Tombelaine. A Norman arch is all that remains from the cathedral, which occupied perhaps the finest position of any cathedral in Christendom, begun 1090, consecrated 1121, and which suddenly fell down, subsiding into utter ruin, in 1790. A stone is inscribed: 'Sur cette pierre, ici à la porte de la cathédrale d'Avranches, après le meurtre de Thomas Becket, Archevêque de Cantorbéry, Henri II., Roi d'Angleterre, Duc de Normandie, reçut à genoux, des legats du pape, l'absolution apostolique, le dimanche 22 Mai, MCLXXII.'

'Le roi se rendit en cérémonie dans la grande église d'Avranches, et posant la main sur l'Evangile, jura, devant tout le peuple, qu'il n'avait ni ordonné ni voulu la mort de l'Archevêque de Cantorbéry, et que, l'ayant apprise, il en avait ressenti plus de chagrin que de joie. On lui récita les articles de la paix et les promesses qu'il avait faites, et il fit serment de les exécuter toutes de bonne foi et *sans mal engin* (absque fraude et malo ingenio). Henri, son fils aîné et son collègue dans la royauté, le jura en même temps que lui ; et, pour garantie de cette double promesse, on en dressa une charte, au bas de laquelle fut opposé le sceau royal. Ce roi, qu'on avait vu naguère si plein de fierté devant la puissance pontificale, engageait les cardinaux à ne l'épargner en rien—*Seigneurs légats*, leur disait-il, *voici mon corps, il est en vos mains ; et sachez pour sûr que, quoi que vous ordonnez, je suis prêt à obéir.* Les légats se contentirent de le faire agenouiller devant eux pour lui donner l'absolution, de sa complicité indirecte, l'exemptant de l'obligation de recevoir sur son dos nu les coups de verges qu'on administrait aux patients.'—*Augustin Thierry.*

15 k., on the road to Granville by the coast is *S.-Jean-le-Thomas*, with a castle ruined by Philippe Auguste. Hence came the St. Johns of Staunton St. John in Oxfordshire, whence sprang the St. Johns of Bletsoe.

127 k. *Pontaubault.*

14 k. S.E. is *S. James*, on a promontory above the deep valley of the Beauvron. Only a fragment remains of the castle built by William the Conqueror. The church is romanesque, with a gothic transept. At 2 k. is the chapel of the ancient abbey of *S. Benoit.* The *Château de la Paluelle* is xvi. c. and xvii. c.

142 k. *Pontorson* (Hotel: *de la Poste*), at the mouth of the Couesnon, which once separated Normandy and Brittany. The interesting church has an early romanesque nave; the rest is xiii. c. transition.

'The nave is without aisles, and vaulted in nearly square compartments, with diagonal ribs; the transverse arches are pointed. The capitals and transoms of some of the doors (which are round-headed) are enriched with grotesque sculpture. The west front forms a sort of porch, with a large open archway; in the real west wall of the nave is a round-headed door with window above. The front is flanked with square turrets. The central tower is massive, and appears to belong to a later style, as does the church, which has aisles.'—*J. L. Petit.*

Nothing remains of the castle, which was defended by Du Guesclin, and where his sister Julienne successfully resisted a nocturnal attack of the English, who had bribed her chambermaids; the faithless women were sewn up in sacks and thrown into the Couesnon.

'Aux portes de Pontorson est la terre du Glaquin; or on sait que le roi donna au vaillant connétable une terre aux portes de cette ville, et parmi les nombreuses formes anciennes du nom des connétables, Glaquin est une des plus constantes.'—*Le Héricher*.

AT PONTORSON.

Tickets are taken at the station at Pontorson for places in the many diligences and open vans which meet the trains. *Mont S. Michel*, about 9 k. distant, is now reached by a causeway across the bay, which possesses many conveniences, though it is less picturesque than the old approach across the sands, where Harold the Saxon bravely saved Norman soldiers from drowning.[1]

[1] See Bayeux Tapestry, 'Hic Harold Dux trahebat eos de arena.'

As soon as the road emerges from the tamarisk-fringed lanes of *Moidrey*, the magnificent rock is seen in full splendour rising beyond the wet sands. Grey and misty in morning light, purple and well defined against the clear skies of evening, it is always sublime, and unparalleled of all monasteries in the picturesqueness of its site. N. of the Alps there is nothing in Europe to compare in interest and beauty with Mont S. Michel—'S. Michel en Péril de Mer,' as Norman sailors call it.

'Le Couesnon—"qui, par sa folie, mit Saint-Michel en Normandie," change fréquemment de cours à marée basse: après avoir coulé à l'est du mont Saint-Michel, il s'était rejeté vers l'ouest et chaque grande marée en déplaçait le lit. De même la Sélune a fréquemment erré sur la plage mobile; parfois elle rase la côte au nord de Tombelène, parfois elle va directement au large. Ce n'est pas tout: les eaux des rivières ne coulent pas seulement à la surface, elles suintent aussi dans les profondeurs des sables, et souvent l'arène, reposant sur une nappe d'eau mouvante, devient fluide elle-même; tout objet lourd s'y engouffre aussitôt. Si l'on en croit les traditions, un navire échoué aux environs du mont, vers la fin du siècle dernier, se serait tellement enfoncé dans la grève, que tout aurait disparu jusqu'à l'extrémité des mâts.[1] Que de fois des voyageurs égarés dans le brouillard ont par malheur posé le pied en dehors du sol affermi et se sont "enlizés" soudain dans un sable sans fond![2] Maintenant le Couesnon est enfermé par des digues, alternativement émergées et sous-marines, qui en conduisent les eaux jusqu'à la base de la roche de Saint-Michel.'—*Elisée Reclus.*

'À une certaine heure tout est désert, morne, immobile dans cette plaine aride; mais attendez seulement quelques instants: un murmure bruira dans l'espace, une ligne blanche frémira à

---

[1] Andoin et Milne Edwards, *Littoral de la France.*
[2] Travellers should read *Les Réprouvés et les Elus* of Emile Souvestre, with its terribly vivid description of being overtaken by the tide on 'La Grève de S. Michel.'

l'horizon, et ce murmure, c'est la voix de la mer; cette ligne blanche, c'est le flux qui arrive; vous avez eu à peine le temps de le reconnaître, de le nommer, que la plage a disparu partout; le mont qui, tout à l'heure, dominait les grèves, ne domine plus que les vagues; en quelques instants le continent est devenu une île.'—*Emile Souvestre.*

The ancient name of Mont-S.-Michel, Mons Tumba, indicates that it had been the receptacle of a venerated tomb at an early age. At the beginning of the VIII. c. S. Michael appeared to S. Aubert, Bishop of Avranches, and urged him to found a convent upon the Mont Tumba. There he found the lines upon which the future abbey was to be erected marked out by supernatural power, and a miraculous spring gushed from the arid rocks to supply water for his monks. The little abbey of Aubert, which soon became a point of pilgrimage, was greatly enriched and enlarged under the different Dukes of Normandy, but especially by the Conqueror, after his invasion of England. The collection of manuscripts formed there in the XII. c. by the abbot Robert de Thorigny, also called Robert du Mont, gave to the convent the name of La Cité des Livres. One of its monks, Guillaume de S. Pair, wrote the chronicle of the abbey in verse. In 1107 Henry II. founded a priory at Pontorson in dependence on the abbey. But in 1203 Philippe-Auguste, at war with John of England, caused Mont S. Michel to be besieged by Gui de Thouars; and as he could not take it he set it on fire. The monastery was entirely destroyed, except its outer walls, but was sumptuously restored afterwards by Philippe-Auguste, by whom the tower of La Merveille and the fortress of the Rocher de Tombelaine were also built. In 1427 the Mount was fruitlessly besieged by the English.

On August 1, 1469, Louis XI. instituted the Order of S. Michel, and held its first chapter at the Mount. The numbers of the Order, limited at first to thirty-six knights, was afterwards increased to a hundred. During the Revolution the buildings of the abbey were preserved to be used as a prison. Afterwards they were given up to the Commission des Monuments Historiques.

MONT S. MICHEL.

The Hotel *Poulard Aîné* is, considering its position, one of the best and most comfortable hotels in France. It is frequented by crowds of tourists in summer, but is always admirably managed by its indefatigable hostess. There are two large *dépendances*, reached by rock staircases—*La maison rouge* and *La maison blanche*, with unrivalled sea-air and their own terraces above precipitous rocks radiant with pinks and valerian. The upper floors are preferable for a long stay. The table d'hôte (excellent) is at the hotel on the lower level, though breakfast may be taken in summer on the terrace or in the summer-houses above. The walls of the dining-room and staircase are covered with an admirable collection of sketches—many from the hands of very celebrated artists—presented to Mme Poulard. It is difficult to persuade your landlady to make a bill: she asks, 'What have you had?' The other hotels on the rock are only suited for pilgrims.

The little town of *Mont S. Michel* is girdled towards the sea by walls, interspersed with towers, chiefly xv. c. It may best be examined from the sands, which are quite safe at low water. On the N.E. is the great wall of *La Merveille*, built in the xiii. c. by Abbot Jourdain, with the picturesque *Tourelle des Corbins* or *du Refectoire* at its E. angle. Continuing to make the circuit of the fortifications from hence, we find, at the base of the turret, the *Fontaine de S. Aubert*, said to have sprung forth at a blow of the staff of the saint. A staircase leads hence to the *Châtelet de la Fontaine*, a beautiful gate flanked by two towers, opposite which on the inside is a fine xiv. c. arch of *La Chartrier*. Under the bare rocks on the W., which support the hôtellerie and infirmerie to the l. of the present approach, is the xvi. c. *Tour Gabrielle*, which formerly supported a windmill, 'the Abbot's Mill.' On the S. side is the xiv. c. *Tour des Fanils*, overlooked by the *Fanils*, or provision warehouses. Then comes the *Tour d'Echauguette*, sustaining an angle of the garden terrace, then the xv. c. bastion, called *La Barbacane*, which defended the entrance to the town.

The tiny town is entered by three gates. The first, *Porte de Bavolle*, leads into the *Cour de Lion*, so called from the lion on the wall on the l. Then the *Porte des Michelettes* (with its original iron portcullis), so called from some cannon left by the English after an ineffectual bombardment in 1429, leads to the court called *Le Boulevard* (containing the hotel), whence the *Porte de la Ville* (xv. c.), with an inner tower called *Tour du Guet*, and preserving its portcullis and the arms of the town (salmon on waves), opens upon the single street. Just inside the last gate is a remarkably picturesque xvi. c. house, often painted, resting on pillars.

MONT S. MICHEL, FROM THE SANDS.

This and many other houses served as hostelleries for pilgrims. Several of them open from an upper story on the terrace of the town wall, where there are many picturesque bits. The street twists round the hill, by the primitive post-office, and then ascends to the abbey by a staircase —*Le Grand Degré*—divided into different landings. A romanesque gateway, in a garden, is a monument of a house built 1366 by Du Guesclin for his wife Tiphaine Raguenel.

The ascent—a very easy one—from the *dépendances* of the hotel, passes a little *Musée*, containing a number of pictures, arms, and other relics connected with the history of the Mount. Following the terrace of the hill and ascending stairs on the l. we reach the little courtyard which encloses *Le Châtelet*, the ancient gate of the keep of 1393, flanked by two tall towers which have preserved their battlements and machicolations.

The Abbaye-Château is open to strangers from 5 a.m. to 6 p.m.

The long staircase of the Châtelet leads to the *Salle des Gardes*, a vast and picturesque vaulted chamber, which forms the vestibule of the building, and where the guides are found. The little door in the corner is the entrance to the porter's lodge. The great door on the right leads to La Merveille, and opens on a sunlit court surrounded by high weather-stained buildings, which is a very favourite subject with artists. The buildings on this side of the rock are of great magnificence.

'Les grands bâtiments qui donnent sur la pleine mer, du côté nord, peuvent passer pour le plus bel exemple que nous possédions de l'architecture religieuse et militaire du moyen âge; aussi les a-t-on nommée de tout temps *la Merveille.'—Viollet le Duc.*

By the door in the l. of the Salle des Gardes we enter upon a great staircase, constructed by the thirty-sixth abbot, Guillaume des Lamps, and flanked on the l. by the stately buildings of the *Logis Abbatial*, begun in 1250 by Richard Tustin, and finished under Pierre Leroy in XIV. c., the architectural change being very visible on the wall. Below the abbatial buildings was the Chapelle S. Catherine (now destroyed), built in 1380 by Abbot Geoffroy de Servon.

The building marked by a stair turret was the abbot's prison. Its lower dungeons, of which the most terrible was *La Trappe*, has given it the name of *Le Grand' Exil*, and to the next building that of *Le Petit Exil*. Both the Exils

LE CHÂTELET, MONT S. MICHEL.

were built by the Abbot Le Vitrier in 1350. A fortified bridge, crenellated and machicolated, which crosses the stairs, formed the approach for the abbots to the lower church.

We now reach the terrace in front of the church. On

the l. is the platform of the *Saut-Gaultier*, raised on three XIII. c. arches. It takes its name from a man who threw himself over the precipice from hence.

'Les auteurs expliquent différemment le nom donné à cette esplanade. L'un dit que, dans les premières années du XVIme siècle, Guillaume de Lamps "fit faire le Saut-Gaultier, ainsi nommé parceque tel fut le bon plaisir de cet abbé." D'autres racontent que cette plate-forme doit son nom au sculpteur Gaultier, prisonnier au Mont S. Michel sous François I. Mais, en réalité, il est beaucoup plus ancien, puisque, au XIII^{mo} siècle, un prédicateur s'écriait, en chaire, assuré d'être compris de ses auditeurs : " Vous êtes semblables à un certain Gaultier, qui, pour montrer à son amante combien il l'aimait, se précipita dans la mer du haut d'un rocher,—d'où le lieu du haut duquel il se précipita est encore nommé par les Normands, chez lesquels il se trouve—le Saut de Gaultier."' '*La Chaire française au* XIIIme *siècle,*' *par Leroy de la Marche.*

It was from this terrace that Barbès tried to escape when imprisoned here during the Revolution, and fell on the rocks, because his cord, made from sheets, was too short by half.

Opposite the Saut-Gaultier is the S.W. entrance to the church (XIII. c.), with a relief above it of the appearance of the archangel to S. Aubert. The grand church itself was only finished *c.* 1113, under the thirteenth abbot, Bernand du Bec, but is almost entirely XI. c.

The nave had formerly seven bays, of which three were burnt in 1776. The present bastard classical W. front is of that date, but is redeemed from ugliness by the golden lichen which has clothed it. It is, however, intended to rebuild it in the style of the XI. c., and to add again the lost bays of the nave. From the platform, called *Beauregarde* or *Mirande*, in front of the church, there is a grand view seawards, with the windings of the Couesnon through the bay.

The interior of the church has been restored. The beautiful granite arches of the choir—a splendid specimen of renaissance gothic—occupy the place of the romanesque choir which fell down in 1421. Some curious reliefs from the earlier church représent Adam and Eve, the Descent into Hades, and the Four Evangelists. It is quite worth while to ascend to the roof, as well for the interest of the view as for the beauty of the flying buttresses, in one of which an *escalier de dentelle* formerly led to the central tower, now destroyed, which was surmounted by a slender spire crowned by a gilt statue of S. Michael. Another statue of the archangel in the church, which had a solemn coronation July 3, 1877, has been removed to the parish church.

By a renaissance door in the N. aisle of the choir we reach the *Cloister*, built 1225-36 by the twenty-first abbot, Raoul de Villedieu. It has no less than 220 tiny columns of rose-granite, of which 100 decorate the side-walls. Between the arches, which are in double lines, are an endless variety of exquisitely sculptured *rosaces*. The roof is of timber. At the S.W. corner is the *lavatarium*, arranged for the monks to wash both their hands and feet.

'Les profils et l'ornementation des arcatures rappelent la véritable architecture normande du XIIIme siècle. Les chapiteaux, suivant le méthode anglo-normande, sont simplement tournés, sans feuillages ni crochets autour de la corbeille. Seuls, les chapiteaux de l'arcature adossés à la muraille sont décorés de crochets bâtards. Les écoinçons entre les archivoltes de l'intérieur des galeries présentent de belles rosaces sculptées en creux, des figures, l'agneau surmonté d'un dais, puis au-dessus des arcs une frise d'enroulements ou de petites rosaces d'un beau travail. Entre les naissances des arcs diagonaux des petites voûtes sont sculptés des crochets. Ce cloître était complètement peint, du moins à l'intérieur et entre les deux rangs de colonnettes.'—*Viollet le Duc.*

At the N.W. angle of the cloister was the *Chartier.* On the E. is the entrance to the *Dormitory*, a vast hall built by Robert des Chambres, 1225. It has a timber roof, and a pulpit for morning and evening prayer.

A more ancient cloister with a double gallery, dating rom 1106 to 1123, called *Le Promenoir*, served for the walks of the monks. Hence a long gallery led to a terrible iron cage in the thickness of the wall.

The *Crypte de l'Aquilon* is perhaps the most picturesque point of the whole building, and has been the oftenest painted. It is situated beneath the Promenoir, and is of the same date. The terrible *In Pace*, reached from hence, served as the prison of Barbès. *Les Oubliettes* are two fearful prisons. The vaults near this—*Le Charnier*—were used as the monks' cemetery. There is a mortuary chapel of XIII. c., dedicated to *S. Etienne.* Close by is the *Chapelle de Notre Dame des Trente Cierges*, so called from the thirty candles which always burnt there before an image of the Virgin. Since 1817 this chapel has been occupied by a huge wheel, by which the prisoners, working six at a time, mounted their provisions.

Passing through the gallery of the Salle des Chevaliers, we reach the *Crypte des Gros Piliers*, a magnificent, massive subterranean church of XV. c., beneath the choir. Here are nineteen enormous columns, which sustain the apse of the church. Five encircling chapels are hewn out of the rock, the whole having been executed under Abbot André de Laure, 1421.

The *Refectory*, dating from the first years of xiii. c., occupies the central floor in the great tower of La Merveille, beneath the dormitory and above the almonry. Like them, it has two naves, divided by tall columns with an octagonal base and capital richly adorned with foliage. It is due to Roger II., the eleventh abbot. This room served also as a kitchen till the xv. c., and was divided by a partition-wall, of which traces remain. The magnificent hall, known as the *Salle des Chevaliers*, was the *Chapter-House*, where all the different priors of Mont S. Michel, scattered over France and England, met annually in council on the 18th of June, the fête of S. Aubert. In 1469 they gave up the hall to the knights, who, in their turn, held their conferences there. It is a superb gothic hall of 1215-20, divided into four aisles by three ranges of circular monolith pillars, with richly sculptured capitals. In the time of the knights it was used as a museum.

'On dirait que toute la pompe féodale de la vieille France s'est refugiée dans cette belle galerie du Mont S. Michel. On y voit les trophées héraldiques de tous les chevaliers de l'ordre du roi, depuis sa création jusqu'à l'institution de celui du S. Esprit, par Henri III. Les casques, les scimiers des chevaliers sont placés sur la sommité de leurs stalles, dont ils forment le coronnement, et tout cela produit de chaque côté de la galerie une longue file de bannières, d'écus blasonnés, de casques, voiles, de casques flottants, cimiers et lambréquins découpés de dorures et de toutes couleurs, et qui produisent un effet très noble et très pittoresque.'—*Marquise de Crequi,* '*Mémoires.*'

The architecture here remains in its pristine perfection, utterly unimpaired by time or restoration. From a little gallery there is a lovely view towards the islet of Tombelaine.

Descending to the lower floor of La Merveille, we find *Les Celliers*, or *Le Magazin Général*, which was an immense store-room. These vaulted halls are also called *Les Montgommeries*, from a fruitless attack of the Calvinists in 1591, under their leader Montgomery, of which a monk, who was an eye-witness, has left a curious account:—

'Le pêcheur tombe presque toujours de mal en pire. . . . Cela est si commun qu'il n'est besoing d'en apporter autre preuve que celle qui suit d'un meschant et abominable criminel appelé Goupigny, qui pour ses forfaits exécrables devoit estre condamné à mort en la ville de Caen, où il estoit prisonnier, mais par je ne sçay quelle nouvelle invention trouva moyen de se sauver, et pour estre en plus grande seureté se retira en ce château avec Monsieur de Beausuzay, qui en estoit lors gouverneur, se reputant heureux de trouver refuge pour sauver sa misérable vie: mais à peine eut-il passé quelques mois que, oublieux de la mort qu'il avoit évitée commence à tramer de plus grandes meschancetez, trahissant la place qui naguerre l'avoit sauvé du gibet, et pour cest effait complota avec Monsieur de Sourdeval, hérétique, moyennant quelque somme d'argent, de lui livrer la place, luy donnant le jour et l'heure pour exécuter ceste horrible trahison en la manière qui suit. C'est que le dit Goupigny devoit monter le dit Sourdeval et ses gens, du costé des grandes salles, par le moyen d'une grande roue et cordages qui servoient d'ordinaire pour monter les grosses provisions du monastère. Mais Dieu ne permit point que la chose en allat ainsy; car le traistre ayant tiré l'argent du sieur Sourdeval descouvrit lui mesme à Monsieur de Beausuzay et à toute la garnison du château ce qui se passoit, pour faire le bon valet, car c'est ainsy que se gouvernent les gens sans âme, tournant à droit et à gauche.

'Cependant voicy le jour assigné venu. Les sieurs de Sourdeval et de Montgomery avec plus de deux cents hommes paroissent à l'heure préfixe, un jour de Saint-Michel, en Septembre, sur les huict heures du soir, l'an 1591, en intention de mettre tout au feu et au sang. Monsieur de Beausuzay d'autre costé donne ordre que le traistre de Goupigny se trouvât à la dite roue d'où il leur crioit qu'il n'y avoit que craindre, qu'ils montassent au plus viste. Vous eussiez veu aussy tost les ennemis s'accrocher à la corde deux ou trois à la fois à l'envie l'un de l'autre, et celuy-ci les tiroit en haut, leur faisant grand accueil, puis soudain les menoit dans le corps de garde où le gouverneur les faisait poignarder. Et cependant le dit Goupigny continuoit d'en monter d'autres ; puis après d'autres, jusqu'au nombre de 78, lesquels à mesme temps les soldats du château lardoient de coups d'espées amoncelens les corps les uns sur les autres (chose horrible à dire) comme on fait des buches de bois et fagots dans le bucher, pensans attirer les dits sieurs de Sourdeval et Montgomery pour les arranger aussy avec les autres en lieu plus éminent.

'Mais voylà qu'ils commencèrent à se deffier, voyans que pas un de leurs gens ne leur parloit, ce qui fut cause qu'ils demandèrent au dit Goupigny qu'il eut à jetter en bas du rocher un des religieux pour signe que ses gens estoient maistres de la place, et aussy tost le gouverneur fit revestir un des corps morts des habits d'un religieux qu'ils jettèrent ainsy du haut en bas ; pour lors le dit Sourdeval s'escria d'aise : *Allons, Montgomery, c'est à bon ; regarde comme les moynes volent*, et soudain s'approchèrent pour monter comme les autres ; mais le comte de Montgomery, plus sage et prudent, luy persuada de ne point monter qu'un nommé Rablotière, l'un de leur plus affidé, ne leur parlast. On fit venir celuy-cy, qu'expres on n'avoit fait encore mourir, et Monsieur de Beausuzay, gouverneur, luy promit de lui donner la vie, s'il vouloit crier à Monsieur de Sourdeval, son maistre, qu'il montast en assurance et qu'il n'y avoit rien à craindre ; mais il fut si fidelle à son maistre, qu'il n'en voulut rien faire, ainsi desguisant sa voix, lui fit entendre la trahison. Cet acte si fidelle pénétra le coeur du gouverneur, qui lui donna la vie, et les dit sieurs de Sourdeval et Montgomery, avec ce qui leur restoit de gens, s'en retournèrent plus vistes que le pas.'

To the E. of Les Celliers, beneath the Salle des Chevaliers, is the *Aumonerie*, occupying the rest of the lower story of La Merveille, divided by a single row of massive pillars. Beneath the chimney is one of the many secret passages provided for escape in case of a successful siege.

Hardy pedestrians, who do not mind occasional wading, will certainly cross the sands to the desolate granite island of *Tombelaine*, which abounds in rare wild flowers. There are some remains of ancient fortifications. It was here that the traitor Goupigny was killed soon after his treachery. The island is now uninhabited; but the hermit-fisherman, commonly known as 'Le Marquis de Tombelaine,' lived here till April 3, 1892, when, as he was crossing the sands, he was drowned by a sudden incursion of the tide. The family of Tombelaine, going over to England at the Conquest, have left their name to Tombland at Norwich.

Beneath the western precipices of the Mount itself is the picturesque *Chapelle S. Aubert*, perched on a rock. Formerly, it is said, this rock formed the summit of the Mount, but it became detached and fell to its present site in answer to the prayers of S. Aubert that his workmen might have a level site to build their church upon.

The railway, leaving Pontorson, reaches—

155 k. *La Boussac.*

3 k. S. is the very picturesque ruined *Château de Landal*, of xv. c., and, near it, the *Chapelle de Broualan*, founded in 1483 by a Dame de Landal, in fulfilment of a vow for the safe return of her husband from Palestine. The local tradition says that two oxen unattended drew all the materials of the work, and that a single cow nourished the workmen with her milk.

'L'édifice, bâti en grand appareil et en beau granit du pays, se compose d'une abside à pans, décorée de pinnacles fleuris, et d'une nef divisée en deux parties par une large arcade qui porte un fronton couronné d'un charmant campanile à trois baies, orné de colonnettes et d'aiguilles fleuronnés. Une petite tourelle octagone contenant un escalier, appliqué extérieurement au plan méridional de la nef, donnait accès au campanile. La partie orientale de la nef, qui comprend la choeur, est d'un style plus pur et plus soigné que l'autre, dont les détails accusent le xvie. Les autels, au nombre de trois, avec leurs contre-retables délicatement sculptés, sont tous en granit et du même temps que la chapelle. Une crypte assez profonde existe sous le maître-autel adossé au chevet.'—'*Bretagne contemporaine.*'

163 k. *Dol*[1] (Hotel: *de la Grand Maison*—tolerable) is a dull little town, though the houses have a quaint character, many of them having porticoes through the lower story, and supported by pillars with carved capitals. The town arose in the vii. c. around a little monastery founded by Samson, a British monk. Nominoë, chosen king of the Bretons in 845, raised Dol to the rank of an episcopal city, but the bishopric was suppressed in 1790.

The former *Cathedral of S. Samson*, now the parish church, being built of granite, is untouched by time, and is remarkable for its vigour of design. It stands alone on the outskirts of the town, and was executed almost entirely on one plan, and, as it appears, by the same workmen. It is happily unrestored, and has the rare charm of bearing completely the stamp of its period (xiii. c.); for, except the façade and side portals, all is of the earliest gothic. In the interior, the pillars are very remarkable—a central column, with four smaller surrounding ones, entirely detached. The choir, of five bays, was finished before 1324, when Bishop Jean de Bosc was buried there. The great window of the chevet has splendid xiii. c. glass. The rectangular form of the choir, the apsidal chapel (of S. Samson), and many points of internal decoration, recall English cathedrals, especially Salisbury. The S. portal was

[1] Originally *Dolomhoir*—the hill by the river.

added by Bishop Etienne Coeuret (1405-29). In the N. transept is the renaissance tomb of Bishop Thomas James, 1503. It bears the signature of Jean Florentinus, a pupil of Michel Colomb, employed on the tomb of Louis XII. at S. Denis. The huge holy water basins look as if they were intended for baptism by immersion. Few places have more local saints than Dol. They include S. Samson (bishop 565), S. Magloire (586), S. Budoc (VII. c.), S. Senior (who ordained

STREET IN DOL.

S. Patrick, the apostle of Ireland), SS. Jumael, Leucher, Thurian (749), Genevé, Ugnac, and Gilduin the deacon.[1]

The plain called *Marais de Dol* is protected from the inundations of the sea by a dyke 36 k. long. It is overlooked on the N. by the hill called *Mont Dol*, with a church partly transition, partly XV. c., and a fountain, which is supposed to bear the footprint of the archangel Michael. It was once an island, like Mont S. Michel or

[1] Consult *Les Vies des Saints de Bretagne*, by the Abbé Trevaux.

Tombelaine, but fifteen thousand hectares of the surrounding marshes have been reclaimed by a series of dykes begun in the XI. c. The number of fossil bones of elephants, stags, etc., deposited here by the sea, make the place very interesting to geologists.

A PEASANT OF DOL

A little S. of Dol, near the church of *Carfantain*, with a XIII. c. spire, is the menhir called *La Pierre du Champ-Dolent*, ten mètres high, and surmounted by a calvary. Whether the name commemorates human sacrifice, or only a place of sepulture, is unknown. Owing to the cross which surmounts it, it has preserved a sacred character.

[A line runs N.W. from Dol to (23 k.) *S. Malo* (Hotels: *de l Univers; Franklin; Continental; de France*), a seaport and bathing-place picturesquely situated on a granite peninsula near the mouth of the Rance. Châteaubriand describes it—

'S. Malo is a single rock. Formerly its huge mass rose from the midst of a salt marsh, but it became an island through an incursion of the sea in 1709. . . . Now the rock of S. Malo is only united to the mainland by a causeway, poetically called the furrow, or *sillon*. The *sillon* is lashed on one side by the open sea and on the other is washed by the tide, which beats round it on entering the harbour. A tempest almost entirely destroyed it in 1730. At the ebb of the tide the harbour is left dry, and on the east and north shores of the sea is covered with the finest sand. One can then make the circuit of my paternal nest on foot. Close in shore, and in the offing, are scattered rocks, forts, and inhabited islands—Fort Royal, La Conchée, Cezembre, and the Grande Bé, where my tomb is to be. I chose it well, though ignorantly, for Bé, in Breton, means a tomb.

'At the extremity of the *sillon*, where a cross is erected, there is a mound of sand on the edge of the open sea. This mound is called La Hoguette, and is crowned with an old gibbet. The posts of this gibbet served us for playing at four corners, and we disputed the possession of them with the sea-birds. It was not, however, without something of fear that we lingered near this place.

'There also stretch the *Miels*, or downs, where sheep graze; to the right are the meadows at the foot of Paramé, the high road to S. Servan, the new cemetery, a calvary, and several windmills, supported on posts, like those which are raised over the tomb of Achilles at the entrance of the Hellespont.'

The town originated in a monastery founded in the VI. c. by the monk Aaron, who was succeeded as abbot by S. Malo, first bishop of Aleth (S. Servan), whence the episcopal see was transferred to S. Malo in 1144. The town is celebrated for the constant success with which it has courageously resisted different sieges by the English, and for the great injuries it has at divers times inflicted upon the fleets and armies of England.

'Bretons et insulaires, les Malouins se sont fait une histoire tout à fait distincte de celle du reste de la France. De 1390 à

1594, ils avaient même réussi à se constituer en république indépendante. Plus tard, ils s'adonnent avec une étonnante énergie au commerce pendant la paix, à la piraterie pendant la guerre. Avec Cartier ils découvrent le Canada : avec Porée ils abordent aux Malouines, aujourd'hui plus connues sous le nom d'îles Falkland ; avec Duguay-Trouin ils s'emparent de Rio-de-Janeiro ; ils visitent un si grand nombre de terres lointaines, que de nos jours encore le nom de *maloon*, Malouines, est usité par les Anglais et les Américains pour désigner une île perdue dans l'Océan. Ils devinnent si redoutables pour l'Angleterre que celle-ci envoie successivement quatre expéditions contre eux sans réussir à brûler leur ville ; ils accumulent tant le trésors qu'ils prêtent 30 millions à Louis XIV. Entre tous les Français ils se distinguent par la force, la ténacité, souvent par l'orgueil. Les deux Malouins les plus illustres du siècle, Lamennais et Châteaubriand, peuvent être pris comme de vrais représentants le leurs compatriotes. La Bourdonnais, Maupertuis, Broussais étaient aussi les enfants de S. Malo.'—*Elisée Reclus.*

The (former) *Cathedral*, almost in the centre of the town, replaced in XII. c. the church of S. Vincent, founded by Bishop Hélocar in the IX. c. You descend a flight of steps into the dark interior. The central nave, with two domical bays, is of XII. c.; the rest of the nave and transept renaissance. The façade was rebuilt in 1713, and the Chapelle du S. Sacrament added 1718; the delicate crocketed spire (on the XV. c. tower) in 1859. The graceful choir, with a flat E. end, is attributed to Bishop Rouxelot de Limoëlan, 1310. The tomb of Bishop Josselin de Rohan is of 1388; that of Bishop Hochet 'par les Malouins reconnaissantes,' of 1878. Amongst the numerous local saints were S. Malo (627), S. Maelmon (638), and S. Gurval (640), bishops of Aleth ; also S. Lunaire, S. Colaphin, S. Armael, S. Enogat, S. Geifroi, and S. Jean de la Grille, bishops of S. Malo. The town retains its ramparts ; many houses are XVI. c.

On outlying rocks, covered with yellow seaweed, is the picturesque *Château*, chiefly of the time of François II., except the donjon. One of the two entrance towers is called *Quiquengrogne*, because the imperious Queen Anne, who had had some disputes with the bishop, caused to be engraved upon it, ' *Qui qu'en grogne, ainsi sera, c'est mon bon plaisir.*' A peninsula at low water, an island at high tide, is the *Grand Bé*, a delightful spot, uninhabited, and covered with wild flowers. Here, in the most romantic situation, facing the open sea, a low granite cross marks the grave of Châteaubriand, solitary in death, as he affected to be in life. He wrote:—

'I shall repose on the shore of that sea which I have loved so well. If I die out of France, I request that my body may not be brought back to my native country until fifty years have elapsed from its first inhumation. . . . The idea of a corpse travelling post fills me with horror, but dry and mouldering bones are easily transported. They will feel less fatigue on that last journey, than when I dragged them hither and thither, burdened with the load of my cares and sufferings.'

Châteaubriand was born in the house which is now the Hôtel de France.

'The house which my parents occupied was situated in a dark and narrow street of S. Malo, called the Jews' Street. This house is at the present day converted into an inn. The apartment in which my mother was confined looks upon a deserted portion of the town walls, and through a window of this chamber can be seen the sea, which spreads away, breaking upon a rocky coast, till it is lost to view. . . . I was almost dead when I came into the world. The roar of the waves, lashed by a storm, precursor of the autumnal equinox, prevented my cries being heard.'

From the Grand-Quai omnibuses (20 c.) start every hour to make the round of the port to—

S. Servan (Hotels: *de l'Union; du Pélican*), a modern town, occupying the site of the ancient Aleth. At the entrance of the glacis of the fort is the ruined cathedral of *S. Pierre d'Aleth* chiefly romanesque. The parish church only dates from 1742 The grand and massive *Tour du Solidor*, at the mouth of the Rance, was built by Duke Jean IV. at the end of the XIV. c.

A steamer leaves the outer port of S. Malo every hour except 12 o'clock, and crosses the bay in 10 min. to *Dinard* (Hotels: *Grand; des Bains; du Casino; de la Plage*), a favourite bathing-place, much frequented by English. It is a bright little town, with terraces above the bay. In fine weather the colour of the sea is glorious, and contrasts vividly with the golden seaweed with which the rocks are covered. A priory, founded

1334, is now the house of the English consul. 4 k. S. is the church of *S. Lunaire* (xv. c. and xvi. c.), which contains the xiii. c. tomb of S. Lunaire.

4 k. N. of S. Malo is *Paramé* (omnibus every half-hour, 35 c. Hotels: *Grand; de la Plage; des Bains*), a pleasant bathing-place; and farther in the same direction (14 k.) *Cancale* (Hotels: *de l'Europe; du Centre*), famous for its oyster beds.

[A line runs S. from Dol to (58 k.) Rennes by—

CHÂTEAU DE COMBOURG.

16 k. *Combourg*. The castle, chiefly xiv. c. and xv. c., has a donjon built by Gingoneus, Bishop of Dol, in 1016. After the death of his brother, who perished upon the scaffold in the Revolution, the seigneurie came to the author François-René de Châteaubriant, whose great-nephew is still its owner.

'Si mes ouvrages me survivent, si je dois laisser un nom, peut-être un jour, guidé par ces mémoires, quelque voyageur viendra visiter les lieux que j'ai peinte. Il pourra reconnaître le château, mais il cherchera vainement le grand mail ou le grand bois; le berceau de mes songes a disparu comme ces songes.

Demeuré seul debout sur son rocher, l'antique donjon pleure les chênes qui l'environnaient et le protégeaient contre la tempête. Isolé comme lui, j'ai vu comme lui tomber autour de moi la famille qui embellissait mes jours et me prêtait son abri ; heureusement ma vie n'est pas batie sur la terre aussi solidement que les tours où j'ai passé ma jeunesse, et l'homme resiste moins aux orages que les monuments élevés par ses mains.'—*Mémoires d'outre tombe.*

35 k. *Betton.* 7 k. N.E., at *S. Sulpice*, are ruins of an abbey founded in 1115 by Raoul de la Fustaie, disciple of Robert d'Arbrissel. Most of the remains are XII. c.]

191 k. *Dinan* (Hotels : *d'Angleterre*—very good, clean and reasonable—much the best ; *de la Bretagne*). This will be found a pleasant halting-place for a few days. The hotels are outside the town, which occupies a promontory above the Rance, and has its origin in a castle built by the Vicomte Hamon in the x. c. Here the Saxon Harold, whilst aiding him in the siege of the place, was knighted by Duke William (the Conqueror). The town and its environs have many English residents. Pleasant avenues of elms, with a view into the rich surrounding gorges, skirt the ramparts, which have some remains of the fifty-six towers which once adorned them. In the heart of the town many fine old timber houses remain, with broad porticoes overhanging the footways, and giving shelter to the numerous wares of street-vendors. The large church of *S. Malo* is chiefly of XII. c. In a fine situation farther on is the very stately church of *S. Sauveur*, with a portal and the lower part of the W. front of XII. c. The rest is of different dates from XII. c. to XVIII. c. The very handsome interior has much good glass, and many admirable gothic and renaissance tabernacles and orna-

ments. In the N. transept is the black marble tomb of the heart of Du Guesclin, 1380. He was originally buried at Le Puy, but removed to S. Denis, where his body 'rests among the kings,' but he bequeathed his heart to the

TOUR DE L'HORLOGE, DINAN.

Dominican church of Dinan, where his first wife, Tiphaine Raguenel, was buried. Behind the church is a pleasant *Public Garden*, looking down on the Rance. Below this, one of the oldest streets in the town leads down the hill to the *Porte de Jerzuel*. Several other gates remain. At the end of the W. wall, separated from the town by a moat, is the *Château*, now a prison. There is a miserable statue of Du Guesclin in a neighbouring square. The picturesque *Tour de l'Horloge* has a clock given by Queen Anne in 1507.

CHÂTEAU DE LA GARAYE.

There is a great charm in the walks round Dinan—the wooded country, deep glens, bright rivers, and variety of old buildings. In the hollow beyond the Porte S. Louis is (1 k.) *Lehon*, where a wooded mound is crowned by the ruins of a castle besieged and taken by Henry II. of England. The fortifications enclose a modern chapel of S. Joseph Consolateur. The picturesque old parish *Church* has a quaint tower and a romanesque nave and portal. On its S. side is a chapel containing tombs of the Seigneurs of Beaumanoir, including the hero who commanded at the romantic 'Combat de Trente.'[1] Four of the statues are of knights, the fifth of a prior of Lehon. Just below are the picturesque XIII. c. and XIV. c. remains of the *Priory of S. Magloire*, founded by Nominoë *c.* 850. The beautiful priory church—gothic, with a Norman front—was restored in 1894; on the N. is a simple renaissance cloister. The gateway of the Priory is passed on the left below the church. A lofty ancient *Bridge* crosses the Rance. The view looking back up the village street is well worth painting.

[3 k. N.E. (beyond the railway), approached by an avenue of trees on the r. of the road to S. Malo, are the XV. c. ruins of the *Château de la Garaye*, which has become celebrated from the touching story of its last proprietors, the Comte Claude-Marot and his wife, *née* de la Motte-Picquet, as told by Mrs. Norton in 'The Lady of La Garaye':—

> 'Oh! loved and reverenced long that name shall be,
> Though, crumbled on the soil of Brittany,
> No stone, at last, of that pale ruin shows
> Where stood the gateway of his joys and woes.
> For, in the Breton town, the good deeds done
> Yield a fresh harvest still, from sire to son:
> Still thrives the noble hospital that gave
> Shelter to those whom none from pain could save.
> Still to the schools the ancient chiming clock
> Calls the poor yeanlings of a simple flock;
> Still the calm refuge for the fallen and lost
> (Whose love a blight and not a blessing crost)
> Sends out a voice to woo the grieving breast,—
> "Come unto me, ye weary, and find rest!"
> And still the gentle nurses—vowed to give
> Their aid to all who suffer and yet live—
> Go forth in snow-white cap and sable gown,
> Tending the sick and hungry in the town.
> And show dim pictures on their quiet walls
> Of those who dwelt in Garaye's ruined halls.'

See ch. v.

An avaricious peasant will admit visitors to her kitchen-garden, where the ruins are situated—a small tower, and a wall with windows rich in details of xv. c. sculpture. Beautifully situated, to the l. of the S. Malo road, is the still-inhabited *Château de la Coninnais*, also xv. c.]

[The pleasantest excursion to be made from Dinan is by taking the early morning train to Dinard. An omnibus meets the train, and allows a sufficient sight of the pretty, bright little place, before reaching the quay whence the steamer crosses the estuary to S. Malo. The views from the boat are enchanting, of the mouth of the Rance, S. Servan, with its fort, church, and grey tower; then S. Malo itself, with its ramparts, churches, and its rocks covered with golden seaweed. The landing-place at low tide is at the end of the island of Grand Bé (see p. 331), whence a causeway leads across the seaweed-covered rocks to the town. But an enchanting morning should be spent on the island itself—a wild spot, overgrown with sea-loving flowers, and with the tomb of Châteaubriand in an incomparably grand position—before S. Malo is entered by a postern gate. After visiting the château and cathedral, the tourist may saunter through the old streets to the quay, and take the little afternoon boat (from the end of the quay to the r.), which ascends the Rance in 2 hrs. (3 fr. and 2 fr.). The boat passes S. Servan and its grand Tour S. Solidor on l. There is nothing very remarkable in the scenery, but the open creeks, rocky islets and wooded banks of the river, and the picturesquely-placed villages and manor-houses, have a great charm. If the tide does not allow of the farther ascent of the river, passengers are landed 6 k. or 7 k. from Dinan, but diligences and open vans in this case meet the steamer, and the fare is included in that of the boat. The drive is a most pleasant one. Ascending the river from S. Malo and returning thither does not allow time for seeing Dinan, but visitors *from* S. Malo may return by the railway, which passes at 17 k. *Châteauneuf,* where the ruins exist of a castle demolished in 1594. Near this, on the E., is *La Mare de S. Coulban,* and the curious and interesting xiii. c. church of *S. Suliac,* containing the tomb of that sainted abbot under an altar dedicated to him. When a wail is heard from the marsh the peasants cross themselves, for it is the cry of an unworthy priest, overwhelmed by the waters at the moment of celebrating mass, and condemned to repeat eternally his 'Dominus vobiscum,' which has ever remained without an answer: this cry is called 'Le beugle de S. Coulman.'[1]]

200 k. *Corseul.* 3 k. S.W. is the village which marks the site of the ancient capital of the Curiosolites, where several Roman roads converged and a number of Roman remains have been found. A Roman inscription is built into one of the pillars of the church of Corseul, which contains a most curious granite font, sustained by four dwarfs—either intended for baptism by immersion or as a bénitier of xii. c. or xiii. c. On a hill half a league from Corseul is the ruin called a temple of Mars—a Roman wall 30 ft. high.

230 k. Lamballe. See ch. v.

[1] See De la Bigue Villeneuve, *Ille et Vilaine.*

CHAPTER VII.

PARIS AND LE MANS TO QUIMPER, BY CHÂTEAU-GONTIER, SÉGRÉ, CHÂTEAUBRIANT, REDON, VANNES, L'ORIENT, AND QUIMPERLÉ. CHEMIN DE FER DE L'OUEST.

LE MANS (see ch. v.) is 211 k. from Paris.
Leaving Le Mans, the line passes r. the ruined *Tour aux Fées*, dating from Roman times; then the *Bois de Teillais*, where Charles VI. saw the apparition which was one of the causes of his madness.

230 k. *La Suze.* The xv. c. château was founded xi. c., the church (altered) in xi. c.

[A line leads S. to La Flèche by—
12 k. *La Lude* (see ch. v.).
33 k. *La Flèche* (Hotel: *des Quatre Vents*) had its origin in a famous fortress built upon the Loir in the xi. c. by Jean de Beaugency, who had married Paule, granddaughter of the famous Comte de Mans, Herbert *Eveille-Chien*. Under his son, the famous warrior-count Hélie, whose virtues were sung by the troubadours, a walled town and priory arose near the castle. Eremburga, daughter of Hélie, brought the Seigneurie of La Flèche to the house of Anjou, and thus to the English Plantagenets. In the xvi. c. it belonged to the house of Bourbon. Antoine de Bourbon and Jeanne d'Albret lived here till a few months before the birth of Henri IV., who had an especial affection for La Flèche, to which he bequeathed his heart. The Vendéens gained a victory over the Bleus at La Flèche, Dec. 1793.

The *Prytanée*, or college of La Flèche, founded 1607, and formerly under the direction of the Jesuits, has produced many illustrious scholars, including Gresset, the Chancellor Voysin, and Séguier. It was turned into a military school by Napoléon I., and is now employed for sons of officers killed upon the field of battle. The chapel, of 1607-22, contained the hearts of Henri IV. and Marie de Medicis preserved in metal cases till the Revolution. The hearts were then publicly burnt; but their ashes, collected by a royalist, are placed in a gilt heart which may be seen in the l. transept. The *Salle des Actes*, where the collegiate prizes are distributed, is adorned with an allegorical painting of Henri IV. crowned by Victory. The king is commemorated by a statue on the '*place*' which bears his name.]

254 k. *Juigné-sur-Sarthe* has a handsome château, rebuilt XVII. c., which has belonged to the family Le Clec from the XIV. c.

259 k. *Sablé* (Hotel: *Notre Dame*) has a château built by the Duc de Guise on the site of a demolished castle, in 1720.

3 k. from Sablé is the famous monastery of *Solesmes*, founded XI. c. Its modernised buildings are deeply interesting as containing the marvellous XV. c. sculptures known as *Les Saints de Solesmes*, chiefly united in the two groups representing the Burial of Christ and the Burial and Coronation of the Virgin.

[For a detailed account of Solesmes, and for the line from Sablé to Angers, see *South-Western France*.]

(8 k. from Sablé, on the way to La Flèche, is *La Chapelle du Chêne*, with a famous pilgrimage chapel, rebuilt 1868-73, on the site of a miracle-working oratory of the Virgin, where a statue had been erected in the branches of an oak in 1494.)

[For the line from Sablé to Sille le Guillaume see ch. v.]

273 k. *Chemazé.*

[A branch of 14 k. leads N. to *Craon* (pronounced Cran). Its XVI. c. château replaces a castle built by Lambert, Comte de Nantes, in 846, and destroyed under Henri IV. 14 k. W., at

La Roë, are the ruins of an abbey founded by Robert d'Aubrissel, before the foundation of Fontevrault. The façade and nave are of 1140, the rich choir of xv. c. Near (10 k. from Cráon) *S. Quentin*, on the road to Segré, is the picturesque and beautiful *Château de Mortier-Crolle*, attributed to Pierre de Rohan, marshal of France under Louis XII.]

282 k. *Gennes-Longuefuve.* (For the line hence to Laval see ch. v.)

290 k. *Château Gontier* (Hotels: *de l'Europe, du Dauphin*) takes its origin from a fortress on the Mayenne built by Foulques Nerra, Comte d'Anjou, in the xi. c. The formerly collegiate church of *S. Jean*, which was within the enclosure of the castle, is a valuable, though over-restored, specimen of xi. c. Under the choir and its aisles is an interesting romanesque crypt. The church of *Bazouges* (1 k. N.W.) has an xi. c. portal.

The line passes (l.) the xv. c. *Château de S. Ouen* before reaching—

308 k. *La Ferrière*, which has a modernised château of xiv. c. and xv. c.

314 k. *Segré* (Hotels: *de Beaurepaire ; de la Croix Verte*) has small remains of its ancient fortifications, as the dower-town of Berengaria of Castille, widow of Richard Cœur de Lion. 8 k. W. is the fine modern *Château de la Mabouliere* (M. de Falloux).

[For the line from Segré to Angers see *South-Western France.*]

340 k. *Pouancé*, the seat of an ancient barony, has remains of a castle of xiii. c. and xiv. c.

356 k. *Châteaubriant* (Hotel: *de la Poste*) on the Chère, an ancient barony, which owes its origin to the castle built

here by one Briant in the XI. c. The old castle is an irregular quadrilateral, with a square donjon tower on the N.E. Here Sybilla, wife of Geoffroy IV., who was taken prisoner in the Crusades, died of joy on receiving him safe home from captivity. The *Château Neuf*, partly used as a gendarmerie, is a handsome renaissance building, begun by Jean de Laval in 1524. The church of *S. Nicolas*, founded XI. c., and rebuilt by Jean de Laval and Anne de Montmorency in the XVI. c., has been recently pulled down and replaced by a modern edifice. On the N.W. of the town is the curious priory church of *S. Jean de Béré*, founded by Briant II. in 1114. The church of *La Trinité* was founded in 1262 by Geoffroy IV., who was buried there with many of his descendants, and the beautiful Françoise de Foix, wife of Jean de Laval. The priory of *S. Michel des Monts* was founded in 1204 by Geoffroy II.

[For the lines to Vitré and to Rennes see ch. v. For the line to Nantes see *South-Western France*.]

367 k. *S. Vincent des Landes*, where the line diverges l. to S. Nazaire (see *South-Western France*).

392 k. *Guémené Penfao*. Near this is the *Château de Bruc*, which has been inhabited by the family of that name from the XII. c.

415 k. *Redon* (Hotels: *de France; du Lion d'Or*), on the Vilaine, owes its origin to the abbey of S. Sauveur, said to have been originally founded by S. Convoïon. The formerly abbatial church of *S. Sauveur* has an isolated XIV. c. tower with a tall stone spire, the only important romanesque tower in Brittany. The triple romanesque nave has been much modernised. The choir, which has

a lofty triforium, is a noble specimen of XIII. c. In the first chapel r. of choir is a tomb, supposed to be that of François I., Duc de Bretagne. The central chapel has the xv. c. tomb of Abbot Raoul de Pontbriand. The *Chapelle de Notre Dame de Bon Secours* (N. aisle of choir) was built in the xv. c. by Abbot Yves le Sénéchal, who is buried there. It is curiously fortified externally, its windows protected by machicolations and its walls pierced with loopholes. The XVII. c. buildings of the abbey are occupied by the Institution de S. Sauveur. The ramparts remain, constructed in XIV. c. by Abbot Jean de Tréal.

[For the line from Redon to Rennes see ch. v.]

[18 k. on the line to (81 k.) Nantes is *S. Gildas des Bois*, retaining the fine XIII. c. church of a Benedictine monastery founded by Simon de la Roche-Bernard in 1026. 9 k. E. of this is the XVIII. c. *Château de Carheil*, which belonged to Mme Adelaïde, and was bequeathed by her to the Prince de Joinville.]

431 k. *Malausac* has an old castle and picturesque houses.

3 k. N.E. are the remains of the convent of *Bodélio*.

5 k. N.W. is *Rochefort-en-Terre*, a very picturesque village in a gorge beneath a precipitous rock, crowned by the ruins of a XIII. c. castle. The once-collegiate church *of Notre Dame de la Tronchaye* is chiefly xv. c. Statues of Claude de Rieux, 1532, and Suzanne de Bourbon, Dame de Rochfort, taken from their tombs at the Revolution, are used as S. Joseph and the Virgin. Several houses are xv. c. and XVII. c.

Near the farm of *Grée-Mahe* remains of an ancient villa and temple have been discovered. 3 k. N. is the parched and desolate plain called *La Lande de Lanvaux*, strewn with megalithic remains, but without any regularity or order. Near the wood of *Misny* is the fine menhir of *La Roche Béguë* (5 mèt.).

Near the village of *S. Jean de la Bande* is the menhir called *Le Chapeau Rouge*.

The desolation of the Lande de Lanvaux is accounted for by the legend that SS. Peter and Paul, wandering on foot through the country, and drenched to the skin, asked leave to dry themselves at a rich peasant's fire. He turned them with ignominy from his door; but one Misery, the poorest peasant in the country, gave them shelter and fed them. Being asked what blessing he would receive as a reward, he begged that if any one climbed his single apple-tree—of the fruit of which he was always robbed—he might be forced to stay there till he (Misery) gave him leave to come down. The rich peasant, coming to steal the poor man's apples, was the first to be kept in this durance. But when Death came to call Misery to follow him, the peasant persuaded him to get him first one of the apples from his tree, and there he kept him till Death had promised to let him live on till the Last Judgment. In his fury at being obliged to make this promise, Death laid waste the whole Lande de Lanvaux: only Misery lives on.

444 k. *Questembert* has several curious old houses and ancient chapels. The district abounds in crosses, adorned with rude sculpture in high relief. At 7 k. beyond Questembert the line passes (l.) the hamlet of *La Vraie Croix*, where a xvii. c. chapel has a fragment of the true cross in a xiii. c. reliquary. Another chapel, of *S. Isidore*, belonged to a hospital of the Knights of S. John of Jerusalem. A second chapel of the Knights is at *Gorvello*, 5 k. S.W. : in its graveyard are two menhirs.

[For the line from Questembert to La Brohinière, on the main line from Paris to Brest, passing Ploermel (for Josselin —well worth visiting), see ch. v.]

458 k. *Elven*. There is an omnibus from the station to the village, 5 k. N. The (rebuilt) church retains its choir of 1526. In the churchyard is an ossuary containing the

portrait of a woman. It is supposed to represent a girl of holy life, whose uncorrupt body was found here many years after her death, and who was venerated as a saint, till her remains were dispersed at the Revolution.

'Le village d'Elven donne une représentation vraiment saisissante de ce que pouvait être un bourg du moyen âge. La forme des maisons basses et sombres n'a pas changé depuis des siècles. On croit rêver quand on voit, à travers les baies incrustées et ans châssis qui tiennent lieu de fenêtres, ces groupes de femmes à l'oeil sauvage, au costume sepulchral, qui filent leur quenouille dans l'ombre, et s'entretiennent à voix basse dans une langue inconnue. Il semble que tous ces spectres grisâtres viennent de quitter leurs dalles tumulaires pour exécuter entre eux quelque scène d'un autre âge dont vous êtes le seul témoin vivant. Cela cause une sorte d'oppression. Le peu de vie qui se communique autour de vous dans l'unique rue du bourg porte le même caractère d'archaïsme et d'étrangeté fidèlement retenu d'un monde evanoui.'—*Octave Feuillet*, '*Roman d'un jeune homme pauvre.*'

The district is full of megalithic remains, the most important being the dolmen called *La Loge du Loup*, near the village of *Les Princes*.

2 k. S.W. of Elven (a pleasant drive from Vannes) are the ruins of the famous castle of *Largouët*, or *Le Tour d'Elven*, built by Odon de Malestroit in the xiv. c., and dismantled in 1496 by order of the Duchess Anne. For the sake of water to the moat it is situated (unusual) in a hollow. The donjon tower, added by the Maréchal de Rieux in the xv. c., is octagonal and exceedingly imposing. Henry VII. was at one time imprisoned in the castle, through jealousy of his title of Earl of Richmond, an appanage of the Dukes of Brittany.

'La tour d'Elven se dégagea soudain de la feuillée, et se dressa à deux par de nous avec la soudaineté d'une apparition. Cette tour n'est pas ruinée : elle conserve aujourd'hui toute sa hauteur primitive, qui dépasse cent pieds, et les assises régulières de granit qui en composent le magnifique appareil octagonal lui donnent l'aspect d'un bloc formidable taillé d'hier par le plus pur ciseau. Rien de plus imposant, de plus fier et de plus sombre que ce vieux donjon impassible au milieu des temps et isolé dans l'épaisseur de ces bois. Des arbres ont poussé de toute leur taille dans les douves profondes qui l'environnent, et leur faîte touche à peine l'ouverture des fenêtres les plus basses. Cette végétation gigantesque, dans laquelle se perd confusément la base de l'édifice, achève de lui prêter une couleur de fantastique mystère. Dans cette solitude, au milieu de ces forêts, en face de cette masse d'architecture bizarre qui surgit tout à coup, il est impossible de ne pas songer à les tours enchantées où de belles princesses dorment un sommeil séculaire.'—*Octave Feuillet.*

'La tour d'Elven si belle quand on regarde les deux cents pieds d'élevation qui restent à ses murailles, quand on entre dans son enceinte, qui était une ville entière, et que l'on voit la fenêtre à laquelle s'accouda prisonnier un roi d'Angleterre.'[1]—*Emile Souvestre.*

In the courtyard of the XVII. c. *Château de Kerfily* (3½ k. N.) are the ruined tower and portal of an older castle. The line passes (r.) the XV. c. *Chapelle S. Anne,* with fine stained glass, before reaching—

469 k. *Vannes* (Hotels: *de France; du Commerce; du Dauphin*)—in Breton, *Gwened* (white wheat)—capital of the Département du Morbihan. Vannes, capital of the Venètes in Celtic times, claims not only to have colonised the Adriatic, but to have given a name to Venice. Its citizens were the fighting men of Brittany, the last inhabitants of Gaul to submit to Caesar, who said that they had bodies of iron and hearts of steel. Having only been conquered 37 B.C., they threw off the Roman yoke in 409, and were governed for many years by independent counts. Vannes was a principal residence of the Ducs de Bretagne. It is a very dull town. A few XVI. c. houses cluster around

[1] The Earl of Richmond, afterwards Henry VII.

the *Cathedral of S. Pierre*, a poor building, dating from XIII. c. to XVIII. c., and quite without beauty. The disposition of the choir is singular, projecting to the first bay of the nave, with its altar under the cross. The circular chapel of the Sacrament was built by the Archdeacon Daniels, who is buried there. At the E. end of the church, approached by a narrow passage, is the long narrow chapel of S. Vincent Ferrier, 1630, commemorating the great Spanish Dominican preacher, invited by Duke Jean V. to fix his residence in Vannes, where he died in 1419. He was canonised in 1456, and was buried in the N. transept, where the Duchesse Jeanne de France, daughter of Charles VI., by her own desire, was laid at his feet. His bones, however, are for the most part preserved in the *trésor*, whence Philip II. of Spain vainly endeavoured to carry them off. It is asserted that as he was saying mass here, he went to fetch his gloves and umbrella from Rome without any one perceiving his absence. His chapel contains two tombs of bishops—Sebastien de Rosmadec, 1646, and François d'Argouges, 1716, with a kneeling figure. Other saints of Vannes, many of whom have reliquaries or shrines here, are SS. Paterne (1st bishop, IV. c., invoked in drought), S. Guenuin, S. Ignoroc (bishop, VII. c.), S. Meriadec (bishop, 666), S. Gobrien (bishop, 735), S. Cadoc, and S. Belo. Here also is buried S. Guenaël, the sainted abbot of Landevenec.

The N. portal is of 1514. Near it are some picturesque remains of a XIII. c. *cloister*, which combine well with the XII. c. N.W. tower. Opposite the W. door of the cathedral is the XIII. c. *Chapelle du Présidial.* The Episcopal Palace was formerly a Carmelite convent. Several fragments remain of the ancient walls, especially the *Porte S. Paterne,* commonly called Porte Paten, often from its use *Porte Prison,* leading to the cathedral, and the xiv. c. *Tour du Connétable.* The *Place des Lices* was the site of the famous palace of the Dukes of Brittany, called the Château de l'Ermine. It was on this Place that S. Vincent Ferrer used to preach in 1417—in Spanish, the only language he knew, but which everybody miraculously understood. Here also, in 1380, the Battle of the Five was fought—five French and five English knights—in the presence of Duke Jean IV. and the Duke of Buckingham. The French were victorious.

The *Porte S. Vincent,* surmounted by a statue of the saint, is xvii. c. It leads to the port. Through it, the relics of S. Vincent are borne annually on his feast-day and carried round the walls.

To the left is the *Tour du Connétable,* where Olivier de Clisson was shut up in 1387.[1] After the battle of Auray Duke Jean IV. had given the seigneury of Gavre, near Clisson's property of Blain, to the Englishman Sir John Chandos, upon which Clisson took service with the king of France, who made him Constable. But the duke appointed a great parliament to be held at Vannes, to which, with all his other lords, Clisson was summoned, and received with great hospitality. Then the duke pretended to desire his advice as to his newly built Château d'Ermine, and persuaded him to enter this tower to examine the masonry, when he was seized and immured there till he was ransomed. The tower is now used to contain the *Musée Archéologique,* which is of the utmost interest, being one of

---

[1] Voltaire's tragedy of *Adelaide du Guesclin* is founded on a terrible drama of the Tour du Connétable.

the richest in Europe in Celtic antiquities, the result of excavations in the tumuli of Western Brittany. Several picturesque houses are XVI. c. and XVII. c. 15, Rue des Orfèvres contains the room of S. Vincent Ferrier, now converted into a chapel. At the corner of Rue Noé are two quaint-coloured figures known as 'Vannes et sa femme.'

The Hôtel de France is believed to occupy the site of the Château de la Motte, the palace of Waroch, Comte de Vannes, the father of Tryphena, sixth wife of Comorre, the Blue Beard Comte de Comorre, who cut off her head, which was restored, with her life, by S. Gildas le Sage.

'There is no more charming walk than that eastward of the town: on one side, above winding river and shady walks and picturesque houses, rise the grey walls and towers of the old fortifications; on the other, terrace upon terrace of greensward, with stately avenues, lead to a broad close, or green, from whence you look across Lombardy poplars towards Nantes. Heather, woods, pastures and rivers make up a wide, invigorating prospect. How every inch of ground here teems with historical associations! It was at Vannes that Caesar first encountered the Gauls, then, as now, "ad bellum mobiliter celeriterque excitari"; then, as now, "subita et repentina consilia," in that sea-fight he so graphically describes.'—*Autumn in Western France.*

At *Tréorante*, near Vannes, is the tomb of S. Ouenne, daughter of Hoël III., of the VII c.

A little N.E. of Vannes, on the Elven road, is the great rock of *Hesquéno*, whence, by the moor of *Bohalgo*, a pedestrian may reach the 'Grotto of Jean II.'

On the peninsula of *Séné*, which produces the sailors called Sinagots, is *Limur*, with a chapel dedicated to S. Ufévrier. The foot of her statue is full of pins; for a girl who can plant a pin there firmly (as in the shrine at Ploumanach) will find a husband before the end of the year; but if the pin does not remain fast she will have to go without.

On a market-day the market-place is worth visiting.

'Le dialecte qui se distingue le plus nettement des autres est celui de Vannes. . . . Par suite de l'écart des traditions et des coutumes, une certaine rivalité s'est établie entre les habitants des divers pays, Tréguier, Léon, Cornouaille, et Vannes. Souvent même les animosités sont devenues des haines, et les Bretons de divers dialectes, tout en se vantant de leurs vertus locales, s'appliquent mutuellement des épithètes fort malveillantes : Voleur comme un Léonard ! traître comme un Trégorrois ! sot comme un Vannetais ! brutal comme un Cornouaillais.'—*Elisée Reclus.*

> 'La langue du pays, c'est la chaîne éternelle
> Par qui sans efforts tout se tient ;
> Les choses de la vie, on les apprend par elle,
> Par elle encore on s'en souvient.'[1]
> *Brizeux,* '*Histoires Poëtiques.*'

Very few now remain of the peasantry who were so characteristic even twenty years ago ; and the costumes, till lately so picturesque, are now almost extinct even amongst ' Les plus bretonnants des Bretons.'

'The old-fashioned Breton combs his long black hair, and walks about unashamed in his *bragou-bras*,—turns his back on the future, and looks only on the past, on his dead ancestors and the cross, and profoundly distrusts all improvement in this world. A grand, sublime, miraculous Past, is contrasted in his mind with a poor uninteresting Present, its mere appendix, and a Future without form or hope till the Last Day ; the past is to him the great reality of the world—the reality, not of dilettantism, of forced reverence, of partial or fictitious interest, but of lifelong faith.'—*Dean Church,* '*Essays.*'

4 k. from Vannes is the nearest island in the Gulf of Morbihan, the little *Île de Gouleau* (omnibus), much frequented by bathers.

[1] The natives say Adam and Eve spoke Breton in Paradise. See *Origines Gauloises.*

S. GILDAS DE RHUIS.

There are public carriages (2 fr. and 1 fr. 50 c.) from Vannes to (24 k. S.W.) *Sarzeau,* where Le Sage, the author of *Gil Blas,* was born in 1688. (Inn with good food.) On the S. of the Bay of Morbihan is the Peninsula of *Rhuis,* which forms a natural dyke, only leaving a narrow canal by which the Morbihan communicates with the Atlantic. 3 k. S.E. of Sarzeau are the ruins of the summer palace of the Dukes of Brittany, the *Château de Sucinio*—'Souci n'y ôt'—an abode of pleasure. Now the site, by the seashore, is dreary in the extreme. The castle was built (1250) by Jean de Roux. Amongst the changes upon the primitive construction are embrasures for cannon. Here Breton legend places the home of Count Raymondin, whose wife was Melle de Lusignan, the fairy Melusine, who had the power of changing herself into a serpent every Saturday. Raymondin was called 'Comte de Forêt.'

7 k. from Sarzeau, at the S.W. extremity of the Presqu'île, which is now so bare and was once covered with forest, is the abbatial church of *S. Gildas-de-Rhuis* (a good and pleasant pension is kept by nuns), belonging to a monastery founded in the VI. c. by S. Gildas[1] le Sage, a missionary from the monastery of S. Hydultus, in Cornwall, who became the apostle of Brittany and the chief counsellor of Waroch, Count of Vannes. He was persuaded by the wicked Comorre, Count of Cornouaille, to bring about a marriage between him and Count Waroch's beautiful daughter Tryphena. One day, some months after their marriage, Comorre found Tryphena embroidering a little cap. 'For whom are you working?' 'For the son whom I hope to give you.' Then Comorre, who had already killed five wives when they were with child, determined on the death of Tryphena. She fled to her father's, but was captured and beheaded here, just outside the walls of Vannes. Then Gildas, having cursed the murderer to his face, performed a great miracle, for he restored the head of Tryphena to its place, and brought her back to life, and—after her child was born—placed her in a convent, and took her son, whom she had called Tremeur, to bring up in the monastery of Rhys.[2]

In the XII. c. Abelard governed the monastery, but was forced

---

[1] S. Veltas in Breton.
[2] See Luzel, *Contes du Pays d'Amor*; Alfred Fouquet, *Légendes du Morbihan,* and *Les Fantômes Bretons.*

to fly by his monks, who, weary of his strict rule, attempted to poison him. The monastic buildings, of XVIII. c., are now inhabited by sisters of charity, who take boarders during the bathing season. In the XII. c. choir of the church is the tomb of S. Gildas, who died in 570 in his island hermitage of Huath, desiring his monks to place his body in a boat, with the stone which had served him in life as a pillow under his head, and then drop it in the open sea, when God would work His will with it. But when the saint was in the boat the monks quarrelled, the English monks claiming his remains for the Cornish S. Hydultus, where he had been educated, the Bretons for Rhuis. But whilst they were disputing, the boat and its holy freight sank in the waves and was lost to sight; after which the Cornishmen gave it up, but the Bretons, searching, after long prayer and fasting, found the boat with the body of S. Gildas safely come to shore near the oratory of S. Croix.

In the Chapelle de la Vierge is the tomb of S. Gingurien. Near the altar is that of S. Gonsten, once a pirate of Ushant, converted by S. Gildas to become a lay brother in the monastery. In the N. transept are the tombs of S. Félix and the Abbot Rioc. Five tombs in the choir (XIII. c. and XIV. c.) are of the house of Bretagne, four of them to children of Jean I., who died at Sucinio, the fifth to Jeanne de Bretagne, daughter of Jean de Montfort, who died 1388. In the *trésor* are relics of S. Gildas in XV. c. reliquaries. In the garden the door is pointed out by which Abelard fled to the sea and eventually to Cluny.

'Près de S. Gildas les pêcheurs de mauvaise vie et qui se soucient peu de salut de leur âme sont quelquefois réveillés la nuit par trois coups que frappe à leur porte une main invisible. Alors ils se lèvent, poussés par une volonté surnaturelle ; ils se rendent au rivage, où ils trouvent de longs bateaux noirs qui semblent vides, et qui pourtant enfoncent dans la mer jusqu'au niveau de la vague. Dès qu'ils y sont entrés, une grande voile blanche se hisse seule en haut du mât, et la barque quitte le bord comme emportée par un courant rapide. On ajoute que ces bateaux, chargés d'âmes maudites, ne reparaissent plus au rivage, et que le pêcheur est condamné à errer avec elles à travers les océans jusqu'au jour du jugement. Qui ne reconnait dans cette fable la tradition celtique rapportée par Procope.'—*E. Souvestre,* '*Les Derniers Bretons.*'

The excursion to S. Gildas may be continued by carriage to (5 k.) *La Butte de Tumiac* (Tumulus Iacchi), a very remarkable tumulus 260 mèt. in circumference, 20 mèt. in height. The sepulchral cell it encloses has supplied many ornaments to the museum at Vannes. 3 k. farther (35 k. from Vannes) is *Port-Navalo,* a little fishing town. A boat hence to Auray (12 fr.) crosses in 2½ hrs. in fine weather.

A boat (12 fr. to 15 fr.) may be taken at Vannes to explore the sacred district of the Morbihan and cross to Locmariaker (20 k.), whence Carnac and Plouharnel may be visited, returning to Vannes by the railway; but this excursion is more easily and pleasantly managed in a carriage from Auray.

483 k. *S. Anne.* An omnibus (50 c.) meets trains for (3 k.) the famous *Chapelle S. Anne,* celebrated for its pilgrimages since 1623, when the sainted mother of the Virgin is supposed to have appeared to a peasant named Yves Nicolazic, to ordain them. In obedience to her will he constructed a rude chapel at the spot called Bucenno, where a mutilated image was found in the soil, to which he was guided by a miraculous light. This famous image was destroyed in the Revolution, and only a single fragment of it remains in the pedestal of the present statue; but the chapel, often renewed, and rebuilt 1866, is still visited, with its miraculous fountain, by vast crowds, especially in the week after Pentecost. But alas! their thousands no longer arrive on foot, but in cheap excursion trains, with—'Pélerinage à S. Anne d'Auray: billet d'aller et retour à prix reduit.' At the *pardon* the 'Santa Scala' is crowded with the faithful ascending on their knees.

488 k. *Auray,* 2½ k. from the town (Hotels: *du Pavillon*—

tolerable, civil landlady; *de la Poste*, carriages for excursions for the whole day to Carnac or Locmariaker, 12 fr.).

Auray, in Breton 'Alvé,' is chiefly celebrated for its battle in 1364, in which Charles de Blois[1] was killed, and which secured the ducal crown to the house of Montfort. The town, built partly on a platform, partly on a declivity towards the Loch, has little interest. A pleasant walk may be taken by turning up behind the hotel to the promenade, and descending the winding paths thence to the river, which is crossed by a fine old bridge; thence returning by the steep streets. There are some xv. c. houses in the suburb beyond the Loch.

'Auray est la première station d'ostréiculture de la France, non par la qualité, mais par la quantité de ses mollusques.'— *Elisée Reclus.*

Beyond the railway, 2½ k. beyond the town, is *La Chartreuse*, which replaces the church of S. Michel-du-Champ, erected by Jean IV. on the battlefield where he had been victorious over Charles de Blois; the buildings are now occupied by deaf and dumb under the care of the Soeurs de la Sagesse. To the N. of the church is a *Chapelle Sépulcrale*, erected over the royalist prisoners put to death by the republicans, August 25, 1793—'Pro Deo, pro rege, nefarie trucidati.' The first stone of the mausoleum was laid by the Duchesse d'Angoulême in 1823. The chiefs Sombreuil, de Soulanges, Talhouët, d'Hervilly, and Mgr. de Hercé, are represented on the sarcophagus, with the young Gesril de Papen, who, after having swum at the peril of his

---

[1] Charles de Blois claimed Brittany as the husband of Jeanne de Penthièvre the lame daughter of the second son of Duke Arthur II. (the eldest son, John III., having died childless). Montfort claimed it as son of Duke Arthur's third son, Jean, Comte de Montfort, who had died in 1345.

life to cause the English fire to cease, returned to constitute himself prisoner. Not far distant, overlooking the marsh of Kerso, is a *Chapelle* Expiatoire, on the spot where the royalists fell. Near this, on the r. of the old road to Auray, is a stone cross marking the battlefield of 1364. The souls of those who died in the battle unshriven are supposed to wander till the Last Day, each in a straight line across the plain; and woe to him who crosses their path!

The excursion to the Chartreuse and Chapelle Expiatoire may be continued to S. Anne d'Auray.

At *Brech*, near the mill of *Pont-de-Brech*, is a rocking-stone. Here also is the fountain where the greyhound of Charles de Blois abandoned him to follow Montfort—an evil augury of the result of the battle.

Near (4 k. S.E.) *Kerisper* is an interesting XVI. c. chapel, with a timber *jubé* and the hollowed stone which is believed to have served as a boat to S. Avoye on her passage to Brittany from Wales. Near (9 k.) *Baden* are the dolmens of *Craffel* and *Toulvern*.

The whole district W. of Auray is full of curious megalithic remains.[1]

'Innombrables sont les pierres taillées devant lesquelles le paysan passe en se signant, qu'il y voie l'oeuvre du diable, ou bien, au contraire, qu'une légende lui ait appris à y vénérer le haut fait d'un ange ou d'un saint. En plusieurs endroits, notamment aux environs d'Auray, les paysans atteints de rhumatismes vont se coucher sur un autel creusé en forme de coupe, tout en invoquant S. Étienne; ailleurs ils traitent la migraine en se frottant à le front avec des cailloux sacrés. Jeunes hommes et jeunes filles se livrent parfois à des danses symboliques autour d'un menhir.'—*Elisée Reclus*.

[1] Genesis (xxxi. 47) speaks of such stones. The tomb of Mina, mother of Mahomet, is a peulven. When a painter wants to represent Brittany, says Adrien Oudin, he draws a peasant under the shadow of a great stone.

A carriage should be taken for the day to Carnac,[1] for which excursion fine weather is almost a necessity. Drivers engaged at the hotel at Auray know the best point to stop at (long before reaching the village of Carnac). Those who are unequal to much walking should make the carriage wait here, while they visit the finest part of the megalithic remains, not ten minutes' walk distant. Good

AT CARNAC.

walkers should let the carriage go on to wait for them at the inn at Carnac.

Guides are wholly unnecessary: there is only one path. The carriage stops by a cottage, and thence a field-path to the l. leads to the *Stones*. It is a wild and beautiful spot. The stones, which are of a delicate green-grey colour, rise like an army in battalions from the heather. They are in three immense groups, always quite distinct — the *Alignements* (or single stones in avenues) *de Menec, de*

---

[1] From *carn*—a mass of stones, and *ac*—a town.

Keriescan, and *de Kermerio*. Some regard the alignements as cemeteries, but they more probably had reference to and served for religious and political solemnities. Here we may imagine the barefooted Druid priestesses of Sein, robed in white, and with their sacred reaping-hooks hanging from their golden girdles, bearing the selago gathered on the sixth day of the moon, with solemnities unseen by any human eye, but as a memorial of which a stone was always erected. Once there were from twelve to fifteen thousand stones, but numbers have perished. Legend says that they were the soldiers of a pagan army who pursued S. Cornely, and would have caught him before he reached the sea, but he exerted his saintly power and turned them all into stone. 'Çà, Monsieur,' say the peasants, 'çà sont les soldats qui poursuivaient Saint Corneille, le bon patron de notre paroisse; comme il allait être pris par eux, et qu'il était arrêté par la mer, il les changea en pierres ainsi que vous les voyez.'

The first group of stones gives perhaps the best impression of Carnac to those who cannot visit it in detail. The stones are far smaller than those of Stonehenge, and far less architectural in character, but their vast multitude, and the wild charm of their situation, make them most interesting.

'Elles restent débout, malgré l'assaut des siècles, ces grandes pierres mystérieuses, éparses dans la lande de Carnac. La pluie a creusé des rigoles dans leurs flancs massifs; la mousse et le lichen masquent les teintes claires de leur granit. Ils sont là pourtant, ces témoins, ces fantômes. Nul n'a pénétré le secret de leur naissance, nul ne prévoit leur mort; mais, à les contempler toujours fiers, toujours muets dans leur immobilité farouche, on croirait volontiers qu'ils ont assisté aux premiers ébats de l'humanité, et qu'ils ne s'émietteront qu'avec sa ruine.'[1]—*Adrien Oudin*.

Some of the finest stones are where the little path first enters the lines. Beautiful Cornish heather, beloved by bees, grows abundantly around the stones. Beyond the first group, a curious tumulus may be visited in the grounds of the *Château de Kercado*, belonging to the Comte de

STONES OF CARNAC.

Perran. A very narrow entrance leads to its lofty chamber twelve feet in diameter.

Keeping the mound of Mont S. Michel in sight, it is easy, in this treeless district, to find one's way thither across the fields and through the yard of a farmhouse. A lovely little gothic fountain, of miraculous properties, is passed near the foot of the mount.

From the mound or galgal of *Mont S. Michel* there is

[1] Visitors should read the *Carnac* of Auguste Brizeux.

a fine view over the country, strewn at intervals with its strange armies of green-grey stones, mysterious and indescribable, and over the sea, with the curious peninsula of Quiberon and the strange, long, narrow isthmus which leads to it. The mound is artificial, and composed of masses of stones heaped one on another. It contains a double dolmen-chamber (now closed), supposed to have been used as a hermitage by one of the early missionaries from Britain. A number of stone weapons, jasper necklaces, etc., were found in it. The best are in the museum at Vannes. On the mound are ruins of a lighthouse, a XVII. c. granite cross, and a chapel, to which sailors' wives come to pray that their husbands' voyages may be prosperous.

Descending the mount on the W., a walk of about $1\frac{1}{2}$ k. brings us to *Carnac*, a large village (Hotel : *des Voyageurs* —a humble but clean country inn). The parish *church*, of 1639, has a singular N. porch, surmounted by a baldacchino of open work in stone. It is said that the porch is built from menhirs and the altars from dolmens. Remains of frescoes tell the story of S. Cornely, patron of horned animals, who was none other than S. Cornelius, pope at the time of the conversion of Brittany to Christianity.

'On faisait dire à Saint Burtot, à Saint Cornélie, des messes pour le repos de son mari défunt ; on les payait quatre fois plus, s'il agissait de guérir ou sa vache, ou son veau.'

'Au moment où la nouvelle mariée, à Carnac, sort de l'église, on lui présente une énorme branche de laurier, chargée de pommes, ornée de beaux rubans ; à l'extrémité de la branche est un oiseau lié par une faveur, auquel elle donne la liberté. Pour lui rappeler ses devoirs, on lui fait présent d'une quenouille qu'elle est obligée de filer.

'Dans le Morbihan, après avoir conduit dans le lit nuptial les amants qui se sont unis, le garçon d'honneur, le dos modestement tourné, tient une chandelle à la main, et ne s'enfuit, ne disparaît que quand elle lui brûle les doigts.'—*Cambry*.

There is a picturesque belief that here, on the night of All Souls', the tombs are opened, the church lighted up, and that Death, robed as a priest, preaches to thousands of kneeling skeletons. Hither, at the Pardon (Sept. 13), numbers of sick animals are brought, and are led round

VIEW FROM MONT S. MICHEL, CARNAC.

the church, and to the statue of the saint. Then, late at night, they are taken to the *Fountain of S. Cornely*, down a bye-road to the l.—one of the largest of the miraculous springs in these parts—and their cure is looked for.

At the other (the E.) end of the village is the *Musée Miln*, containing the interesting objects found in Carnac, collected by the Englishman, James Miln, who died in 1881. Amongst them is a curious dwarf skeleton with a very large head.

From Carnac one may return to Auray by Plouharnel, visiting the dolmens of *Kergavat, Mané-er-Roch* and *Mané-Kérioned*[1] on the way, all of more or less interest. Formerly local superstition consecrated most of these ancient remains to the saints, but now this is changed.

'De siècle en siècle le culte a pu continuer sans que les paysans se soient aperçus du changement des dieux. Cependant mainte pierre jadis consacrée aux saints est vouée maintenant aux puissances infernales; pour mettre un terme à l'habitude, générale autrefois, de déposer de la nourriture sur les tables des dolmens, le clergé breton déclara solennellement, en 1658, que ces offrandes ne pouvaient profiter qu'au diable. Encore au dernier siècle un coin de terre était réservé par les cultivateurs au malin esprit; c'était à ce prix qu'il consentait à ne pas dévaster la ferme.'—*Elisée Reclus.*

It is possible, but not enjoyable, to visit Locmariaker, 16 k. distant, on the same day as Carnac. The way thither passes (1 k.) *Boiscenno,* where remains of a Gallo-Roman town, with baths, temples and dwellings have been discovered. At 7 k. is *La Trinité sur Mer,* with its oyster-beds. At 8 k. the mouth of the Crach is crossed by the ferry-boat of *Kerisper.*

A second excursion should be made from Auray (16 k) to *Locmariaker*—Lieu de la Belle Marie. Tolerable pedestrians should be put down by the carriage about 1 k. before reaching the village, where there is a ruined dolmen—*Mané-er-Hroeck* or the Fairies' Mount—a little to the r. of the road. Hence a field-path opposite the

[1] 'De nos jours encore le dolmen est révéré comme la tombe d'un homme puissant, et quand une pierre est placée sur la fosse d'un riche, la langue bas-bretonne emploie toujours le mot de dolmen pour signaler le monument, en opposition aux simples buttes de terre qui recouvrent le cercueil du pauvre.'—*Elisée Reclus.*

dolmen (public, though would-be guides try to prevent strangers from using it) leads direct to the giant dolmen called *La Table de César*, or *Table des Marchands—Dol-ar-Marc'hadourien*, probably the finest dolmen in existence. Close to it a huge menhir, the largest known, broken into four pieces, lies upon the ground, and is known as *Men-er-Hroeck*—the Fairies' Stone. It must originally have been sixty-seven feet high, about seven feet thick, and 250,000

LA TABLE DES MARCHANDS.

kilogrammes in weight. The Table des Marchands, like the other dolmens acquired by the State, has an attractive surrounding of heath and broom. Hence there is a path direct to Locmariaker. A little to the N.W. of the village is the tumulus of *Mané-Lud* or *Mané-en-Hellud*—the Mount of Ashes—with a chamber which can be entered by a staircase.

A little farther N.W. is a barrow, with the hamlet of

Nelud at its foot. W. of this is the dolmen called *Dol-er-Hroeck*—the Fairies' Table. Lastly, to the W. of the village, is the ruined dolmen called *Mané-er-Retual*, and, near the sea, the monument called *Les Pierres Plates* or *Men Platt*.

'Si vous interrogez les gens du pays, ils répondront brièvement que ce sont les maisons des Torrigans, des Courils, petits hommes lascifs qui, le soir, barrent le chemin, et vous forcent de danser avec eux jusqu'à ce que vous en mouriez de fatigue. Ailleurs, ce sont les fées qui, descendant des montagnes en filant, ont apporté ces rocs dans leur tablier. Ces pierres éparses sont toute une noce petrifiée. Une pierre isolée, vers Morlaix, témoigne du malheur d'un paysan qui, pour avoir blasphémé, a été avalé par la lune.'—*Michelet.*

Locmariaker is a poor fishing village, with a small inn (*Hôtel Marchand*—where a good luncheon may be obtained).

A boat—8 fr. and *bonne main*—may be taken from Locmariaker to Gavr-Innis, and it is the best starting-point. The boatmen are often very inefficient, and it is well to remember that the sea of the Morbihan, even when it looks absolutely calm from the mainland, is often tremendously rough, owing to the currents as the sea washes in between the islands. Sail-cloth is given to cover the passengers, but they are often soaked through by the waves before they return. Thirty minutes is the nominal time taken in crossing to Gavr' Innis—only 4 k. distant, but the time taken in returning, with contrary tides, is often an hour and a half. With a good boatman, one who 'has salt water round his heart,' as the expression is,[1] there is no danger.

There is no beauty, except in the glorious colour of the waves, in the curious inland *Sea of Morbihan*. It is difficult to believe that it has 363 islands, as one conceals

[1] 'Dour vor èn dre 'é halon'—the Breton expression for being 'a born sailor.'

another. Probably not above sixty are more than islet rocks. None rise to any great height, but the *Île aux Moines* is 6 k. in length, and the *Île d'Artz* 3 k. The latter is especially full of old-world traditions. The Ankou, or Banshee of the Morbihan, frequently announces the loss of a sailor-husband to his wife at home.

'À l'île d'Artz, on aperçoit quelquefois, à ce que disent les habitants, de grandes femmes blanches qui sortent des îles voisines ou du continent, marchent sur la mer, et viennent s'asseoir au rivage. Là on les voit, tristes et penchées, creuser le sable avec leurs pieds nus, ou effeuiller entre leurs doigts les fleurs de romarin qu'elles ont cueillées sur la dune. Ces femmes sont des enfants de l'île mariées ailleurs, et qui, mortes dans le péché, loin du sol chéri, y reviennent pour demander à leurs parents des prières.

'Quelquefois aussi, dans les longues nuits d'hiver, quand le vent rugit sur les flots, les femmes de l'île d'Artz qui ont leurs maris en mer sont réveillées en sursaut. Elles entendent comme le bruit triste et monotone de l'eau qui tombe goutte à goutte à pied de leurs lits; alors elles regardent épouvantées, et si le bruit n'a point de cause naturelle, si la place n'est pas mouillée, malheur! car c'est *l'intersigne* du naufrage, et la mer vient de faire des veuves.'—*E. Souvestre*, '*Les Derniers Bretons.*'

Most of the islands are perfectly bare and colourless, and without any picturesqueness of form. Long before reaching it, the flat line of an island broken by a great tumulus indicates *Gavr'Innis*—the Goat's Island.

The landing-place is near a great fig-tree and a cottage, whence a girl comes to show the tumulus (entrance, 50 c. each person).

'Le mieux conservé et le plus beau des monuments mégalithiques du monde entier, celui qu'un de nos anciens présidents appelait, dans son language imagé, *la perle des antiquités celtiques.*'—*Closmadeuc*, '*Revue Archéologique,*' iv.

The tumulus to the S. of the island is composed of piled-up stones, and is entered on the E. by a gallery 13 mèt. long, composed of two ranges of menhirs, forming the walls, and a number of dolmens placed upon them horizontally. The paving-stones are placed horizontally between the menhirs, and always in the same direction. The passage leads to a tiny chamber surrounded by eight menhirs, adorned with rude sculpture of concentric circles, parallel lines, arches, and spirals. Some of the stones employed here are of a kind unknown upon the island.

[A line runs S.W. from Auray down the Presqu'île de Quiberon.

14 k. *Plouharnel Carnac*. *Plouharnel* (Hotel: *de Commerce*) has many megalithic remains. 3 k. S.E. is Carnac (see above).

Another excursion from Plouharnel may be made by (1 k.) *S. Barbe*, with a ruined cromlech, and (2½ k.) *Crucuno*, with the gigantic dolmen of the *Roche aux Fées*, to (5½ k.) *Erdeven*, with its extraordinary lines or avenues (alignements) of (1030) half-ruined menhirs. The stones are sometimes fifteen feet high, often lower. None are wrought. Some lie on the ground; some are slightly buried. The lines of Carnac and Erdeven must have had the same end and the same cause: they have the same orientation, and the same number of lines, composed of the same elements. The excursion may be prolonged to (9½ k.) *Etel*, a little port, and (13½ k.) *Belz*, 1 k. W. of which is the great dolmen of *Kerlutu*. 1 k. N. of this are the little village and island (connected with the mainland by a causeway) of *S. Cado*, with a romanesque chapel, a remnant of a priory founded by the sainted monk, son of a Welsh prince, who established himself here in the V. c. or VI. c. Legend tells that the causeway was formed in one night by the devil, at the request of the saint, who promised in return the first soul that crossed it, and sent a cat across at daybreak.' The devil then wished to destroy his work, the saint rushed upon him to hinder this, and fell in the struggle, leaving a lasting mark in the rock. This mark—*la glissade de*

S. Cado—is now covered by an iron grating and surmounted by a calvary.

Leaving Plouharnel, the line crosses the causeway near (XVIII. c.) *Fort Penthièvre* to the peninsula of Quiberon.

23 k. *Quiberon* (Hotel: *Penthièvre; du Commerce*), a pleasant bathing-place, chiefly celebrated for the melancholy landing of the disunited royalists (June 27, 1795) and their defeat by Hoche.]

[The upper part of the *Gulf of Morbihan* (10 k. long and 17 k. wide) may be best visited by boat from Auray, with its principal islands—the *Île d'Arz*, with a priory church, partly XI. c.; and the *Île aux Moines*, with a cromlech and several dolmens. This island is cultivated by women; all the men are sailors.

'The islands of the Breton archipelago here lie as thickly together as those of the Aegean, and, according to local tradition, are as numerous as the days of the year. In some cases they are mere uninhabited island-rocks; in others, little oases of verdure, with châlets and gardens, farm-buildings and corn-fields; and, seen on a bright autumn day, the sky blue and warm, the sea smooth and bluer still, they reminded me of the exquisite scenery of the Greek seas.'—*Autumn in Western France.*

'Je n'oublierai jamais le jour où je partis de grand matin d'Auray, la ville sainte des chouans, pour visiter, à quelques lieues, les grands monuments druidiques de Loc Maria Ker et de Carnac. Le premier de ces villages, à l'embouchure de la sale et fétide rivière d'Auray, *avec ses îles du Morbihan, plus nombreuses qu'il y a de jours dans l'an*, regarde par-dessus une petite baie la plage de Quiberon, de sinistre mémoire. Il tombait du brouillard, comme il y en a sur ces côtes de la moitié de l'année. De mauvais ponts sur des marais, puis le bas et sombre manoir avec la longue avenue de chênes qui s'est religieusement conservée en Bretagne; des bois fourrés et bas, ou les vieux arbres même ne s'élèvent jamais bien haut; de temps en temps un paysan qui passe sans regarder, mais il vous a bien vu avec son oeil oblique de l'oiseau de nuit. Cette figure explique leur fameux cri de guerre, et le nom de *chouans*, que leur donnait les *bleus*. Point de maisons sur les chemins; ils reviennent chaque soir au village. Partout de grandes landes, tristement parées de bruyères roses et de diverses plantes jaunes ; ailleurs, ce sont des campagnes blanches de sarasin. Cette neige d'été, ces couleurs sans éclat et comme flétries d'avance, affligent l'oeil plus qu'elles en le recréent.'—*Michelet.*

The water enters from the sea by a very narrow channel between the points of *Port Navalos* and *Kerpenhir.*]

[Steamers ply daily between Auray and *Belle-Ile-en-Mer* (30 k. from the entrance of the Morbihan, 6 k. from Quiberon), in Breton *Guerveur.* The island—where the Druids had their principal school—measures 18 k. by 10 k.; its principal village is *Le Palais.*]

[For the line from Auray to S. Brieuc see ch v.]

514 k. *Hennebont* (Hotels: *de France; de Commerce*). This old town, often mentioned in Froissart, retains its three divisions. We enter by the *Ville Neuve,* and after crossing the Blavet find the *Vieille Ville* and the *Ville Close.* The latter retains much of its ancient fortifications and one very fine *Gateway,* flanked by round towers. Beyond this is the large unfinished church of *Notre Dame de Paradis,* built 1513-30. The central nave, without a vault, ends in a five-sided chevet, pierced with two ranges of windows; the side aisles end in a straight wall.

'On doit réserver son admiration pour le portail, où se découpe une ogive élégante, entourée de riches moulures, et surmontée d'un clocher svelte et gracieux. Il est flanqué de deux petites tours avec lesquelles il communique par des galeries, ou plutôt des ponts légers, jetés bien au-dessus du toit de la nef. Un de ces ponts est abattu, et sa destruction affaiblit un peu l'effet général de la façade.'—*Prosper Merimée.*

Very little remains of the castle, which was bravely defended by the Countess Jeanne de Montfort (in full armour) against Charles de Blois, in the xiv. c. There are many old timber houses of xvi. c. and xvii. c. in the Place de l'Église, Rue des Lombards, and Rue de la Prison. In the Rue Neuve, a house is inscribed ' Le Livec, 1600.'

At 1 k., on the l. bank of the Blavet, stood the Cistercian *Abbaye de la Joie*, founded at the end of the xiii. c. Nothing remains except a parlour belonging to its later buildings, decorated in the time of Louis XV.

6 k. S. is *Kervignac*, with a xv. c. church, two gothic chapels, and a dolmen containing a circular chamber.

An excursion may be made from Hennebont to *Les Pierres de Plouhinec*.

' Plouhinec est un pauvre bourg au delà d'Hennebon, vers le mer. On ne voit, tout autour, que des landes ou de petits bois de sapins, et jamais la paroisse n'en a eu assez d'herbe pour élever un boeuf de boucherie, ni assez de son pour engraisser ni descendant des Rohans.

' Mais, si les gens de pays manquent de blé et de bestiaux, ils ont plus de cailloux qu'il n'en faudrait pour rebâtir Lorient, et l'on trouve au delà du bourg une grande bruyère dans laquelle les Korigans ont planté deux rangées de longues pierres qu'on pourrait prendre pour une avenue si elles conduisaient quelque part.'—*Emile Souvestre*.

522 k. *L'Orient* (Hotels: *de France ; de Bretagne*), the capital of Morbihan. A dull, ugly, dusty, unhealthy town, especially subject to cholera. The port, founded here in the end of the xvii. c. by the East India Company, has become a great military port since their failure in 1769. The town is devoted to ship-building. Its buildings are of no interest. In the cemetery is the tomb of Brizeux, the Breton poet.

4 k. S.W., at the end of the promontory which closes the bay of L'Orient on the N., is *Port Louis*, founded a century earlier. 6 k.

N. of this is the church of *Merlévenez*, attributed to the Templars. The nave, aisles, and transept are XII. c. or XIII. c.; the octagonal tower and spire are of 1533.

6 k. W. of L'Orient is the romanesque church of *Ploeneur*, near which are the tumulus called *Butte à Madame* and several dolmens and menhirs. At the hamlet of *Lannênec* (1½ k. W.), where was formerly a monastery of S. Nennoch, a stone trough is shown as the boat of S. Nennoch, in which he crossed to Brittany from England. At the end of the commune of Ploeneur, 6 k. S. of L'Orient, is the *Chapelle de Notre Dame de Larmor*, a quaint building of different dates, with a spire of 1615.

Steamers ply to (22 k. from L'Orient, 14 k. from Port Louis) the *Île de Croix*, abounding in megalithic remains, and with a rocky, caverned coast. In the arm of the sea called *Le Coureau de Croix*, which separates the island from the mainland, a picturesque ceremonial takes place on S. John's Day, when the clergy of the neighbouring parishes, escorted by a flotilla of fishing-boats, bless the waters, that the fishery may be abundant.

532 k. *Gestel*.

6 k. N. is *Pontscorff*, with the curious rectangular *Chapelle S. Jean*, built by the Templars. The *Maison des Princes* is a very richly decorated building of the renaissance, bearing the arms of the house of Rohan. The town is intersected by the Scorff.

> 'Ne crains rien si tu n'as ni parure ni voile;
> Viens sous ta coiffe blanche et ta robe de toile,
> Jeune fille de Scorff.'—*Brizeux*, '*Marie*.'

4 k. S. of Gestel is *Guidel*, in a district abounding in dolmens.

542 k. *Quimperlé*[1] (Hotel: *Lion d'Or*—very good, comfortable, and well situated, once the home of the abbots of S. Croix). An unusually quiet and silent, but pretty little town, chiefly built on a promontory at the junction of the Elle and Izol, as its name, Kemper-Elle, 'the meeting of

---

[1] Quimperlé, Bey, Moëlan, and Chobars, were the communes most devoted to the Revolution.

the Elle,' signifies. It first arose around the hermitage of the Welsh prince Gunthiern. In the *Ville haute*, old houses and convents cluster around the xiv. c. and xv. c. church of *S. Michel*, which has a good tower and a beautiful N. portal with lace-like decorations. At the E. end two arches connect it picturesquely with neighbouring houses, that on the N. being a good specimen of xv. c.

'Parmi les petites villes que l'on rencontre presque à chaque pas dans la Bretagne comme témoignage de la civilisation et de l'importance primitive du vieux duché, il n'en est point dont l'aspect soit à la fois plus coquet, plus paisible et plus doux que Kemperlé. Née d'une abbaye, cette gracieuse bourgade semble avoir conservé la sérénité du cloître. Seulement, les cellules se sont insensiblement transformées en maisonettes riantes entourées de jardins, où chaque famille vit à part, d'une existence silencieuse et murée.'—*Emile Souvestre.*

In the *Ville basse*, where the hotel is situated, is the very curious ancient basilica of *S. Croix*, which belonged to a Benedictine abbey founded by S. Gunthiern in 550, and rebuilt in 1029 by Alain, Comte de Cornouaille. It was much injured by the fall of its central tower in 1862, but has been restored upon the old lines, in imitation of the church of the Holy Sepulchre at Jerusalem. The interior is most curious—a Greek cross, with a raised choir between massive pillars. The xi. c. crypt below has two ranges of columns with Byzantine capitals, and a subterranean corridor repeats the circular aisle of the upper church. In the crypt is the tomb of S. Gurloës, the first abbot of Quimperlé, who died in 1057. His hands hold a cross, his feet rest on a dragon, and a little plate upon his breast collects the sous of the faithful. The Bretons, who call him S. Urlou, invoke him against the gout, which they call *mal de S. Urlou*. A second tomb in the crypt bears the statue and arms of Abbot Henri de Lespervez, 1434.

'La forme de l'église, très rare en France, offre comme la réunion de la Rotonde et de la Croix. Qu'on se représente un choeur circulaire, dont le coupole s'appuie sur d'énormes massifs. Autour du choeur règnent les bas-côtés, qui lui sont concentriques. À l'est est l'apside, se terminant par un hémicycle sortant de la circonférence; au sud, une chapelle semicirculaire, ou pour mieux dire un croisillon. Au nord et à l'ouest, les deux autres branches de la croix se terminent carrément; mais ces parties ont été refaites. Entre chaque massif, un escalier conduit des bas-côtés dans le choeur, élevé d'environ quatre pieds au-dessus de leur niveau. L'apside orientale est encore plus haute. On y arrive des bas-côtés par deux escaliers; un troisième donne dans le choeur.'—*Prosper Merimée.*

Not far from S. Croix is the picturesque ruined front of the church of *S. Columban*, with a flamboyant window and gothic niches. This church served as the palace chapel of the dukes of Brittany, when they lived here for hunting in the forest of Carnoët. There are some ruins of a *Dominican Convent*, where Jean de Montfort, husband of the famous Jeanne la Flamme, was buried beneath the high altar. The XVI. c. chapel of *S. David* contains a S. Sepulcre of the same date.

The virtues of the fountain of *Serignac* have a great local reputation.

'Puisque la fontaine de Serignac, où j'ai bu trois fois de l'eau à l'heure de minuit, ne m'a pas guéri de la fièvre tierce, je cesse tout remède, et je me décide à la mort, disait un paysan du district de Quimperlé.'—*Cambry.*

4 k. S. of the town begins the forest of Carnoët, an old hunting ground of the dukes of Brittany, who had a magnificent castle there, which has been demolished for the sake of its stone. At the S. extremity of the forest are remains of the abbey of

S. Maurice, founded 1170 by Duc Conan IV., and where S. Maurice, a monk of Langonnet, was buried in 1191. His relics are preserved in a chapel in the midst of the ruined church. In the buildings, turned into a dwelling-house, is a chapter-house of XIV. c. or XV. c. Over the doorway of S. Maurice was engraved the proud inscription—'Cette maison durera jusqu'à ce que la fournoi ait bu la mer, et que la tortue ait fait le tour du monde.'

Dependent on the abbey of Quimperlé was the Priory of *Lan Ninnocht*, of which Déric, in his *Ecclesiastical History*, says that it was the oldest monastery for women in Gaul.

'Non loin de Quimperlé, dans la commune de la Clohars-Carnoët, s'étend la lande Minars, où errent, sous la forme de haridelles, les spectres des notaires et des procureurs "qui ont fait des fautes dans leurs additions." Il paraît qu'on rencontre beaucoup de ces ombres fécondes.'—*Adrien Oudin.*

3 k. N.E. is the *Chapelle de Rosgrand*, with a graceful renaissance timber *jubé*.

[An excursion should certainly be made N. from Quimperlé to—

18 k. *S. Fiacre*, a beautiful xv. c. chapel. Its spire has a flamboyant gallery. On the wall of the chevet are the arms of Jean de Bonteville, Baron du Faouet. In the interior is a magnificent screen of 1440. Some of its sculptures are very grotesque—a wolf in a pulpit dressed as a monk, a fox trying to persuade some hens to come to listen to him, the hens pursuing the fox and pecking him, the fox lying dead and the hens eating him, etc. On the inner side of the *jubé*, theft, gluttony, luxury, dancing, etc., are represented. The latter is indicated by a *sonneur*—a Breton piper, and alludes to the excesses which accompany the 'pardons.' The stained glass is almost equally fine, and represents the life of Christ, the legend of S. Fiacre, and a number of saints, whose names are inscribed in the phylacteries which they hold. The windows are due to Androuet de Quimperlé, 1552.

21 k. *Le Faouet*, a picturesque place, with ancient Halles and many old houses. The church, partly XIII. c., has a polygonal choir of XVI. c. It is 1½ k. hence to the famous sanctuary

of *S. Barbe* (turning l. by the Halles, where a blue Virgin is painted on the wall). It is a very curious place. The paved path ends near a stone cross. To the l. is the cottage of the guardian of the chapel, and, opposite it, a belfry, where four stone pillars support a roof over the bell which each pilgrim sounds on the day of the pardon. An arch connects it with the *Chapelle S. Bernard*, on a point of rock, and, by a broad flight of mossy stone steps, with the *Chapelle S. Barbe*, also built on a projecting spur of rock above the Elle. Its position involved its direction from S.E. to N.W.; and, the principal entrance being S.W., the high altar is opposite, on the N.E. It was built in 1449 to fulfil a vow of Jehann de Toulboden that he would build a chapel to his patron saint if she would arrest a rock which seemed about to fall upon the place where he had taken refuge during a terrible storm which overtook him while hunting in the valley of the Elle. The outside of the chapel of S. Bernard has rings at intervals, holding which pilgrims make the dangerous external circuit at the pardon.

'The rose-tinted, lichen-crusted church, the frowning brown rocks all around, tapestried with ivy and other clinging greenery, and then the broken massive time-stained steps, with their heavy green-grey balústrades, bits of lady-fern and ivy-leaved toad-flax nestling here and there in the chinks, making a background for red cranesbill and yellow hawkweed blossoms, are full of exquisite colour.'—*Katherine S. Macquoid.*]

[A road runs N.W. from Quimperlé to—

18 k. *Gourin*, passing (l.) at 11 k. *S. Hervé*, with an interesting xv. c. chapel. One of the fine stained windows represents the legend of the saint, which tells how, when a wolf ate up the ass which he employed to cultivate his ground, he forced the wolf to take its place, and kept it thenceforth in the same shed with his sheep. For this reason S. Hervé is invoked for the protection of flocks from wolves, and shepherds bring him lambs as offerings. Near Gourin is the ruined *Château de Kerbiguet.*]

[A road leads E. to (30 k.) Concarneau (see later) by (17 k.) *Pont-Aven* (*Hôtel des Voyageurs*—of Mademoiselle Julie Guillou—a capital country inn, much frequented by artists and adorned with many of their works). This is a very pretty spot,[1] where the little river Aven falls into a narrow estuary of the sea 7 k. distant. The rocks have great picturesqueness of form and character, the country is full of interest, and artists may well make its comfortable hotel a centre. On a neighbouring hill is the curious chapel of *Tre Malo.* 4 k. S., on the r. bank of the river, which almost encircles it, is the picturesque *Château du Hénan,* of XV. c. and XVI. c.

A little r. of the road to Concarneau is the deserted village of *Nizon,* with a curious calvary, and near it the ruined *Château de Rustéphan,* originally built by Etienne, Comte de Penthièvre, in XII. c. The ruins are XV. c. They are haunted by the priest Jannik Flécher, a peasant who was forced to take orders because he had dared to win the affection of Geneviève, youngest daughter of the lord of the château, who died of love for his sake. Her bier, surrounded by burning torches, is sometimes seen in the ruined hall, or, at the full moon, she is seen upon the walls, in her green satin dress embroidered with gold. Pont-Aven is a very cheap place of residence. The author of *Quatre Dons* says:—

'Si j'avais trois cents écus de rente, j'irais demeurer à Quimper, où se trouve la plus belle église de la Cornouaille, et où les maisons ont des girouettes sur les toits; si j'avais deux cents écus, j'habiterais Carhaix, à cause de ses moutons de bruyère et de son gibier; mais si je n'avais que cent écus, je voudrais tenir ménage à Pont-Aven, où on a le beurre pour le prix du lait, la poule pour le prix de l'oeuf, et la toile pour le prix du lin encore vert. Aussi y voit-on de bonne fermes, où l'on sert du porc salé trois fois la semaine, et où les bergers eux-mêmes mangent du pain de métail à discretion.'

Many curious dolmens and menhirs, and the rocking-stone of *Trégunc,* are passed between Pont-Aven and Concarneau. A little E. of Pont-Aven is *S. Léger,* where, in the wood, is a miraculous fountain with an image of the saint, where many hundreds of babies are bathed at the pardon.]

557 k. *Bannalec* ('the place of broom'), famous for

---

[1] A place of twelve fairs and fifty-two markets.

the beauty of its women. 2 k. S.E. is the old *Château de Quimerc'h.*

568 k. *Rosporden*, burnt by the Spaniards in 1594, with the exception of the beautiful church, which is chiefly xiv. c., with a flamboyant apse and a graceful spire. It stands picturesquely on the edge of a pool. The country is prettily wooded.

17 k. N.W. is *Scaër*. The church, partly romanesque, is dedicated to S. Candide; from its tower there is a very wide view. The misused and neglected miracle-working *Fountain of S. Candide* is said to have sprung from the earth at a single blow of her staff; it is sixty feet long, sixteen wide, and seven deep, and, winter or summer, is never without the same quantity of beautifully clear water. In the churchyard is a fine xvi. c. cross.

At a marriage at Scaër two candles are lighted. One is placed before the husband, the other before the wife. That which is least bright is the candle of the one who will die first. Fire and water have still—as of old time—a great part in Breton ceremonies.

'Dans ce pays, la première nuit des noces est à Dieu, la seconde à la Vierge, la troisième au patron de mari; celui-ci n'approche de sa femme que dans la quatrième nuit.'—*Cambry.*

A line leads S. to (15 k.) *Concarneau* (Hotel: *Grand*), a small fortified seaport in a cove opening on the bay of La Forest. The inhabitants are chiefly occupied in the sardine fishery, in which five hundred boats are employed. The *Ville close* retains its walls, surrounded by the sea at high tide. The *Aquarium* is worth visiting:—

'La richesse de la faune marine de Concarneau est si grande qu'on a cru devoir faire choix de ce coin du rivage pour y établir le premier vivier de poissons, de crustacés et de mollusques pour l'étude comparée et l'élève de ces animaux: le laboratoire et l'aquarium est mis à la libre disposition des savants, et plusieurs y ont déjà fait des recherches de la plus haute importance ; la nature elle-même sert de champ d'observation dans ces vastes bassins qu'alimente directement le flux, qu'abaisse le reflux et où croissent les algues de la mer voisine.'—*Elisée Reclus.*

288 k. *Quimper* (Hotels: *de l'Epée*—large, good, and reasonable; *de Provence; de France*), on the Odet and Steyr, the ancient capital of Cornouaille, now capital of the Département de Finisterre, prettily situated below a wooded hill—*le Mont Frugy*. The principal thoroughfare—*le Mail* —is bordered on one side by handsome hotels, and on the other by the river Odet, which makes Quimper an estuary port. The fabled founder of the town was the escaped Trojan Chorinaeus. It was the Curiosolitum of Caesar, but early writers and bishops of the IX. c. speak of it as Civitas Aquilae: *Kemp-ër* is the eagle's camp.

The noble *Cathedral of S. Corentin*,[1] the largest and most beautiful church in Brittany, was begun in 1239 and only finished in 1515. It has a great charm, from the harmonious yellow-grey colour of the stone of which it is built, and the distant effect of its two lofty west towers, with their noble spires. The façade is of great heraldic interest. In the centre is the lion of Montfort bearing the banner of Brittany, with the device of Jean V., '*Malo au riche duc*,' and many bishops and seigneurs of the district are represented by their arms and mottoes. The point of the gable is surmounted by an equestrian statue of King Grallon.

'Tous les ans, à Quimper, le jour de S. Cécile, à deux heures après-midi, tout le clergé montait sur la plate-forme, où l'on

---

[1] S. Corentin, bishop in the v. c., in the time of King Grallon, lived at one time as a hermit at Plomodiern. His name, from *cor*, 'head,' and *d'en*, 'excellent,' expresses his character. He was also called Charaton, from *char*, 'great,' and *rat*, 'thought.'

trouvait la statue équestre du roi Gralon, entre les deux tours de la cathédrale; on y chantait un hymne à grand chorus, accompagné de musiciens. Pendant ce temps, un des valets de ville montait en croupe sur le cheval, tenant une bouteille, un verre, une serviette; cet homme alors versait une rasade, la présentait

CATHEDRAL OF QUIMPER.

au roi, l'avalait, essuyait la bouche du prince, et lançait le verre dans la place. On se précipitait pour le recevoir; celui qui le rapportait sans qu'il fut rompu, devait avoir une gratification de cent écus, ce qui n'est jamais arrivé. La cérémonie se terminait en plaçant une branche de laurier dans la main du roi

Gralon. . . . Gralon sera le Bacchus ou le Mars des bretons.'—*Cambry*, '*Voyage dans le Finistère.*'

The towers were begun in 1424, but the spires are only of 1854. The two side portals are of 1424-45. That of Notre Dame on S. has good sculpture. The choir has not the same axis as the nave, but inclines first to the N.E., and, towards the extremity, bends again, which is probably due to the insecurity of the foundation near the river. The rich high altar is a fine modern work. In the *trésor* are preserved *les trois gouttes de sang*. Legend tells that a native of Quimper, going on pilgrimage, left his money in the care of a comrade. When he came home and asked for it back, the comrade denied having received it, and offered to swear to the same upon the crucifix of S. Corentin. He gave his staff to the pilgrim to hold. The staff was hollow, and contained the stolen coin, and at the moment when the traitor took the false oath it opened, and the money was scattered on the pavement; at the same moment the feet of the Crucified, fastened by a single nail, came apart, and three drops of blood fell upon the altar. The series of tombs of the bishops of Cornouaille—several of whom, Corentin, Conogan, Menon (VII.), Tugean, have been canonised—and the pictures of Dargent, deserve attention. Making the round of the church, we should observe—

Under the tower. Tomb of Bishop Raoul de Moël.
Baptistery. xv. c. statue of S. John, in alabaster.
Fifth Bay, Chapel of SS. Crispin and Crispinian. Tomb of Bishop de Ploeuc, 1739.
Third Chapel, of S. Roch. S. Roch in his Hermitage, and S. Roch Blessing the Plague-stricken, by *Yan Dargent*.
Fourth Chapel, of S. Corentin. The Apotheosis of S. Corentin,

and the Meeting of S. Corentin and S. Primel under an Oak, by *Dargent.*

After the Sacristy door, Chapel of Notre Dame des Carmes. Tomb of Bishop Sargent, 1871.

Chapelle des Anges. Tomb of Bishop Geoffroy le Marhec, 1383. Against a pillar is the statue of Jean Discalcéat, the barefooted, called 'Le petit S. Jean' by the faithful, of whom Albert the Great reports that if he found any vermin in his habit, he always took them up carefully and placed them in his sleeves or hood.

Second Chapel after Apse, of S. Paul. Tomb of Canon Pierre de Quenquis, XIV. c. The Conversion of S. Paul, and S. Paul on Areopagus, by *Dargent.*

Chapel of S. Jean. Tomb of Bishop Bertrand de Rosmadec, with a fine XV. c. statue.

Chapel of S. Joseph. The Flight into Egypt and the Death of S. Joseph, by *Dargent.*

Chapel of S. Anne. The Education of the Virgin by S. Anne, by *Dargent.*

First Chapel after Transept, of S. François. The Transfiguration, by *Le Febvre.*

Last Chapel, of the Madeleine. Tomb of Bishop Alain de Maout.

The space between the Odet and Steyr was formerly called Terre au Duc, because the ducal officers resided and exercised their powers there. Beyond the Promenade of Penity—where, on the l. bank of the Odet, once stood a beautiful chapel, famous for its glass—is the suburb of *Locmaria*, once celebrated for its china factory. Here is an interesting church, built 1030 by Alain Canhiart, Comte de Cornouaille. It is an interesting simple building of XI. c., with the additions of a restored choir and gothic porch. Close to the Hôtel de Ville is the *Musée*, which well deserves a visit on account of its curious life-size models—representing all the Breton costumes—marvellously lifelike and full of character. There is the usual picture-gallery. Quimper was the birthplace of the painter Valentin.

> 'Les grotesques figures qu'on aperçoit sur les plus anciens édifices de Quimper ont un caractère d'originalité, de plaisanterie, de gaieté, qui ne le cède à rien. C'est un malheureux qui souffre, et dont la risible grimace est à moitié cachée par un mouchoir ; c'est un lourdeau qui sollicite un juge, qui lui répond, en lui montrant sa bourse ; c'est un monstre à tête de pongo, presque aussi longue que son corps décharné, qui pose sur un bouclier ; un cordelier à figure benigne, étendant des mains bénites sur la tête des passants. On y voit l'ange de Tobie, la folle, un homme séparant en deux un lion dont il déchire les mâchoires, et regardant d'un air féroce un burlesque guerrier qui le menace d'un massue ; ce matamore armé porte un de ces étuits insolens et menteurs que nos pères étalaient, en forme priape, au défaut de la cuirasse et des cuissarts.'—*Cambry.*

In a fountain at Quimper was said to swim a miraculous fish, always living and always whole, though S. Corentin daily cut it in half to supply his food for the day. This fountain still exists, on the road to L'Orient. Nothing remains of the famous church of S. Guéodet—Notre Dame au Gué de l'Odet, famous for its glass—where, after the destruction of Is, a sacred candle was always kept burning. When this was extinguished it was believed that the water of a well adjoining the church would rise, and Quimper would be submerged. In 1792 the candle was extinguished.

> 'A cette époque, deux enfans, entrant un jour au Guéodet, s'en emparèrent et se placèrent à la bouche du puits. Là, munis d'une chandelle allumée, ils éteignirent la bougie sacrée, en regardant dans le puits pour voir si l'eau s'élevait, résolus à rallumer la sainte bougie, dès qu'ils apercevraient quelque mouvement dans le puits terrible. Ils furent trouvés dans cette occupation, et chassés de la chapelle. Il y avait certes un grave symptôme dans la doute philosophique de ces deux enfants

jouant ainsi avec une croyance populaire; cela faisait comprendre que la destruction de la foi catholique n'était pas loin.'—*Cambry*.

Quimper is a centre for many interesting excursions:—

18 k. S., descending the Odet by boat, is *Loctudy*, which takes its name from S. Tudy, abbot in the VI. c., who built a monastery, on the site of which a church was built the Templars in 1187—a very curious building, which retains traces of the earlier edifice. It consists of a nave, aisles making the circuit of the choir, and three apsidal chapels. Three tombs are xv. c. In the churchyard is the little transition chapel of *Notre Dame de Portzbihan*, and at the entrance of the churchyard a menhir, supporting a cross. There is a ferry from Loctudy to the *Island of Tudy*, where S. Tudy had a hermitage and founded his first monastery.

[A line runs S. to (18 k.) *Pont l'Abbé* (Hotels: *Duhamel; des Voyageurs*), a quaint little place on the river Abbé (2 k. from the bay of Benodet (which preserves, more than most places, its ancient Breton costumes. The church belonged to a Carmelite convent, founded by Hervé, Baron de Pont l'Abbé, and Perronelle de Rochefort, his wife, in 1383, but was restored in xv. c. and xvi. c. There is a very beautiful and picturesque xv. c. *Cloister*, now a school, which bears the arms of its builder, Bishop Bertrand de Rosmadec, who has such a fine tomb in Quimper Cathedral. The Mairie is established in the remains of the xiii. c. château.

Near Pont l'Abbé is the *Île Chevalier*, where some ruins are shown as belonging to one of the castles of King Grallon.

The excursion should be continued (by carriage 8 frs., or place in the *courier* 2 frs.) to Penmarc'h. The road, at 2½ k., skirts the grounds of the desolate and decaying *Château de Kernuz*. Then it passes between two dolmens. The latter part of the road runs through an excessively wild district, sprinkled with menhirs, with occasional dolmens. There are striking views across the yellow corn plains to the pink-grey church of S. Nonne, backed by the line of the distant sea, with its belt of rocks, on which the breakers lash themselves high in foam.

'C'est la vraie "fin des terres," où le vent et la houle

s'élancent avec plus de fureur que sur tous les autres rivages de France.'—*Elisée Reclus*.

At 12 k. (30 k. from Quimper) we reach the first ruins of *Penmarc'h*. Its name signifies a horse's head, and is taken from the form of a neighbouring rock. The whole plateau of 'the Horse's Head,' covered with ancient buildings, is now a waste; but Penmarc'h is said to have been once as large as Nantes is now: it could equip 3000 men, possessed a fleet of 800 boats,

PENMARC'H.

and had its Jewellers' Street and Drapers' Street. The whole district is covered with remains—houses, many of them much isolated and fortified, chapels, and churches. Here and there is an old grey wayside cross. Till 1556 Treoultré Penmarc'h was a large town, with 10,000 inhabitants. It lived upon its cod fishery. In 1566 the sea made a sudden incursion, the harbour was choked up and the cod-fishery destroyed, and before the place had rallied from these the brigand chieftain Guy Eden Fontenelle and his followers came over from Donarnenez, insinuated themselves into the good graces of the inhabitants, and then, when they were least suspected, massacred 5000 men, outraged the women, and filling 300 ships of Penmarc'h with all the spoils of the place, carried it off.

The church of *S. Nonne*,[1] entirely XVI. c., is a fine building, with an ossuary at its E. end, and a churchyard porch on the W. On the wall of the tower are a number of curious ships in relief, though they have been much scratched away in 'restoration.' The interior is still striking, the old pavement having fortunately been left, from want of funds for its removal.

The church of *S. Guénolé*[2]—the first inventor of cider—is the ruin of an admirable XV. c. building, and highly picturesque. Its remains are a massive tower and a little chancel and apse, in which service is held once a month. Here also ships are carved on the external walls. Near this are the remains of the *Manoir de Kervervé*.

'Guénolé n'avoit pour tout habit qu'une tunique de peaux de chèvres, qui cachoit un rude cilice. . . . Il mêloit avec son pain une certaine quantité de cendres et la faisoit doubler pendant le carême. Pour se rapprocher davantage à la vie de Jésus-Christ, il ne mangeoit que deux fois la semaine dans le temps consacré à la pénitence. Il couchoit sur les écorces d'arbres ou sur le sable, et il n'avoit qu'une pierre pour chevet. Depuis l'âge de vingt ans jusqu'à sa mort, il ne s'assit jamais dans l'église. Il disoit son office les bras étendus vers le ciel, ou à genoux, ou debout. Il recitait tous les jours le psautier; il faisoit cent génuflexions le jour et autant la nuit. La prière lui était familière jour et nuit: uni à Dieu par la contemplation, il sembloit n'avoir plus rien de terrestre.'—*Déric*, '*Hist. Ecc. de Bretagne.*'

The ruined church of *Kérity*, dedicated to *S. Thumette*, one of the Virgins of S. Ursula, belonged to the Templars, who had a commanderie here; the remains are XIII. c. The curious alabaster

---

[1] Also known as S. Melarie. She was daughter of the Welsh prince Brecan, sister of S. Keine and S. Ninnoc, and mother of S. David. Her tomb is in the parish church of Dirinon.

[2] S. Guénolé was a holy hermit dressed in skins, the son of S. Fracan and S. Guen, brother of S. Jacut and S. Guethenoc, master of S. Rioc, S. Idunet, S. Ratian, etc. He founded the monastery of Landevenec, and died 504. (See Lobineau, 'Les Saints de Bretagne.')

statue of S. John, formerly here, is now in the church of Penmarc'h: it has its beard, hair and eyebrows gilt; a garland of boughs, on which birds perch, surrounds the saint: he holds a lamb. The statue is perhaps of Spanish origin, and was wrecked on the coast. The church of *S. Pierre* (close to Kérity) is xv. c. Near the sea are *Notre Dame de la Joie* and *S. Fiacre*.

Between the Pointe de Penmarc'h and the *Anse de la Torche*

NOTRE DAME DE LA JOIE.

(4 k. N.) the shore is bordered by rocks of great picturesqueness. In the Anse de la Torche is the rock which gives it the name, separated from the mainland by the *Saut-du-Moine* (so called because S. Viaud, when he arrived from Ireland, is supposed to have leapt across it in safety). But the finest cliffs are those called *des Etaux*, or *Tal-Yvern*, with caverns which can only be reached at low tide. Of these the *Grotte de Philopex* served as a refuge to Girondin fugitives in 1793.

A cross near the shore marks the spot where two ladies and three children, sitting unsuspecting on a rock, were swept away by a wave. 'Who has ever passed along this funereal coast,' says Michelet, 'without exclaiming or feeling, " Tristis usque ad mortem " ? ']

[A line leads N.W. to (24 k.) *Douarnenez*[1] (Hotels: *du Commerce*—best, clean and tolerable; *des Voyageurs*), a large fishing town on the bay of the same name. Its narrow, rugged, tortuous white streets all lead down to the port with its long pier. The vast bay is almost land-locked. The only sands are 2 k. distant, so that the place is most inconvenient for bathing. Sardines are the principal object of commerce.

An interesting sight is the evening departure of the fishing-boats, more than a hundred at a time following one another, with chocolate-coloured sails.

> 'Ah! quel bonheur d'aller en mer !
> Par un ciel chaud, par un ciel clair,
>   La mer vaut la campagne ;
> Si le ciel bleu devient tout noir,
> Dans nos cœurs brille encore l'espoir,
>   Car Dieu nous accompagne,
> Le bon Jésus marchait sur l'eau,
> Va sans peur, mon petit bateau.'
>
> Auguste Brizeux, '*Hist. poëtiques.*'

A more curious sight than the boats at such times are the hundreds of unmarried girls, who come down dressed in their best, to sit in a long row on the pier wall to watch the proceedings and be inspected, and, if possible, admired. Sometimes there are nearly a thousand in this 'girl-show'—so many that it seems impossible the town can produce them all—wearing white lace caps of different patterns and shawls of every shade of blue and green. Boys come in troops and throw squibs, producing sudden flights, with much screaming and laughter. Many of the girls are very handsome, and all court observation.

[1] Perhaps from *daou-ar*, 'two lands,' because the land, which was one, became two after the submersion of 401.

'Grâce à l'extrême variété de fonds, aux multiples dentelures de la côte, aux îles et aux écueils parsemées le long du littoral breton, la végétation marine est très-riche, et, par une conséquence naturelle, la faune aquatique est représentée par un grand nombre d'espèces, foisonnant en multitudes : jadis le saumon était la nourriture la plus commune des paysans de Quimper et de Châteaulin, et l'on raconte qu'en plusieurs districts maritimes du pays les domestiques de ferme ne se louaient qu'à la condition de ne pas manger de saumon plus de trois fois par semaine. Aussi, malgré ses dangers, la pêche a-t-elle été toujours des plus actives dans les mers qui baignent la presqu'île de Bretagne. Des milliers d'embarcations sont équipées pour la pêche du hareng, de la sardine, du maquereau, de la langouste, de l'huitre ; et même les marins bretons, familiarisés avec les périls de la mer, vont en grand nombre pêcher la morue sur les bancs de Terre-Neuve ou les parages islandais. Les populations agricoles prennent aussi part à ces expéditions lointaines. Chaque année des centaines de jeunes gens consacrent l'hiver à la culture des champs, aux semailles, à la récolte du varech ; puis, dès le mois de février, ils s'engagent comme matelots sur les navires en partance pour les mers boréales. Les quatre départements de la Bretagne donnent à la marine commerciale la cinquième partie de ses équipages.'—*Elisée Reclus.*

The name of Douarnenez, signifying 'island-land,' comes from the *Île Tristan*, which can be reached on foot at low tide. There was a priory here dedicated to S. Tutuarn, in which the brigand Fontenelle established himself for three years, as in a fortress, and devastated thence the surrounding country. The island (properly Ile Tutuarn) is said to take its present name from the brave Tristan des Léonais, one of the knights of the Round Table, who partook with the fair Yseult the 'draught of love' intended for the King Marc'h. This King Marc'h (the name signifying *horse*), who had his residence on the site of the village of Plomarc'h, on the E. of Douarnenez, like King Midas, put to death all his barbers, for fear they should reveal that his ears were those of a horse. At last a hairdresser was spared on promise of silence, but he could not keep the strange secret, and confided it to the sand of the sea-shore. Forthwith three reeds sprang up, from which bards made strings for hautboys which proclaimed, 'Marc'h, the King of Plomarc'h, has the ears of a horse.'

'In the Bay of Douarnenez, when the storm is rising, the fishermen hear in the whistling, moaning gale, the *crierien*, the voices of the shipwrecked, shrieking for burial; and tell that on All Souls' Day, *le jour des morts*, you may see the pale spirits rising on the crests of the waves and scudding like the spray before the wind, in the *Baie des Trépassés*: it is the annual gathering of those who have lived on these shores, the drowned and the buried, and they seek each other among the waves. There also they believe that the demons who wait for the lost soul show themselves in visible form about his door during his agony; they tell of fishers' boats deeply laden with their invisible freight of spirits, gliding off to the ocean.'—*Dean Church, 'Essays.'*

A little E. of Douarnenez is *Plomarc'h*, where some substructions were attributed to the palace of King Marc'h. The neighbourhood abounds in woodpeckers and kingfishers.

6 k. E. of Douarnenez is the *Manoir de Kervénargen*, where the proscribed Girondists, Buzot, Pétion, Guadet, Barbaroux and Louvet found a temporary refuge in 1793. Near this are a number of menhirs and the *allée-couverte* of *Ty-ar-C'houriquet*.

The road from Douarnenez to (28 k.) Châteaulin, passes (3 k.) *Kerlas*,[1] with a fine XVI. c. and XVII. c. church with a spire, and a cemetery cross of 1645. At *Plouré*, near Douarnenez, in the Chapelle des Morts, is a copy of Canova's 'Christ,' given by Cardinal Fesch to the famous doctor Laënnec, who bequeathed it to his parish church.

10 k. from Douarnenez, on the road to Audierne, is *Comfort*, where the *Chapelle Notre Dame*, an admirable little building of XVI. c., contains a *roue de fortune*—a circle of wood hung with bells—which the sacristan sets in motion at certain points in the service. In the churchyard are a calvary and menhir.

The railway reaches—

39 k. *Pont-Croix*. The collegiate church of *Notre Dame de Roscudon*, called *Ilis-ar-Verc'hez* by the peasants, is chiefly XII. c., with a central tower and spire of XV. c., flamboyant

---

[1] Ker, or Kar, means a stone or altar.

windows, a fine gothic porch, and some good glass of 1554. A road turns S.E. from hence to (33 k.) Pont-l'Abbé (see p. 381), by (27 k.) *Plonéour Lanvern*, 4 k. W. of which, at *Tréguennec*, is the *Chapelle S. Viaud*, much frequented by pilgrimage for the cure of fever; and 2 k. farther S. the *Chapelle Notre Dame de Tronoan*, a fine gothic building in a desolate district.

43 k. *Audierne* (Hotel: *Batifoulier*—primitive, but clean. Diligence to Quimper, 3 fr. 50 c.). This little port and quay on the Goayen, 1 k. from its mouth, is a much prettier place than Douarnenez. The neighbouring hamlet of *S. Tugean* has a fine xv. c. and xvi. c. church, partly renaissance. A mysterious pointed iron key of the saint is preserved in a reliquary, and is used on the day of the *pardon* to prick a number of small loaves, which, it is supposed, can never, from that time, grow mouldy, and a fragment of which, thrown to a mad dog, will put it to flight. In another reliquary are preserved the teeth of S. Tugean, which are believed to cure all aching teeth that are touched by them. Tourists may stay at Audierne to explore the curious neighbouring district.

A carriage—a covered car—should be engaged at Audierne for a visit to the Pointe du Raz—the Land's End of France, and a luncheon basket with hard-boiled eggs, bread and wine should be taken from the hotel. The road, which passes over high corn-land, is for the most part uninteresting. Near the village of *Primelin* is the *Chapelle S. Théodore*. At the foot of a windmill is a dolmen, rising above a stone trough, in which fever-stricken patients are stretched for cure. The road now descends into a little bay, and, mounting the opposite hill, reaches, at 10 k., *Plogoff*. Here the church is dedicated to S. Ké, or Collédoc, a Welsh bishop who came to be a hermit in Brittany in the vi. c., and who possessed a miraculous bell, which warned him of the good acts he had to perform and the evil he had to avoid. The story of his life is bound up with that of King Arthur, and, after the king's supposed death, in 542, it is he who is said to have persuaded Guinevere to resist the blandishments of Lancelot and remain in her convent at Amesbury. There is a pretty chapel of *S. Collédoc*, with an old stone cross on the l. of the road before reaching (13 k.) *Lescoff*, where there are several menhirs. A little beyond this, cultivation ceases.

'Les bords ne sont pas moins désolés que ceux de Spitzberg: pas une arbre sur les hauteurs voisines, nulle culture au vent de la mer: c'est la région de la mort. Puis le continent s'amincit; ce n'est plus qu'une péninsule, même qu'une simple corne de rochers s'avançant au loin dans les eaux. Là le spectacle de la mer bouleversée par la tempête est vraiment formidable: quoique le sentier suive la crête du promontoire à 80 mètres de hauteur, on y est cependant couvert de l'embrun des vagues, et l'on sent distinctement le sol frémir sous ses pieds.'—*Elisée Reclus*.

At 15 k. we reach the lighthouse of the *Pointe du Raz* or *Cap Sizun*, ever surrounded by crowds of beggars and guides, who live in constant idleness on the chance of what they can pick up,[1] but—when they get nothing—give you the same friendly 'Bon-jourc'h.'

A few minutes' walk from the lighthouse brings us to the cliffs above the sea. The scenery is not to be compared to that of the English Land's End, but is wild and savage. The rocky promontory—'la proue de l'ancien monde'—is lashed by grand breakers, and has a definite end, with nothing beyond it. It is perfectly safe in calm weather, and guides are absurdly unnecessary, as there is only one well-defined path. In a storm the waves are sublime, but indeed the scene is grandest when you cannot see it, when it is next to impossible to stand against the wind and the storm. There is an islet lighthouse, very necessary at this, the most dangerous point of the whole French coast.

'C'est un proverbe breton: "Nul n'a passé le Raz sans mal ou sans frayeur." Et encore, "Secourez-moi, grand Dieu, à la Pointe de Raz! mon vaisseau est si petit, et la mer est si grande."'
—*Michelet*.

'It is a coast of a terrible name for shipwrecks. Much has been done and is doing with lighthouses, but nothing can prevent the deadly *Chaussée des Seins*, as they call the reef of rocks beyond the island, and the perilous *Bec du Raz*, which is the name of the channel between the island and the point, from

---

[1] 'Chercheurs de pain à qui une compatissante moitié de ménage donne de quoi fumer une pipe et boire un coup.'

devouring their yearly tale of lives. On either side of the point the waters are full of fish, so that smacks pass to and fro continually in the Bec du Raz; as do greater craft often, to avoid the long circuit outside the Chaussée. The Breton fisherman has a prayer for the passage, and a proverb which says, "Whoso steers not wisely in the Raz is a dead man."'— *Cornhill Magazine.*

'Rien d'effrayant comme le passage entre le Raz et l'île de Sein; la moindre erreur, une fausse manoeuvre, vous précipitent à

THE POINTE DU RAZ.

jamais dans des gouffres, sur des rochers, sans aucun espoir de salut.'—*Cambry.*

Far out in the open sea is the *Île de Sein*, the *Sena* of Pomponius Mela, where every family still eats, on Holy Thursday, the *repas du navire*, a little boat made of pastry. It hangs over each dining-table, and at the end of the meal it is let down, and, the whole family standing round it, the master of the house chants the *Veni Creator*, to which the rest respond in chorus. The old vessel is then burnt and replaced by another till the following year. This is supposed to call down the blessing of heaven upon the fishing boat which is the support of the family, the boat being formed of bread as an emblem of faith and hope, as the words of the Last Supper made bread a consecrated aliment. Many are the curious customs observed on the island.

Sein is said in the v. c. to have been the last refuge of the Druids in Brittany, and it was hence that the famous priestess Uheldeda went to attend the states-general convoked by Conan Meriadech to meet at Rennes, and there in the presence of the assembly cursed the retrogade Conan, and destroyed the mystic plant of Selago which she had brought with her. Here also, after their return, Uheldeda and her companions stabbed themselves, after singing their own funeral requiem, to escape the persecution of Conan Meriadech. Here too, in the VI. c., was born the famous Merlin, the son of 'a demon and a nun,' who hoped to destroy Christianity in his person; but this was prevented by his baptism, and he became the devoted adherent of Uther Pendragon and Arthur.

'Les portes des maisons ne se ferment qu'aux approches de la tempête; des feux follets, des sifflements l'annoncent. Quand on entendait ce murmure éloigné qui précède l'orage, les anciens s'écrièrent : " fermons les portes ; écoutez les Crierien, le tourbillon les suit." Ces *Crierien* sont les ombres, les ossements des naufragés qui demandent la sépulture, désesperés d'être, depuis leur mort, ballottés par les elements.'—*Cambry*.

'Asseyons-nous à cette formidable pointe du Raz, sur ce rocher miné, à cette hauteur de trois cents pieds, d'où nous voyons sept lieues de côtes. C'est ici, en quelque sorte, le sanctuaire du monde celtique. Ce que vous apercevez par-delà la baie des Trépassés, est l'île de Sein, triste banc de sable sans arbres et presque sans abri; quelques familles y vivent, pauvres et compatissantes, qui, tous les ans, sauvent des naufragés. Cette île était la demeure des vierges sacrées qui donnaient aux Celtes beau temps ou naufrage. Là, elles célébraient leur triste et meurtrière orgie ; et ces navigateurs entendaient avec effroi de la pleine mer le bruit des cymbales barbares. Cette île, dans la tradition, est le berceau de Myrddyn, le Merlin du moyen-âge. Son tombeau est de l'autre côté de la Bretagne, dans le forêt de Broceliande, sous la fatale pierre où sa Vyvyan l'à enchanté.

Tous ces rochers que vous voyez, ce sont des villes englouties ; c'est Douarnenez, c'est Is, la sodôme bretonne ; ces deux corbeaux, qui vont toujours volant lourdement au rivage, ne sont rien autre que les âmes du roi Grallon et de sa fille, et ces sifflemens qu'on croirait ceux de la tempête, sont les *crierien*, ombres des naufragés qui demandent la sépulture.'—*Michelet,* '*Hist. de France.*'

The nearest of the headlands seen from the Pointe du Raz is the *Pointe de Van*. Between the Pointe du Raz and the Pointe de Van is a narrow bay called *Baie des Trépassés*—' Dead Man's Bay '—because here it is said that the spirits of the drowned assemble in the night, waiting to be conducted home. This tradition is recorded by Procopius 1300 years ago :—

'Along the ocean shore over against Brittia are many villages inhabited by fishermen, husbandmen, and boatmen, who traffique in the island. . . . They have the employment of conducting soules departed imposed on them by turns ; when any man's time comes, they goe to bed towards night, expecting their fellow conductors, and at midnighte they finde the door opened, and hear a softly voice calling them to the business ; instantly they rise, and go down to the sea-side, finding themselves constrained to goe on, but they perceive not by whom ; boats they find ready, with no men in them, and aboard they goe and sit to their oars. They perceive the boats loaded with passengers even to the decks, and the place of their oares not an inch from the water ; they see nothing ; but after an hour's rowing come to a land in Brittia, whereas in their own boats they have much ado to pass over in a day and a night, having no sailes but rowing only. And they instantly land their fare, and are gone away with their boats suddenly grown light, and swimming with the current, and having all save the keels above water : they see no men leaving the boates, but they heare a voice relating to some, who it seemes stayes there for them, the names of the passengers, with their titles, and additions of what fathers they were, and (if women) what husbands they had.'—*Holcroft's Trans*

One may descend into the Baie de Trépassés by taking the path opposite the chapel of S. Collédoc, on the Audierne road. Here the *Étang de Laoul* is supposed to cover the great town of

Is or Kéris—' which Paris was proud to equal '—a second Sodom, submerged in the v. c. Here, in calm weather, fishermen look through the blue waters, and see, upon the sands of the bay, the ruins of the wicked city, whose bells, ringing under the waves, presage a storm. That which is certain is that a paved way, evidently leading to buildings of Roman times, enters the sea not far from the Baie des Trépassés.[1]

'Is était défendue contre l'océan par une digue puissante, dont les écluses ne livraient passage qu'à la quantité d'eau nécessaire aux habitants. Le roi Grallon présidait lui-même, chaque mois, à l'ouverture de ces écluses; la principale s'ouvrait au moyen d'une clef d'argent qu'il portait toujours suspendue à son cou. Le palais du roi était une des merveilles de la terre; le marbre, le cèdre et d'or y remplaçaient le chêne, le granit et le fer. C'était là qu'il vivait au milieu d'une cour brillante, à laquelle présidait sa fille Dahut ou Ahès; ou cette princesse était alors l'Honoria de l'Armorique. Comme la fille de Valentinien, elle s'était fait une couronne de ses vices, et avait pris pour pages les sept péchés capitaux. Prévenant, dans ses monstreuses inventions, la Marguerite de Bourgogne de la tour de Nesle, elle faisait conduire chaque soir, au fond de sa retraite, quelque jeune étranger qu'un homme noir lui amenait masqué. Le temps s'écoulait en folles orgies jusqu'au point de jour; alors Dahut disparaissait. Le masque remis à l'étranger se resserrait au moyen d'un ressort jusqu'à l'étouffer; et l'homme noir, montant à cheval avec le cadavre, s'efforçait dans les montagnes pour ne reparaître que le soir. On montre encore dans le *Bois élevé* (le Huel-goat) un gouffre d'où sortent, dans les grandes eaux, les bruits les plus lugubres; ce sont, disent les pâtres de l'Arrée, les âmes des amants de Dahut qui demandent des prières.

'Grallon avait promis plusieurs fois de punir les crimes de sa fille; mais l'indulgence paternelle l'avait toujours emporté dans son coeur. Dahut craignit pourtant qu'il ne finît par céder, et elle forma un complot au moyen duquel elle enleva au roi son autorité et la clef d'argent qui en était le symbole. Alors tout tomba dans un inexprimable désordre. Le vieux roi, retiré dans son

---

[1] See Ernest Desjardin's '*Géographie de la Gaule romaine*,' p. 303.

palais presque désert, y cachait sa douleur. Un jour, comme la nuit approchait, il vit paraître devant lui Guénolé, le saint abbé de Landévennec, dont les travaux apostoliques consolaient la Cornouaille de la mort de Corentin. "O roi!" lui dit-il, "hâte-toi de quitter la ville avec tes fidèles serviteurs; car Dahut à ouvert l'écluse à l'aide de la clef d'argent: la fureur des flots n'à plus de frein!" Grallon voulut encore preserver sa fille des suites de sa folle imprudence. Il l'envoya chercher, la prit en croupe sur son cheval, et, suivi de ses officiers, se dirigea vers les portes de la cité. Au moment où il les franchissait, un long mugissement retentit derrière lui; il se detourna et poussa un cri. À la place de la ville d'Is s'étendait une baie immense sur laquelle se refletait la lueur des étoiles. Cependant la vague lui poursuivait lui et les siens, et, dans cette lutte de vitesse, elle gagnait du terrain avec une effrayante rapidité. Elle avançait, avançait toujours, dressant sa crête frémissante et couverte d'écume. La voilà près d'atteindre le roi et ses serviteurs. Tout à coup une voix lui cria: Grallon, si tu ne veux périr, débarrasse-toi du démon que tu portes derrière toi? Dahut terrifiée sentit ses forces l'abandonner: un voile s'étendit sur ses yeux; ses mains, qui serraient convulsivement la poitrine de son père, se glacèrent, et ne lui furent plus d'aucun secours; elle roula dans le flot. À peine l'eurent-ils engloutie qu'ils arrêtèrent. Quant au roi, il arriva sain et sauf à Kemper, et se fixa dans cette ville, qui devint définitivement la capitale de la Cornouaille. Ce fut là qu'il mourut, cassé de vieillesse et riche de mérites.

'Quelques auteurs ont contesté l'existence de ce héros des légendes et de sa ville d'Is. On ne peut douter toutefois qu'une cité puissante n'ait été elevée par les anciens habitants de la Cornouaille dans le bassin de la baie de Douarnenez; outre les chroniques religieuses et les traditions du pays, qui en ont gardé le souvenir, on a découvert sur le sol et jusque sous les flots plus d'un témoignage de ce passé merveilleux. Un petit havre de la côte s'appelle encore *Poul-Dahut*, le gouffre de Dahut.

'Sur les bords de l'étang de Laoual, s'élève une chapelle ruinée, qui passe pour avoir été une dépendance d'Is.'—*Emile Souvestre.*

At *Poul Dahut* (the abyss of Dahut) it is said that Dahut may often be seen sitting like a siren on the rocks; while

Grallon's horse may be met at night galloping furiously over the country.

'Une des légendes les plus répandues en Bretagne est celle d'une prétendue ville d'Is, qui, à une époque inconnue, aurait été engloutie par la mer. On montre, à divers endroits de la côte, l'emplacement de cette cité fabuleuse, et les pêcheurs vous en font d'étranges récits. Les jours de tempête, assurent-ils, on voit, dans le creux des vagues, le sommet des flèches de ses églises: les jours de calme, on entend monter de l'abîme le son de ses cloches, modulant l'hymne du jour. Il me semble souvent que j'ai au fond du coeur une ville d'Is qui sonne encore des cloches obstinées à convoquer aux offices sacrés des fidèles qui n'entendent plus. Parfois je m'arrête pour prêter l'oreille à ces tremblants vibrations, qui me paraissent venir des profondeurs infinies, comme des voix d'un autre monde.'—*Ernest Renan.*

'Oh, bells of Is! oh, bells of Is!
  Deaf were the heart and ears
That never heard you ringing
  Your psalm of vanished years.
That quaint old Breton legend
  Rings through our daily strife:
Its story is an image,
  A parable of life!—
When for a space we listen,
  As at some eventime,
And upward, through the Present,
  The bells of Memory chime.
Pause;—listen in the silence;
  Lest we their message miss!
Ring on—your heart-made music,
  Ring on! sweet bells of Is!'
                        Clifford Harrison.

[A road leads N. from Quimper to—

12 k. *Plogonnec*, which has a fine XVI. c. church, with flamboyant windows. The stained glass is very fine. In several windows the donors are represented.

15 k. *Locronan* (the place of S. Ronan) has a magnificent

xv. c. church. The sculptures of the xvii. c. pulpit represent the story of S. Ronan. In the sacristy is a gilt chalice, given by Marguerite de Foix, second wife of Duc François II. Adjoining the S. aisle is the *Chapelle du Peniti*, built 1530 by Renée de France, Duchess of Ferrara, daughter of Louis XII. and Anne of Brittany, and containing the xvi. c. tomb of S. Ronan, who was buried here in his oratory of the v. c., where the queen of King Grallon, after shutting up her daughter, falsely accused the saint of having transformed himself by witchcraft into a wild beast and having devoured her.[1] When S. Ronan died, as the Bretons were uncertain where to bury him, his body was placed on a cart drawn by two oxen. They made the circuit of what was the daily walk of the saint, and stopped at the hermitage.

'Les roues de la charrette, gênées par un passage étroit, laissèrent des marques sur deux rochers contre lesquels les femmes stériles se frottent pour avoir des enfants, comme sur le clou de S. Guenolé, à Landevennec.'—*Cambry.*

An excursion of 6½ k. may be made to the popular chapel of *S. Anne la Palue*, with a statue of the saint of 1543. The place is famous for its pardon, and is visited by 60,000 or 70,000 pilgrims annually.]

[For the line N. to Landernean and Brest see ch. v.]

[1] See Trevaux, '*Les Vies des Saints de Bretagne.*'

INDEX.

A.

Abbaye Blanche, 155
Aber Bénoit, 301
   -Ildut, 300
   Vrac'h, 303
Abondant, 146
Acquigny, 86
Ailly, 18
Airan, 108
Alençon, 150
Alisay, 40
Allouville, Le Chêne d', 69
Alluyes, 193
Almenêches, 150
Alvimare, 69
Ambrières, 154
Ancourt, 18
Anctoville, 156
Andely, Le Grand, 38
   Le Petit, 36
Andrieu, 126
Anet, 80
Angerville-l'Orcher, 75
Arbrissel, 215
Archelles, 17
Ardennes, abbaye d', 118
Argences, 108
Argentan, 151
Argentré, 211
Argueil, 11
Aron, 200
Arques la Bataille, 15
Arromanches, 129
Artoire, 164

Artz, Ile d', 364, 366
Asnelles, 129
Assé de Beranger, 197
Aubigné (Sarthe), 195
Aubigny, château d', 108
Audierne, 388
Auffay, 60
Aulnay, 27
   -sur-Odon, 126
Aulnaye, abbaye d', 126
Auray, 353
Authie, 120
Auzebosc, 69
Avalon, Ile d', 252
Avenières, Notre Dame d', 204
Avranches, 308

B.

Bacqueville, 19
Baden, 355
Bagnoles les Eaux, 152
Baigneux, château de, 191
Balleroy, 130
Ballon, château de, 194
Bannalec, 374.
Barentin, 60
Barfleur, 131
Batz, Ile de, 264
Baud, 235, 238
Baudemont, château de, 35
Bayeux, 127
Bazenville, 123
Bazoche-Gouet, 183
Beaubec, abbey of, 11

Beaubec-la-Rosière, 11
Beaumesnil, château de, 94
Beaumontel, 94
Beaumont-en-Auge, 99
— -Hague, 133
— -le-Roger, 93
— -le-Vicomte, 194
Beauport, abbaye de, 231, 243
Beauregard, château de, 35
Beauvron en Auge, 102
Beauzeville le Grenier, 70
Bec Hellouin, Le, 90, 94
Bécherel, 218
Bégard, 242
Belair, château de, 234
Belbœuf, 41
Belle Etoile, abbaye de la, 126
Belle-Ile-en-Mer, 367
— -Isle, 248
Bellengreville, 108
Bellevue, 136
Belz, 365
Béniguet, Ile, 297
Bény, 120
Berjou-Cahan, 125
Bernay, 95
Bernières, 120, 123
Bernouville, 5
Berthéaume, Anse de, 296
Bertichère, La, 1
Berville-sur-Mer, 59
Beslé, 220
Betton, 333
Beuvillers, 99
Beuzit-Conogan, 292
Béville sur Mer, 18
Beynes, 139
Bézu S. Eloi, 5
Binic, 231
Bizy, château de, 33
Blainville-Crevon, 11
Blanchelande, abbey of, 132
Blangy, 99
Blossac, château de, 219
Bodilis, 277
Bois des Anges, château de, 301
— de la Roche, château de, 22
Boiscenno, 361
Boisdenemetz, château de, 35
Boisset le Châtel, 95

Boisset les Prévanches, 86
Bolbec, 74
Bonnemare, château de, 6
Bonnetable, 184
Bonneval, 191
Bonneville, 92
— sur Touques, 100
Bon-Port, abbaye de, 41
Boos, 5
Boquen, abbey of, 228
Bord, forest of, 41
Bordeaux S. Clair, 35
Bosc-Bordel, 11
Bouessay, château de, 219
Boullemont, château de, 99
Bourbriac, 233
Bourg-Beaudouin, 5
— -Blanc, 301
— Le Dun, 19
— le Roi, 195
Bourgtheroulde, 95
Boussac, La, 325
Brain, 220
Brametot, 67
Braspartz, 302
Bray, Pays de, 7
— -Ecos, 35
Bréauté, 70
Brêche au Diable, 108
Brécourt, château de, 35
Bréhal, 308
Bréhec en Plouha, 231
Brélèvenez, 249
Brest, 294
Bretagnolles, 86
Breteuil, 93
Bretteville, 67
— d'Orgueilleuse, 120
— sur Laize, 125
— sur Odon, 121
Breuil-Benoît, abbey of, 85
Bréval, 79
Bricquebec, 131
Briec, 274
Brignogan, 286
Brionne, 94
Briouze, 152
Brocelinde, forêt de, 223
Broglie, 96
Brohinière, La, 222

INDEX.

Broons, 228
Broualan, chapelle de, 325
Bruz, 219
Bueil, 79
Buhulien, 242
Bures, 15, 124

C.

Cabourg, 102
Caen, 108
Cagny, 108
Cailly, 60
Cairon, 122
Caligni, 126
Calvados, Roches du, 123
Camaret, 290
Cambes, 120, 122
Cambremer, 102
Cancale, 332
Canon, 108
Canteleu, 59
Cany, 67
Caradeuc, château de, 218
Carambouville, château de, 88
Carhaix, 273
Carheil, château de, 343
Carentan, 130
Carfantain, 328
Carnac, 356, 359
Carnoët, 273
   forest of, 371
Caudebec, 63
Caudebecquet, 65
Cesny aux Vignes, 108
Cesson, tour de, 230
Cérisy-la-Forêt, 130
Chaillot, 21
Challerie, château de la, 154
Chambois, castle of, 148
Chambors, 1
Champ-Dolent, pierre de, 328
Chanteloup, 308
Chapelle Anthenaise, La, 201
Charleval, 5
Chars, 1
Chartres, 171
Châteaubriant, 341
Château d'O, 151

Château Gaillard, 36
Châteaugal, 274
Châteaugiron, 215
Château Gontier, 341
Châteaulin, 290
Châteauneuf, 337
   du Faou, 274
   -en-Thymerais, 147
Châtelaudren, 238.
Châtelier, château de, 219
Châtillon en Vendelais, 211
Châtillon-sur-Seiche, 219
Châtres, 199
Chaumont-en-Vexin, 1
Chaussée Brunehaut, 1
Chaussey, Les Iles, 157
Chaville, 136
Chef du Port, 129
Chemazé, 340
Chène, La chapelle du, 340
Cherbourg, 132
Chesnay, château de, 35
Cheux, 120
Chevalier, Ile, 481
Chevilly, 57
Chrismet, Mont, 124
Clamart, 134
Clécy, 125
Cléden Poher, 273
Clerai, château de, 151
Clermont, abbey of, 205
Clinchamps, 124
Closerie des Poiriers, 205
Coat-Nevenez, château de, 242
Cocherelle, 85
Coëlmalouen, Abbey of, 233
Coëlmen, château de, 231
Coëtirec, château de, 251
Columbes, 21
Combourg, 332
Comfort, 387
Concarneau, 375
Conches, 94
Condé sur Huisne, 181
Condé sur Noireau, 125
Conflans-S.-Honorine, 22
Connerré, 184
Coquainvillers, 99
Corlay, 233
Corps Nuds, 219

Corseul, 338
Coulaine, château de la, 194
Couliboeuf, 103
Coulombs, 147
Courseulles, 123
Courson, 156
Courtalieru, château de, 194
Courville, 180
Coutances, 305
Cran, chapelle de, 274
Craon, 340
Creully, 121
Criel, 18
Croisilles, 125
Croix S. Leufroy, 86
Croix, Ile de, 369
Croth-Sorel, 85
Crozon, 290
Cuy-S.-Fiacre, 9

D.

Dampierre, 9, 15
Dampierre en Chemin, 21
Damville, 89
Dangu, 35
Daoulas, 286
Darnetal, 57
Deauville, 101
Délivrande, chapelle de la, 123
Démouville, 124
Dieppe, 17
Dinan, 333
Dinard, 331
Dirinon, 286
Dives, 102
Dol, 326
Domfront, 153
    en Champagne, 196
Douarnenez, 385
Doudeville, 66
Douvres, château de, 120, 122
Dozulé-Putot, 102, 124
Dreux, 142
Drouains-Blaru, 35
Duclair, 59, 60

E.

Echaffour, 97
Ecos, 35
Ecouché, 152
Ecouis, 5
Ecretteville-les-Baons, 69
Edern, 278
Elbeuf, 95
Elven, 344
Envermeu, 18
Epau, abbaye d', 185
Epernon, 169
Epone, 26
Eragny, 6
Ernée, 201
Erondeville, cross of, 129
Erquy, 229
Esquay sur Seulles, 123
Essai, 150
Essarts de Roi, Les, 164
Essé, 215
Estouteville, 11
Etelan, château de, 59
Etrépagny, 5
Etretat, 70
Evreux, 86
Evron, 197
Ezy-Anet, 80

F.

Falaise, 105
Faou, 288
Faouet, Le, 372
Fécamp, 70
Ferrière, La, 341
Ferrières, priory of, 105
Ferté-Bernard, La, 183
    -Macé, La, 152
    -S.-Simon, La, 11
Feuguerolles-S.-André, 124
    -sur-Orne, 124
Fine Terre, abbaye de, 296
Flèche, La, 339
Flers, 152
Fleury, 134
Fleury-sur-Andelle, 5
Folligny, 308
Folgoët, Le, 281
Fontaine-le-Bourg, 60
    -Daniel, abbaye de, 154, 200
    -le-Dun, 67

INDEX.

Fontaine Etoupefour, château de, 120, 121
   -Guérand, abbaye de, 6
   -Henri, 120, 121
   -Martel, 74
Fontenay, abbaye de, 124
   -le Marmion, 124
Forges les Eaux, 10
Formigny, 129
Fort de Salles, château de, 195
Foucart-Alvimare, 69
Fougeray-Langon, 220
Fougères, 212
Foulletourte, château de, 197
Frenouville, 108
Fresnay le Vicomte, 194
Fresne-Camilly, La, 122
Fresney le Puceux, 125
Fumichon, château de, 99

G.

Gacé, 102
Gaillon, 35
Gainville, 60, 79
Gallardon, 169
Gambais, château de, 142
Gancourt, S. Etienne, 9
Ganne, château, 308
Garaye, château de la, 336
Gasny, 34
Gassicourt, 31
Gauterie, La, 126
Gavr' Innis, 364
Genest, Le, 205
Gennes-Longuefuye, 341
Gerberoi, 8
Giberville, 124
Gisors, 2
Glatigny, château de, 101
Glos-Montfort, 94
Gomfreville-l'Orcher, 59, 76
Gorvello, 344
Gouesnou, 300
Gourin, 373
Gournay, 7
Graincourt, 18
Grance, château de, 274
Grandcamp, 130
Grand Jardin, Le, 99

Grangues, 103
Granville, 156
Graville S. Honorine, 76, 77
Grée-Mahé, 343
Grémonville, 66
Grès de S. Meen, 222
Grignon, 139, 163
Grimbosq, 125
Grisy, 105
Gros-du-Raz, 131
Gruchet La Valasse, 74
Guéméné Penfao, 342
Guémené sur Scorff, 234
Guerche, La, 215
Guern, 234
Guichen-Bourg des Comptes, 219
Guignen, 219
Guimiliau, 276
Guingamp, 238
Guyardière, château de la, 154

H.

Hague, Cap de la, 133
   Dicke, 133
Hambye, abbaye de, 307
Hanvec le Faou, 288
Harcourt, 89
Harfleur, 75
Haute-Bruyère, priory of, 164
   -Perche, château de, 193
Hauteville sur Mer, 307
Hautot sur Mer, 19
   Seine, 59
Havre, Le, 76
Haye Pesnel, La, 308
   du Puits, La, 132
Hébertot, château d', 101
Hédé, 218
Hennebont, 367
Hermitage-Mordelles, 220
Hesqueno, 349
Heuland, Croix de, 101
Heurteauville, 59
Hoc, Pointe du, 59
Hode, Cap du, 59
Honfleur, 100
Hôtot en Auge, 102
Houdan, 142

Houlgate-Beauzeval, 103
Huelgoat, 271
Huguenots, château des, 9

I.

Ifs, 121
    d'Etretat, Les, 70
Iffs, 218
Illiers, 180
    l'Evêque, 85
Ingouville, 77
Isigny, 130
Issy, 134
Ivry la Bataille, 79

J.

Joie, abbaye de la, 368
Joigné-sur-Sarthe, 340
Josselin, 224
Joyeuse-Garde, château de la, 292
Jublains, 199
Jumièges, 61

K.

Keramenac'h, chapelle de, 248
Kerangouez, manoir de, 262
Kérauzern, 249
Kerbiguet, château de, 373
Kercado, château de, 358
Kerfily, château de, 346
Kerfons, chapelle de, 251
Kerfunteun, 253
Kergoat, chapelle de, 292
Kergrist, château de, 251
Kergournadec'h, château de, 278
Kerhuon, 292
Kerisper, 355, 361
Kerity, 383
Kerjean, château de, 277
Kerlas, 387
Kerlivri, château de, 278
Kermaria au Isquit, 231
Kermenguy, château de, 278
Kermerchou, menhir de, 254
Kermerio, manoir de, 356
Kermoran, 296
Kermor-ruy, manoir de, 262

Kernascleden, 235
Kernuz, château de, 381
Keronic, château de, 238
Keroual, château de, 297
Kérouzéré, château de, 264
Kersaint-Plabennec, 301
Kervénargen, manoir de, 387
Kervignac, 368

L.

Lacs, Les, 215
Laigle, 148
Laize la Ville, 124
Lambader, 278
Lamballe, 228
Lampaul, 277
Landal, château de, 325
Landeda, 303
Landeleau, 273
Landerneau, 279
Landévennec, abbaye de, 289
Landivisiau, 277
Langoat, 243
Langon, 220
Langrune, 120, 123
Lanleff, temple de, 243
Lanloup, 231
Lanmeur, 253
Lannenec, 369
Lannilis, 302
Lan-Ninnocht, 372
Lannion, 249
Lanvollon, 231
Lassay, château de, 101
Lasson, château de, 122
Lantheuil, château de, 122
Lanvaux, La Lande de, 343
Largouët, château de, 345
Laval, 201
Lavardin, 196
Lécaudé, 101
Lehon, 335
Lery, 40
Lescoff, 388
Lesneven, 285
Lesquelen, château de, 301
Lessay, 132
Levy S. Nom, 163
Lezardrieux, 244

INDEX.

Liancourt-S.-Pierre, 1
Lignon, chapelle de, 150
Lillebonne, 74
Limes, La Cité de, 18
Limur, 349
Lion sur Mer, 123
Lion d'Or Croissanville, 102
Lisieux, 97
Lison, 130, 304
Lisors, 5
Littry, 130
Livarot, 102
Lochrist, 278
Locmaria, 379
Locmariaker, 361
Locminé, 234
Locquenvel, 248
Locronan, 395
Loctudy, 381
Loges, Les, 70
Londe, La, 95
Longpré, château de, 108
Longuerne-Vieux-Manoir, 11
Longueville, 60
Lorges, château des, 233
Loudéac, 233
Loué, 197
Loup, La Loge du, 345
Loupe, La, 181
Louviers, 39
Louvigné du Désert, 215
Luc, 120, 123
Luc sur Mer, 123
Lude, Le, 195, 339
Luzerne, abbaye de, 308
Lyons la Forêt, 5

M.

Maboulière, château de la, 341
Maillé, 278
Maintenon, 169
Maison des Eaux, abbaye de, 85
Maisons Lafitte, 21
Malausac, 343
Malestroit, 228
Malon, château de, 99
Malville, château de, 223
Mamers, 184.

Manerbe, 99
Manneville la Piparde, 99
Manoir, Le, 123
Manou, château de, 181
Mans, Le, 185
Mantes, 27
Marcilly sur Eure, 85
Marcouf, 131
Margon, 183
Marines, 1
Marolles, 99
Maromme, 60
Martinvaast, 132
Martyre, La, 280
Mathieu, 120, 122
Maule, 27
Maulevrier, 69
Maurepas, 164
Mauron, 222
Mauves, 181
Mayenne, 200
Mayet, 195
Medan, 25
Ménerval, 10
Menesqueville-Lyons, 5
Mériadec, château de, 300
Meslay, 204
Mesléan, château de, 300
Mesnières, 15
Mesnil S. Denis, 163
   sous Jumièges, 59
   -Mauger, Le, 102
Mesnuls, château de, 140
Messac, 220
Meudon, 134
Meulan, 26
Mézaugers, 199
Mezidon, 102
Milesse, La, 196
Miromesnil, château de, 60
Misedon, bois de, 205
Moidrey, 312
Moines, Ile de, 364, 366
Molay-Littry, Le, 130
Molène, Ile. 297
Mondrainville, 126
Mont des Boulards, 7
   S. Catherine, 57
   S. Jean, 196
   aux Malades, 57

INDEX.

Mont S. Michel, 312
    Roty, 9
    à la Vigne, château de, 101
Montagnes Noires, 274
Montauban, 222
Montbizot, 194
Montebourg, 131
Montecler, château de, 199
Monterollier, 11
Montfort l'Amaury, 139
    -sur-Meu, 220
    S. Philbert, 94
    sur Rille, 94
    le Rotrou, 185
Monthorvin, château de, 215
Montivilliers, 76
Montmartin sur Mer, 307
Montmuran, château de, 218
Montreuil le Chetif, 194
Montsurs, 201
Monville, 60
Morbihan, Baie de, 350, 353, 363
Morgny, 11
Morlaix, 255
Mortain le Neubourg, 155
Mortagne, 148
Mortemer, 12
Mortier-Crolle, château de, 341
Mortimer, abbaye de, 5
Mortrée, 151
Motte Broons, château de, 228
Motteville, 66
Mouen, 120, 126
Moult, 108
Moussaye, château de la, 228
Mouteille, 101
Moutiers-en-Cinglais, 125
Mureaux, 26
Mutrécy, 124

N.

Narolles, 99
Navarre, château de, 88
Néant, 223
Neaufles S. Martin, 4
Néauphle-le-Vieux, 137
Nesle-Hodeng, 12
Neubourg, Le, 89

Neufchâtel en Bray, 12
Neufmarché, 7
Neuilly, 130
Neuville Champ d'Oisel, 6
    -Ferrières, 12
Néville, 67
Nizon, 374
Nogent le Roi, 147
    Rotrou, 181
Noin'ot, 69
Nonant-le-Pin, 148
Nonancourt, 147
Norrey, 120, 126
Notre Dame de Barre-y-Va, 66.
    de Bliquetuit, 59
    de la Clarté, 253
    de la Cour, 231
    de la Délivrande, 123
    de Crénénan, 234
    du Désert, 95
    d'Estrées, 102
    des Grâces, 241
    de Larmor, 369
    de Portzbihan, 381
    de Quelven, 234
    de la Roche, abbaye de, 163
    du Roncier, 233
    de Tronoan, 388
    de Vandreuil, 40
Noyal Acigné, 215
    Pontivy, 234
    -sur-Seiche, 219
Noyers, 126

O.

O, château d', 151
Offranville, 60
Oissel, 41
Orbec, 101
Orgeville, 86
Orient L', 368
Orval-Hyenville, 308
Osmoy, 15
Ouessant, Ile d', 296
Ouézy sur Laizon, 108
Ouilly le Vicomte, 99
Ouistreham, 120
Outrelaize, château de, 125

INDEX.

Ouville l'Abbaye, 66
    la Rivière, 19

P.

Pabu, 242
Pacy-sur-Eure, 85
Paimpol, 243
Paluelle, château de la, 310
Panard, château de, 201
Paramé, 332
Parcs Fontaines, 99
Patay, 180
Pavilly, 66
Pédernec, 242
Pelice, abbaye de la, 184
Penmarc'h, 382
Péran, Camp de, 232
Périers, 132
Perros Guirec, 253
Pierre des Druides, La, 2
Pierrefitte, 99
Pierrepont, 122
Pinte Blanche, La, 231
Pitres, 6
Plaisir-Grignon, 137
Pleiber-Christ, 274
Plénée-Jugon, 228
Pleneuf, 229
Plessis, château du, 211
Plessix, château du, 242
Plestin, 253
Pleyben, 291
Ploeneur, 369
Ploërmel, 223
Ploeuc l'Hermitage, 233
Ploëzal, 242
Plogoff, 388
Plogonnec, 395
Plomarch, 387
Plonéour Lanvern, 388
Plouaret, 248
Ploudalmézeau, 300
Ploudaniel, 281
Plouénan, 258
Plounerin, 254
Plouescat, 278
Plougastel, 293
Plougaznou, oratoire de, 271
Plougniel, 247

Plougrescant, 247
Plouguerneau, 303
Plouha, 231
Plouharnel, 365
Plouhinec, Les Pierres de, 369
Plouider, 285
Ploumanac'h, 252
Plounéour-Ménez, 275
    Trez, 285
Plouré, 387
Plourin, 300.
Plouvara Plerneuf, 238
Plouvénez-Lochrist, 278
    -Moëdec, 248
Plouvien, 301
Plouzévedé, 278
Pluvigner, 238
Poillé, 197
Poissy, 22
Pommereaux, 10
Pommerit-Jaudy, 242
Pont l'Abbé, 381
    de l'Arche, 40
    Audemer, 95
    -Authou, 94
    -Aven, 373
    de Braye, Le, 185
    de Brech, 355
    -Croix, 387
    l'Evèque, 99
    de Gannes, 185
Pontanézen, 300
Pontaubault, 310
Pontchartain, château de, 139, 164
Pontgouin, 181
Pontivy, 233
Pontorson, 310
Pontrieux, 242
Pontscorff, 369
Port-en-Bessin, 129
    -Brillet, 203
    Jerôme, 59, 75
    Navalos, 367
    Royal des Champs, 158
Portrieux, 231
Pouancé, 341
Poul Dahut, 394
Pouldour, 254
Prévalaye, château de la, 218
Prie, manoir de, 99

Primelin, 388
Priziac, 234
Puits, château des, 197
Putot, 102
Puys, 18

Q.

Questembert, 344
Quiberon, 366
Quillebeuf, 59, 75
Quimerch, château de, 375
Quimper, 376
Quimperlé, 369
Quinéville, 131
Quinipily, 236
Quintin, 232

R.

Radepont, 6
Radeval, 39
Rambouillet, 164
Rambures, manoir de, 9
Ranes, château de, 152
Raz, pointe du, 389
Redon, 342
Relecq, abbaye de, 275
Rennes, 216
Rhuis, 351
Riberpré, 11
Richebourg, 142
Rigalet, La Lande de, 195
Robertière, château de la, 147
Roc S. André la Chapelle, 227
Roche, La, 279
    château de la, 274
Rochefagu, château de, 242
    Derrien, La, 142
    Guyon, château de la, 34
    -Maurice, château de la, 279
Rochefort-en-Terre, 343
Rochers, château des, 208
Roches, cap des, 18
    château de, 199
Rohan, 227
Rolleboise, 33
Romilly-sur-Andelle, 6
    la Puthenaye, 93
Roque, Pointe de la, 95

Roscanvel, Presqu'île de, 291
Roscoff, 264
Rosay, 32
Rosel, 120, 122
Rosgrand, chapelle de, 372
Rosny, 32
Rosperden, 375
Rost, 120
Rostrenen, 233
Rouen, 42
Rouesse-Vassé, 197
Rozel, Le, château de, 130
Ruffao, château de, 251
Rugles, 93
Rumengol, 288
Rustephan, château de, 374
Ryes, 129

S.

Sablé, 370
S. Adresse, 77
S. Adrien, 235
S. André, 86
    sur Cailly, 60
    de Fontenay, 124
S. Anne, chapelle de, 346
    d'Auray, 353
    la Palue, 396
S. Antonin de Sommaire, 93
S. Armel, 219
S. Arnoult, 101
S. Aubin, 180
    le Cauf, 15
    du Cormier, 218
    sur Mer, 123
    d'Offranville, 60
S. Barbe, chapelle de, 373
S. Benoît, abbaye de, 310
S. Berthevin, 203
S. Brieuc, 229
S. Calais, 185
S. Côme, chapelle de, 290
S. Contest, 120
S. Corentin, 32
S. Coulban, La Mare de, 337
S. Cyr, 137
S. Didier, 215
S. Efflam, 253
S. Eloi, chapelle de, 280

INDEX

S. Etienne, 9
 du Rouvray, 41
S. Evroult Notre Dame du Bois, 97
S. Fiacre, 372
S. Floxel, 131
S. Gabriel, prieuré de, 122
S. Gauberge, 148
S. Georges de Boscherville, 58
 -sur-Eure, 85
S. Germain la Campagne, 97
 de Clairfeuille, 148
S. Germer, 8
S. Gertrude, 66
S. Gildas des Bois, 343
 de Rhuis, 351
S. Herbot, 271
S. Hervé, chapelle de, 242, 373
S. Hilarion, 169
S. James, 310
S. Jaoua, 302
S. Jean du Doigt, 266
 le Thomas, 310
S. Julien de la Côte, 232
S. Languy, chapelle de, 293
S. Laurent en Caux, 19
 -de-Condet, 125
 du Pouldour, 254
S. Léger, 374
S. Lery, 220
S. Lo, 304
S. Lubin 181
 -des-Joncherets, 147
S. Maclou de Folleville, 60
S. Malo, 329
S. Manvieu, 120
S. Marc, Anse de, 294
S. Mards-Orbec, 97
S. Marie aux Anglais, 102
S. Mars sous Ballon, 194
S. Martin de Fontenay, 124
 en Campagne, 18
S. Mathieu, 296
S. Maurice, abbaye de, 372
 d'Etelan, 59
S. Méen, 220
S. Mère Eglise, 130
S. Michel d'Arhès, 273
 en Grève, 253
S. Nicodème, 235

S. Nicolas des Eaux, 235
 de Bliquetuit, 59
S. Ouen des Toits, 205
S. Pair, 157
S. Philbert, 95
S. Pierre sur Dives, 103
 de Mailloc, 101
 de Manneville, 59
 du Vauvray, 39
S. Plancher, 156
S. Pol de Léon, 258
S. Quay, 231
S. Quentin, Gorge de, 108
S. Remy, 125
 sur Avre, 147
S. Renan, 297
S. Romain de Colbosc, 75
S. Saire, 12
S. Samson, 11
S. Sauveur Châteauneuf, 145
 le Vicomte, 132
S. Servan, 331
S. Sever, 156
S. Suzanne, 199
S. Thégonnec, 275
S. Théodore, chapelle de, 388
S. Thois, 274
S. Trouberon, fontaine de, 300
S. Vaast d'Equiqueville, 15
S. Valery en Caux, 67
S. Viaud, chapelle de, 388
S. Victor l'Abbaye, 60
S. Vigor le Grand, 124
S. Vincent des Landes, 342
S. Vougay, 278
S. Wandrille, 65
Saon, 130
Sarceau, château de, 195
Sartrouville, 22
Sarzeau, 351
Saucerie, château de la, 154
Sauchay le Bas, 18
Saulges, 204
Saumont la Poterie, 10
Saussay, 85
 -les-Andelys, 3
Saut Roland, Rochers du, 211
Scaer, 375
Sceaux, 184
Secqueville en Bessin, 126

Seèz, 148
Segré, 341
Sein, Ile de, 390
Senarpont, château de, 15
Séné, 349
Sequeville, 120
Serifontaine, 6
Serqueux, 11
Sigy, 11
Sillé le Guillaume, 196
Solesmes, 340
Sommervieu, 123
Sorel, château de, 85
Sottevast, 131
Sotteville sous le Val, 41
Soquence, 59
Spézet, 274
Stang en Ihuern, 234
Stival, 234
Sucinio, château de, 351
Surdon, 148
Suze, La, 339

Tregunc, 374
Tré Malo, chapelle de, 374
Tremblay, château de la, 164
Trémezan, château de, 300
Trente, Combat des, 224
Tréorante, 349
Trépassés, Baie de, 387, 392
Trévières, 130
Trie-Château, 2
Triel, 25
Trinité sur Mer, La, 361
    de Reveille, La, 97
Tristan, Ile 386
Trouville, 101
    en Caux, 69
Tudy, Ile de, 381
Tumiac, La Butte de, 353

U.

Ussy, 125
Uzel, 233

T.

Tacoignières, 142
Tancarville, 74
Taureau, château du, 257
Thaon, 120, 121
Thevray, Tour de, 93
Thil-Riberpré, 11
Thouars, château de, 191
Thury-Harcourt, 125
Tierceville, 123
Tilly-sur-Seulles, 126
Tolente, 303
Tombelaine, 325
Tonquedec, château de, 249
Torche, Anse de la, 384
Torigni sur Vire, 305
Toulinguet, Pointe de, 290
Touques, 100
Tour, 129
    château de la, 108
Tournerie, château de la, 184
Tourville-sur-Arques, 60
Trappes, 158
Trédrez, 253
Trégastel, 251
Tréguier, 244

V.

Val, 134
Valmont, 67
Val aux Grès, 74
    Richer, 99
Valliquerville, 69
Valognes, 130
Van, Pointe du, 392
Vannes, 346
Varaville, 122
Varengeville, 18
Vassé, 197
Vatteville, 59
Vaudreuil, Le, 39
Vaupillon, 181
Vaux, 26
    château de, 4
Vendeuvre Jort, 105
Venus de Quinipily, 236
Vern, 219
Verneuil, 147
Vernon, 33
Vernonnet, château de, 33
Vernouillet, 25
Verrière, La, 163
Versailles, 137

INDEX.

Versainville, château de, 108
Verson, 126
Vetheuil, 31
Veules, 68
Vienne, château de, 123
Vieux-Fumé, 108
    Pont en Auge, 104
    -Port, 59
Vigny, château de, 1, 26
Villebon, château de, 181
Villedieu-les-Poëles, 156
Villepreux-les-Clayes, 138
Villers-sur-Mer, 103
    -le-Sec, 123
Villetertre, 1
Villiers-Néauphle, 27, 139
Vimont, 108

Vire, 154
Viroflay, 136
Vitré, 206
Vivouin, 194
Voutré, 197

W.

Ws-Marines, 1

Y.

Yffiniac, 229
Yport, 74
Yvetot, 68
Yville-sur-Seine, 59
Yvré-l'Evéque, 185

Hazell, Watson, & Viney, Ld., Printers, London and Aylesbury.

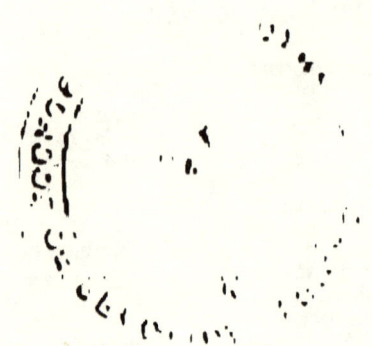

WORKS BY AUGUSTUS J. C. HARE

LIFE AND LETTERS OF FRANCES, BARONESS BUNSEN. *Third Edition.* With Portraits. 2 vols., crown 8vo, 21*s*.

MEMORIALS OF A QUIET LIFE. 3 vols., crown 8vo, Vols. I. and II., 21*s*. (*Nineteenth Edition*); Vol. III., with numerous Photographs, 10*s*. 6*d*.

"One of those books which it is impossible to read without pleasure. It conveys a sense of repose not unlike that which everybody must have felt out of service time in quiet little village churches. Its editor will receive the hearty thanks of every cultivated reader for these profoundly interesting 'Memorials' of two brothers, whose names and labours their universities and Church have alike reason to cherish with affection and remember with pride, who have smoothed the path of faith to so many troubled wayfarers, strengthening the weary and confirming the weak."—*Standard*.

DAYS NEAR ROME. With more than 100 Illustrations by the Author. *Third Edition.* 2 vols., crown 8vo, 12*s*. 6*d*.

WALKS IN ROME. *Thirteenth Edition, revised.* With Map. 2 vols., fcap. 8vo. cloth limp, 10*s*.

"The best handbook of the city and environs of Rome ever published. . . . Cannot be too much commended."—*Pall Mall Gazette*.
"This book is sure to be very useful. It is thoroughly practical, and is the best guide that has yet been offered."—*Daily News*.
"Mr. Hare's book fills a real void, and gives to the tourist all the latest discoveries and the fullest information bearing on that most inexhaustible of subjects, the city of Rome. . . . It is much fuller than 'Murray,' and any one who chooses may know how Rome really looks in sun or shade."—*Spectator*.

WALKS IN LONDON. *Sixth Edition, revised.* With additional Illustrations. 2 vols., fcap. 8vo, cloth limp, 12*s*.

"One of the really valuable as well as pleasant companions to the peripatetic philosopher's rambling studies of the town."—*Daily Telegraph*.

WANDERINGS IN SPAIN. With 27 full-page Illustrations. *Fifth Edition.* Crown 8vo, 7*s*. 6*d*.

"Here is the ideal book of travel in Spain; the book which exactly anticipates the requirements of everybody who is fortunate enough to be going to that enchanted land; the book which ably consoles those who are not so happy by supplying the imagination from the daintiest and most delicious of its stories."—*Spectator*.

GEORGE ALLEN, 156, CHARING CROSS ROAD, LONDON

CITIES OF SOUTHERN ITALY AND SICILY.
With Illustrations. Crown 8vo, 10s. 6d.

"Mr. Hare's name will be a sufficient passport for the popularity of his new work. His books on the Cities of Italy are fast becoming as indispensable to the traveller in that part of the country as the guide-books of Murray or of Baedeker. . . . His book is one which I should advise all future travellers in Southern Italy and Sicily to find room for in their portmanteaus."—*Academy.*

CITIES OF NORTHERN ITALY. Second Edition.
With Illustrations. 2 vols., crown 8vo, 12s. 6d.

"We can imagine no better way of spending a wet day in Florence or Venice than in reading all that Mr. Hare has to say and quote about the history, arts, and famous people of those cities. These volumes come under the class of volumes not to borrow, but to buy."—*Morning Post.*

CITIES OF CENTRAL ITALY. Second Edition. With
Illustrations. 2 vols., crown 8vo, 12s. 6d.

SKETCHES IN HOLLAND AND SCANDINAVIA.
Crown 8vo, with Illustrations, 3s. 6d.

"This little work is the best companion a visitor to these countries can have, while those who stay at home can also read it with pleasure and profit."—*Glasgow Herald.*

STUDIES IN RUSSIA. Crown 8vo, with numerous
Illustrations, 10s. 6d.

"Mr. Hare's book may be recommended as at once entertaining and instructive."—*Athenæum.*

"A delightful and instructive guide to the places visited. It is, in fact, a sort of glorified guide-book, with all the charm of a pleasant and cultivated literary companion."—*Scotsman.*

FLORENCE. Third Edition. Fcap. 8vo, Illustrated,
cloth limp, 3s.

VENICE. Third Edition. Fcap. 8vo, cloth limp, 3s.
Revised, with Illustrations.

"The plan of these little volumes is excellent. . . . Anything more perfectly fulfilling the idea of a guide-book we have never seen."—*Scottish Review.*

GEORGE ALLEN, 156, CHARING CROSS ROAD, LONDON

WORKS BY AUGUSTUS J. C. HARE

PARIS. With Illustrations. Crown 8vo, cloth, 10s.

DAYS NEAR PARIS. With Illustrations. Crown 8vo, cloth, 10s.

NORTH-EASTERN FRANCE. Crown 8vo, cloth, 10s. 6d. With Map and 86 Woodcuts. 532 pages.

Picardy—Abbeville and Amiens—Paris and its Environs—Arras and the Manufacturing Towns of the North—Champagne—Nancy and the Vosges, etc.

SOUTH-EASTERN FRANCE. Crown 8vo, cloth, 10s. 6d. With Map and 176 Woodcuts. 600 pages.

The different lines to the South—Burgundy—Auvergne—The Cantal—Provence—The Alpes Dauphinaises and Alpes Maritimes, etc.

SOUTH-WESTERN FRANCE. Crown 8vo, cloth, 10s. 6d. With Map and 232 Woodcuts. 664 pages.

The Loire — The Gironde and Landes — Creuse — Corrèze — The Limousin—Gascony and Languedoc—The Cevennes and the Pyrenees, etc.

NORTH-WESTERN FRANCE. Crown 8vo, cloth, 10s. 6d. With Map and about 80 Woodcuts. 409 pages.

Normandy and Brittany—Rouen—Dieppe—Cherbourg—Bayeux—Caen—Chartres—Dinan—Brest, etc., etc.

"Mr. Hare's volumes, with their charming illustrations, are a reminder of how much we miss by neglecting provincial France."—*Times*.

"The appreciative traveller in France will find no more pleasant, inexhaustible, and discriminating guide than Mr. Hare. . . . All three volumes are most liberally supplied with drawings, all of them beautifully executed, and some of them genuine masterpieces."—*Echo*.

"Every one who has used one of Mr. Hare's books will welcome the appearance of his new work upon France. . . . The books are the most satisfactory guide-books for a traveller of culture who wishes improvement as well as entertainment from a tour. . . . It is not necessary to go to the places described before the volumes become useful. While part of the work describes the district round Paris, the rest practically opens up a new country for English visitors to provincial France."—*Scotsman*.

SUSSEX. *Second Edition*. With Map and about 50 Woodcuts. Crown 8vo, 6s.

GEORGE ALLEN, 156, CHARING CROSS ROAD, LONDON

WORKS BY AUGUSTUS J. C. HARE

THE STORY OF TWO NOBLE LIVES. CHARLOTTE, COUNTESS CANNING, AND LOUISA, MARCHIONESS OF WATERFORD. In 3 vols., of about 450 pages each. Crown 8vo, £1 11s. 6d. Illustrated with engraved Portraits and 21 Plates in Photogravure from Lady Waterford's Drawings, 8 full-page and 24 smaller Woodcuts from Sketches by the Author.

There is a Special Large-Paper Edition, with India Proofs of the Plates. Crown 4to, £3 3s. *net.*

The Embassy at Paris in the time of Louis XVIII. and Louis Philippe—Life of Lord and Lady Waterford in Ireland—The Famine and Rebellion, etc.—The Story of the Indian Mutiny as told in Lady Canning's Letters and Journals, etc.—Lady Waterford's Art Work—Recollections of her Conversations—Visits from and to the Royal Family, etc.

THE GURNEYS OF EARLHAM: Being Memoirs and Letters of the Eleven Children of JOHN and CATHARINE GURNEY of Earlham (1775-1875), and the Story of their Religious Life under many Different Forms. Illustrated with 33 Photogravure Plates and 20 Woodcuts. In 2 vols, crown 8vo, 25s., about 712 pages.

BIOGRAPHICAL SKETCHES: Being Memorial Sketches of ARTHUR PENRHYN STANLEY, Dean of Westminster; HENRY ALFORD, Dean of Canterbury; Mrs. DUNCAN STEWART; PARAY LE MONIAL. Illustrated with 8 Portraits and 20 Woodcuts. 1 vol., crown 8vo, 10s. 6d.

BY THE LATE AUGUSTUS WILLIAM HARE
RECTOR OF ALTON, BARNES

THE ALTON SERMONS. *Fifth Edition.* Crown 8vo, 7s. 6d.

SERMONS ON THE LORD'S PRAYER. Crown 8vo, 1s. 6d.

GEORGE ALLEN, 156, CHARING CROSS ROAD, LONDON

www.ingramcontent.com/pod-product-compliance
Lightning Source LLC
Chambersburg PA
CBHW032142010526
44111CB00035B/899